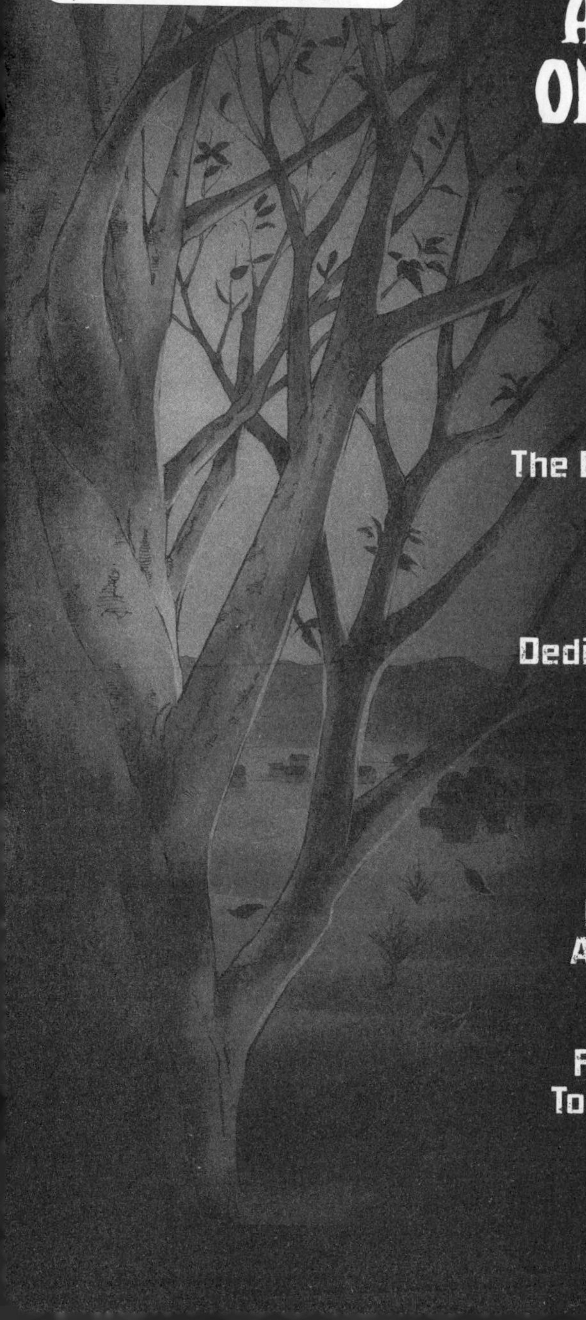

ATTACK ON TITAN

34

HAJIME ISAYAMA

ATTACK on TITAN

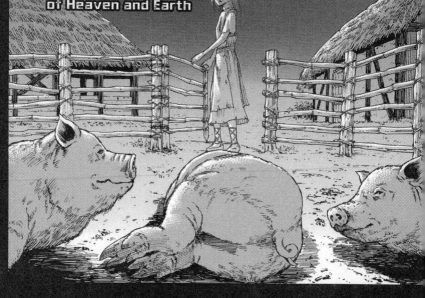

Episode 135: The Battle of Heaven and Earth

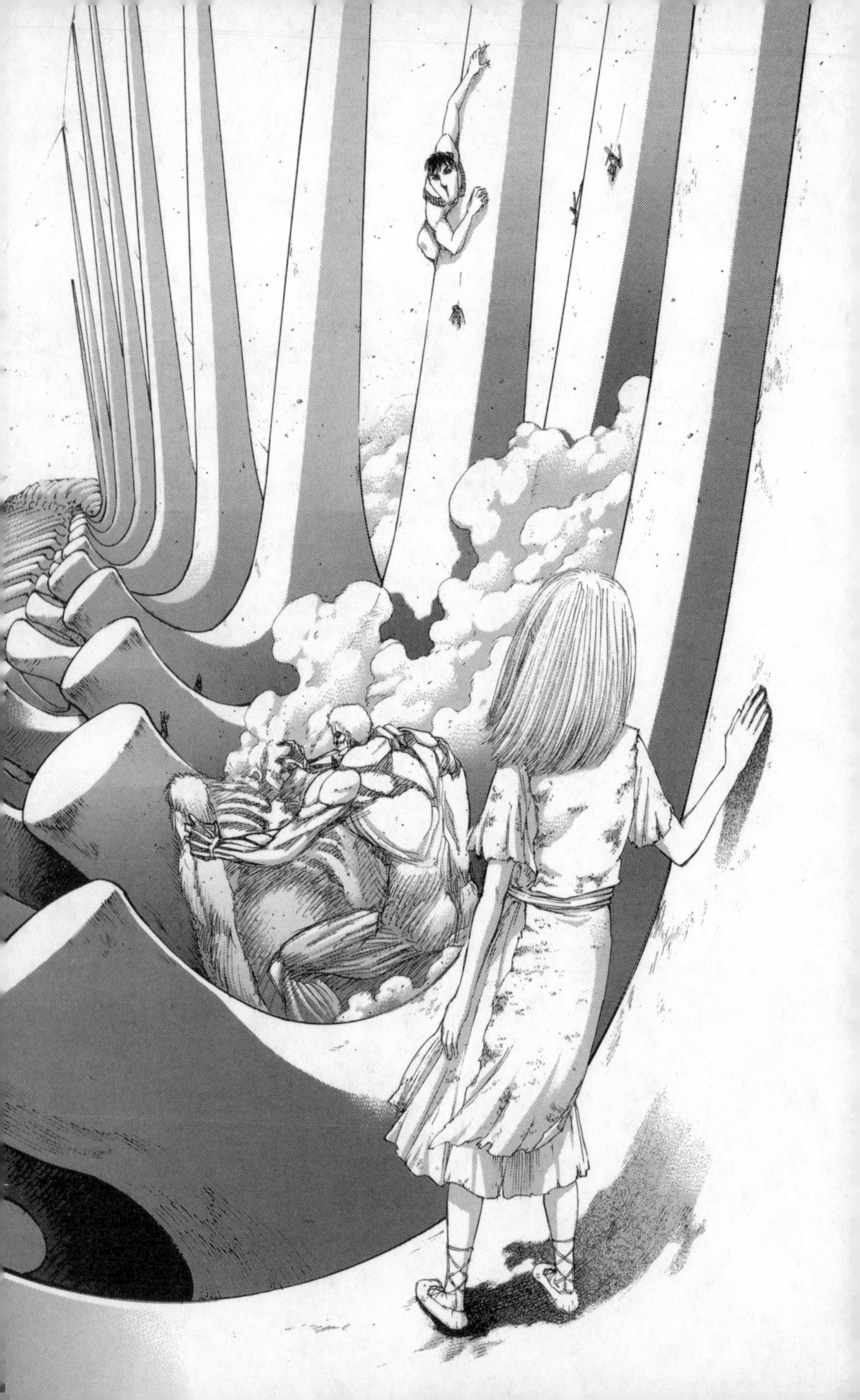

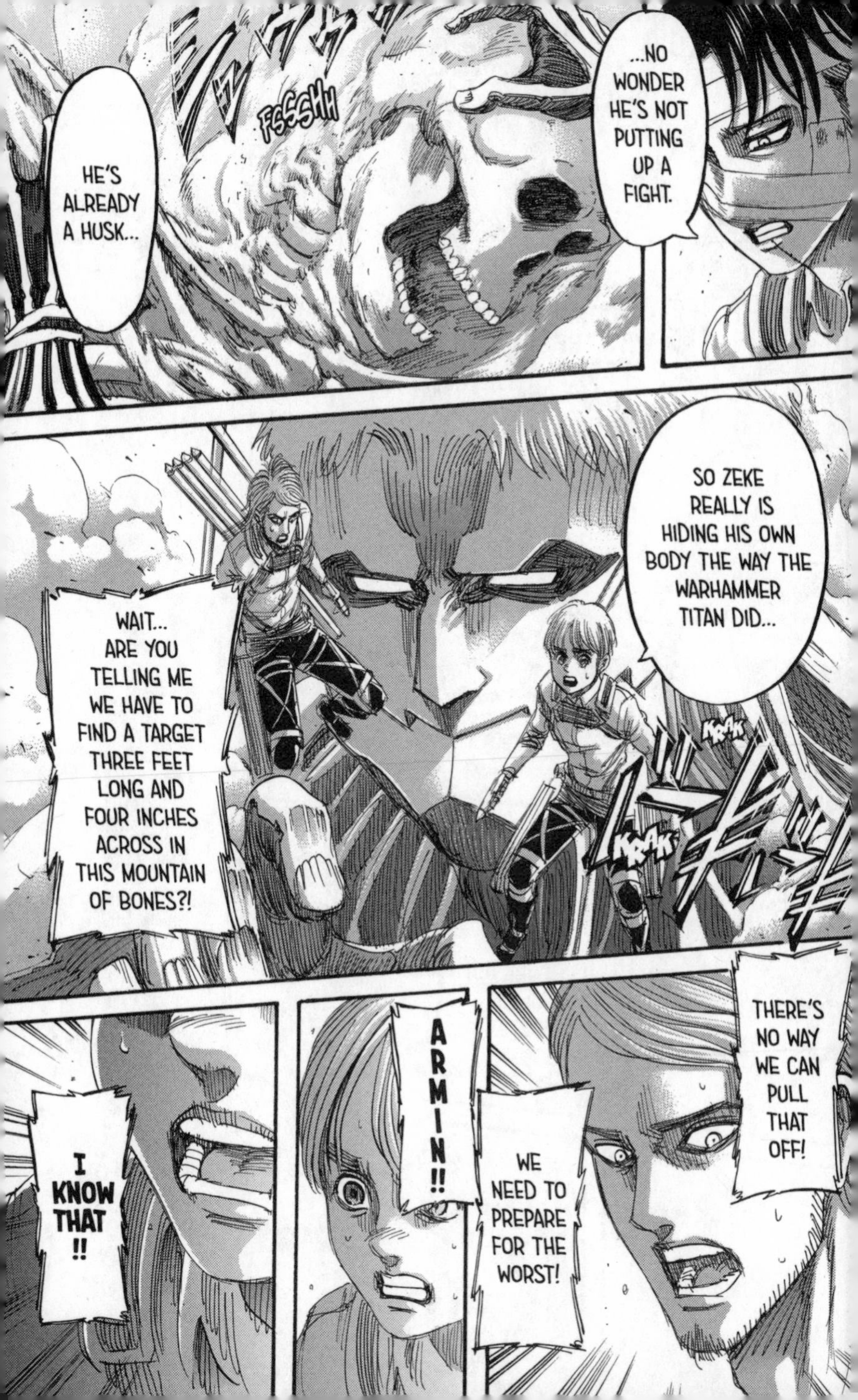
...NO WONDER HE'S NOT PUTTING UP A FIGHT.
FSSSHH
HE'S ALREADY A HUSK...
SO ZEKE REALLY IS HIDING HIS OWN BODY THE WAY THE WARHAMMER TITAN DID...
KRAK
KRAK
WAIT... ARE YOU TELLING ME WE HAVE TO FIND A TARGET THREE FEET LONG AND FOUR INCHES ACROSS IN THIS MOUNTAIN OF BONES?!
THERE'S NO WAY WE CAN PULL THAT OFF!
ARMIN!!
WE NEED TO PREPARE FOR THE WORST!
I KNOW THAT!!

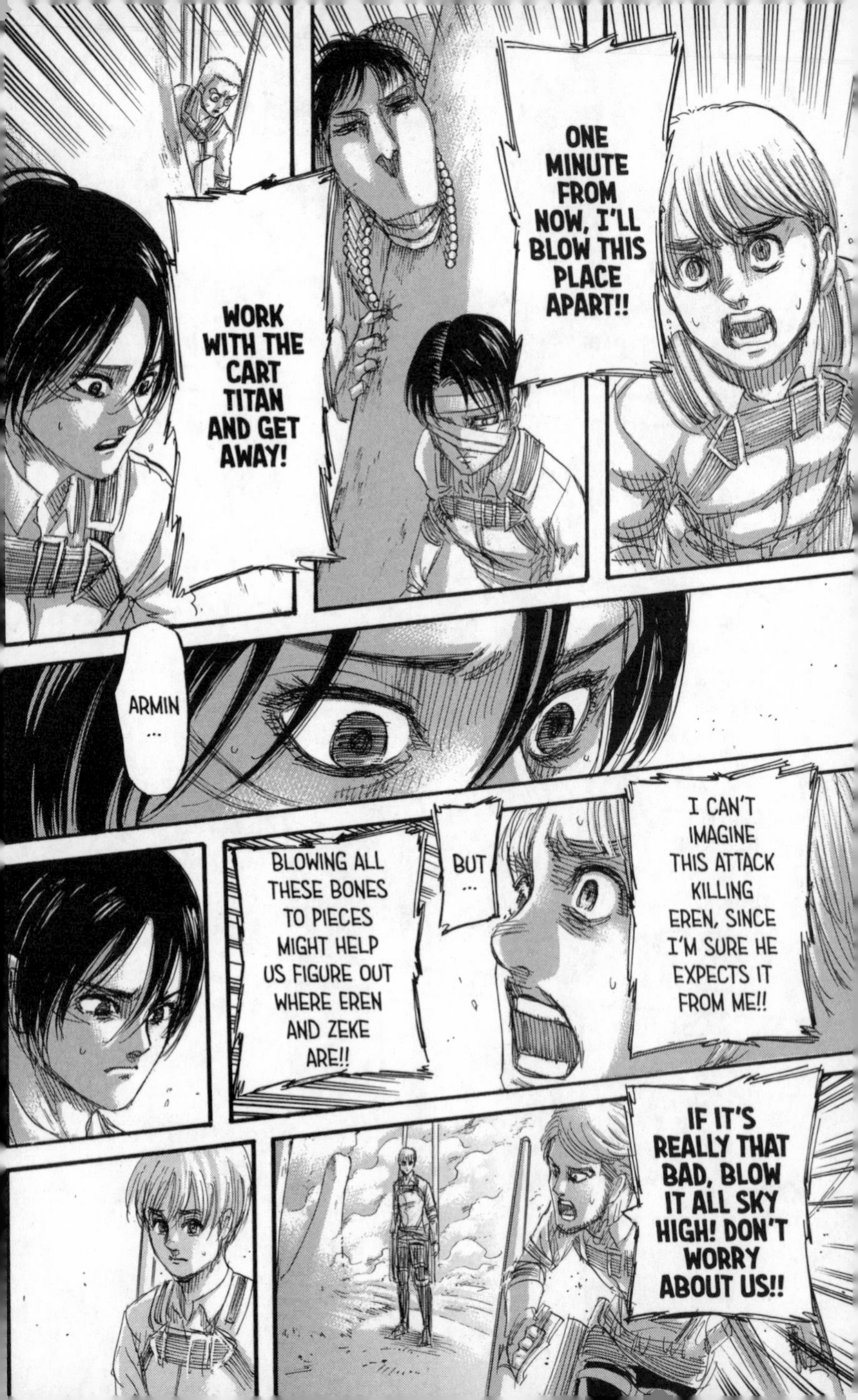
ONE MINUTE FROM NOW, I'LL BLOW THIS PLACE APART!!
WORK WITH THE CART TITAN AND GET AWAY!
ARMIN ...
I CAN'T IMAGINE THIS ATTACK KILLING EREN, SINCE I'M SURE HE EXPECTS IT FROM ME!!
BUT ...
BLOWING ALL THESE BONES TO PIECES MIGHT HELP US FIGURE OUT WHERE EREN AND ZEKE ARE!!
IF IT'S REALLY THAT BAD, BLOW IT ALL SKY HIGH! DON'T WORRY ABOUT US!!

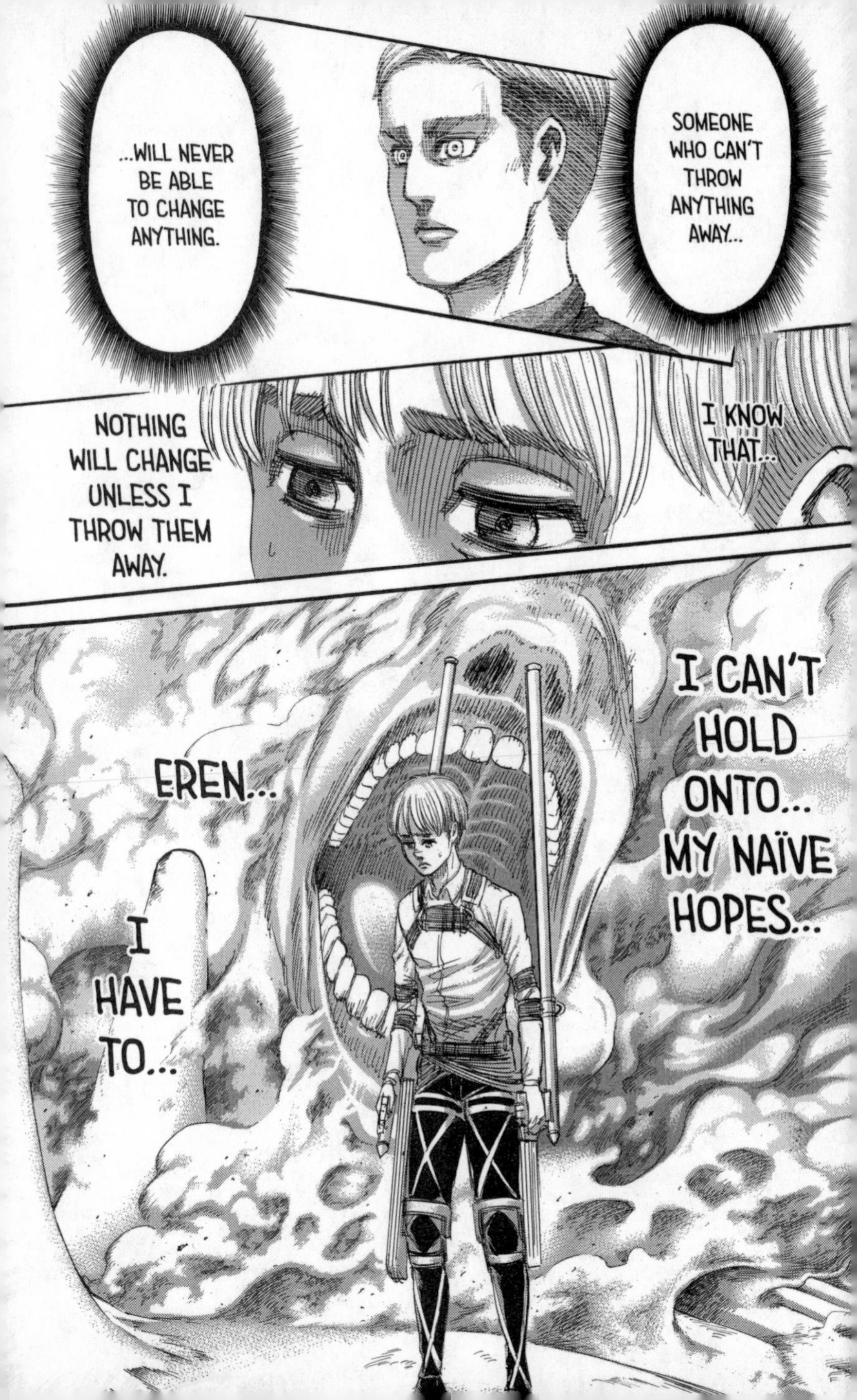
SOMEONE WHO CAN'T THROW ANYTHING AWAY...
...WILL NEVER BE ABLE TO CHANGE ANYTHING.
I KNOW THAT...
NOTHING WILL CHANGE UNLESS I THROW THEM AWAY.
I CAN'T HOLD ONTO... MY NAÏVE HOPES...
EREN...
I HAVE TO...

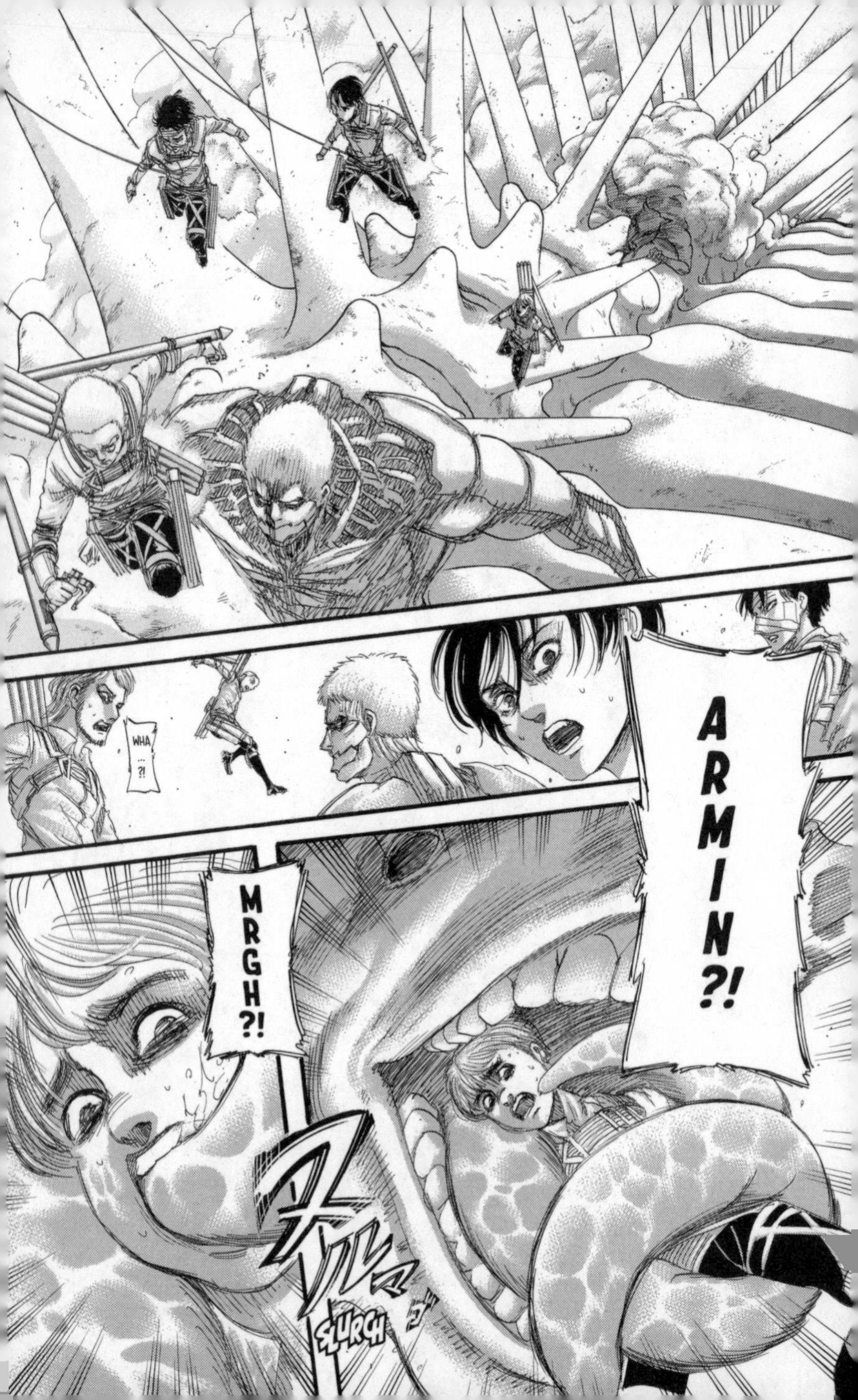
ARMIN?!
WHA ... ?!
MRGH?!
SLURCH

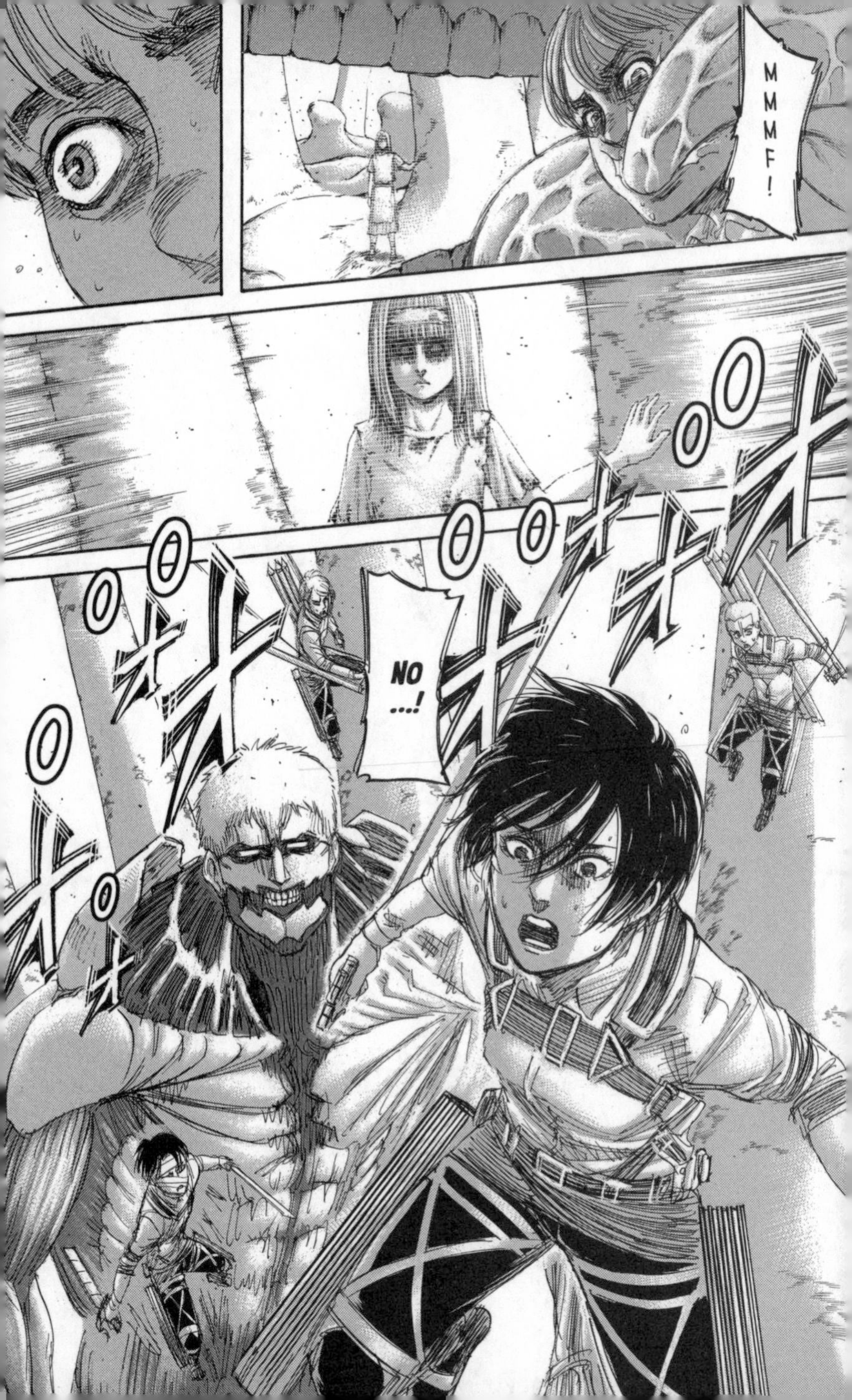
MMMF!
NO ...!

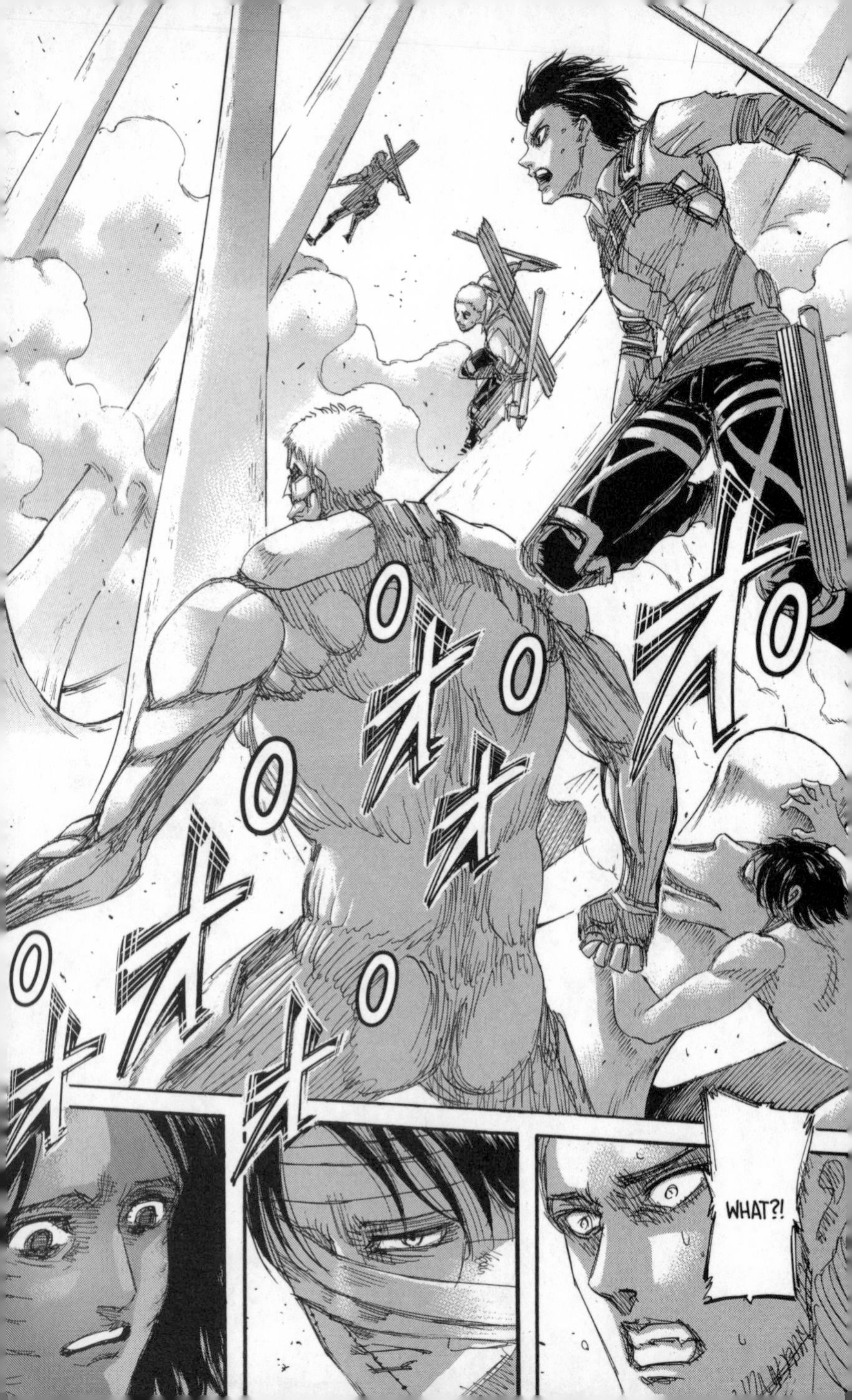
オO
OオOオ
OオOオOオ
WHAT?!

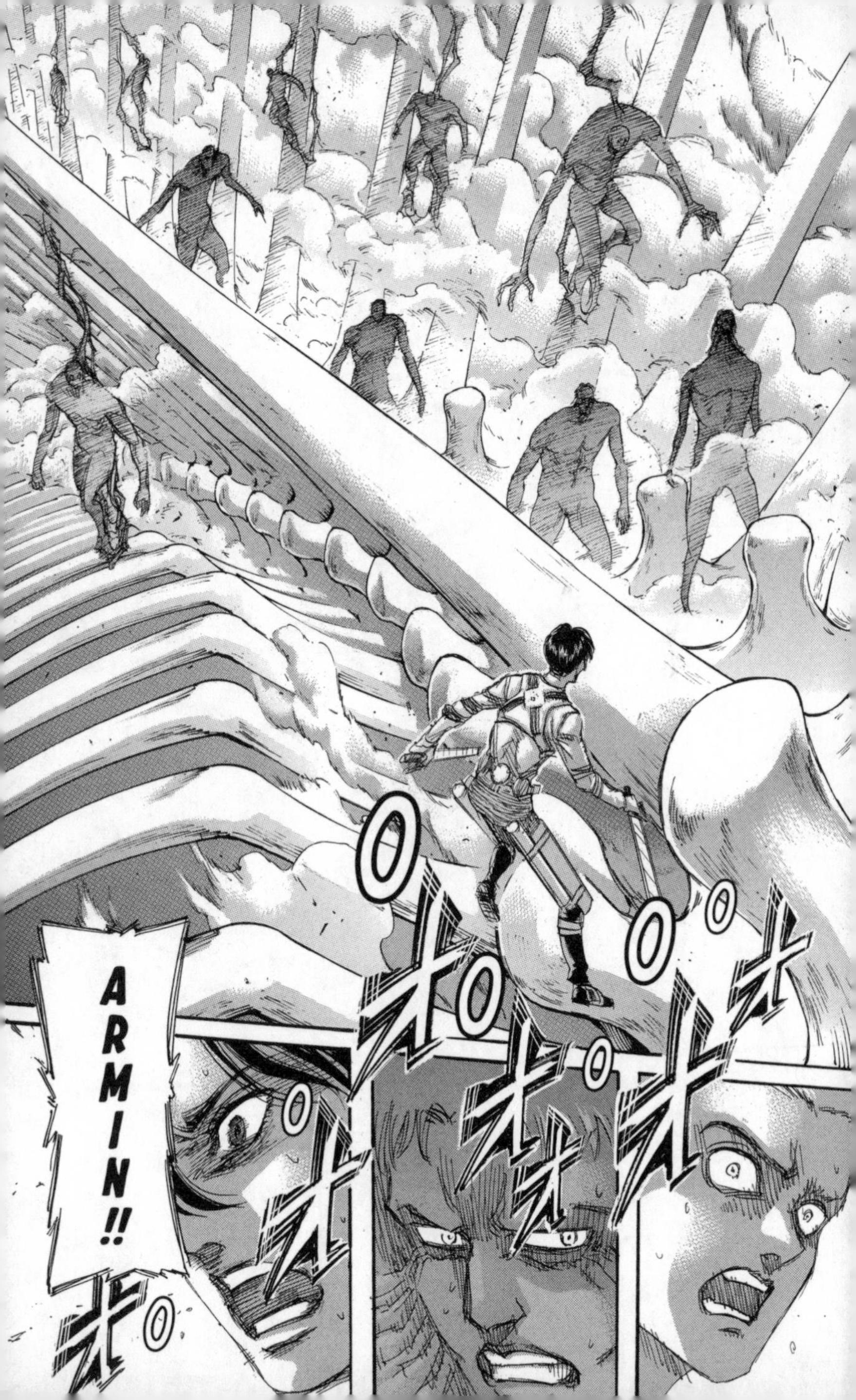
ARMIN!!

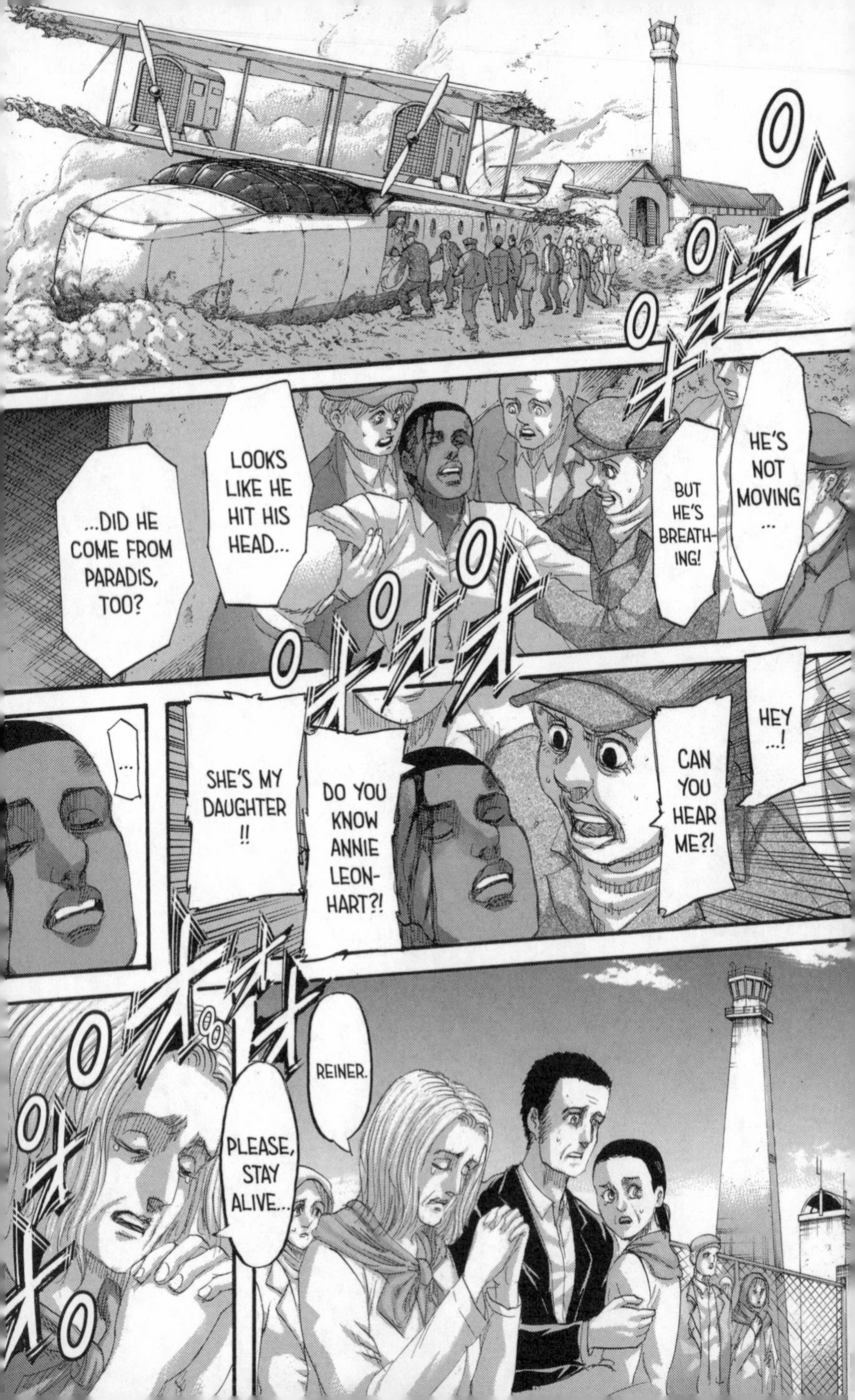
OOOO
HE'S NOT MOVING...
BUT HE'S BREATHING!
LOOKS LIKE HE HIT HIS HEAD...
...DID HE COME FROM PARADIS, TOO?
OOOO
HEY...!
CAN YOU HEAR ME?!
DO YOU KNOW ANNIE LEONHART?!
SHE'S MY DAUGHTER!!
...
OOOO
REINER.
PLEASE, STAY ALIVE...

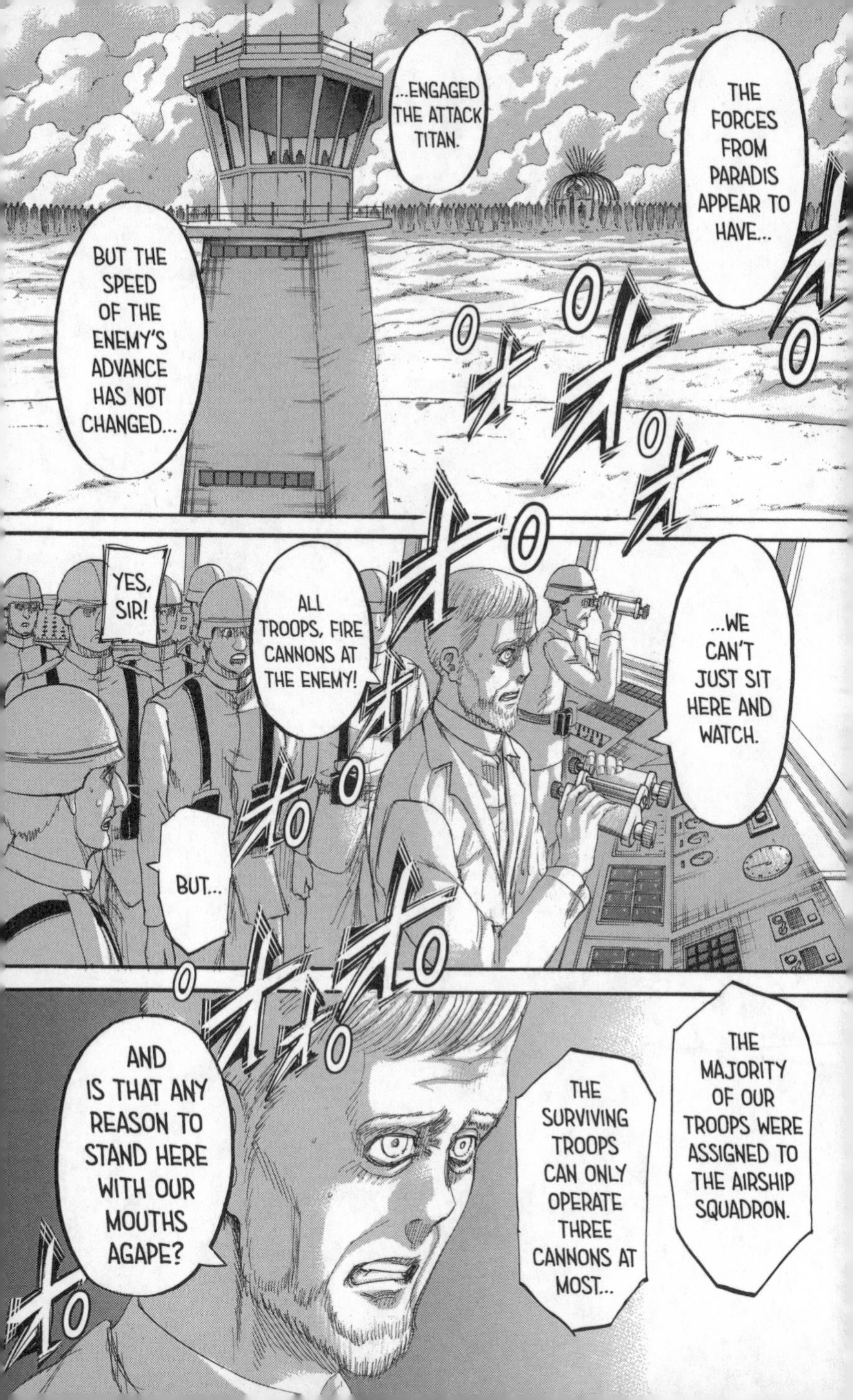
THE FORCES FROM PARADIS APPEAR TO HAVE...
...ENGAGED THE ATTACK TITAN.
BUT THE SPEED OF THE ENEMY'S ADVANCE HAS NOT CHANGED...
...WE CAN'T JUST SIT HERE AND WATCH.
ALL TROOPS, FIRE CANNONS AT THE ENEMY!
YES, SIR!
BUT...
THE MAJORITY OF OUR TROOPS WERE ASSIGNED TO THE AIRSHIP SQUADRON.
THE SURVIVING TROOPS CAN ONLY OPERATE THREE CANNONS AT MOST...
AND IS THAT ANY REASON TO STAND HERE WITH OUR MOUTHS AGAPE?

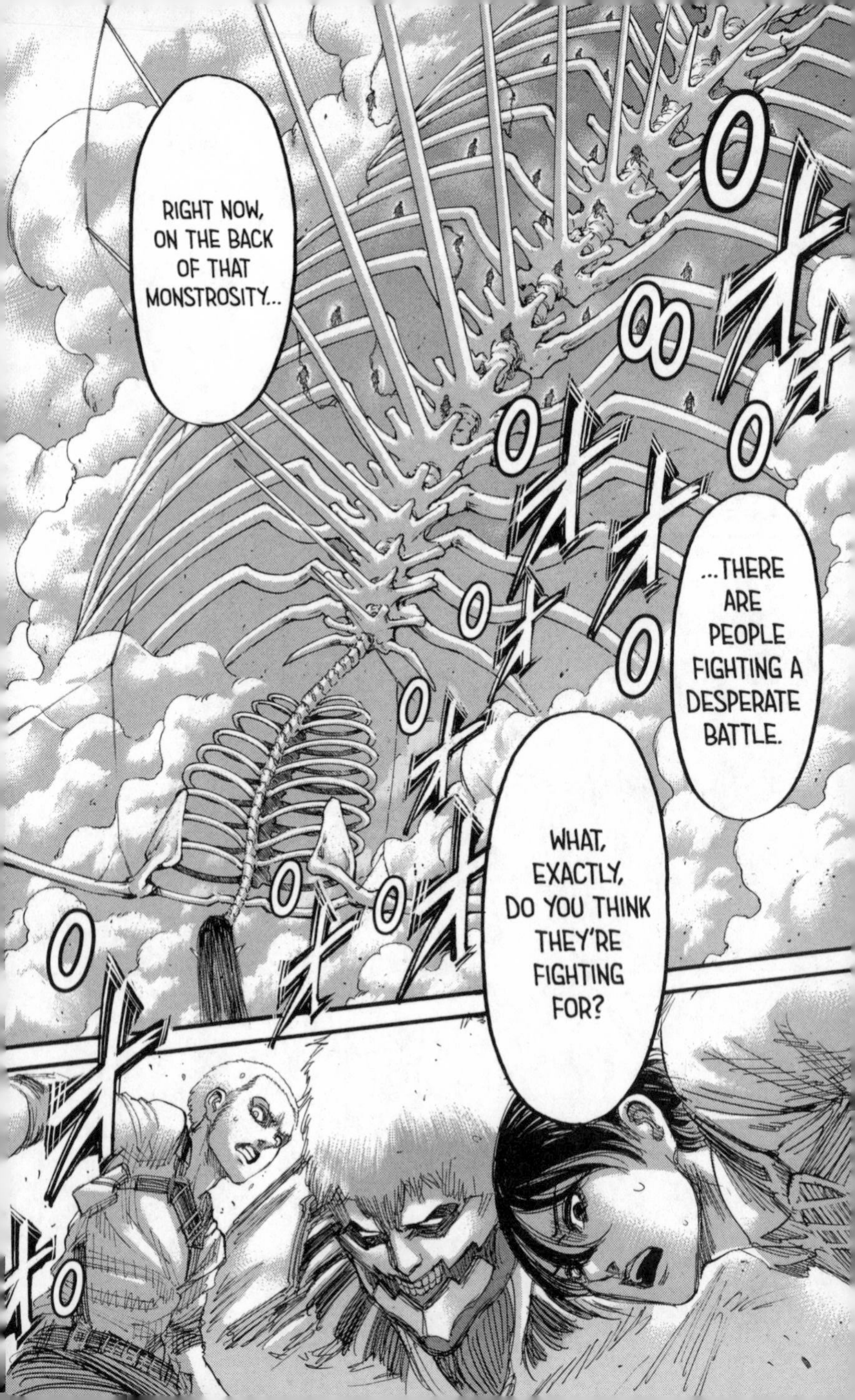
RIGHT NOW, ON THE BACK OF THAT MONSTROSITY...
...THERE ARE PEOPLE FIGHTING A DESPERATE BATTLE.
WHAT, EXACTLY, DO YOU THINK THEY'RE FIGHTING FOR?

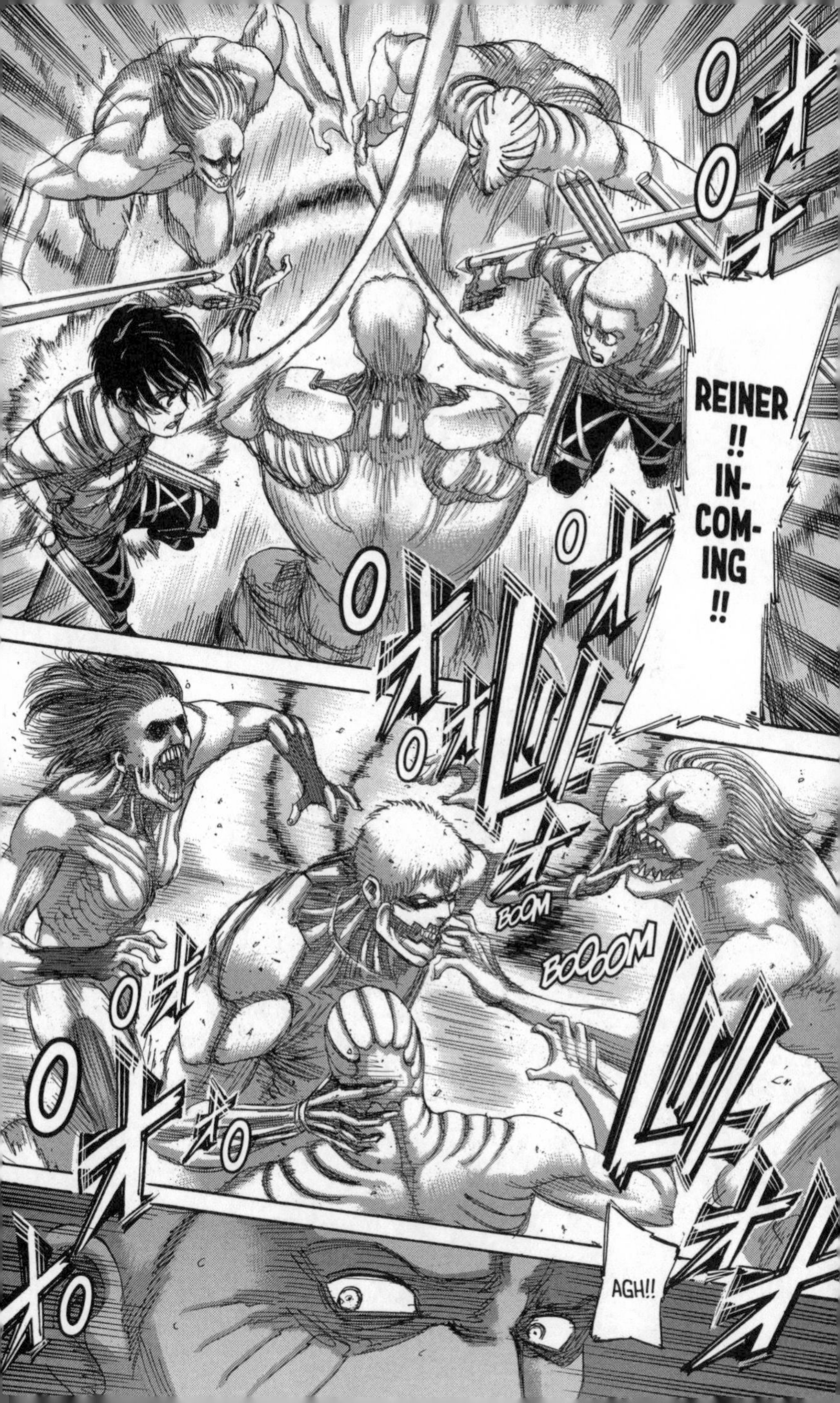
REINER!! INCOMING!!
BOOM
BOOOOM
AGH!!

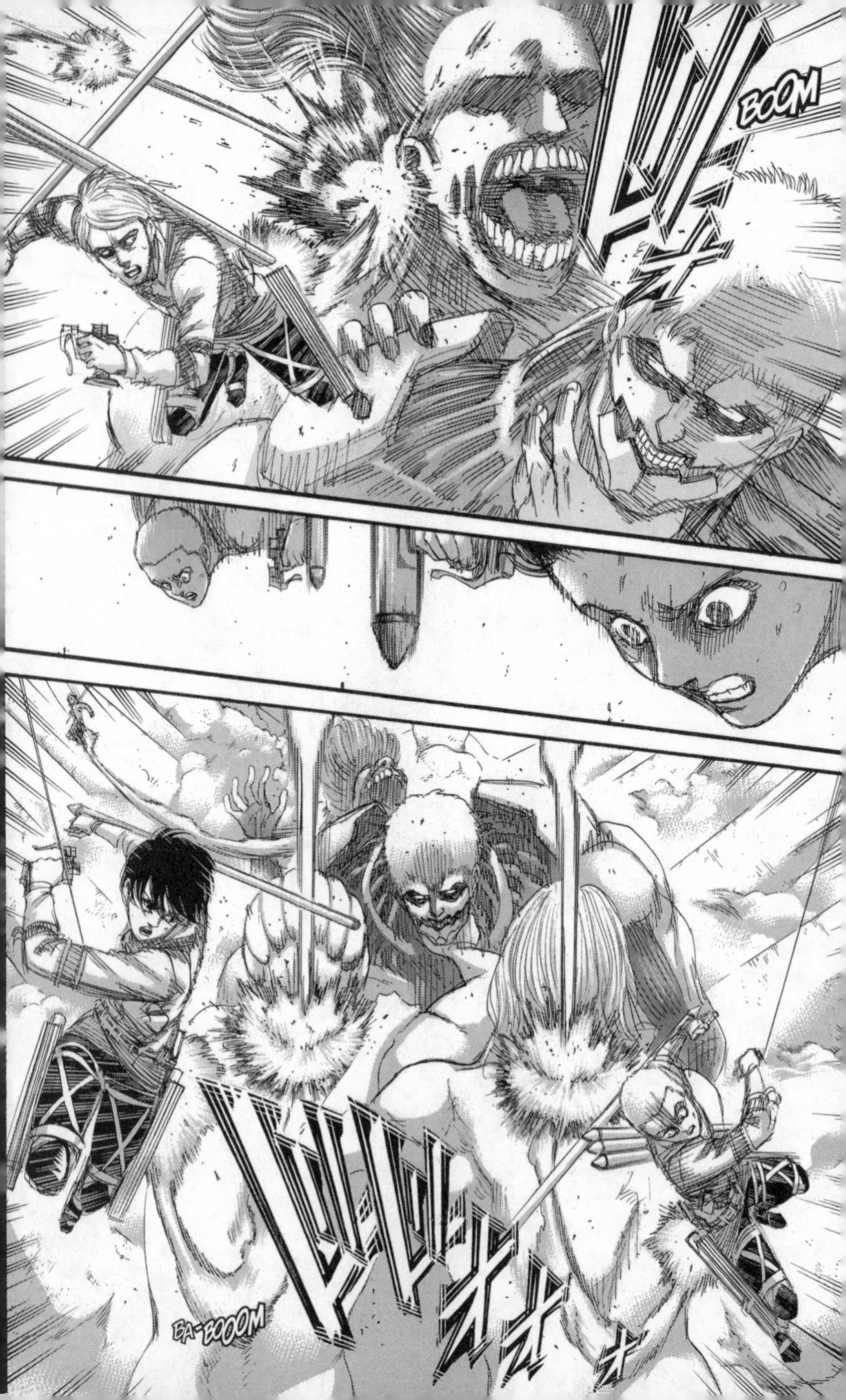
BOOM
BA-BOOOM

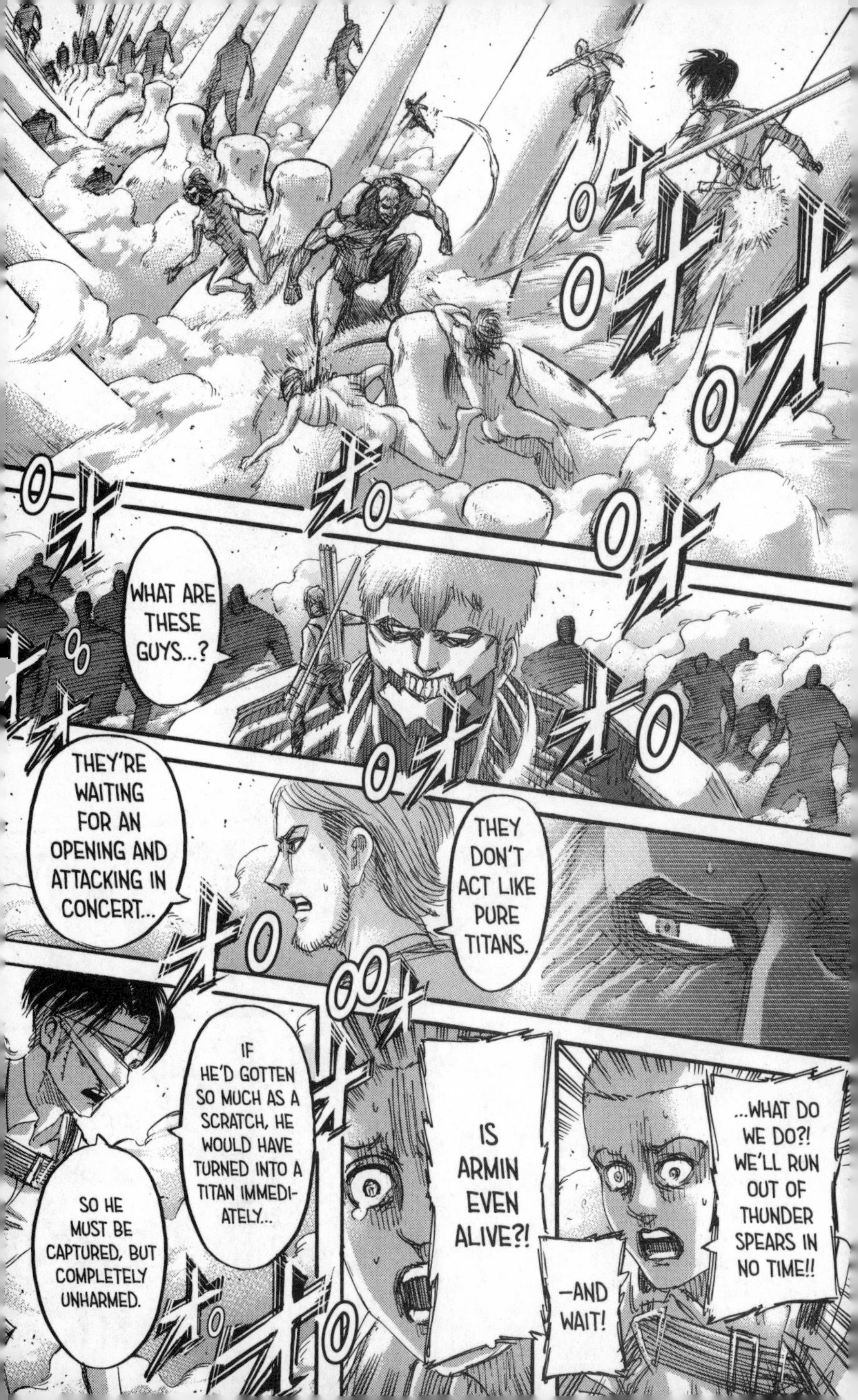
WHAT ARE THESE GUYS...?
THEY DON'T ACT LIKE PURE TITANS.
THEY'RE WAITING FOR AN OPENING AND ATTACKING IN CONCERT...
...WHAT DO WE DO?! WE'LL RUN OUT OF THUNDER SPEARS IN NO TIME!!
—AND WAIT!
IS ARMIN EVEN ALIVE?!
IF HE'D GOTTEN SO MUCH AS A SCRATCH, HE WOULD HAVE TURNED INTO A TITAN IMMEDI-ATELY...
SO HE MUST BE CAPTURED, BUT COMPLETELY UNHARMED.

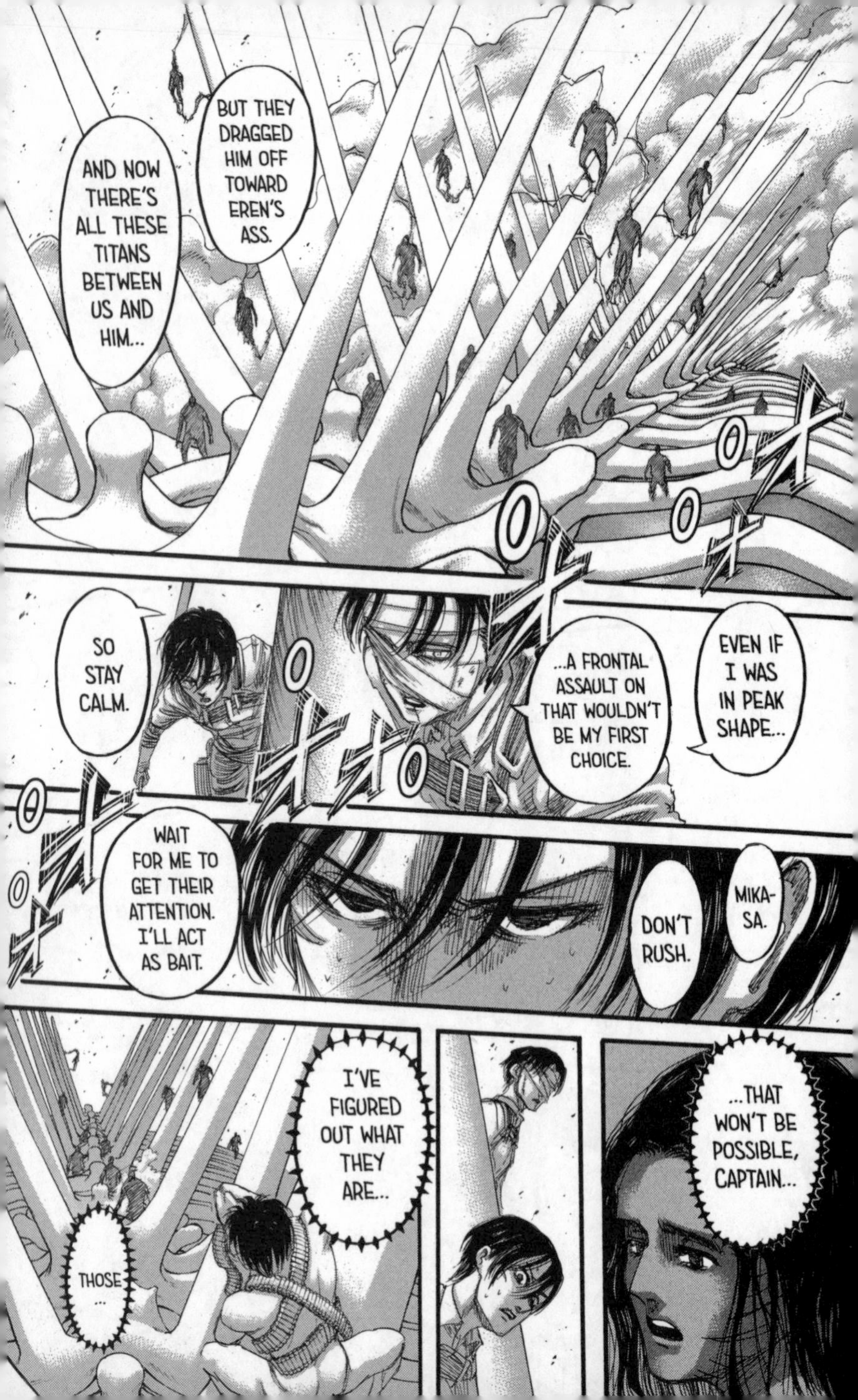
BUT THEY DRAGGED HIM OFF TOWARD EREN'S ASS.
AND NOW THERE'S ALL THESE TITANS BETWEEN US AND HIM...
EVEN IF I WAS IN PEAK SHAPE...
...A FRONTAL ASSAULT ON THAT WOULDN'T BE MY FIRST CHOICE.
SO STAY CALM.
MIKA-SA.
DON'T RUSH.
WAIT FOR ME TO GET THEIR ATTENTION. I'LL ACT AS BAIT.
...THAT WON'T BE POSSIBLE, CAPTAIN...
I'VE FIGURED OUT WHAT THEY ARE...
THOSE ...

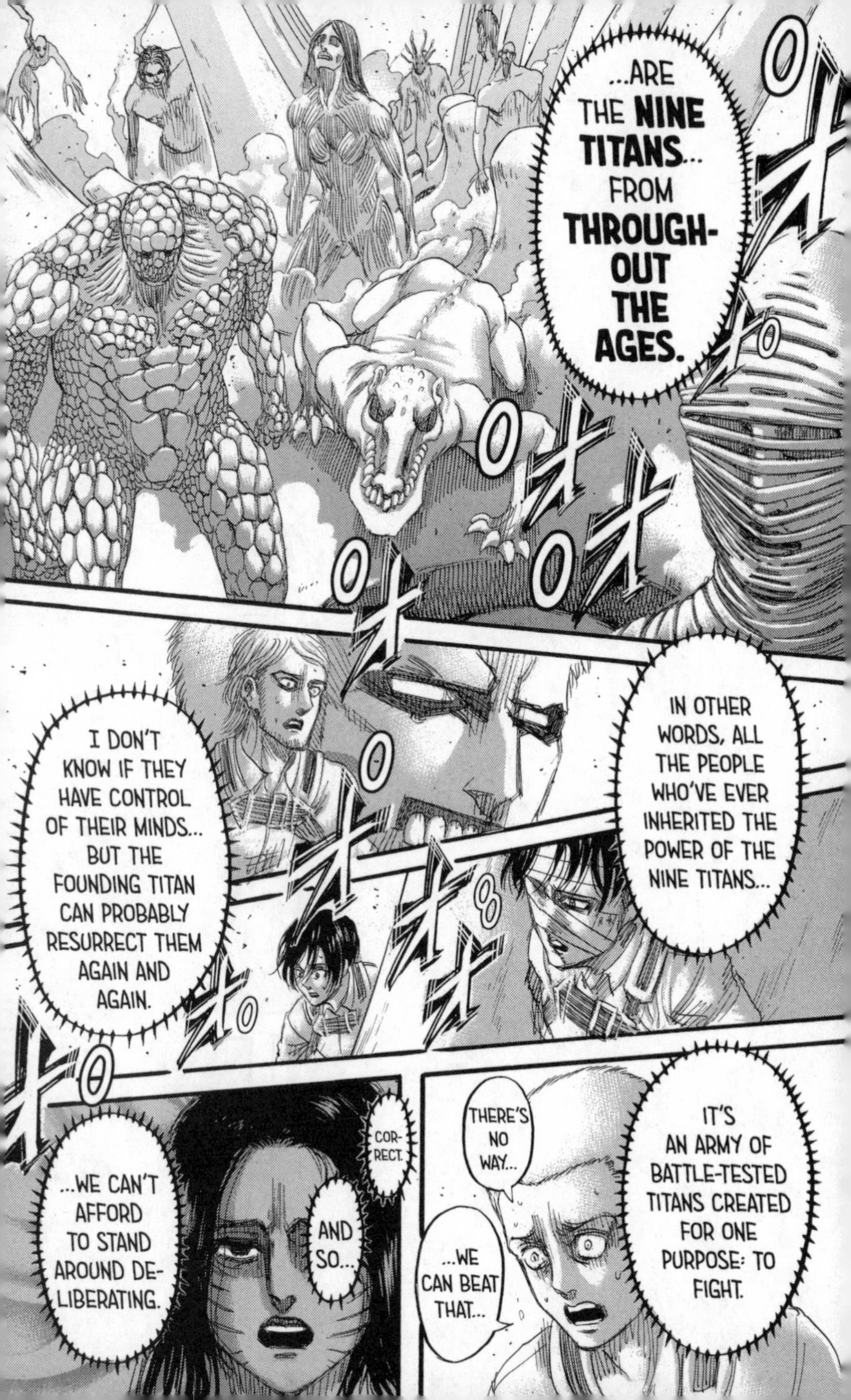
...ARE THE NINE TITANS... FROM THROUGH-OUT THE AGES.
IN OTHER WORDS, ALL THE PEOPLE WHO'VE EVER INHERITED THE POWER OF THE NINE TITANS...
I DON'T KNOW IF THEY HAVE CONTROL OF THEIR MINDS... BUT THE FOUNDING TITAN CAN PROBABLY RESURRECT THEM AGAIN AND AGAIN.
IT'S AN ARMY OF BATTLE-TESTED TITANS CREATED FOR ONE PURPOSE: TO FIGHT.
THERE'S NO WAY...
...WE CAN BEAT THAT...
COR-RECT.
AND SO...
...WE CAN'T AFFORD TO STAND AROUND DE-LIBERATING.

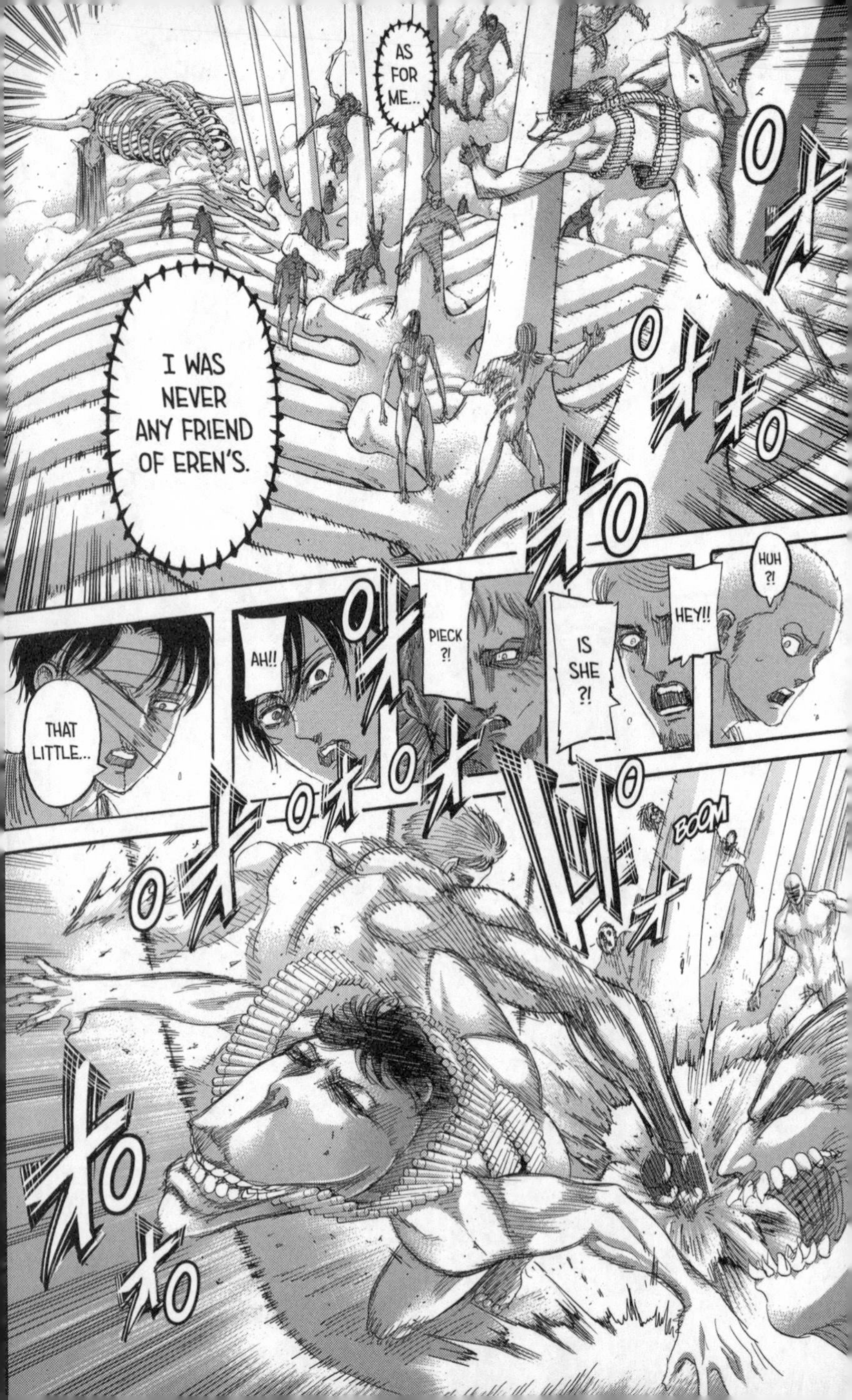

AS FOR ME...
I WAS NEVER ANY FRIEND OF EREN'S.
HUH ?!
HEY!!
IS SHE ?!
PIECK ?!
AH!!
THAT LITTLE...
BOOM

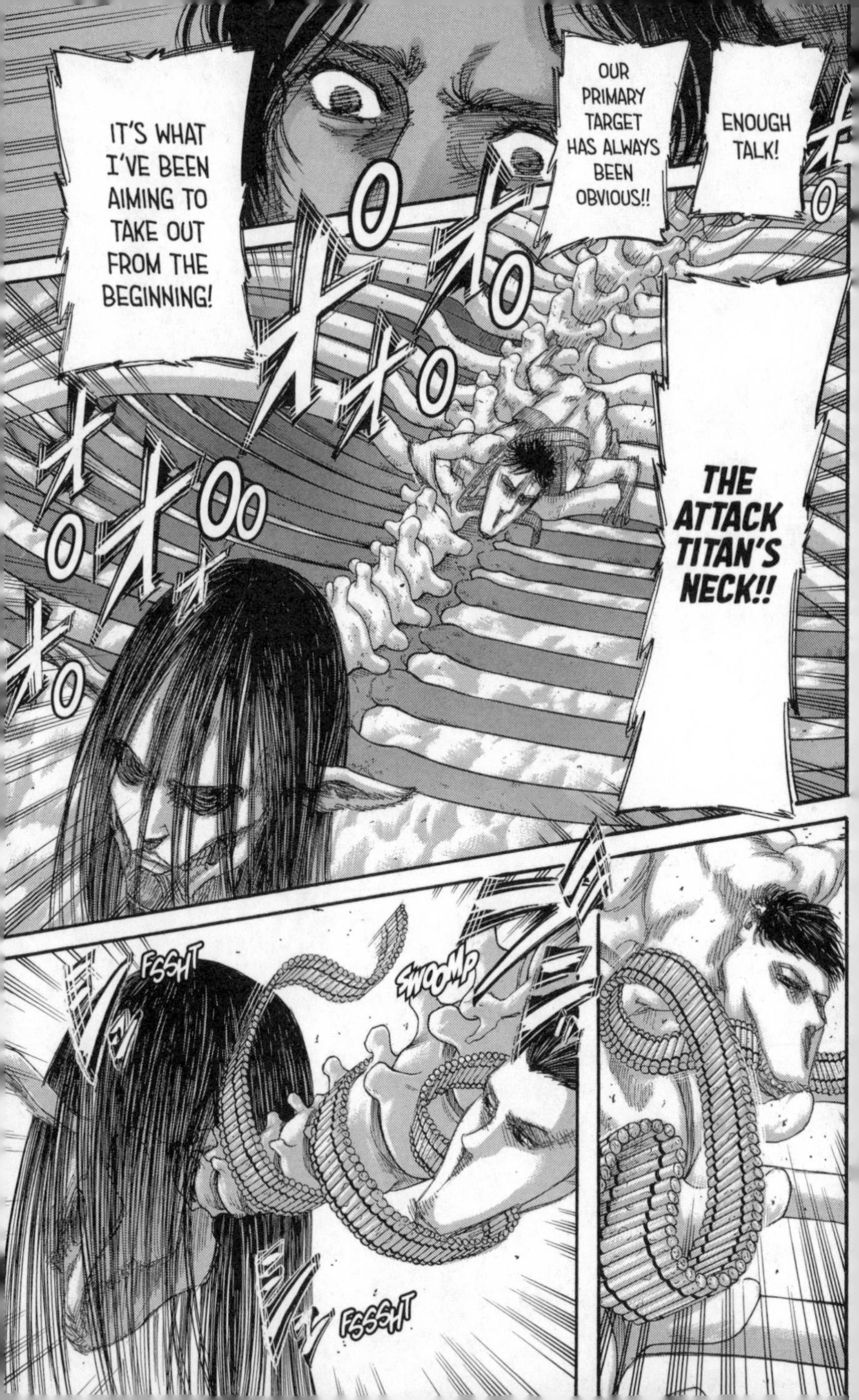
ENOUGH TALK!
OUR PRIMARY TARGET HAS ALWAYS BEEN OBVIOUS!!
THE ATTACK TITAN'S NECK!!
IT'S WHAT I'VE BEEN AIMING TO TAKE OUT FROM THE BEGINNING!
SWOOMP
FSSHT
FSSSHT

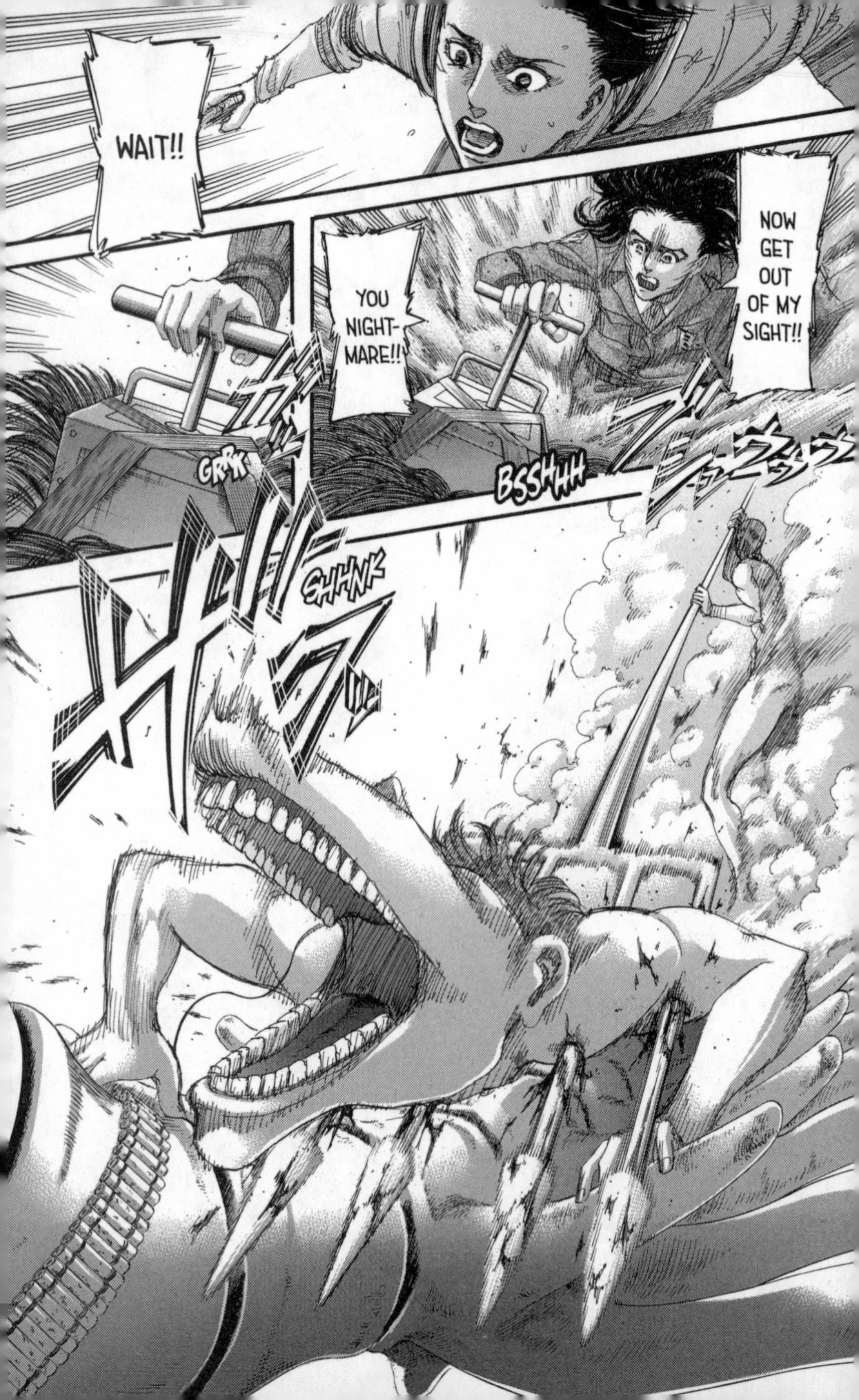
WAIT!!
NOW GET OUT OF MY SIGHT!!
YOU NIGHTMARE!!
BSSHHH
GRRK
SHHNK

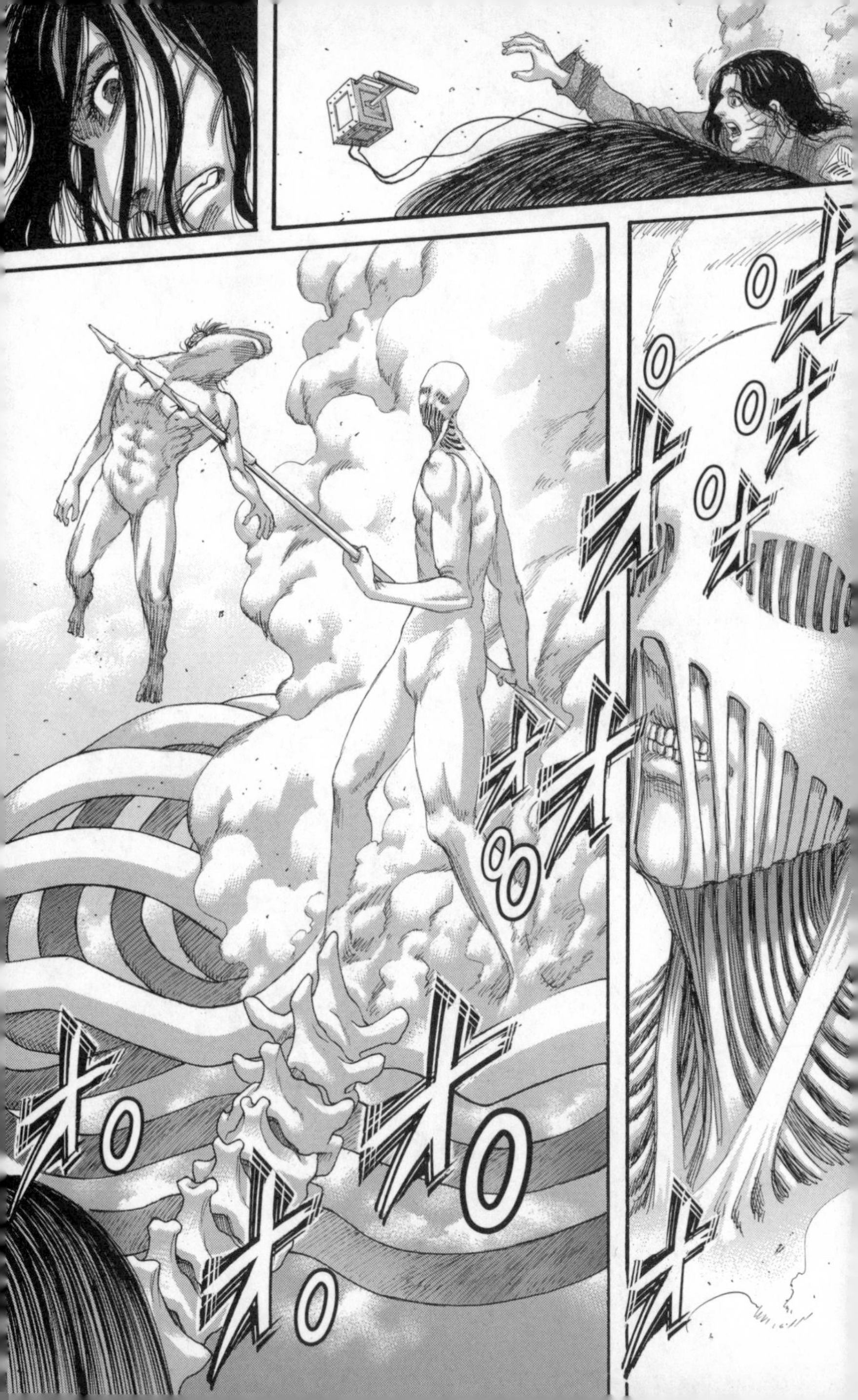

オオオオ
オオオオオ
オオ
オオ

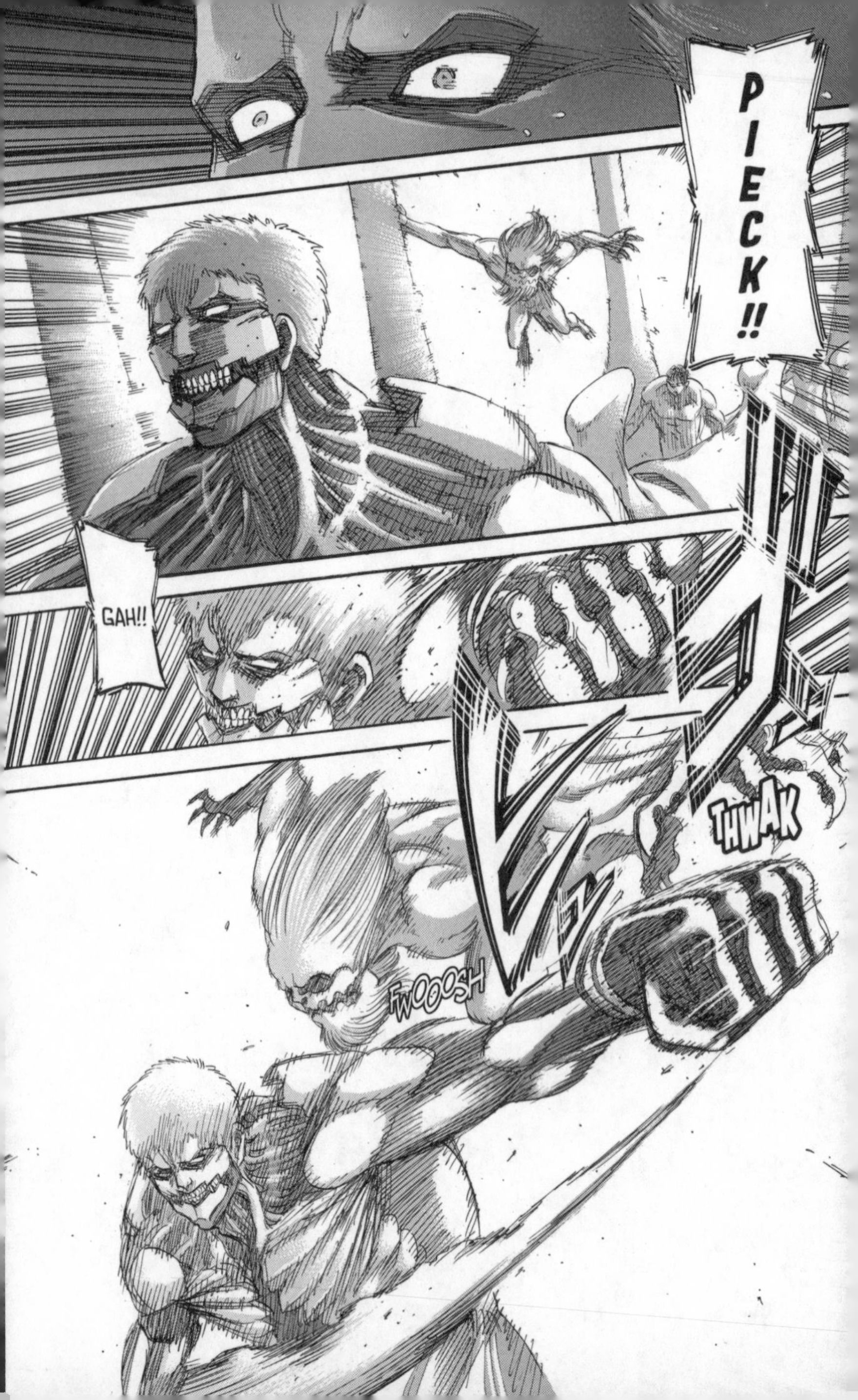
PIECK!!
GAH!!
THWAK
FWOOOSH

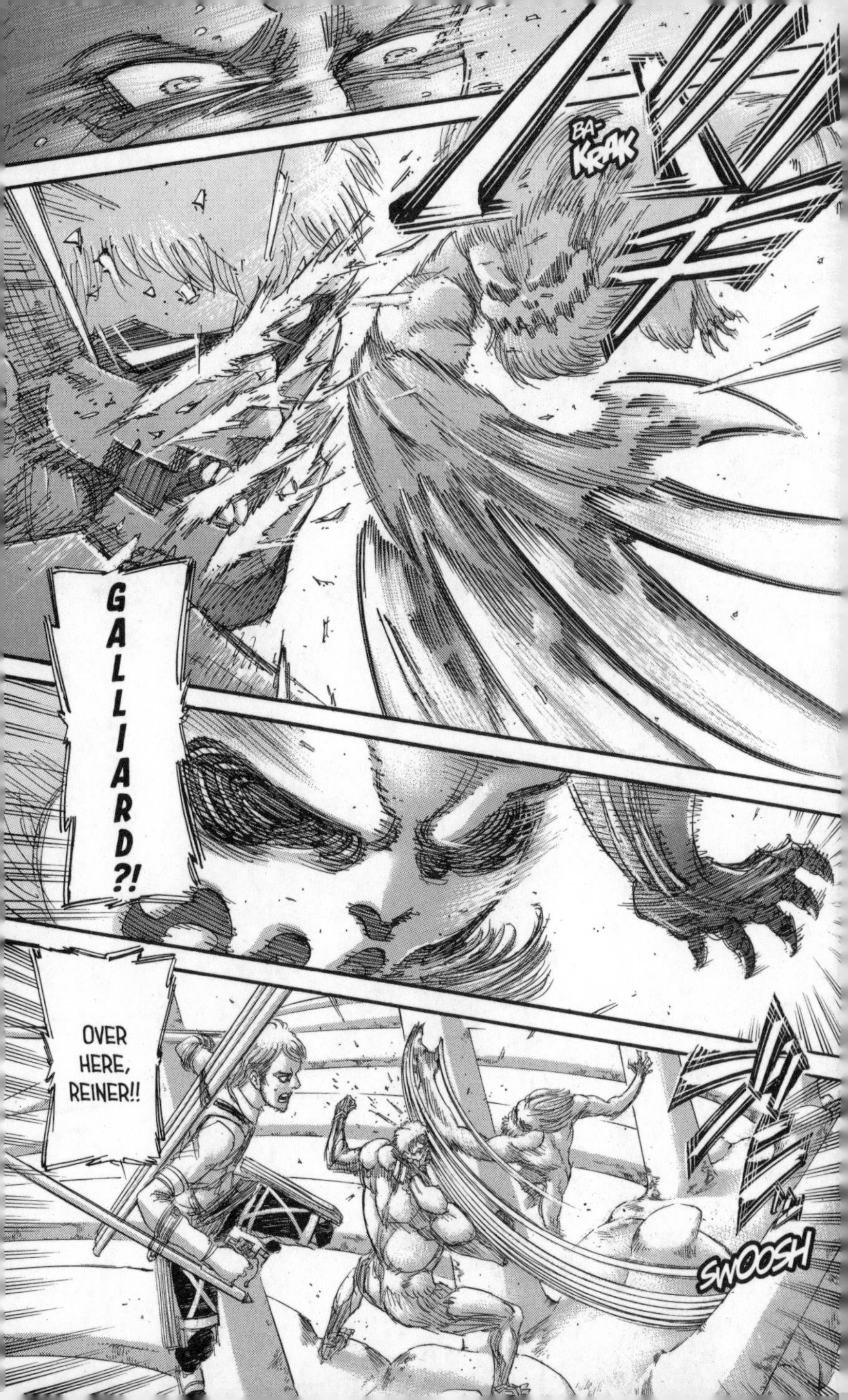
BA-KRAK
GALLIARD?!
OVER HERE, REINER!!
SWOOSH

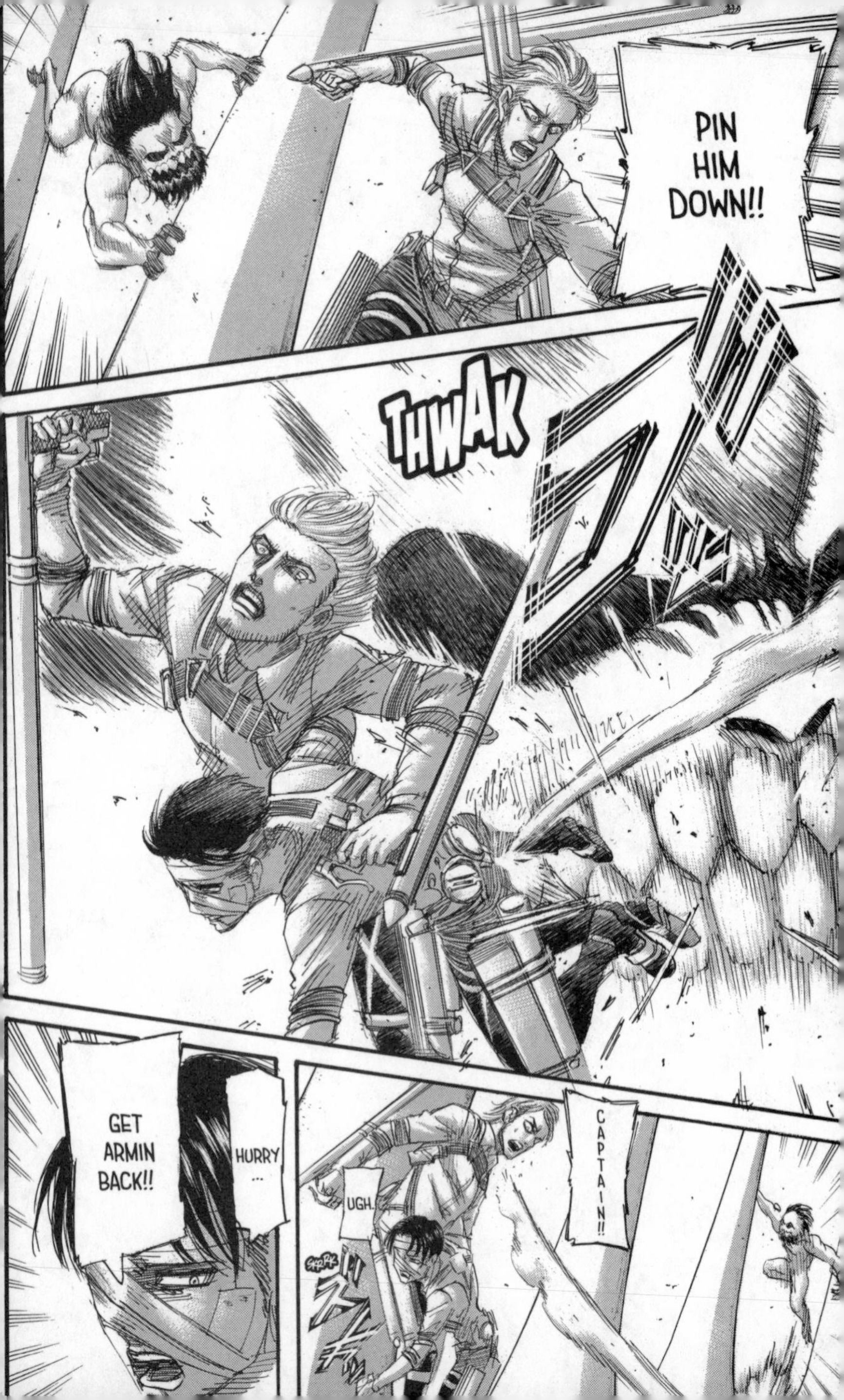
PIN HIM DOWN!!
THWAK
CAPTAIN!!
UGH.
SKRK
HURRY...
GET ARMIN BACK!!

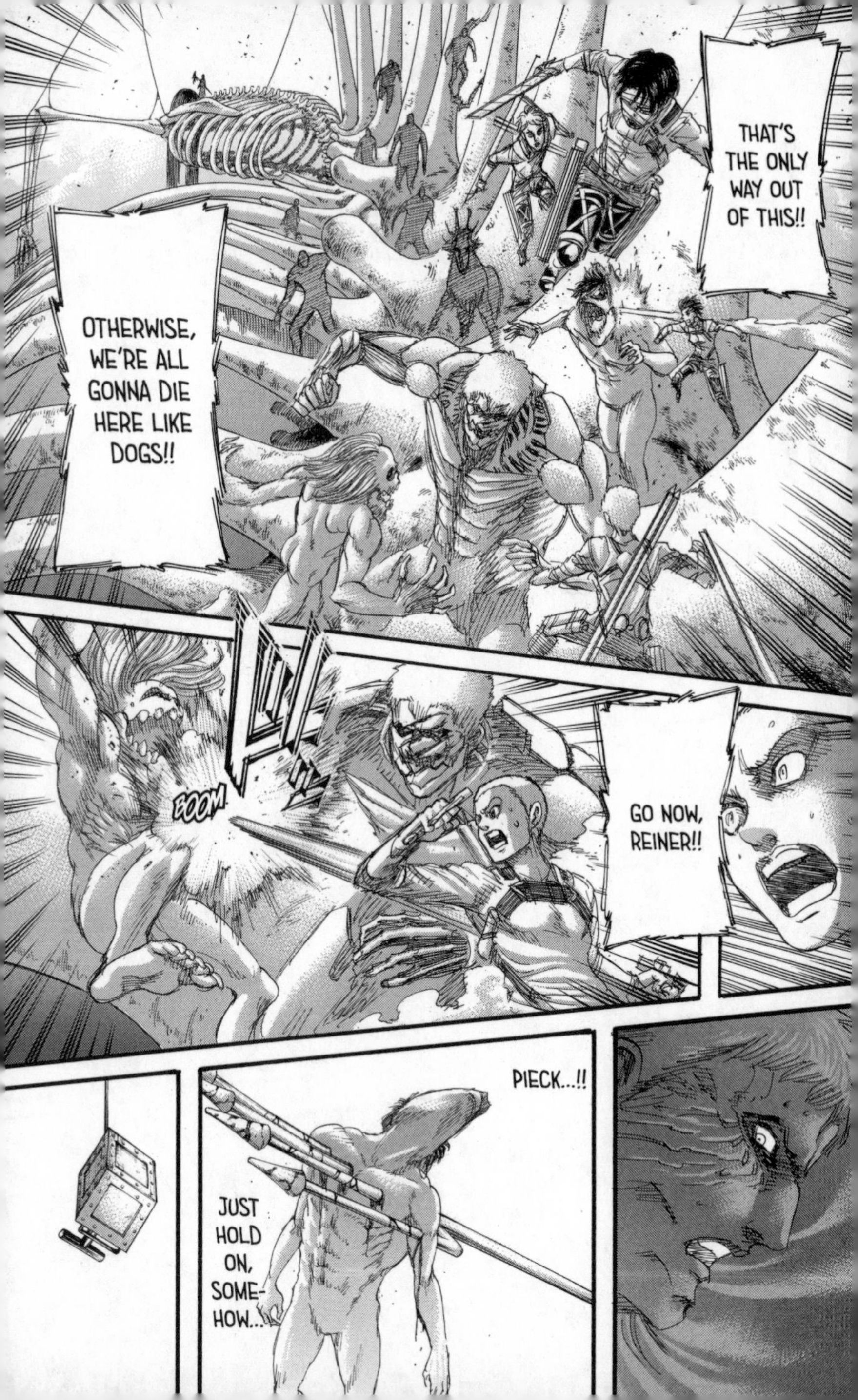

THAT'S THE ONLY WAY OUT OF THIS!!
OTHERWISE, WE'RE ALL GONNA DIE HERE LIKE DOGS!!
GO NOW, REINER!!
BOOM
PIECK...!!
JUST HOLD ON, SOME-HOW...

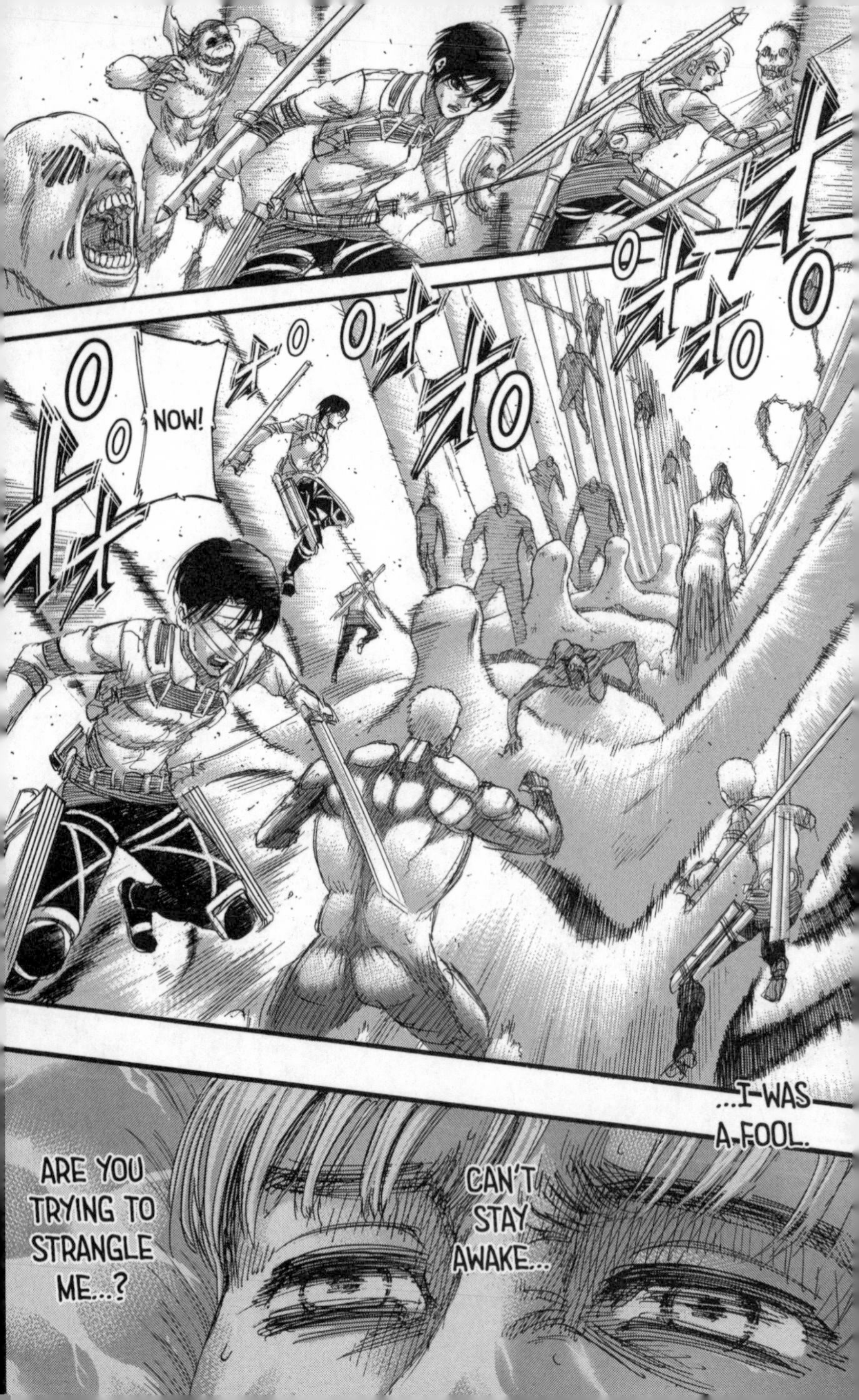
NOW!
...I WAS A FOOL.
CAN'T STAY AWAKE...
ARE YOU TRYING TO STRANGLE ME...?

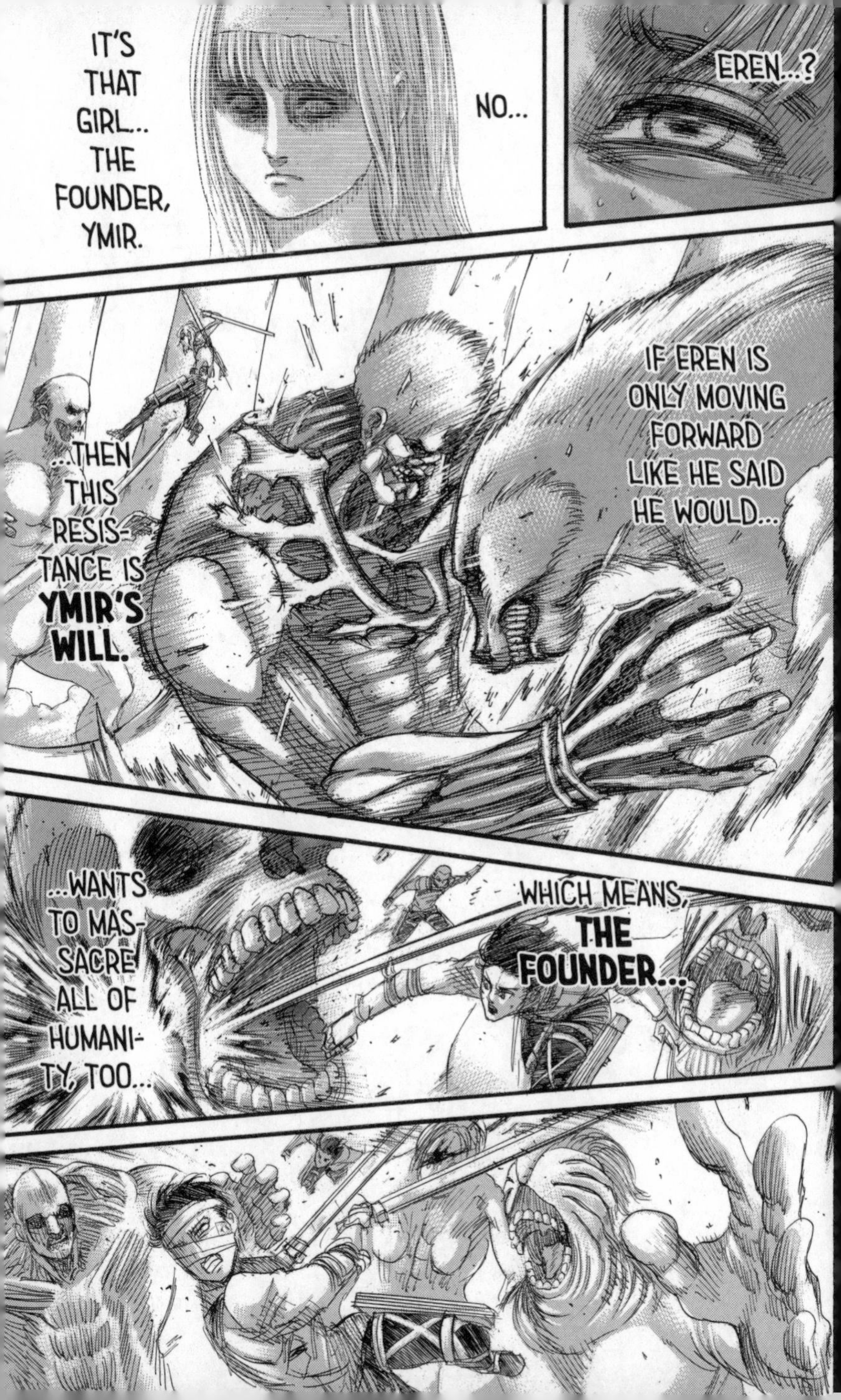
EREN...?
NO...
IT'S THAT GIRL... THE FOUNDER, YMIR.
IF EREN IS ONLY MOVING FORWARD LIKE HE SAID HE WOULD...
...THEN THIS RESIS-TANCE IS **YMIR'S WILL.**
WHICH MEANS, **THE FOUNDER...**
...WANTS TO MAS-SACRE ALL OF HUMANI-TY, TOO...

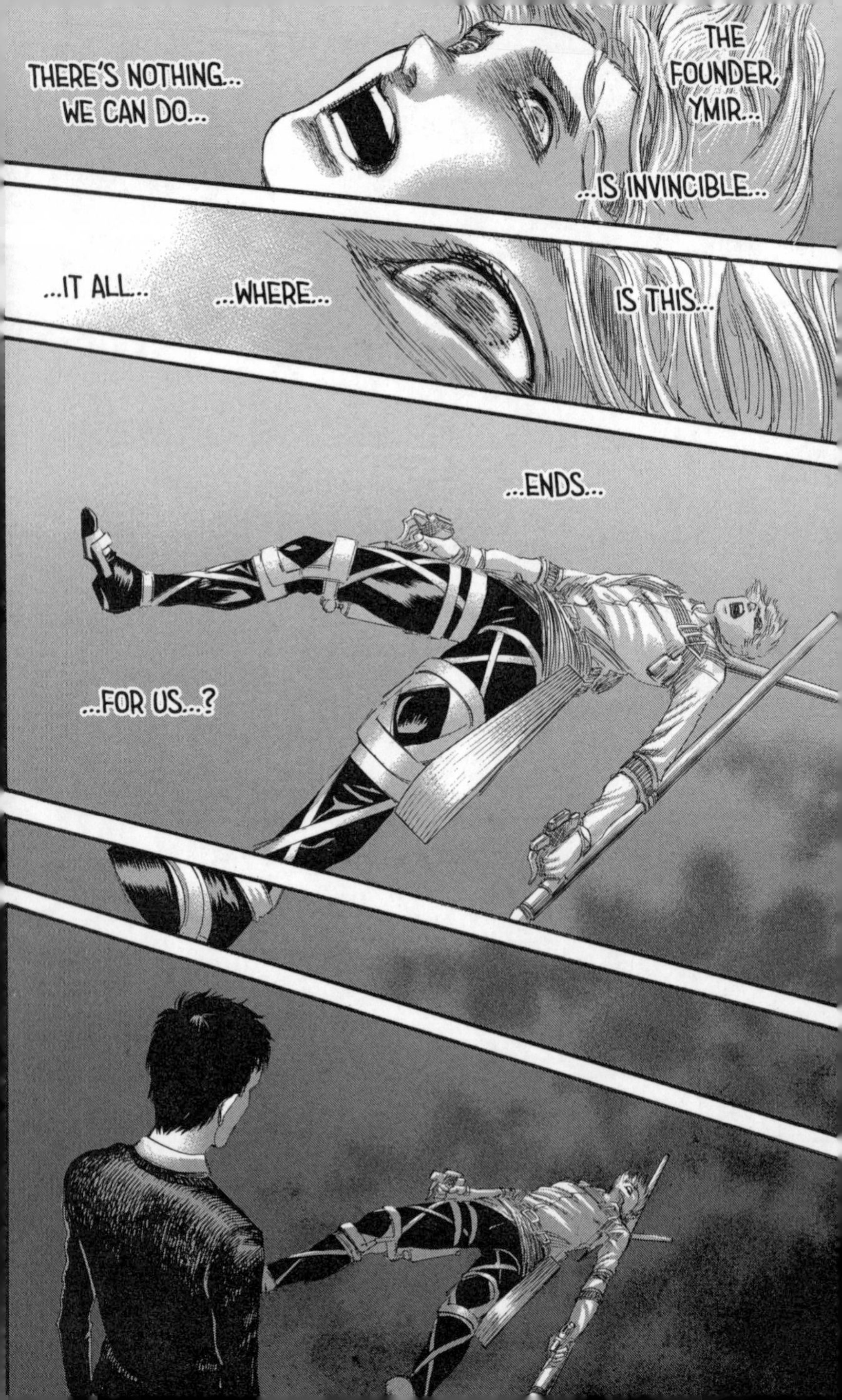
THE FOUNDER, YMIR...
...IS INVINCIBLE...
THERE'S NOTHING... WE CAN DO...
IS THIS...
...WHERE...
...IT ALL...
...ENDS...
...FOR US...?

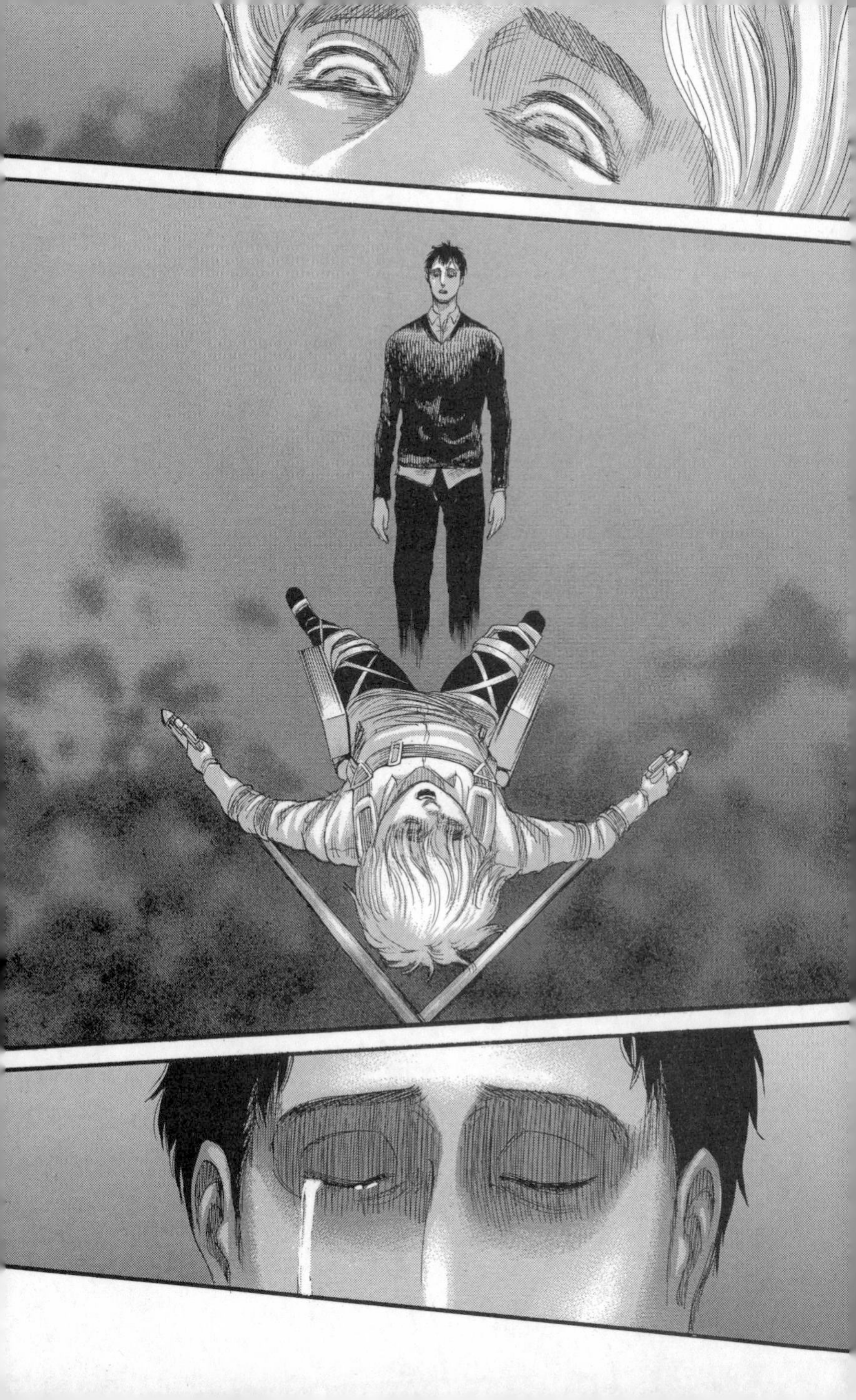

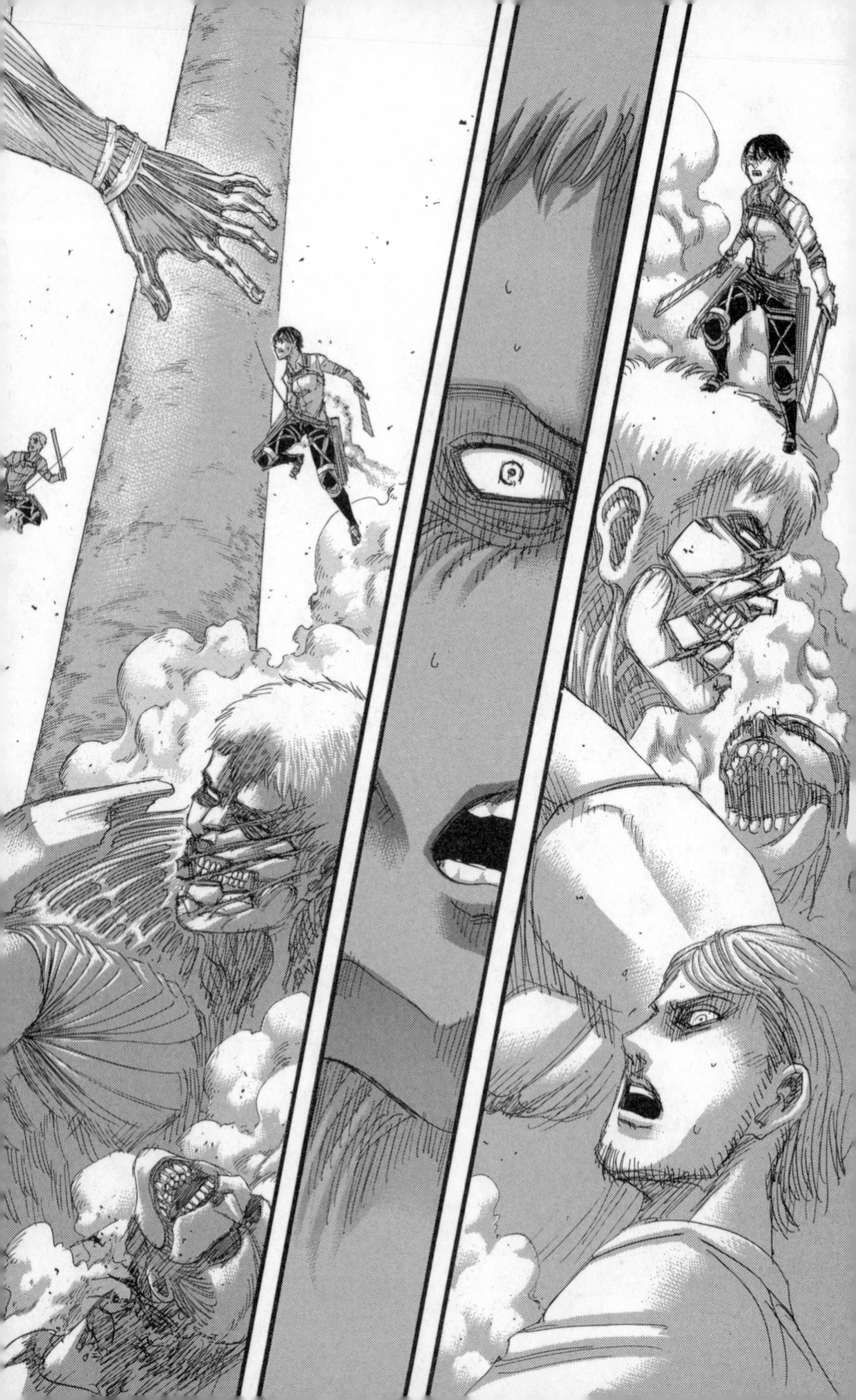

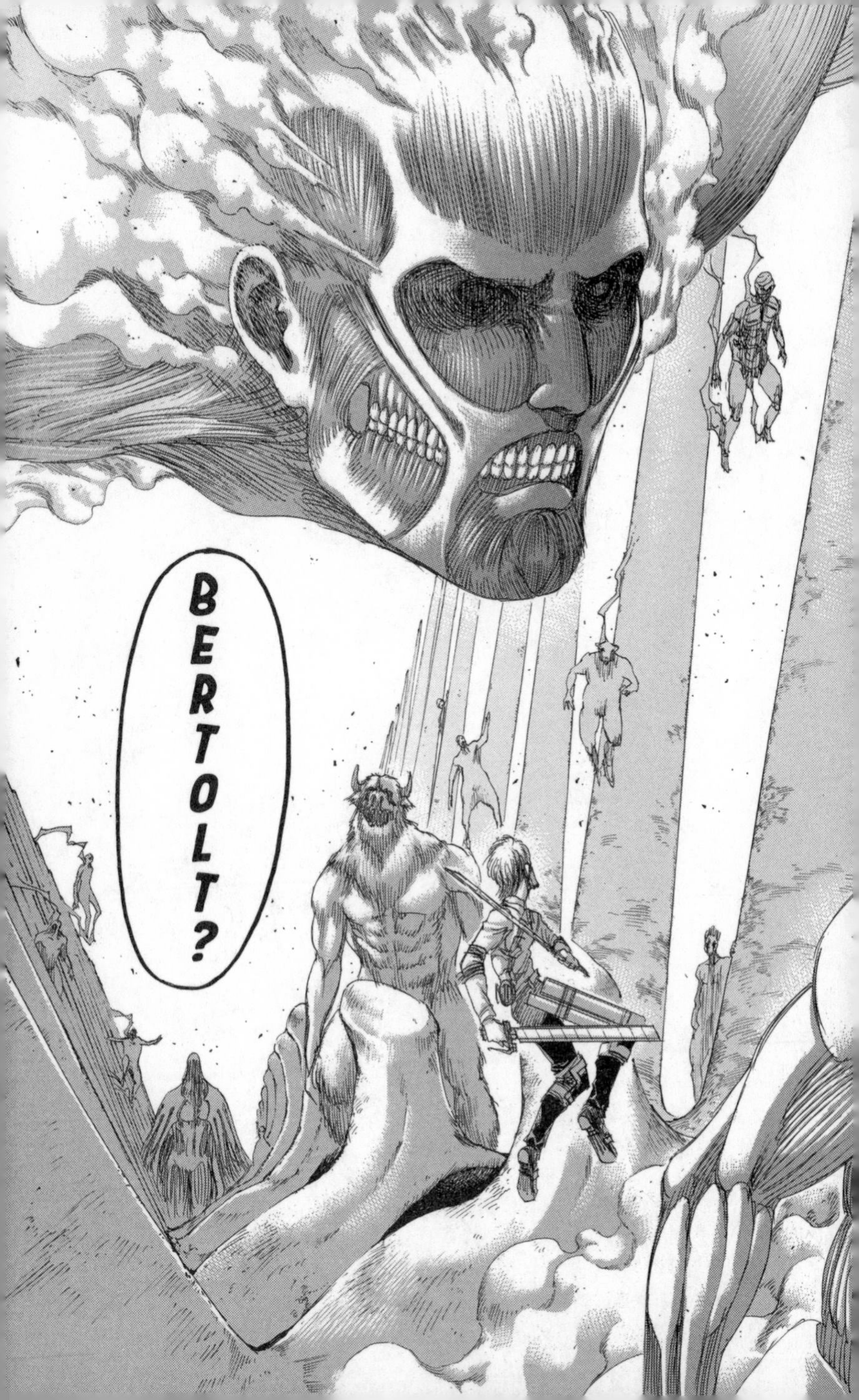
BERTOLT?

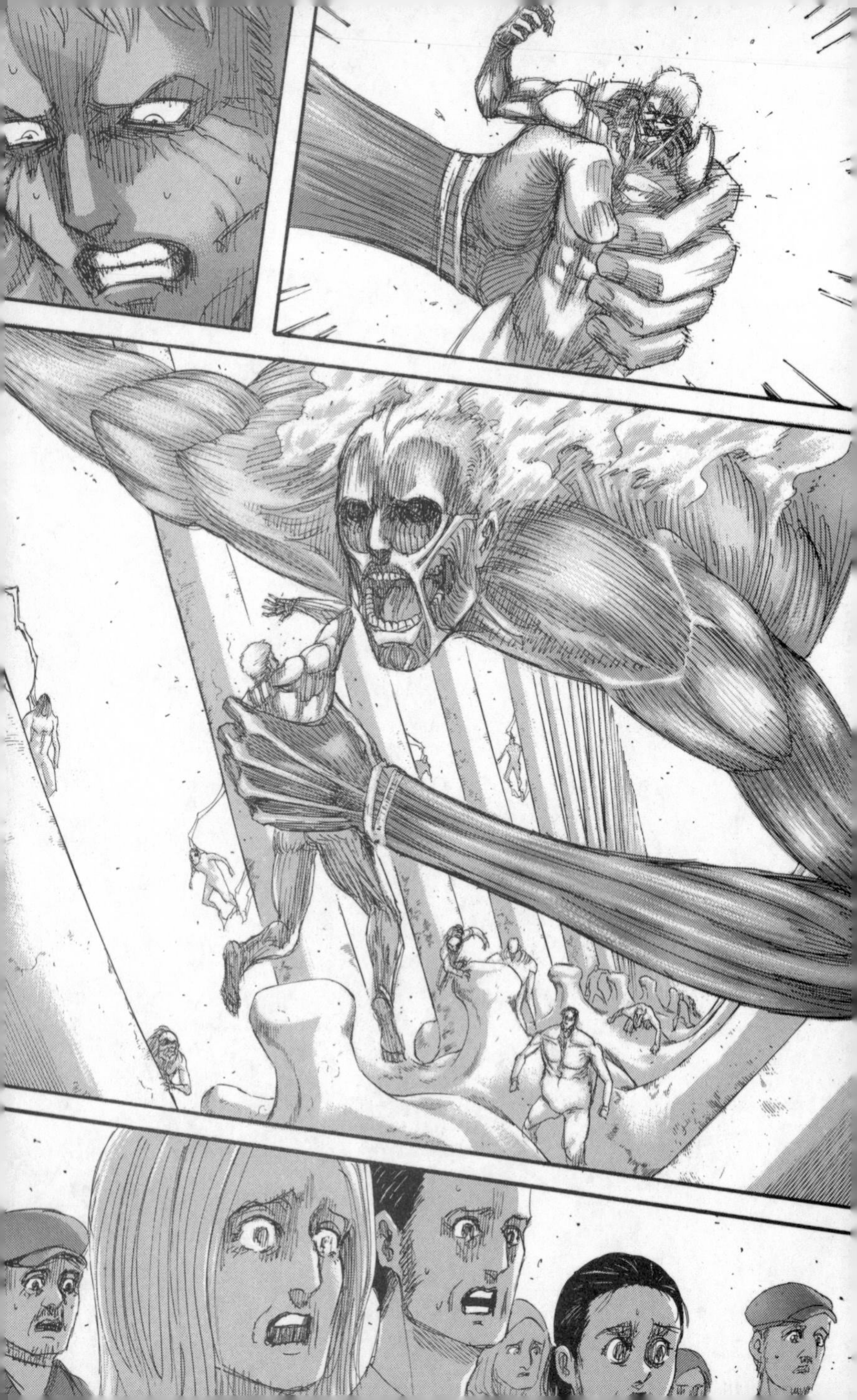

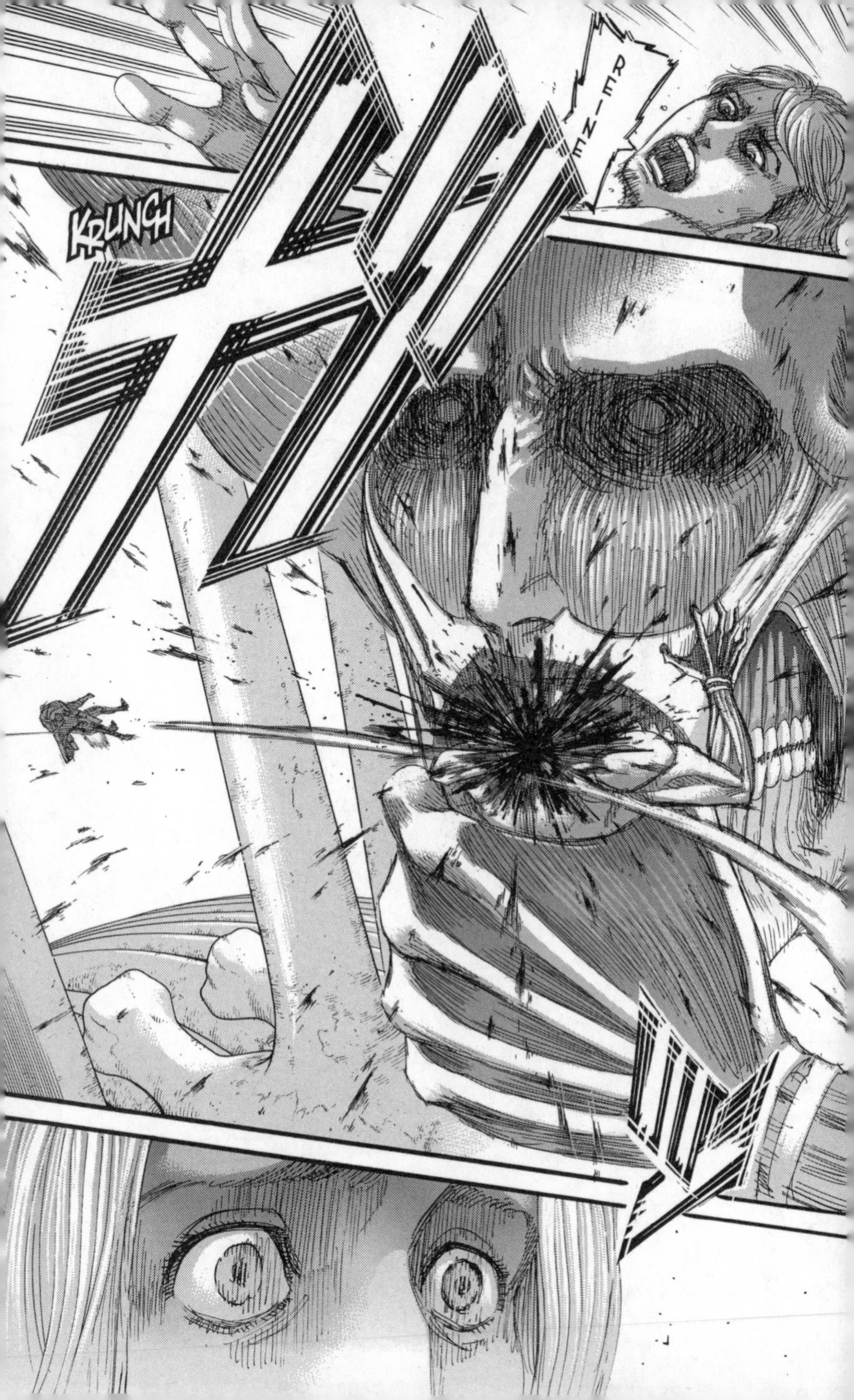
REINE
KRUNCH

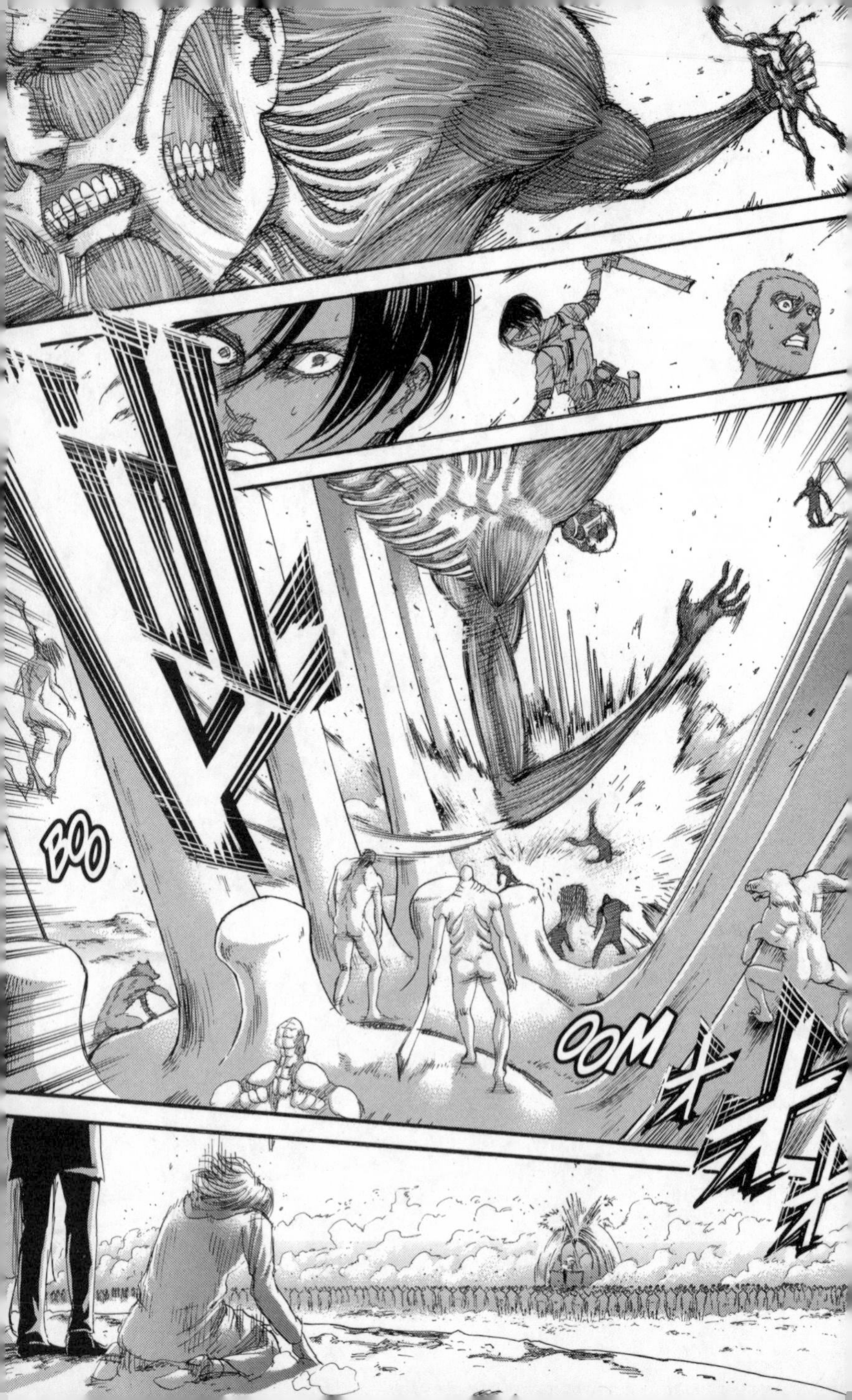
BOO
OOM

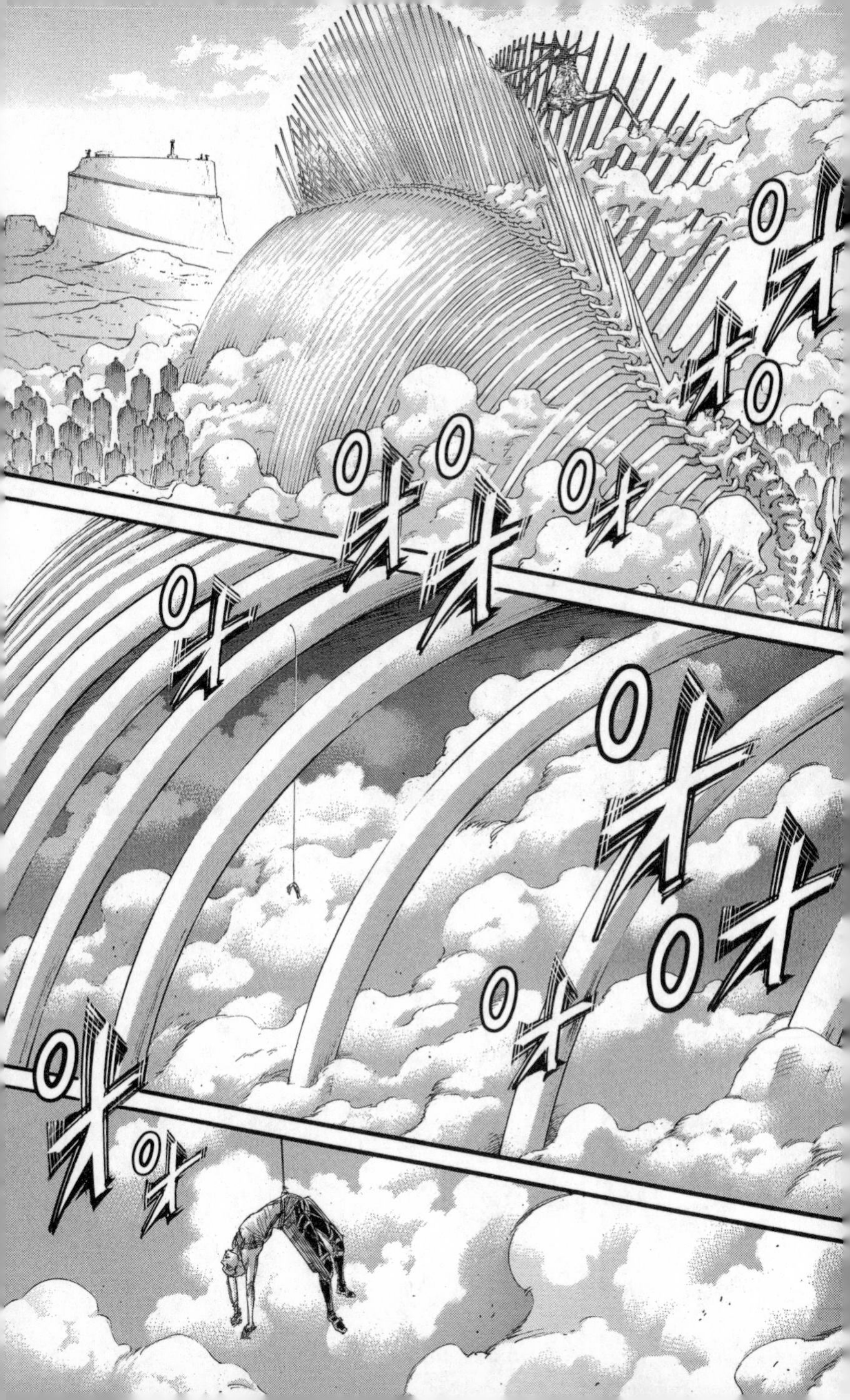

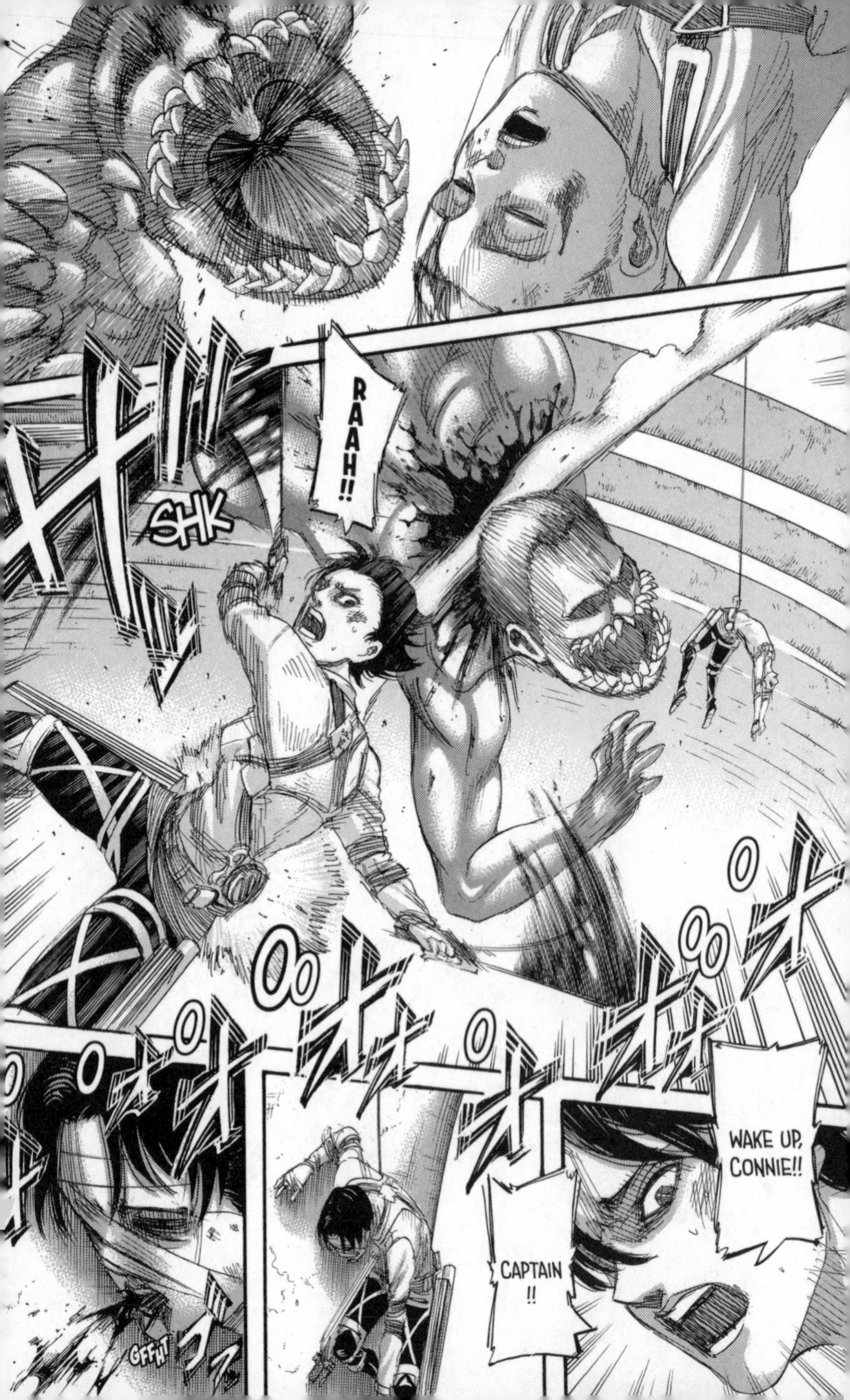
RAAH!!
SHK
WAKE UP, CONNIE!!
CAPTAIN !!
GFFHT

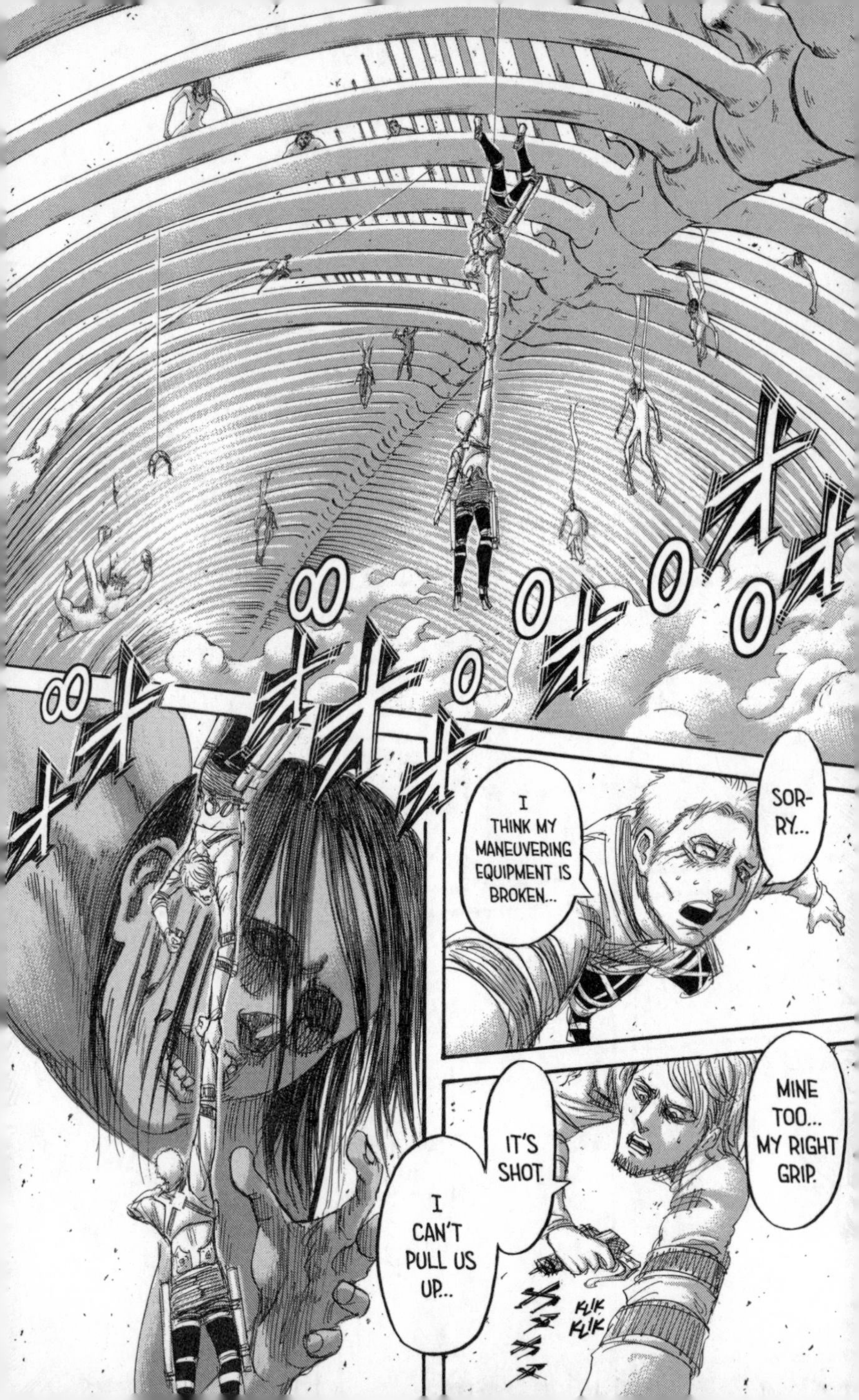
SOR-RY...
I THINK MY MANEUVERING EQUIPMENT IS BROKEN...
MINE TOO... MY RIGHT GRIP.
IT'S SHOT.
I CAN'T PULL US UP...
KLIK KLIK

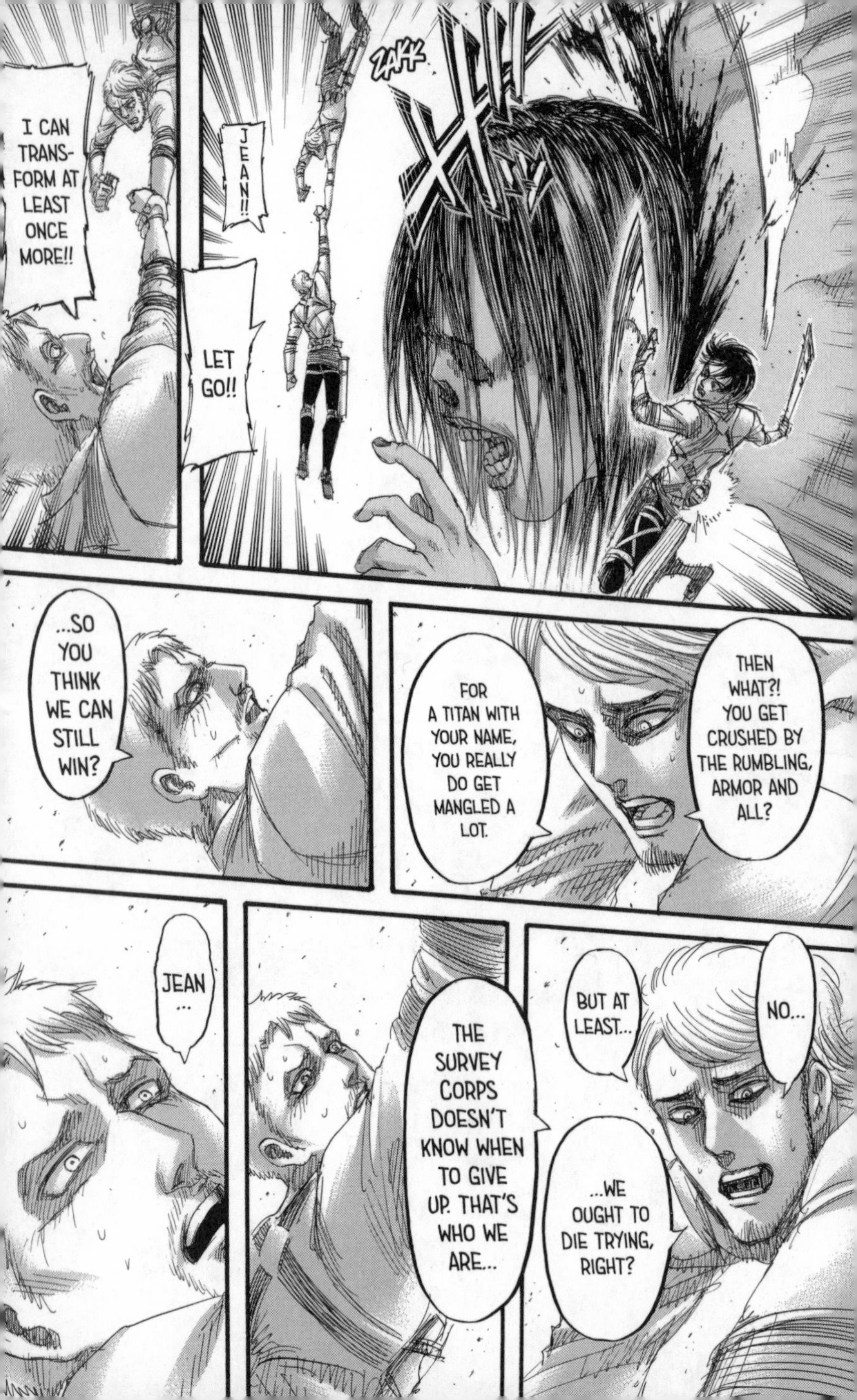
ZAKK
JEAN!!
LET GO!!
I CAN TRANSFORM AT LEAST ONCE MORE!!
THEN WHAT?! YOU GET CRUSHED BY THE RUMBLING, ARMOR AND ALL?
FOR A TITAN WITH YOUR NAME, YOU REALLY DO GET MANGLED A LOT.
...SO YOU THINK WE CAN STILL WIN?
NO...
BUT AT LEAST...
...WE OUGHT TO DIE TRYING, RIGHT?
THE SURVEY CORPS DOESN'T KNOW WHEN TO GIVE UP. THAT'S WHO WE ARE...
JEAN...

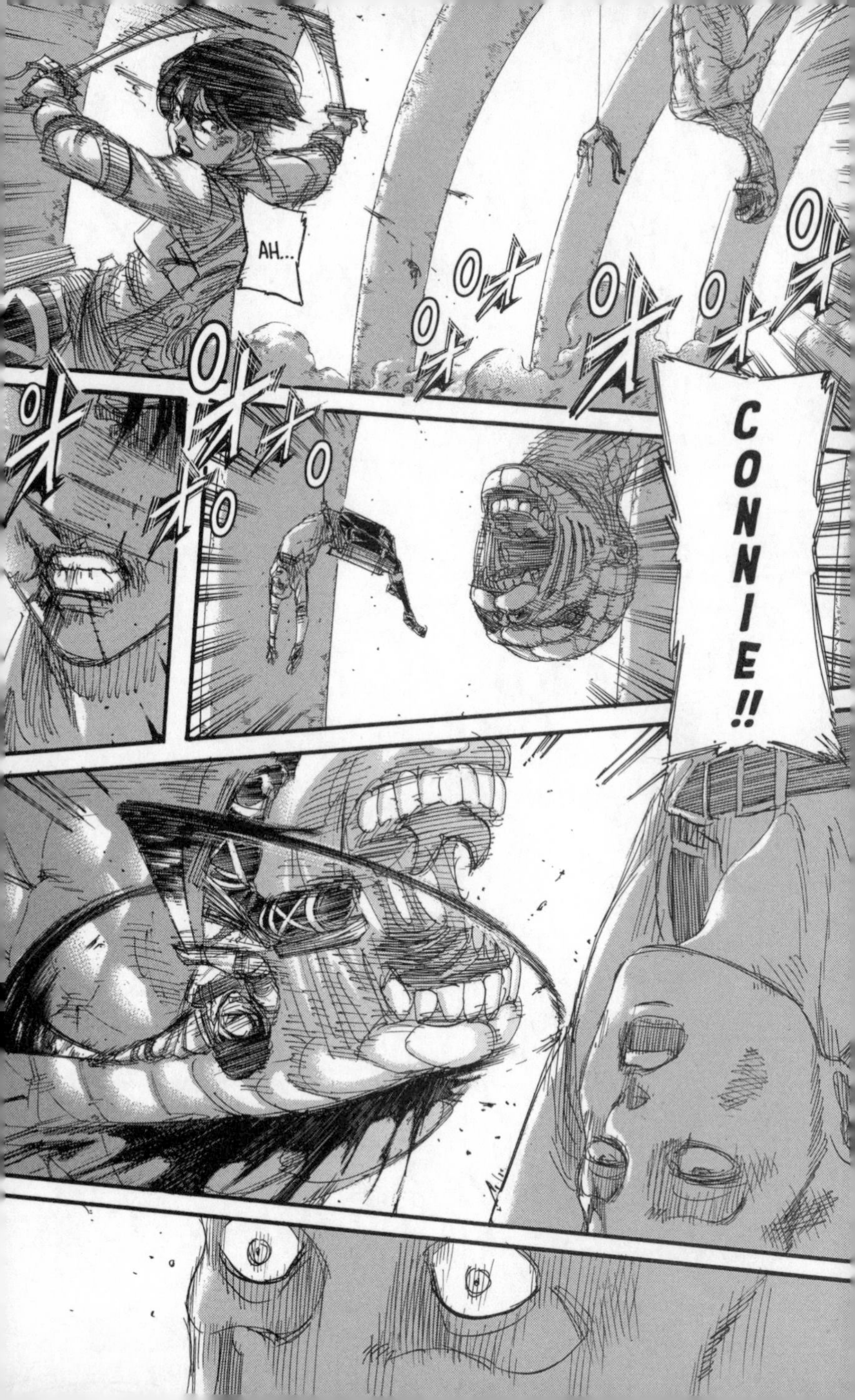

OオOオOオOオ
AH...
OオOオOオOオ
CONNIE!!

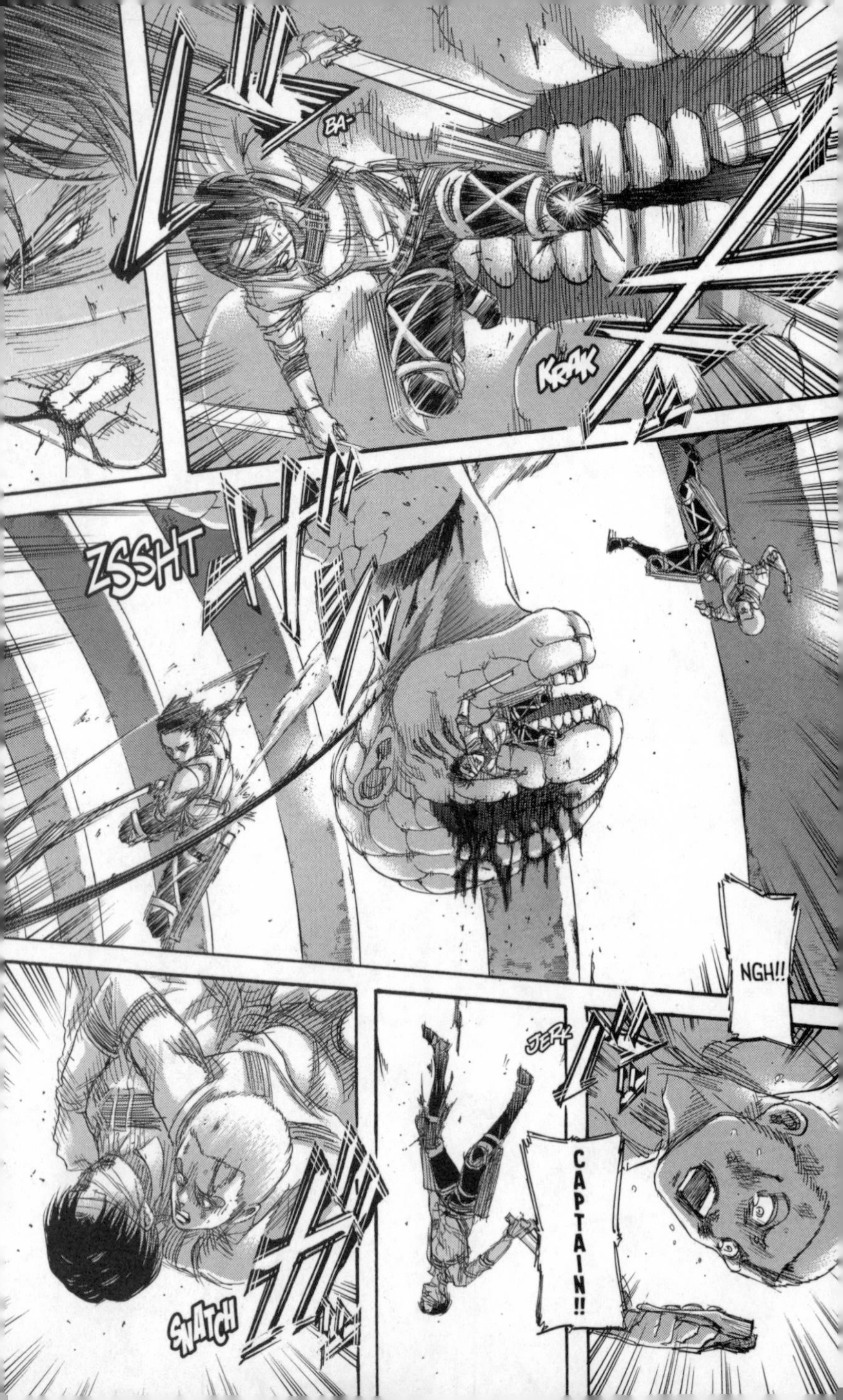
BA-
KRAK
ZSSHT
NGH!!
JERK
CAPTAIN!!
SNATCH

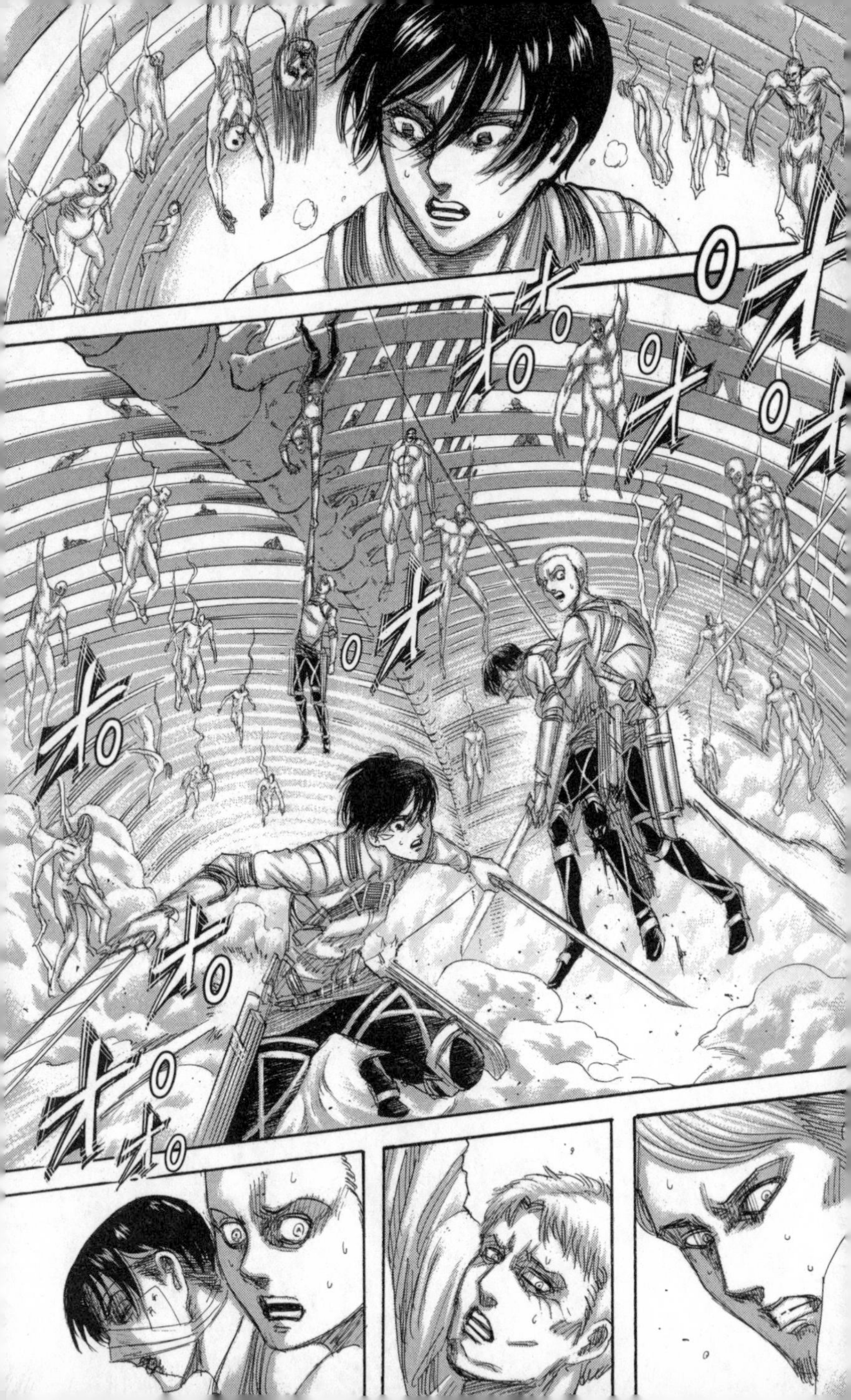

ォオ
オォォ
オォ
オォ
オォ
オォ
オォ

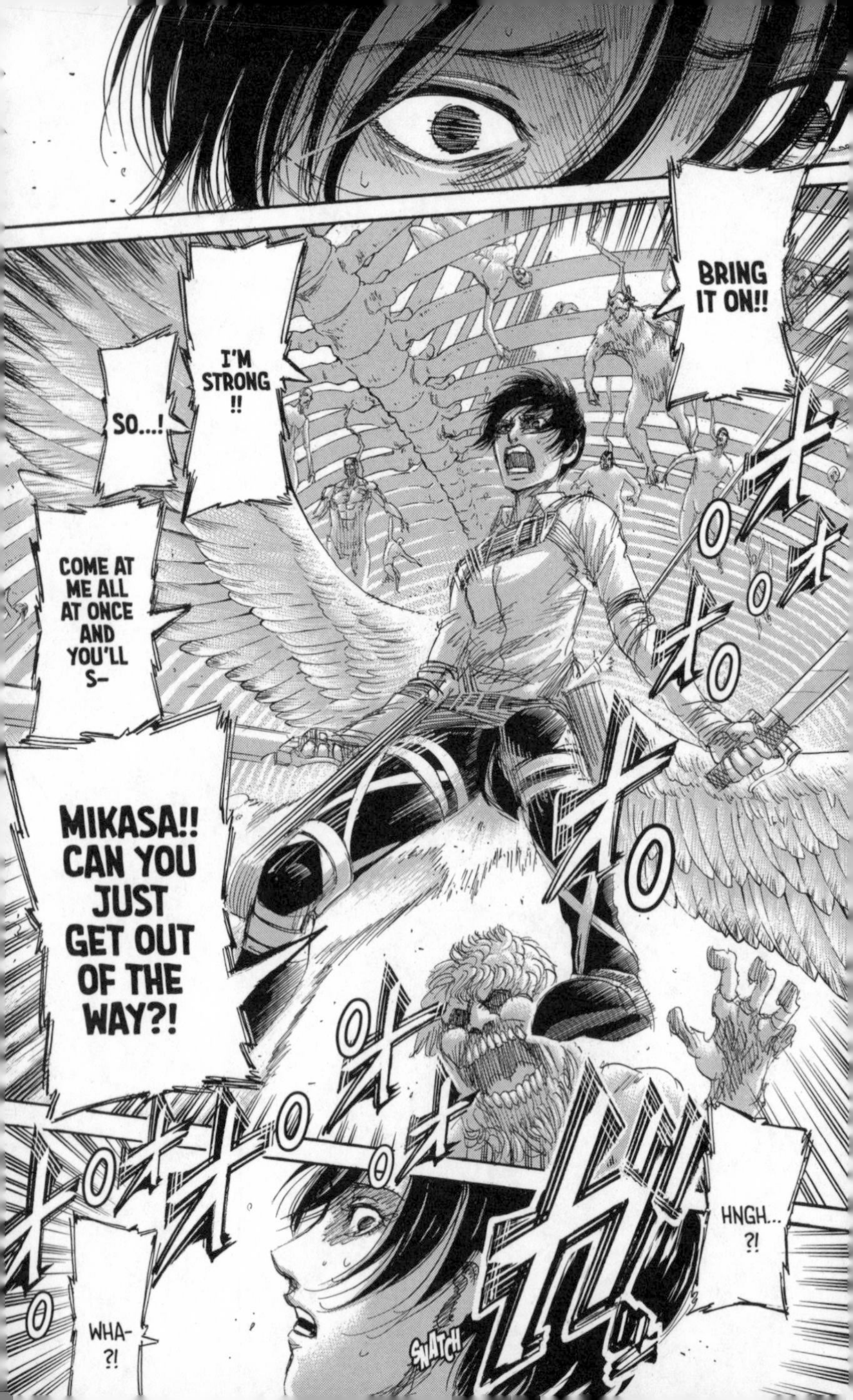
BRING IT ON!!
I'M STRONG!!
SO...!
COME AT ME ALL AT ONCE AND YOU'LL S-
MIKASA!! CAN YOU JUST GET OUT OF THE WAY?!
HNGH...?!
SNATCH
WHA-?!

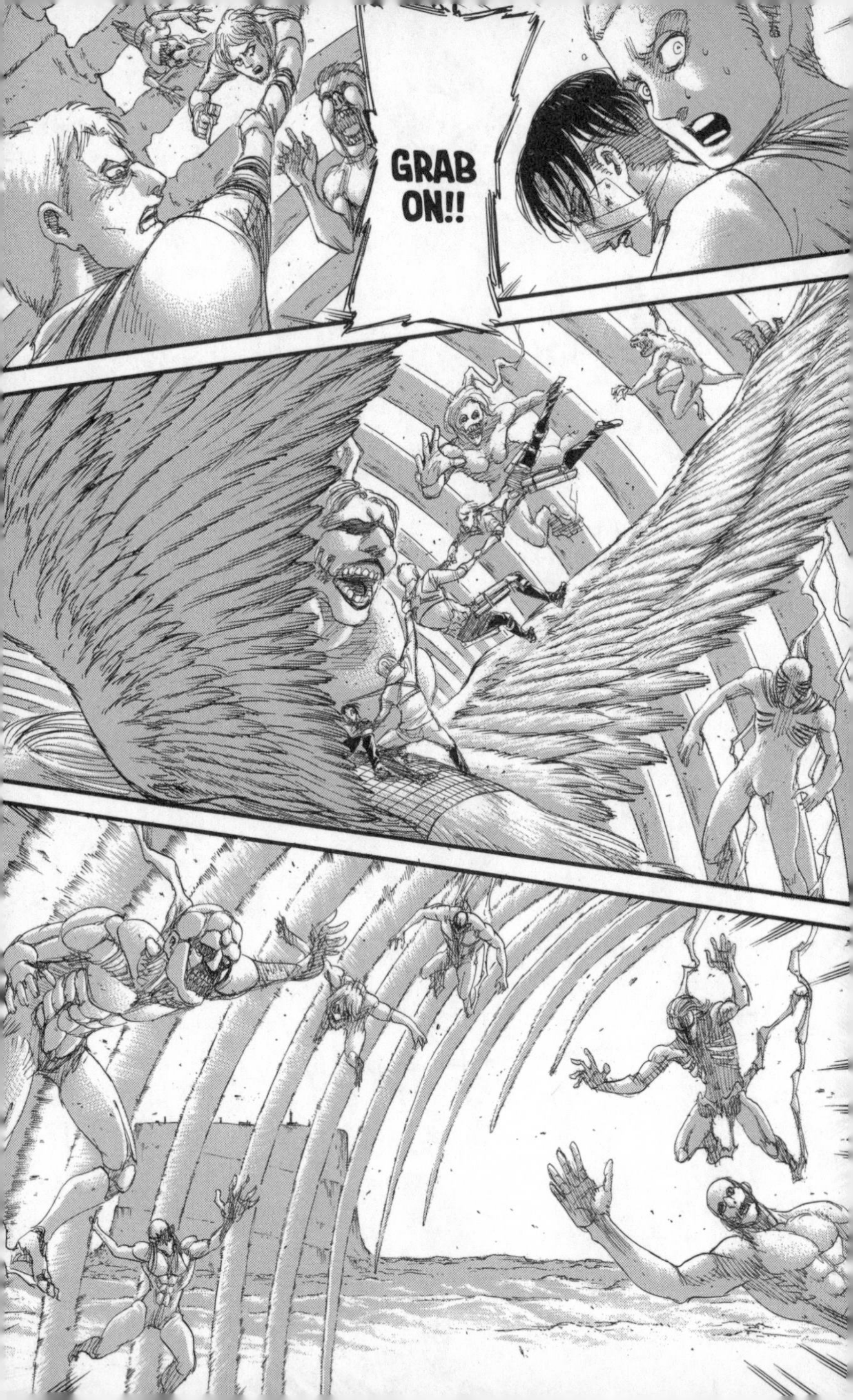
GRAB ON!!

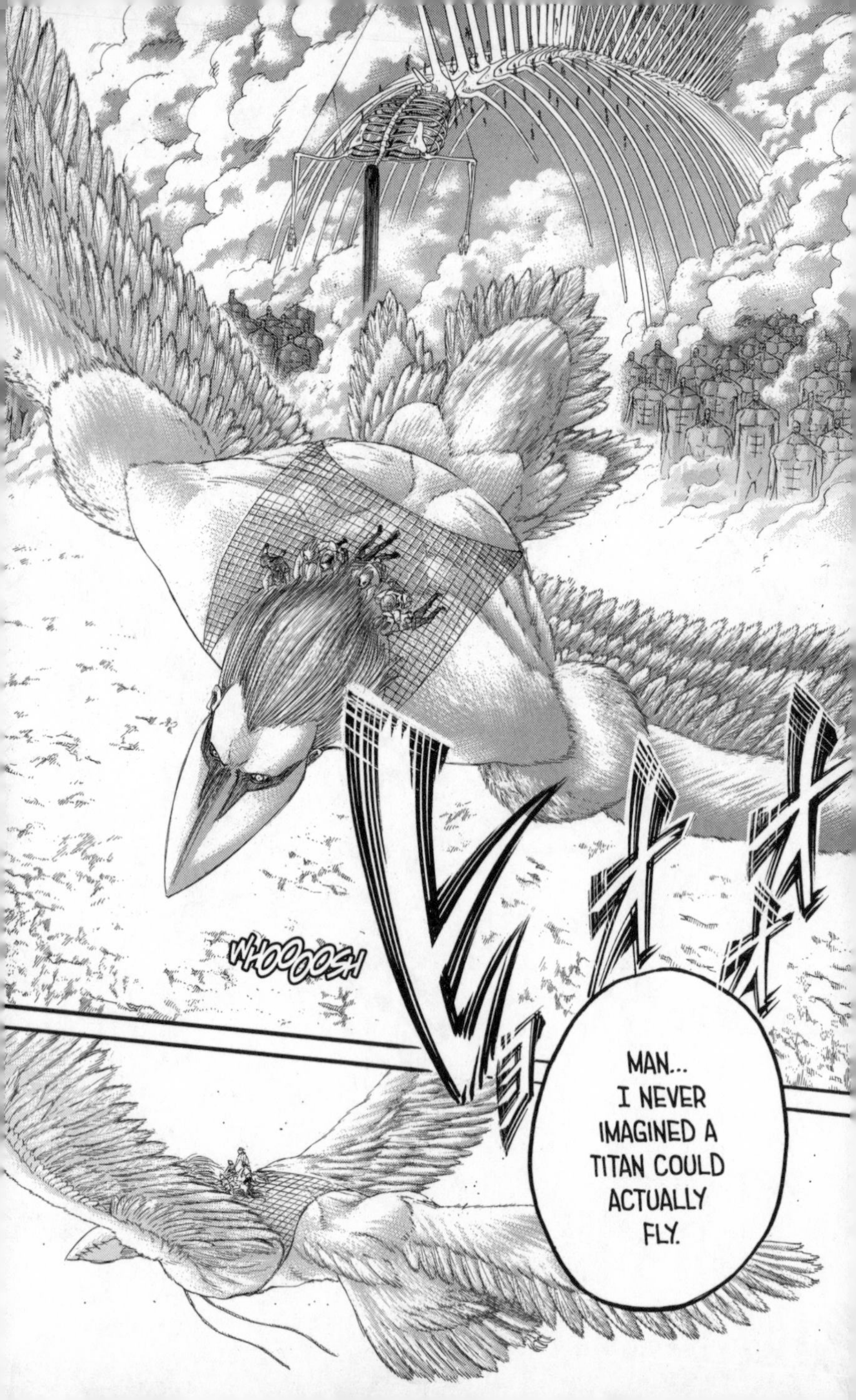
WHOOOOSH
MAN... I NEVER IMAGINED A TITAN COULD ACTUALLY FLY.

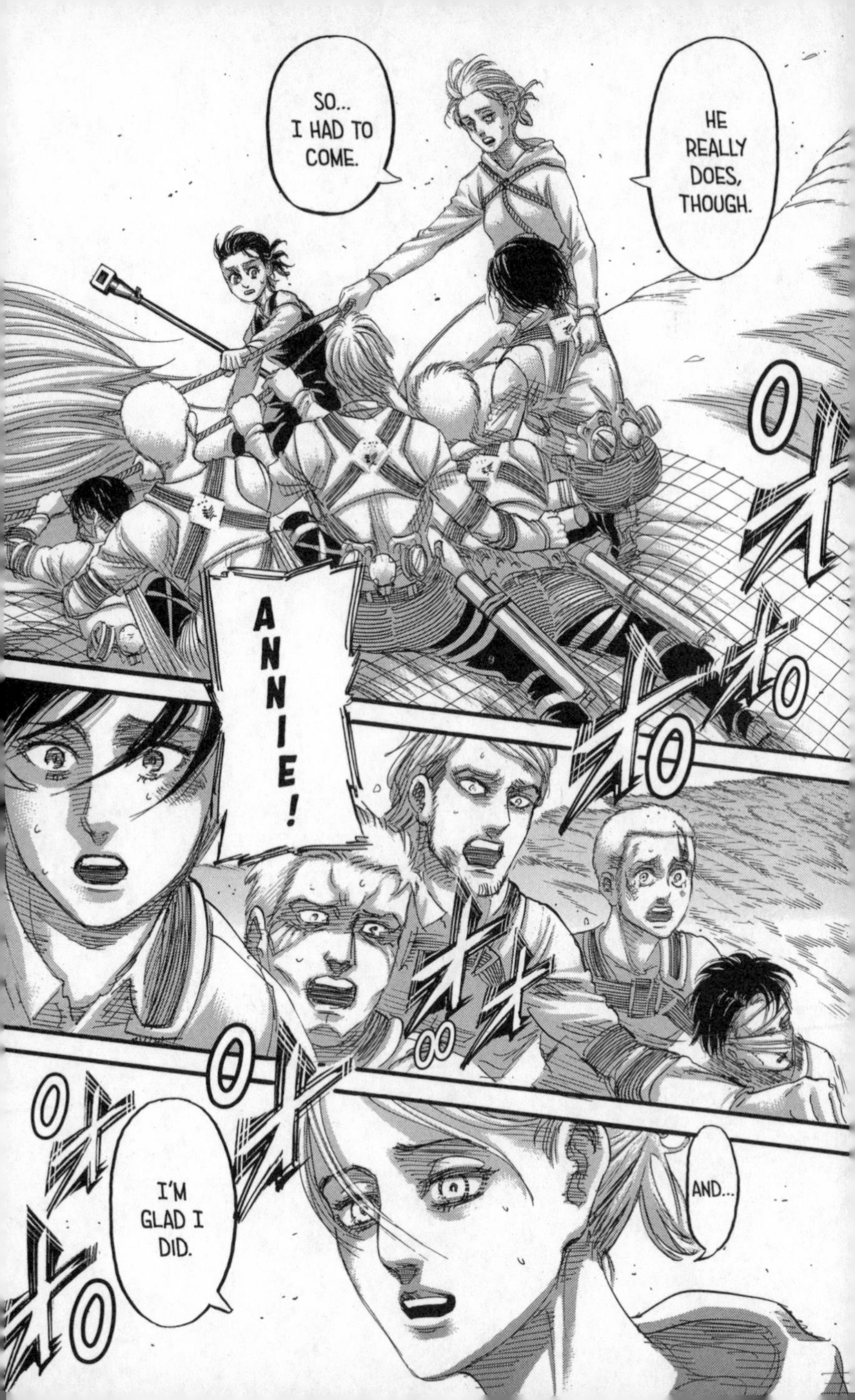
HE REALLY DOES, THOUGH.
SO... I HAD TO COME.
ANNIE!
AND...
I'M GLAD I DID.

ATTACK
on TITAN

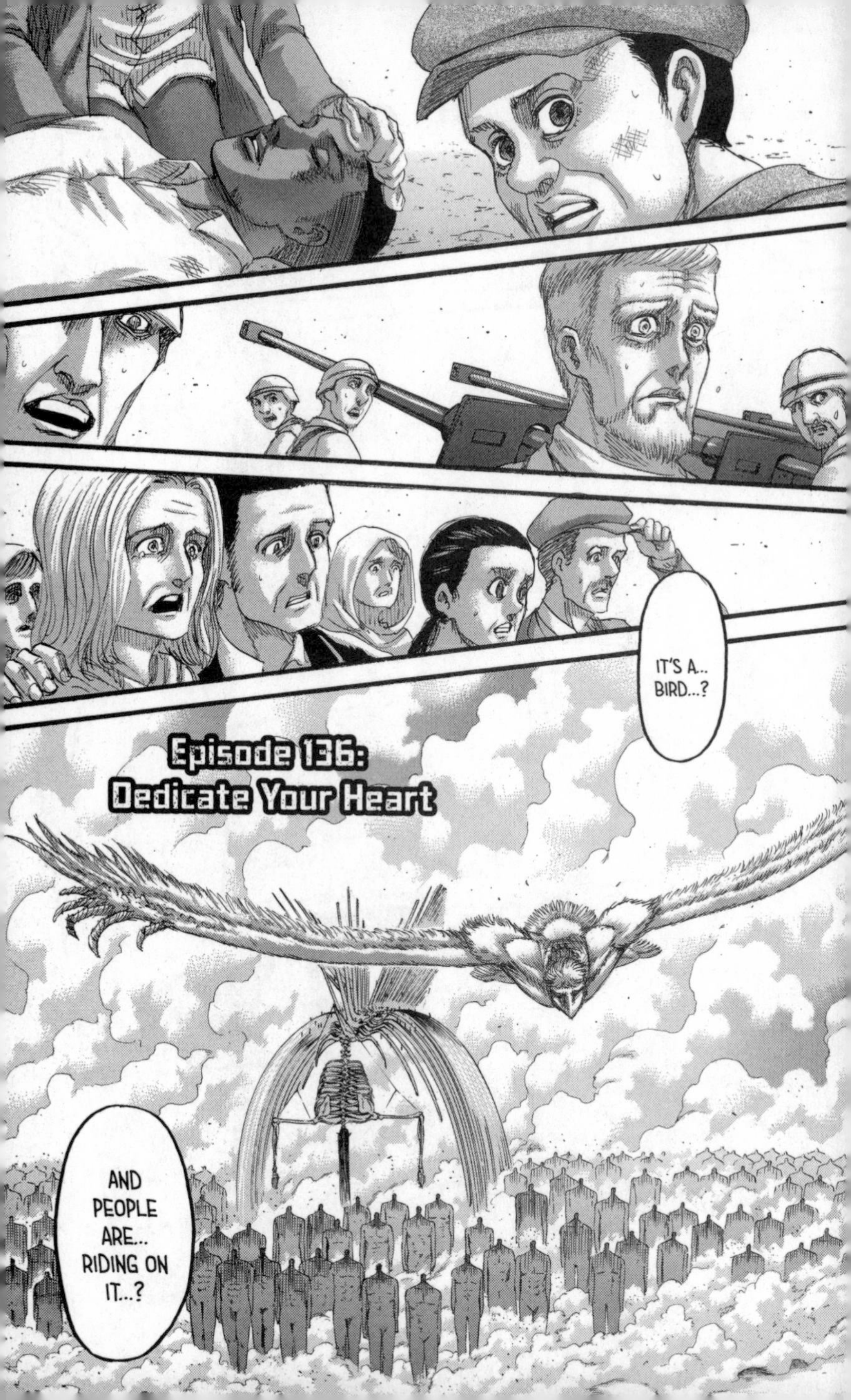
IT'S A... BIRD...?
Episode 136: Dedicate Your Heart
AND PEOPLE ARE... RIDING ON IT...?

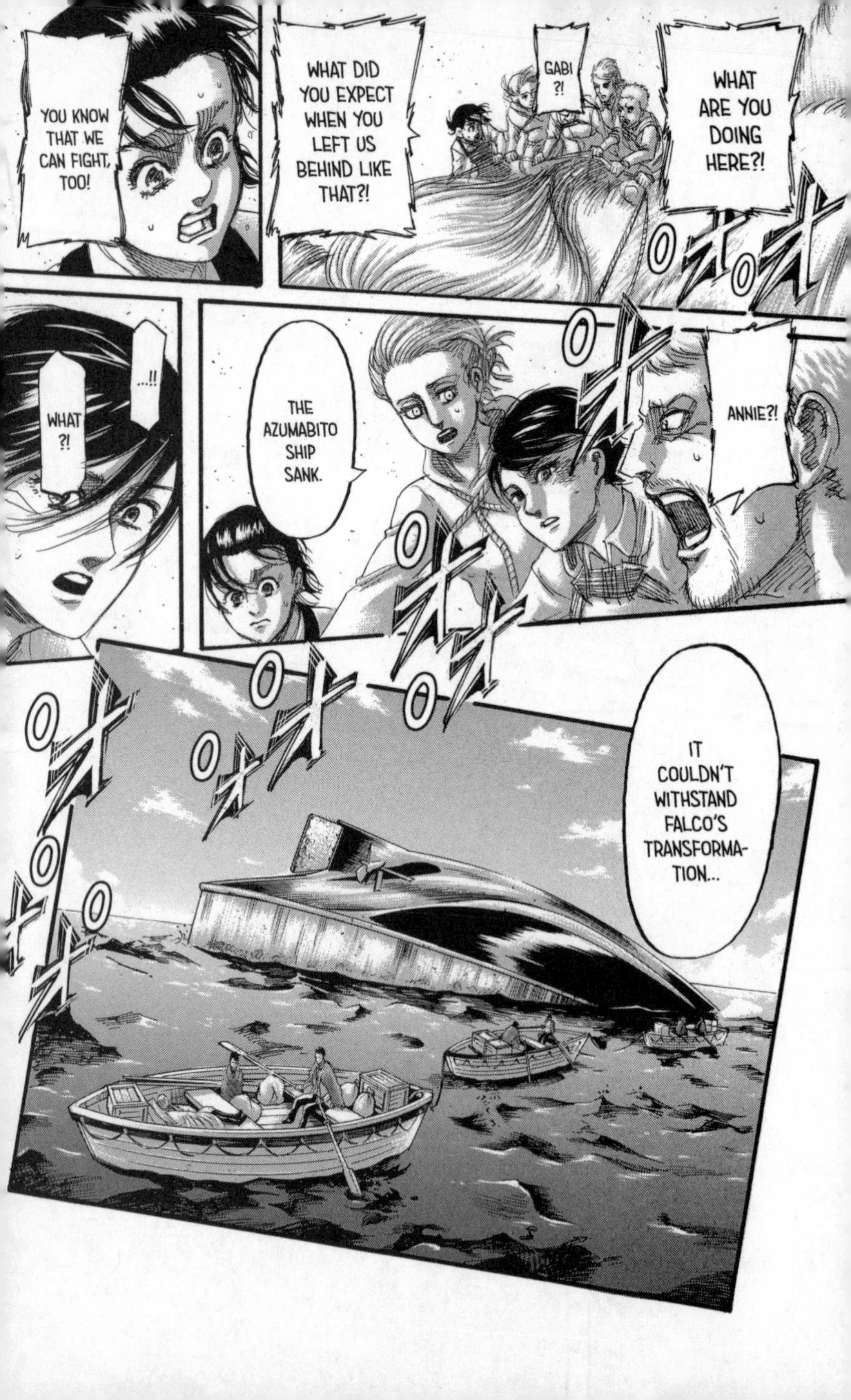
WHAT ARE YOU DOING HERE?!
GABI?!
WHAT DID YOU EXPECT WHEN YOU LEFT US BEHIND LIKE THAT?!
YOU KNOW THAT WE CAN FIGHT, TOO!
ANNIE?!
THE AZUMABITO SHIP SANK.
...!!
WHAT?!
IT COULDN'T WITHSTAND FALCO'S TRANSFORMATION...

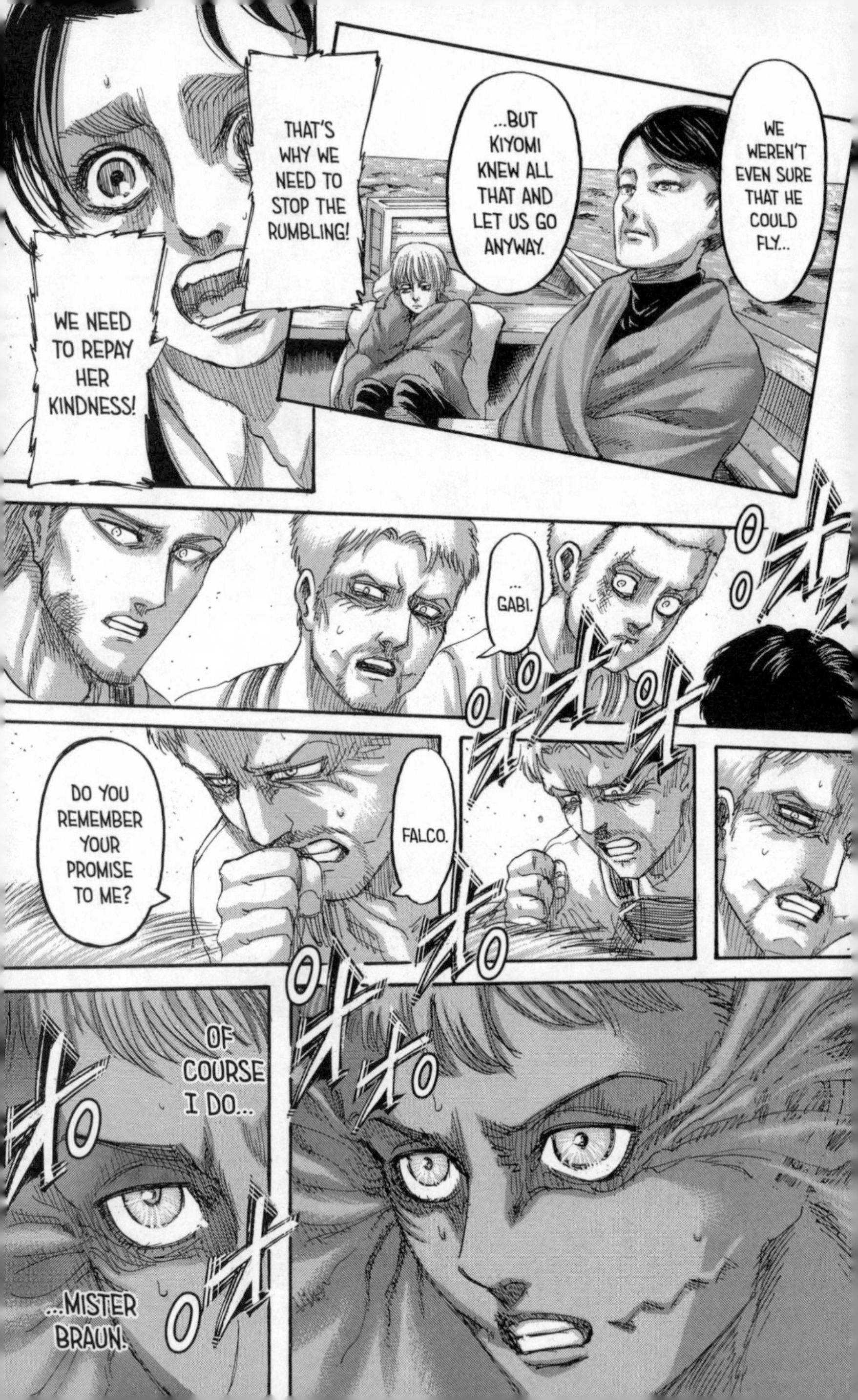
WE WEREN'T EVEN SURE THAT HE COULD FLY...
...BUT KIYOMI KNEW ALL THAT AND LET US GO ANYWAY.
THAT'S WHY WE NEED TO STOP THE RUMBLING!
WE NEED TO REPAY HER KINDNESS!
... GABI.
FALCO.
DO YOU REMEMBER YOUR PROMISE TO ME?
OF COURSE I DO...
...MISTER BRAUN.

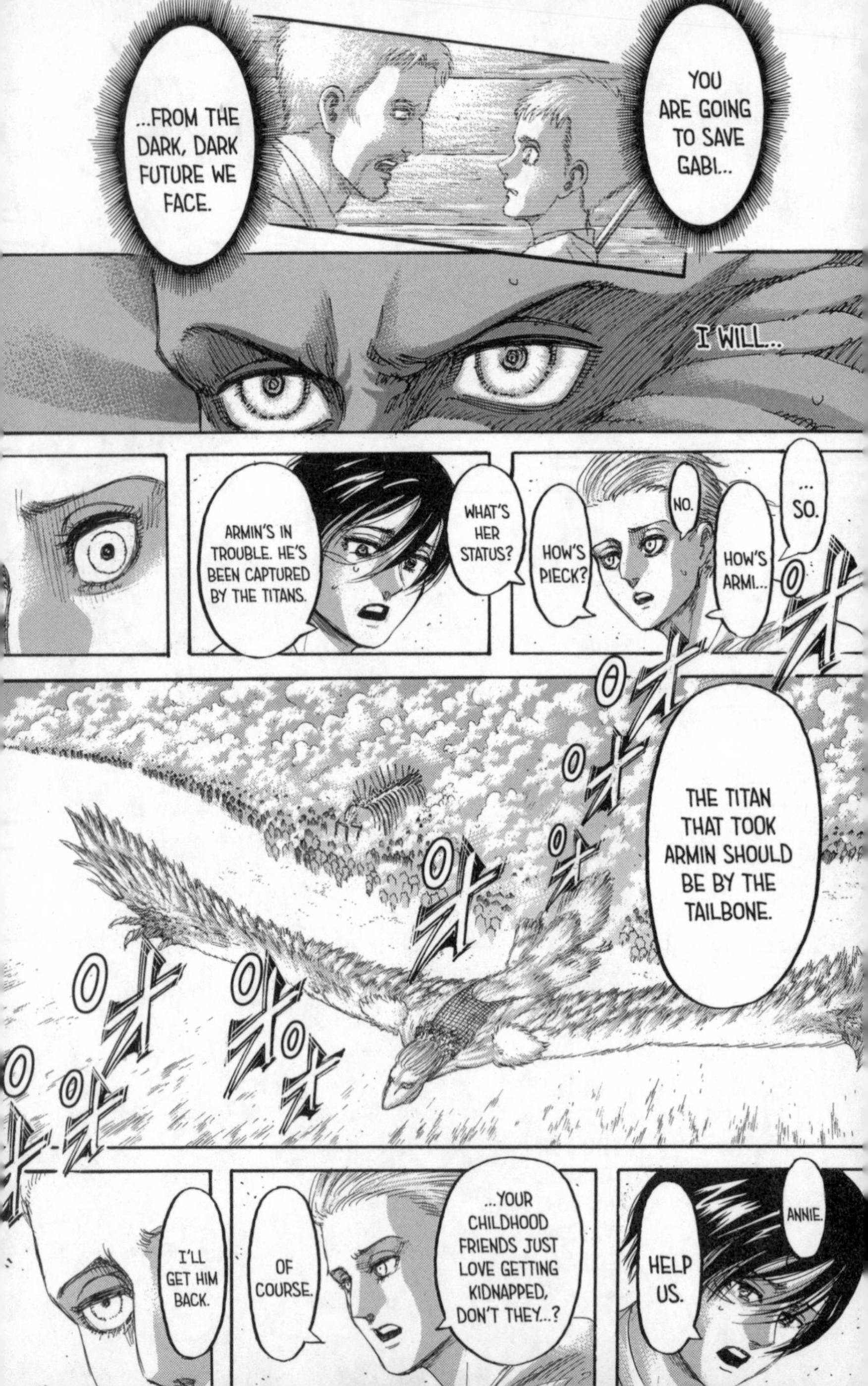
YOU ARE GOING TO SAVE GABI...
...FROM THE DARK, DARK FUTURE WE FACE.
I WILL...
... SO.
NO.
HOW'S ARMI...
HOW'S PIECK?
WHAT'S HER STATUS?
ARMIN'S IN TROUBLE. HE'S BEEN CAPTURED BY THE TITANS.
THE TITAN THAT TOOK ARMIN SHOULD BE BY THE TAILBONE.
ANNIE.
HELP US.
...YOUR CHILDHOOD FRIENDS JUST LOVE GETTING KIDNAPPED, DON'T THEY...?
OF COURSE.
I'LL GET HIM BACK.

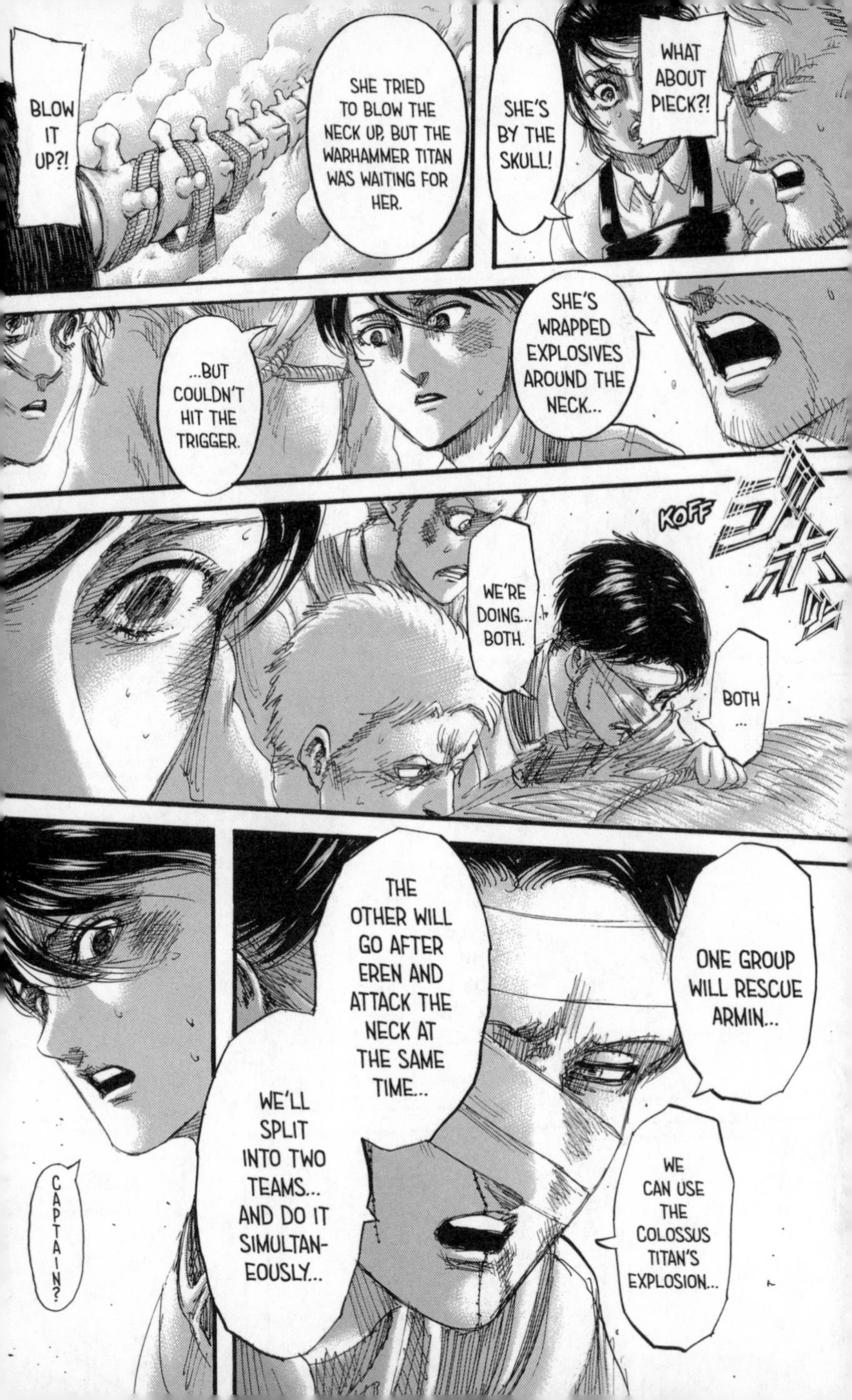
WHAT ABOUT PIECK?!
SHE'S BY THE SKULL!
SHE TRIED TO BLOW THE NECK UP, BUT THE WARHAMMER TITAN WAS WAITING FOR HER.
BLOW IT UP?!
SHE'S WRAPPED EXPLOSIVES AROUND THE NECK...
...BUT COULDN'T HIT THE TRIGGER.
KOFF
BOTH ...
WE'RE DOING... BOTH.
ONE GROUP WILL RESCUE ARMIN...
THE OTHER WILL GO AFTER EREN AND ATTACK THE NECK AT THE SAME TIME...
WE CAN USE THE COLOSSUS TITAN'S EXPLOSION...
WE'LL SPLIT INTO TWO TEAMS... AND DO IT SIMULTANEOUSLY...
CAPTAIN?

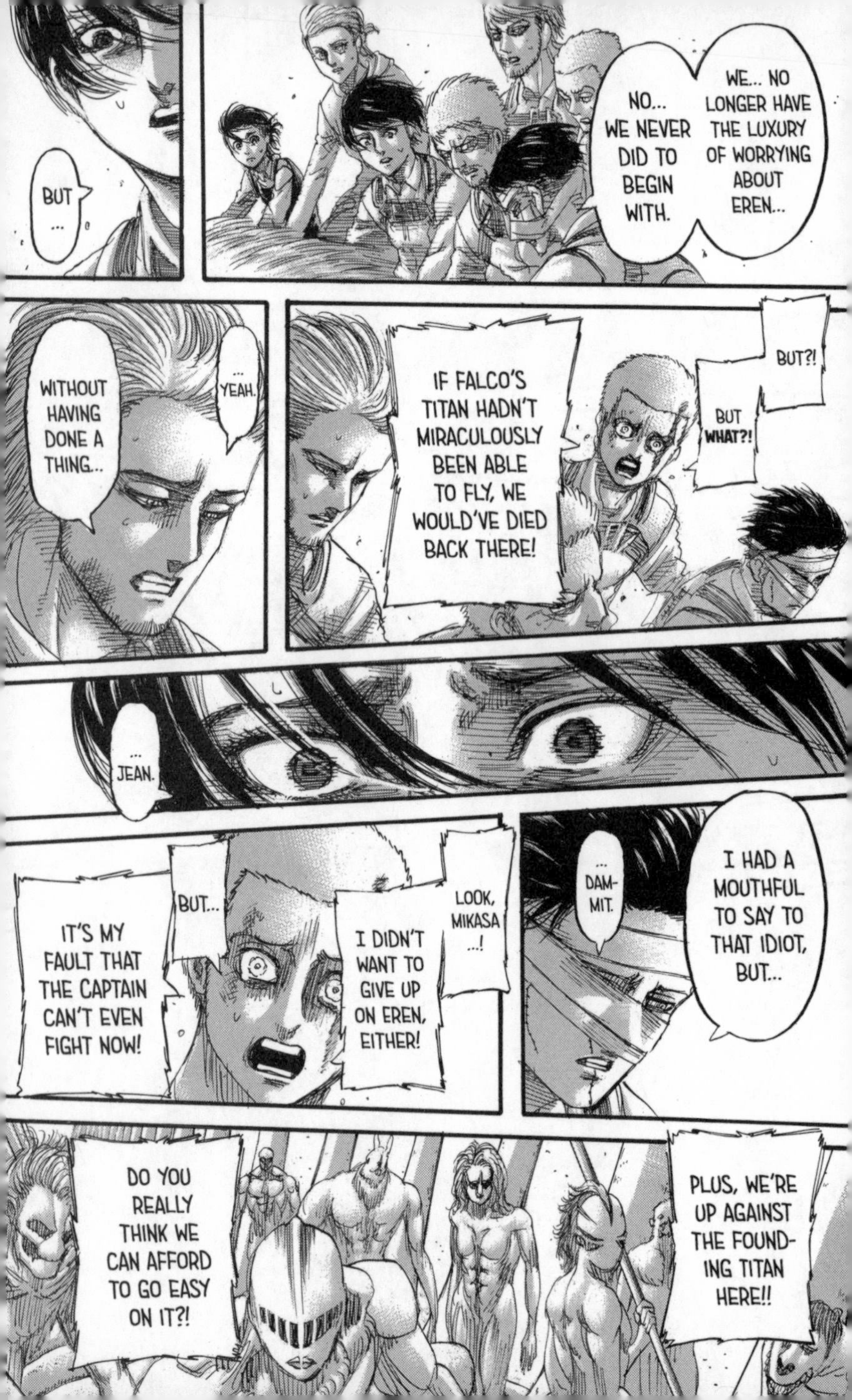

WE... NO LONGER HAVE THE LUXURY OF WORRYING ABOUT EREN...
NO... WE NEVER DID TO BEGIN WITH.
BUT ...
BUT?!
BUT WHAT?!
IF FALCO'S TITAN HADN'T MIRACULOUSLY BEEN ABLE TO FLY, WE WOULD'VE DIED BACK THERE!
... YEAH.
WITHOUT HAVING DONE A THING...
... JEAN.
I HAD A MOUTHFUL TO SAY TO THAT IDIOT, BUT...
... DAM-MIT.
LOOK, MIKASA ...!
I DIDN'T WANT TO GIVE UP ON EREN, EITHER!
BUT...
IT'S MY FAULT THAT THE CAPTAIN CAN'T EVEN FIGHT NOW!
PLUS, WE'RE UP AGAINST THE FOUND-ING TITAN HERE!!
DO YOU REALLY THINK WE CAN AFFORD TO GO EASY ON IT?!

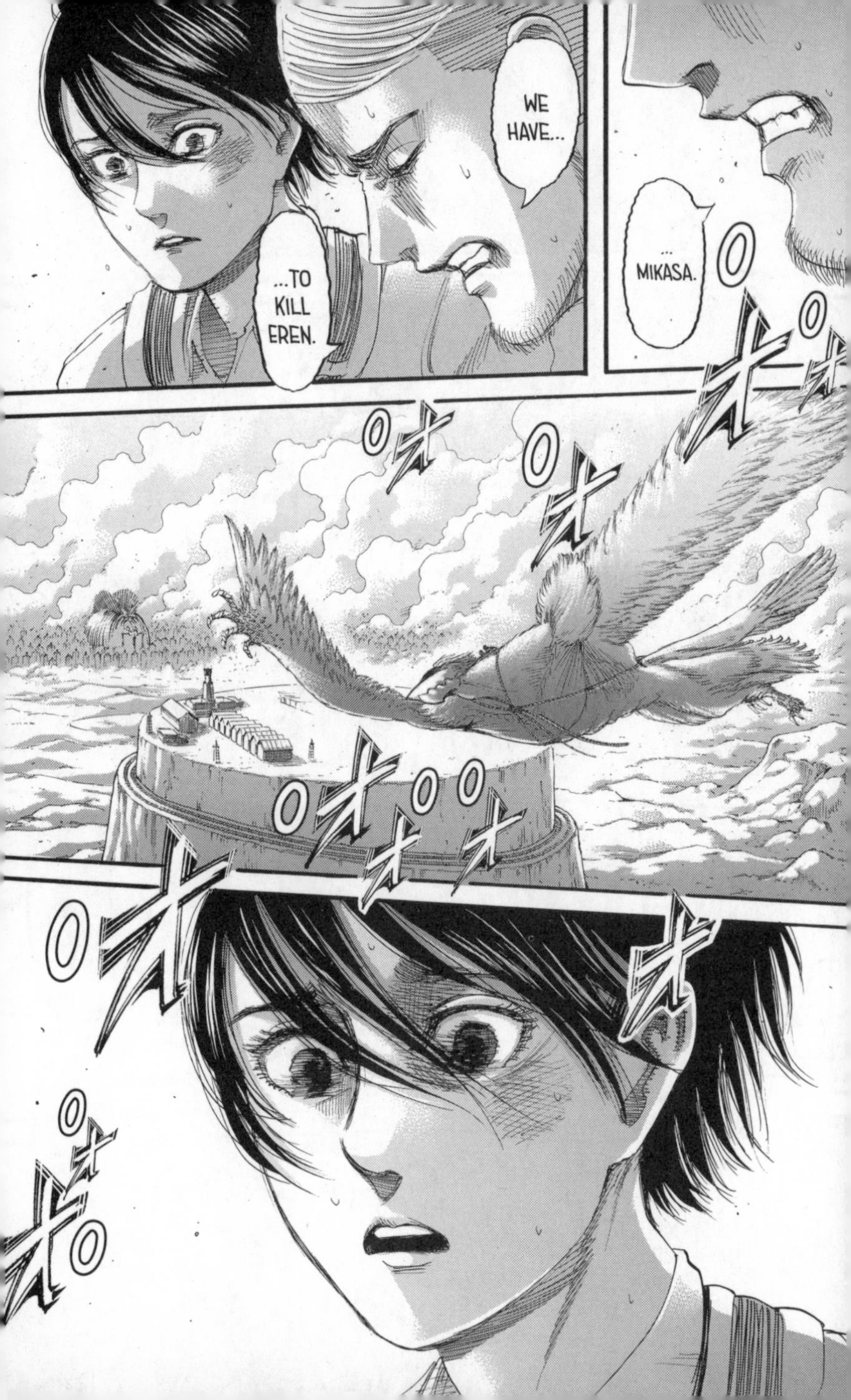
... MIKASA.
WE HAVE...
...TO KILL EREN.

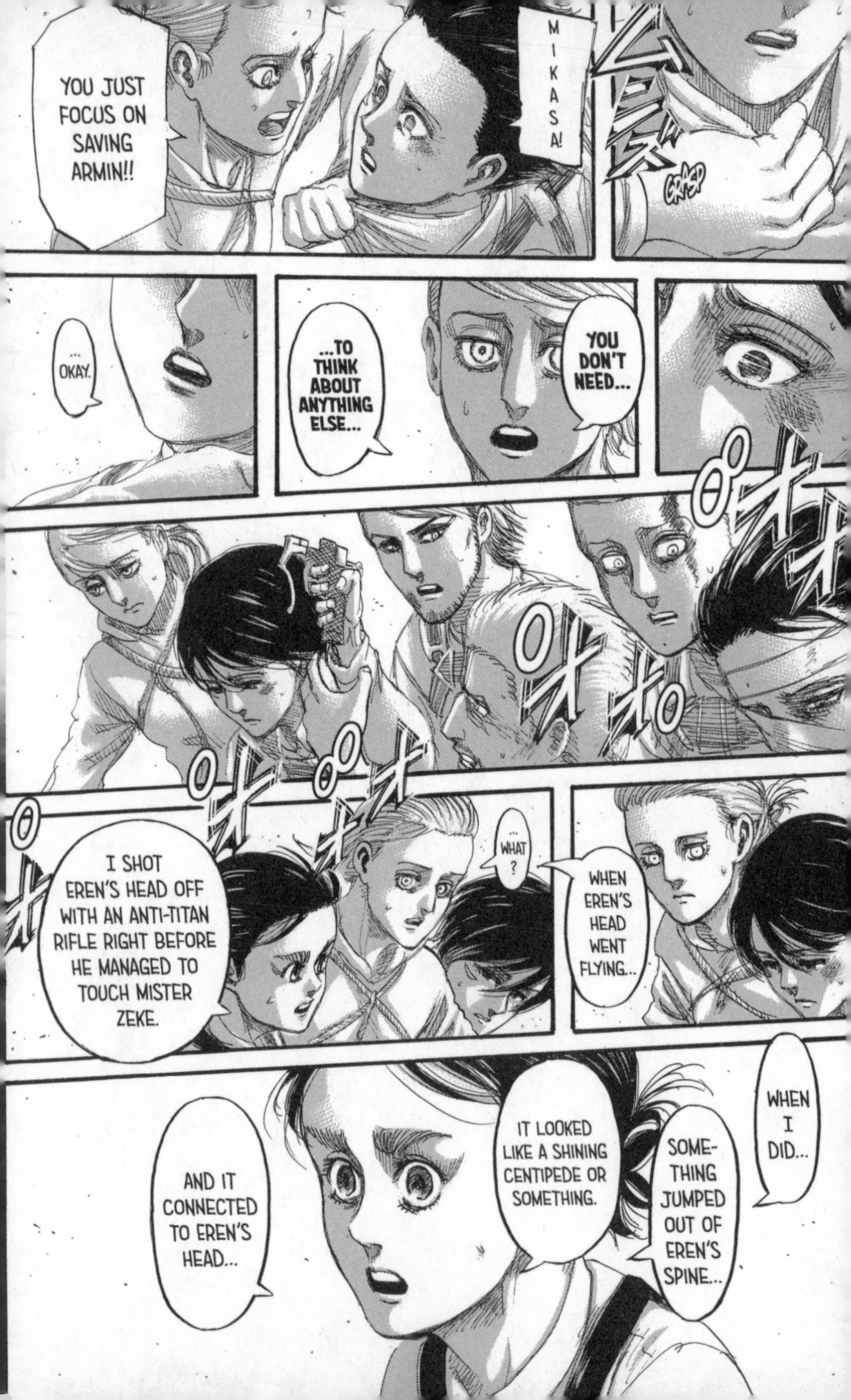
GRASP
MIKASA!
YOU JUST FOCUS ON SAVING ARMIN!!
YOU DON'T NEED...
...TO THINK ABOUT ANYTHING ELSE...
...OKAY.
I SHOT EREN'S HEAD OFF WITH AN ANTI-TITAN RIFLE RIGHT BEFORE HE MANAGED TO TOUCH MISTER ZEKE.
...WHAT?
WHEN EREN'S HEAD WENT FLYING...
WHEN I DID...
SOME-THING JUMPED OUT OF EREN'S SPINE...
IT LOOKED LIKE A SHINING CENTIPEDE OR SOMETHING.
AND IT CONNECTED TO EREN'S HEAD...

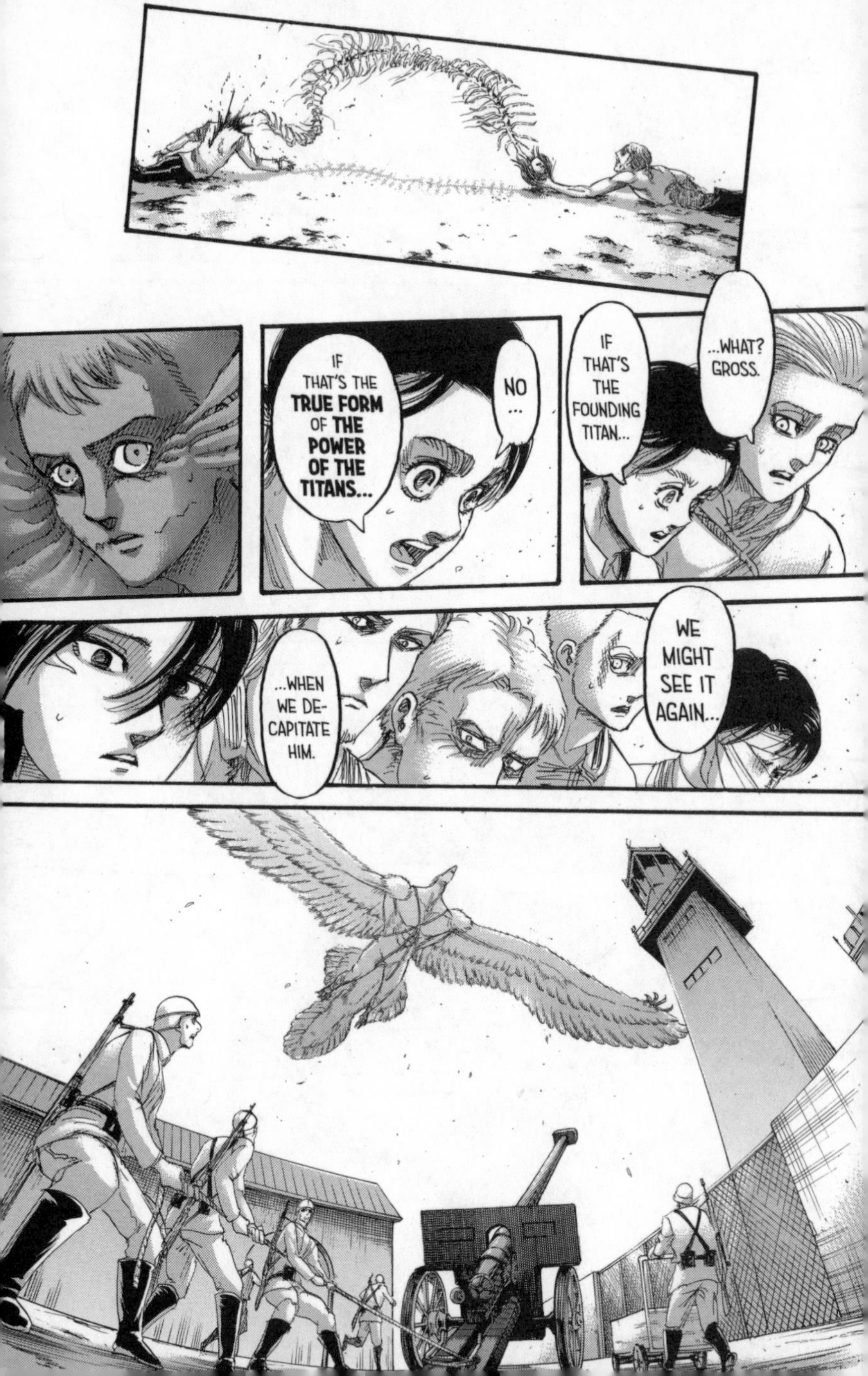
...WHAT? GROSS.
IF THAT'S THE FOUNDING TITAN...
NO ...
IF THAT'S THE TRUE FORM OF THE POWER OF THE TITANS...
WE MIGHT SEE IT AGAIN...
...WHEN WE DE-CAPITATE HIM.

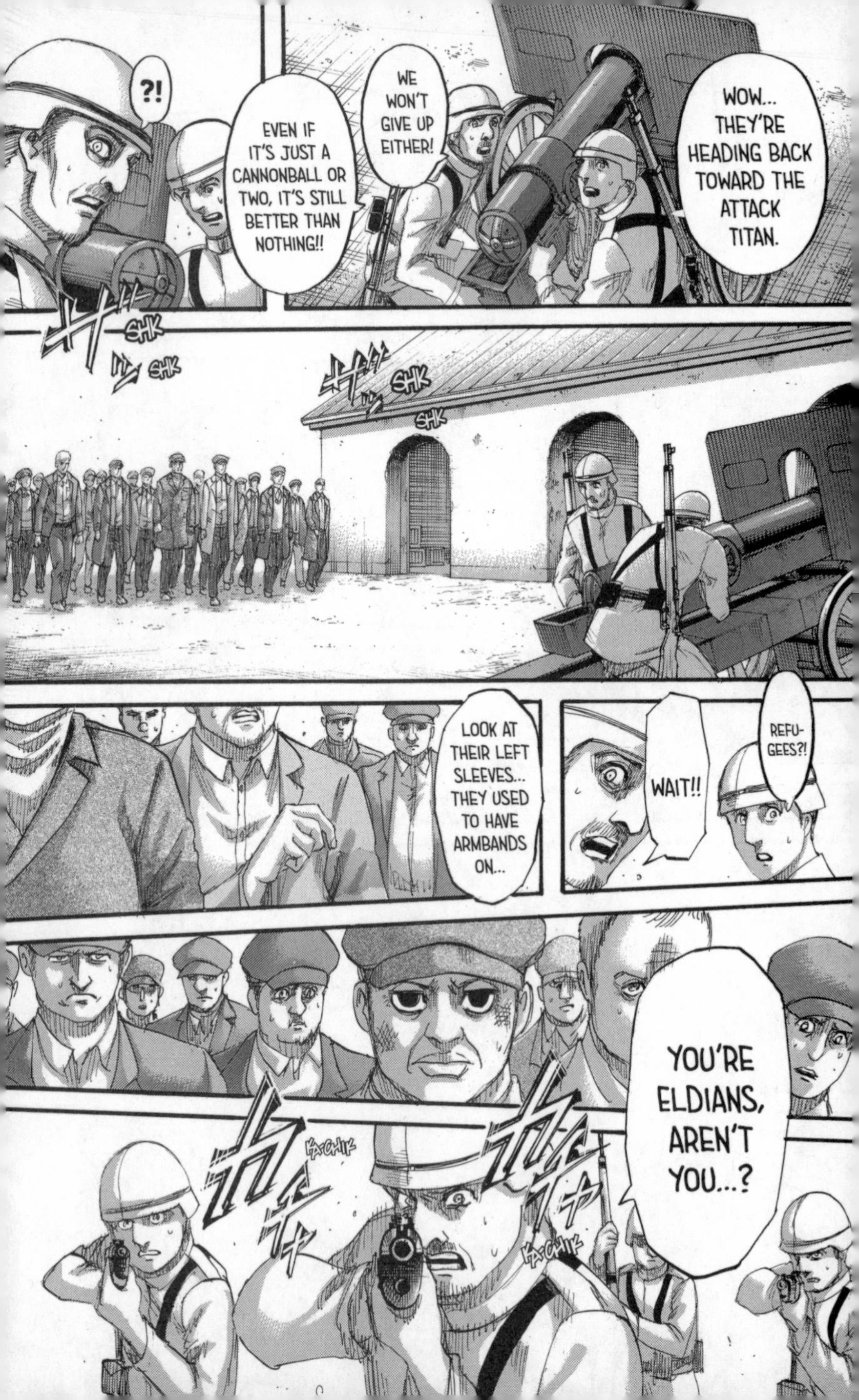
WOW... THEY'RE HEADING BACK TOWARD THE ATTACK TITAN.
WE WON'T GIVE UP EITHER!
EVEN IF IT'S JUST A CANNONBALL OR TWO, IT'S STILL BETTER THAN NOTHING!!
?!
SHK
SHK
SHK
SHK
REFU-GEES?!
WAIT!!
LOOK AT THEIR LEFT SLEEVES... THEY USED TO HAVE ARMBANDS ON...
YOU'RE ELDIANS, AREN'T YOU...?
KA-CHIK
KA-CHIK

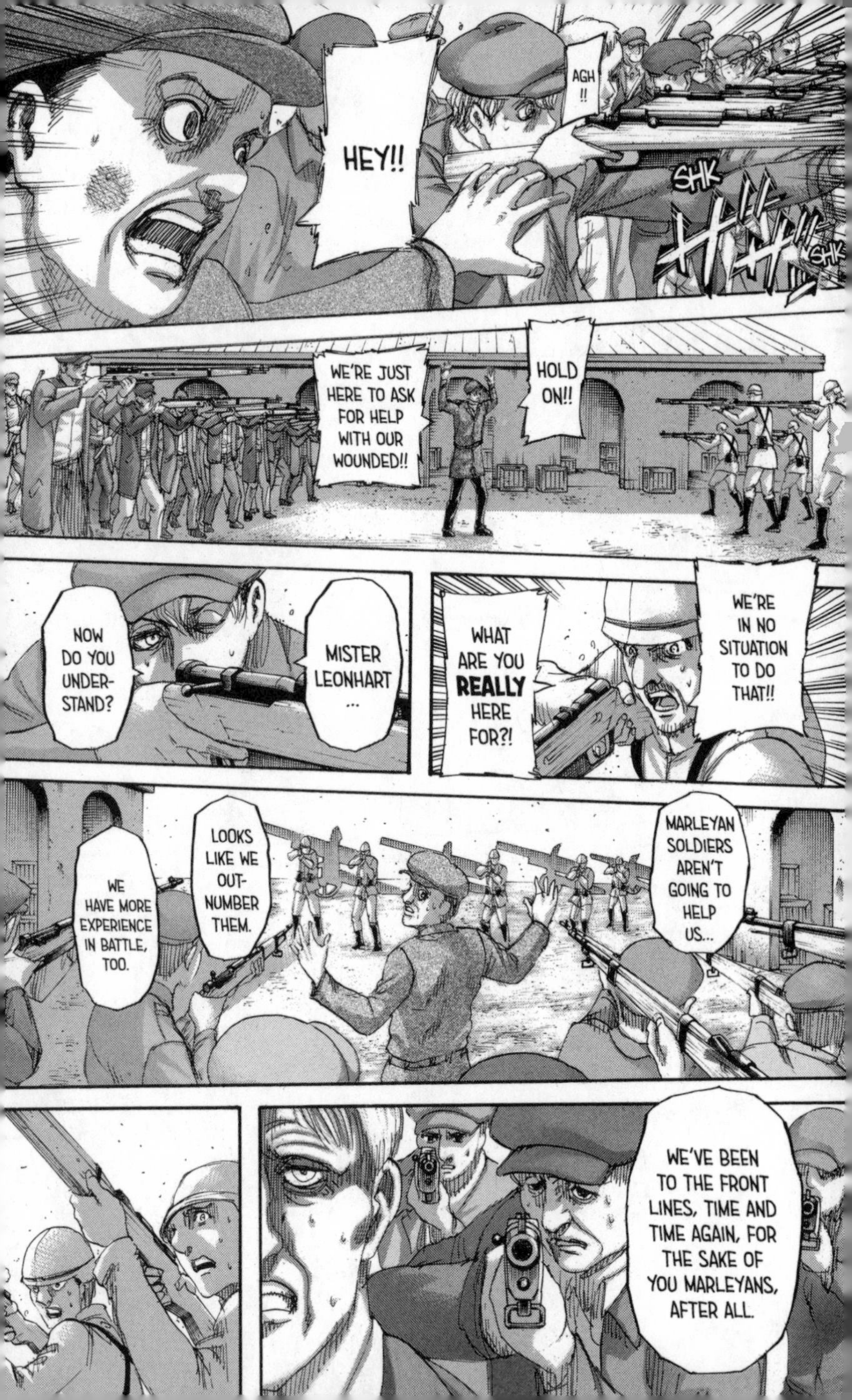
AGH!!
SHK
SHK
HEY!!
HOLD ON!!
WE'RE JUST HERE TO ASK FOR HELP WITH OUR WOUNDED!!
WE'RE IN NO SITUATION TO DO THAT!!
WHAT ARE YOU **REALLY** HERE FOR?!
MISTER LEONHART ...
NOW DO YOU UNDER-STAND?
MARLEYAN SOLDIERS AREN'T GOING TO HELP US...
LOOKS LIKE WE OUT-NUMBER THEM.
WE HAVE MORE EXPERIENCE IN BATTLE, TOO.
WE'VE BEEN TO THE FRONT LINES, TIME AND TIME AGAIN, FOR THE SAKE OF YOU MARLEYANS, AFTER ALL.

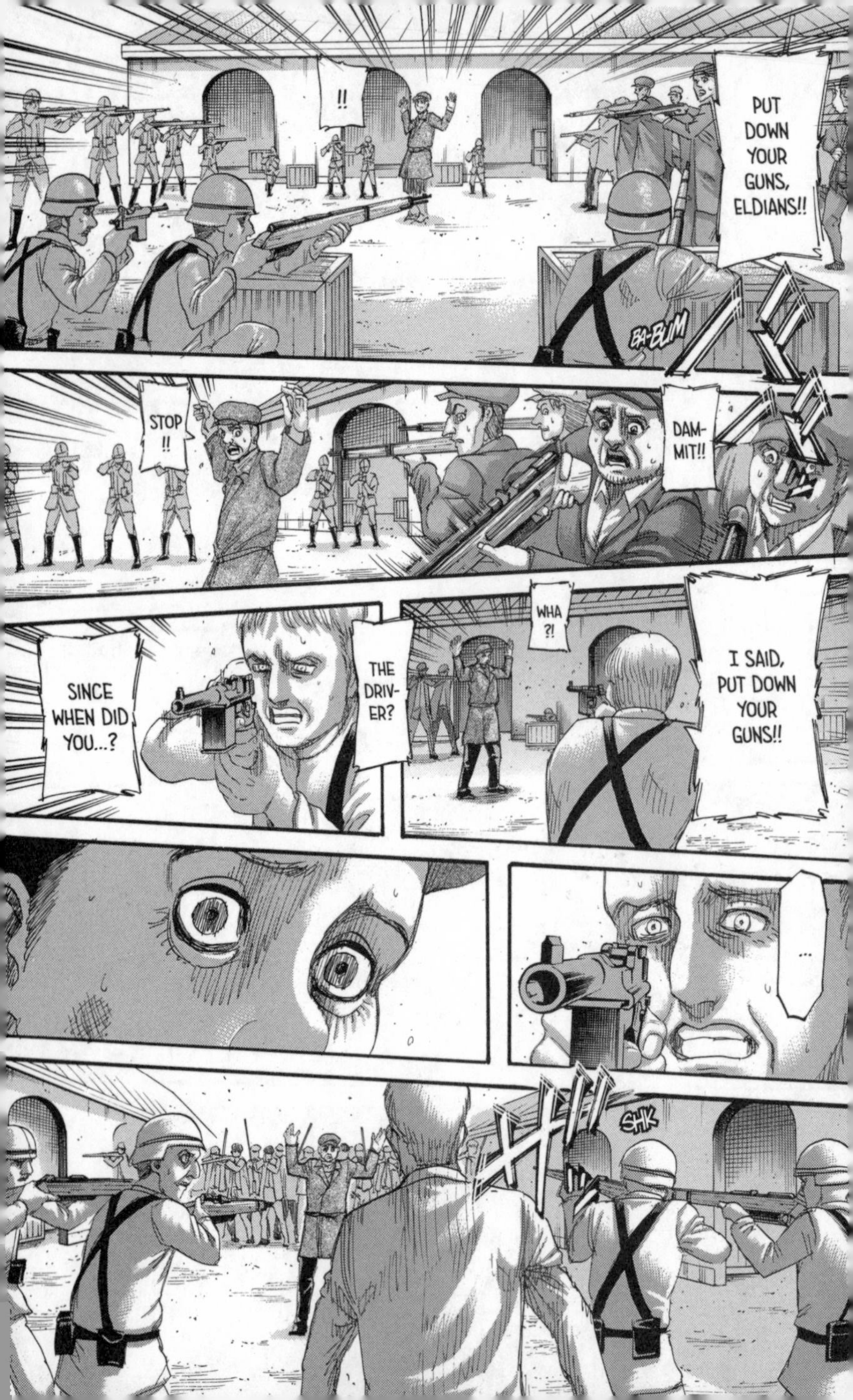
PUT DOWN YOUR GUNS, ELDIANS!!
!!
BA-BLUM
DAM-MIT!!
STOP !!
I SAID, PUT DOWN YOUR GUNS!!
WHA ?!
THE DRIV-ER?
SINCE WHEN DID YOU...?
...
SHK

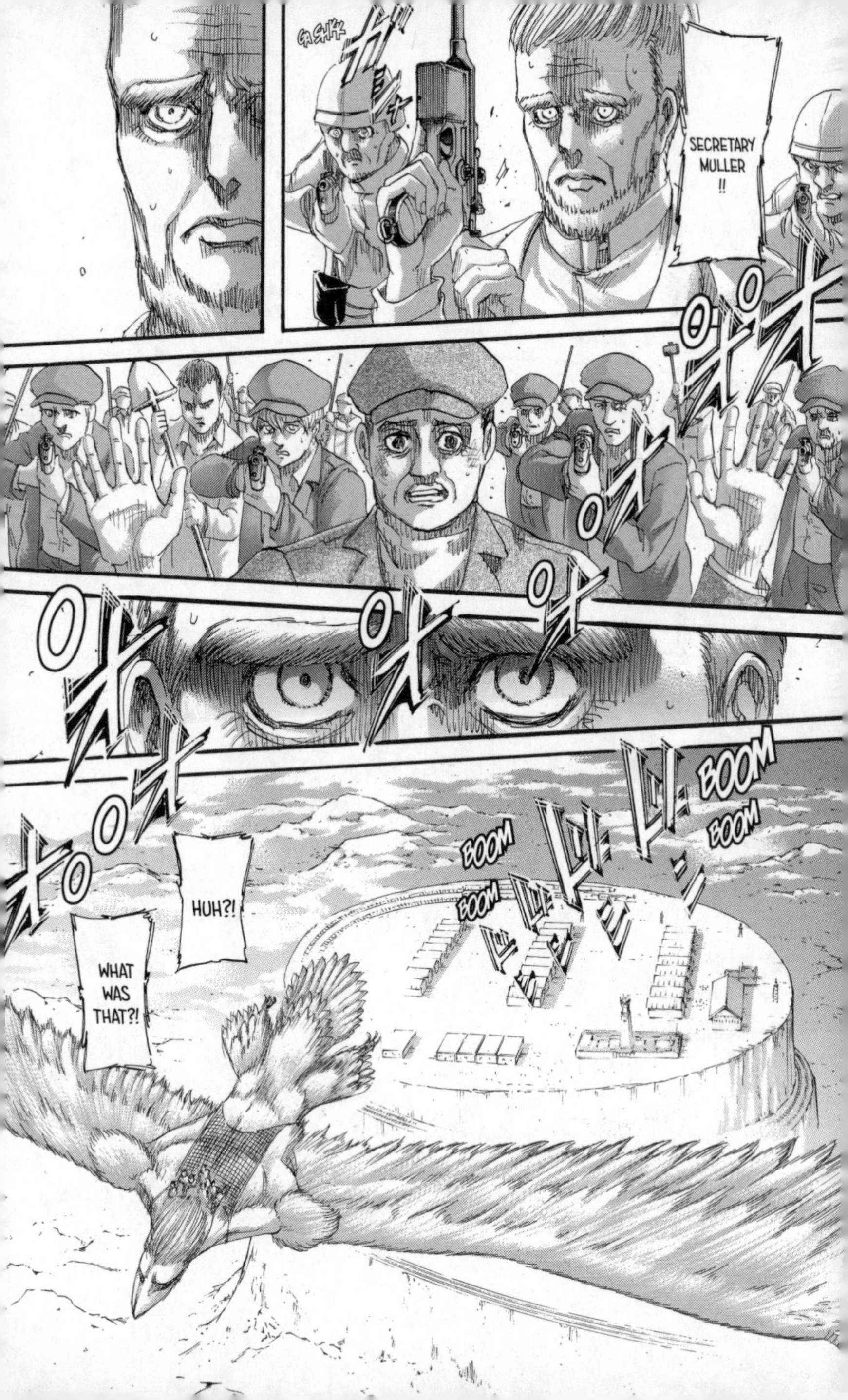
SECRETARY MULLER !!
GA SHK
BOOM
BOOM
BOOM
BOOM
HUH?!
WHAT WAS THAT?!

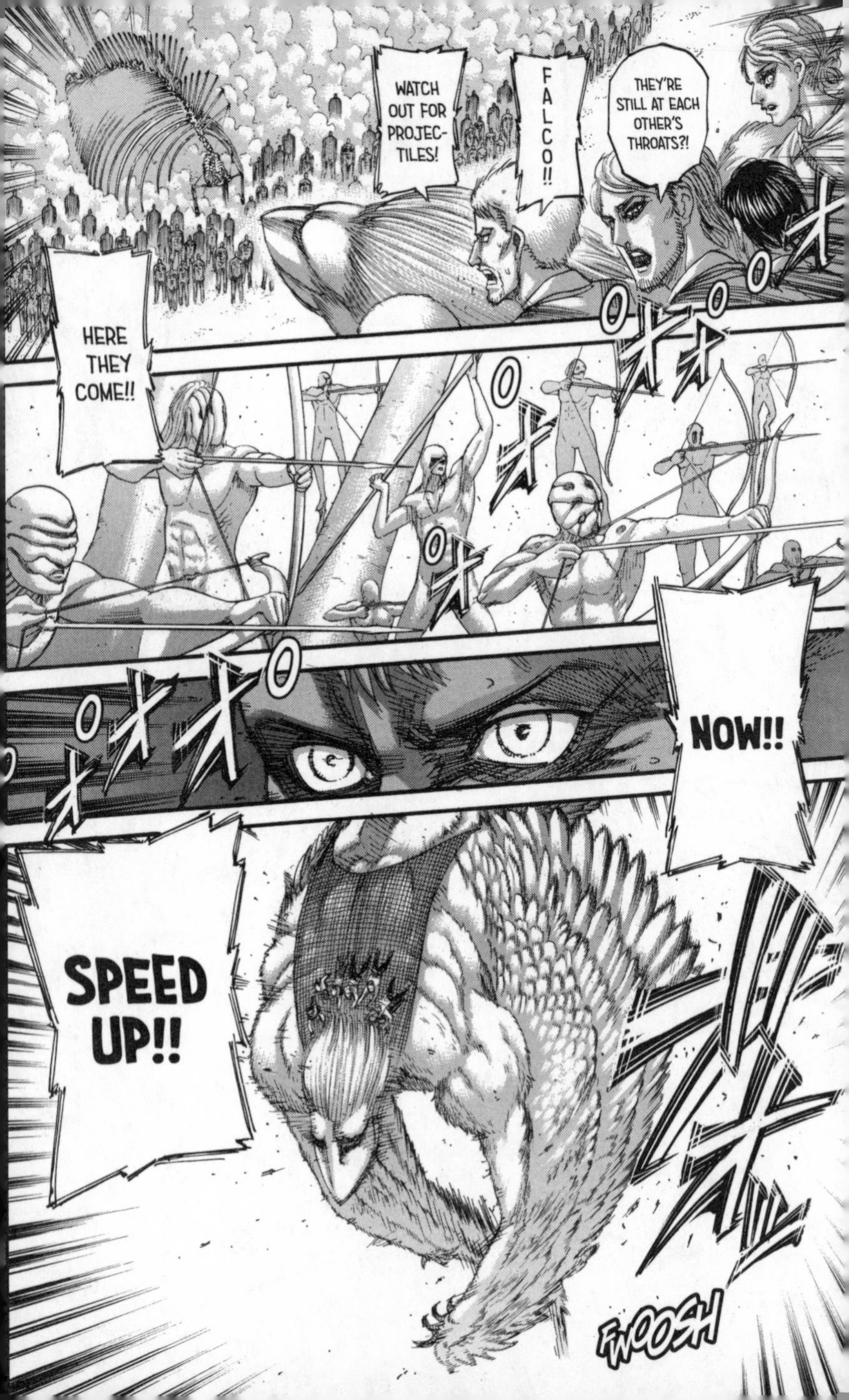
THEY'RE STILL AT EACH OTHER'S THROATS?!
FALCO!!
WATCH OUT FOR PROJEC-TILES!
HERE THEY COME!!
NOW!!
SPEED UP!!
FWOOSH

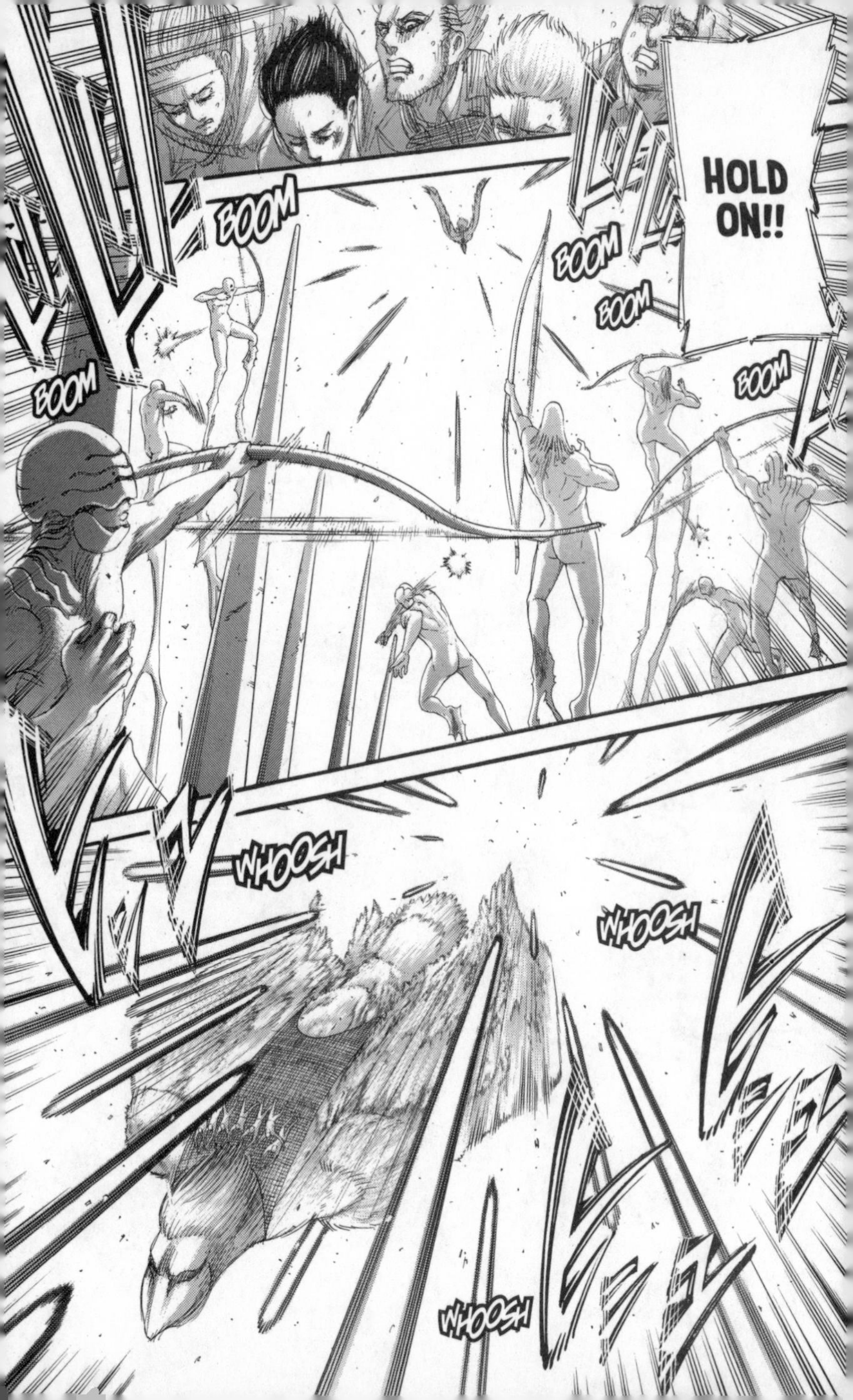
HOLD ON!!
BOOM
BOOM
BOOM
BOOM
BOOM
WHOOSH
WHOOSH
WHOOSH

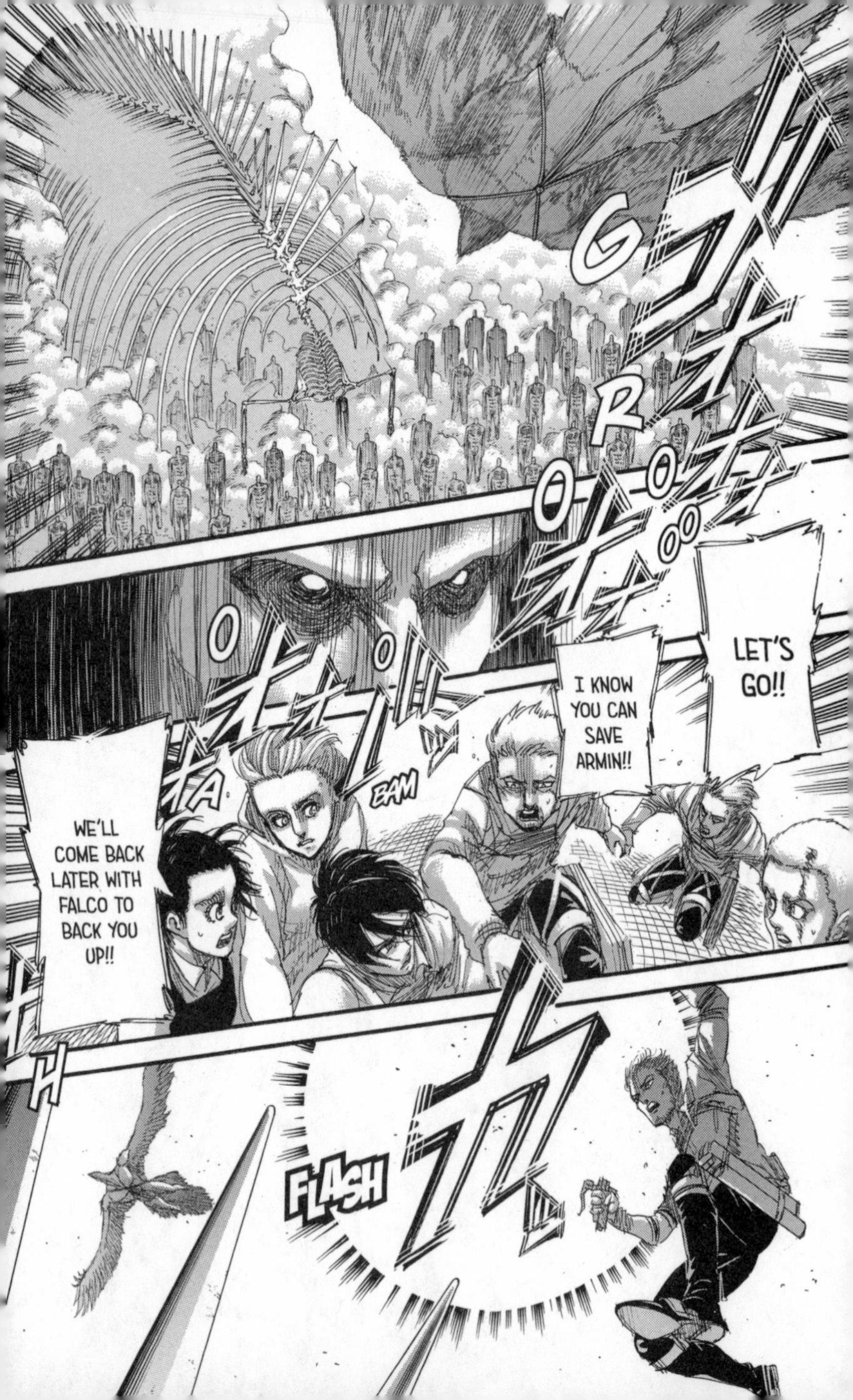
GROOOO
LET'S GO!!
I KNOW YOU CAN SAVE ARMIN!!
BAM
WE'LL COME BACK LATER WITH FALCO TO BACK YOU UP!!
FLASH

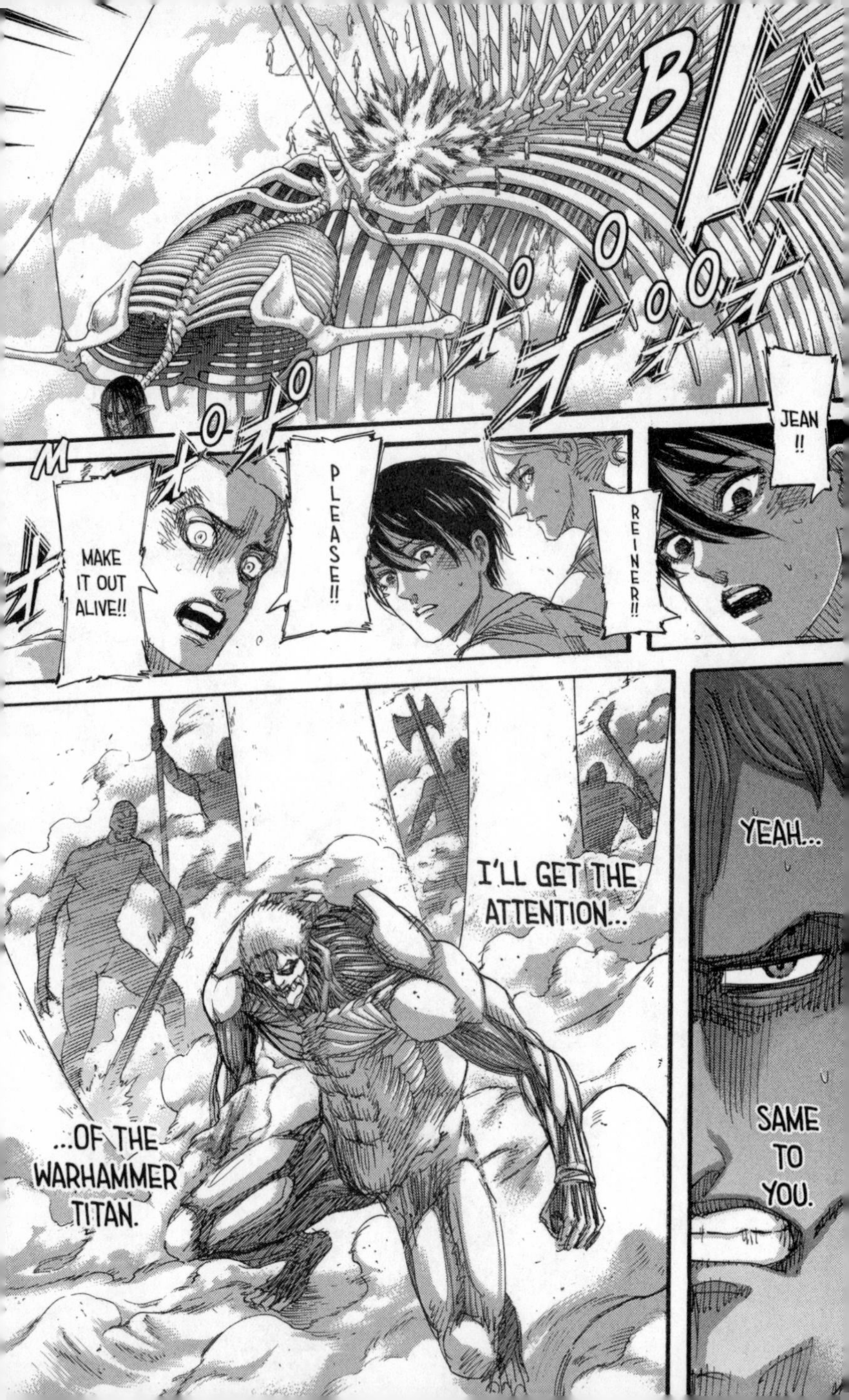
JEAN!!
REINER!!
PLEASE!!
MAKE IT OUT ALIVE!!
YEAH...
SAME TO YOU.
I'LL GET THE ATTENTION...
...OF THE WARHAMMER TITAN.

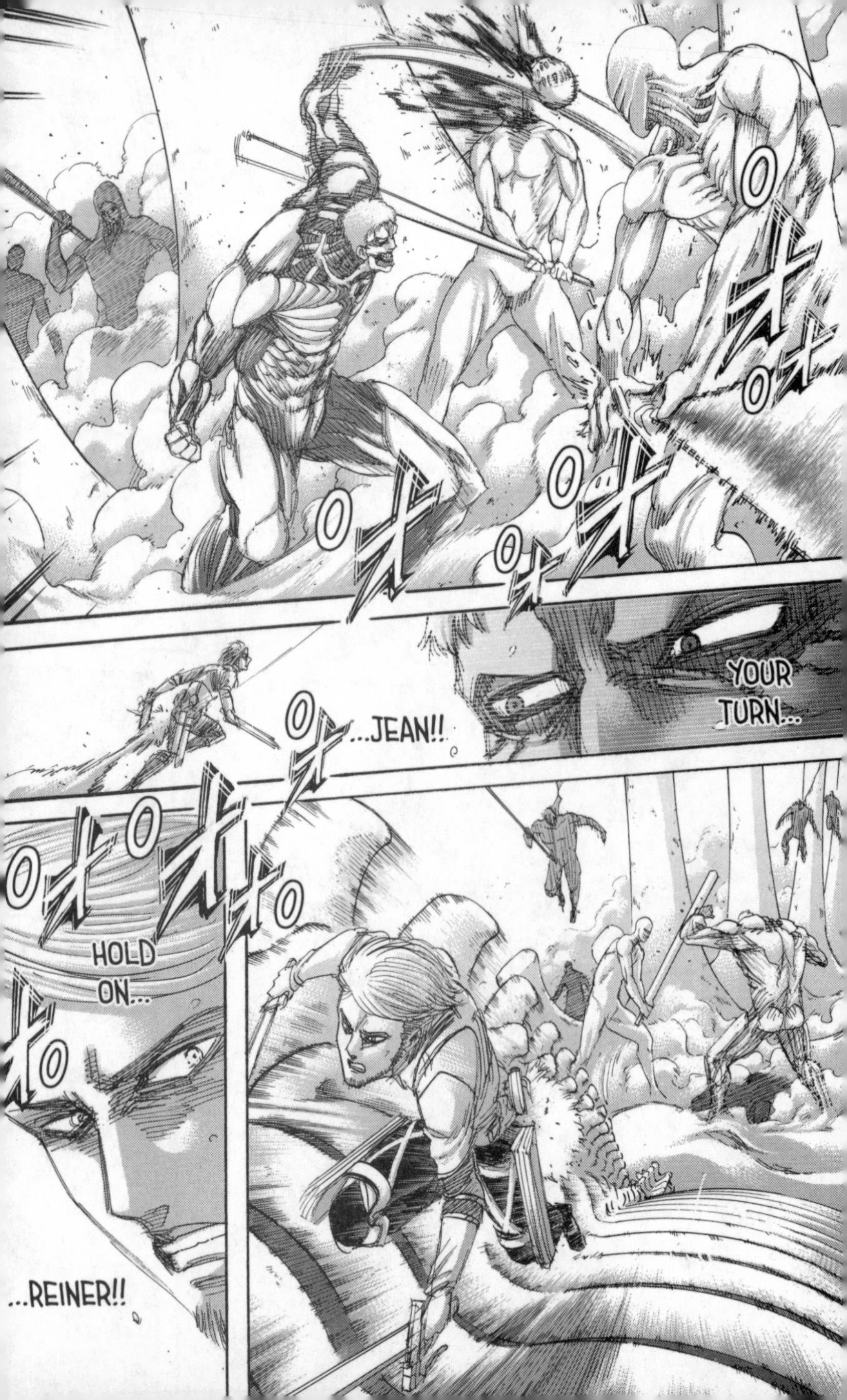
YOUR TURN...
...JEAN!!
HOLD ON...
...REINER!!

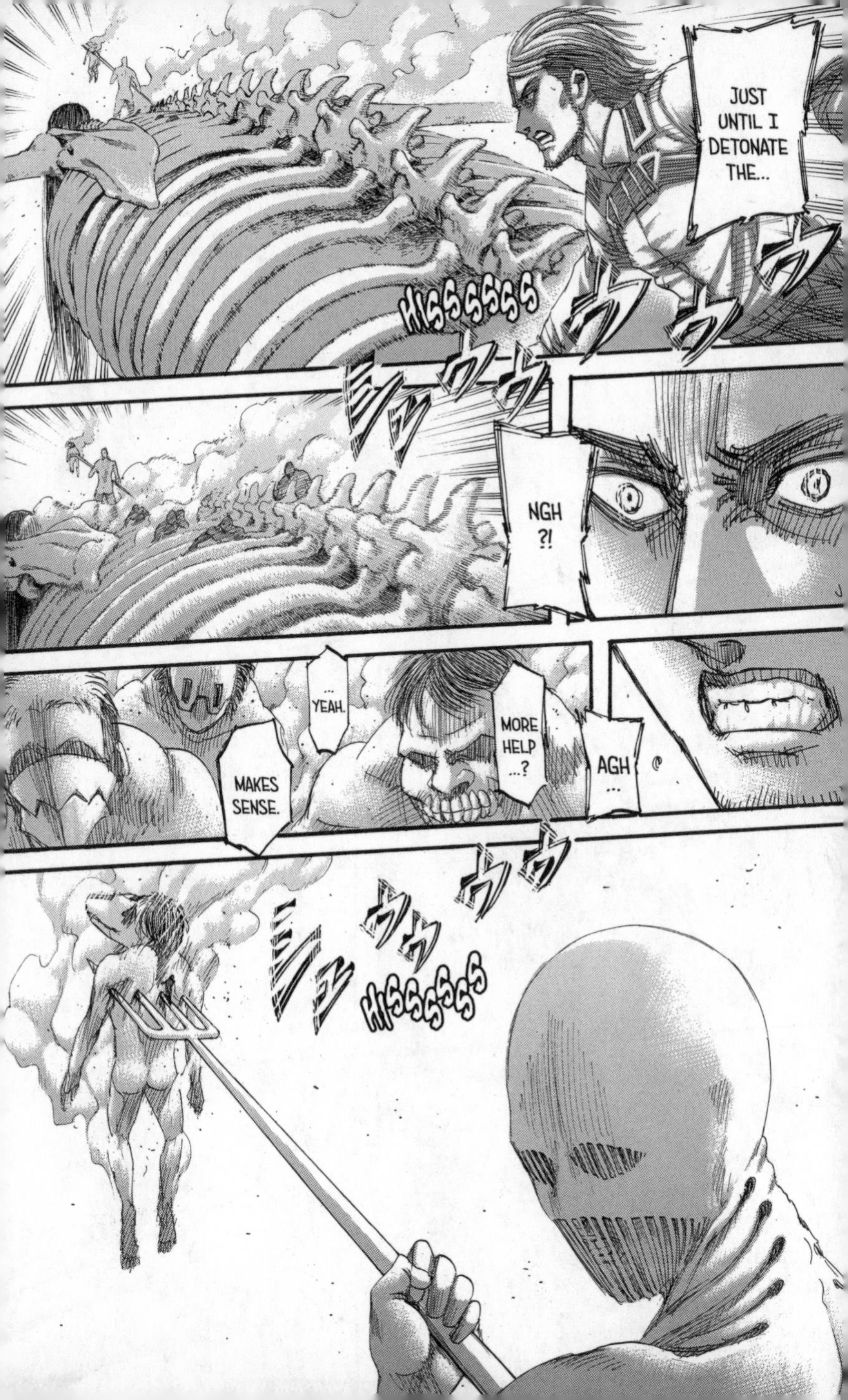
JUST UNTIL I DETONATE THE...
HISSSSSSS
NGH ?!
AGH ...
MORE HELP ...?
... YEAH.
MAKES SENSE.
HISSSSSS

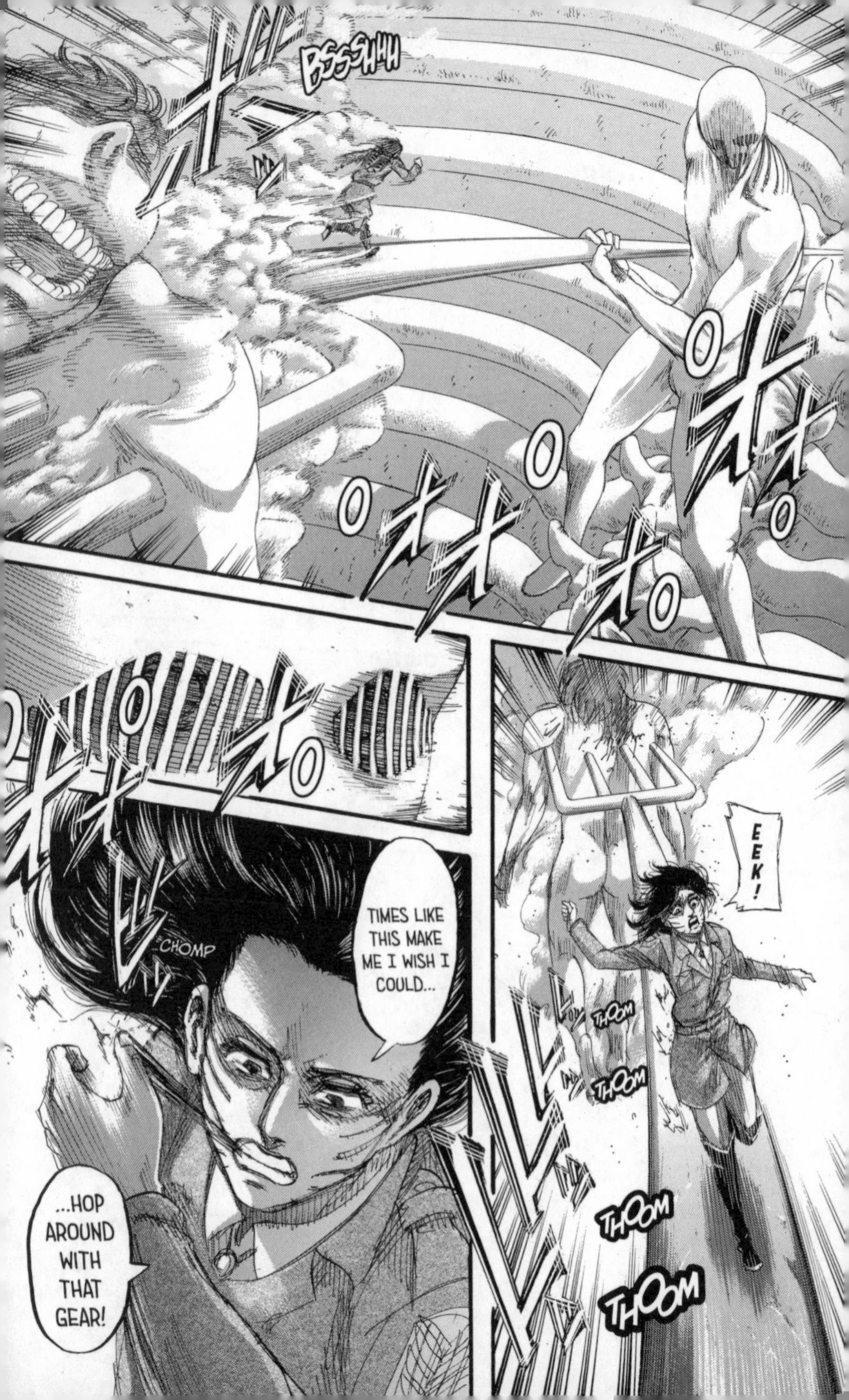
BSSSHHH
EEK!
THOOM
THOOM
THOOM
THOOM
CHOMP
TIMES LIKE THIS MAKE ME I WISH I COULD...
...HOP AROUND WITH THAT GEAR!

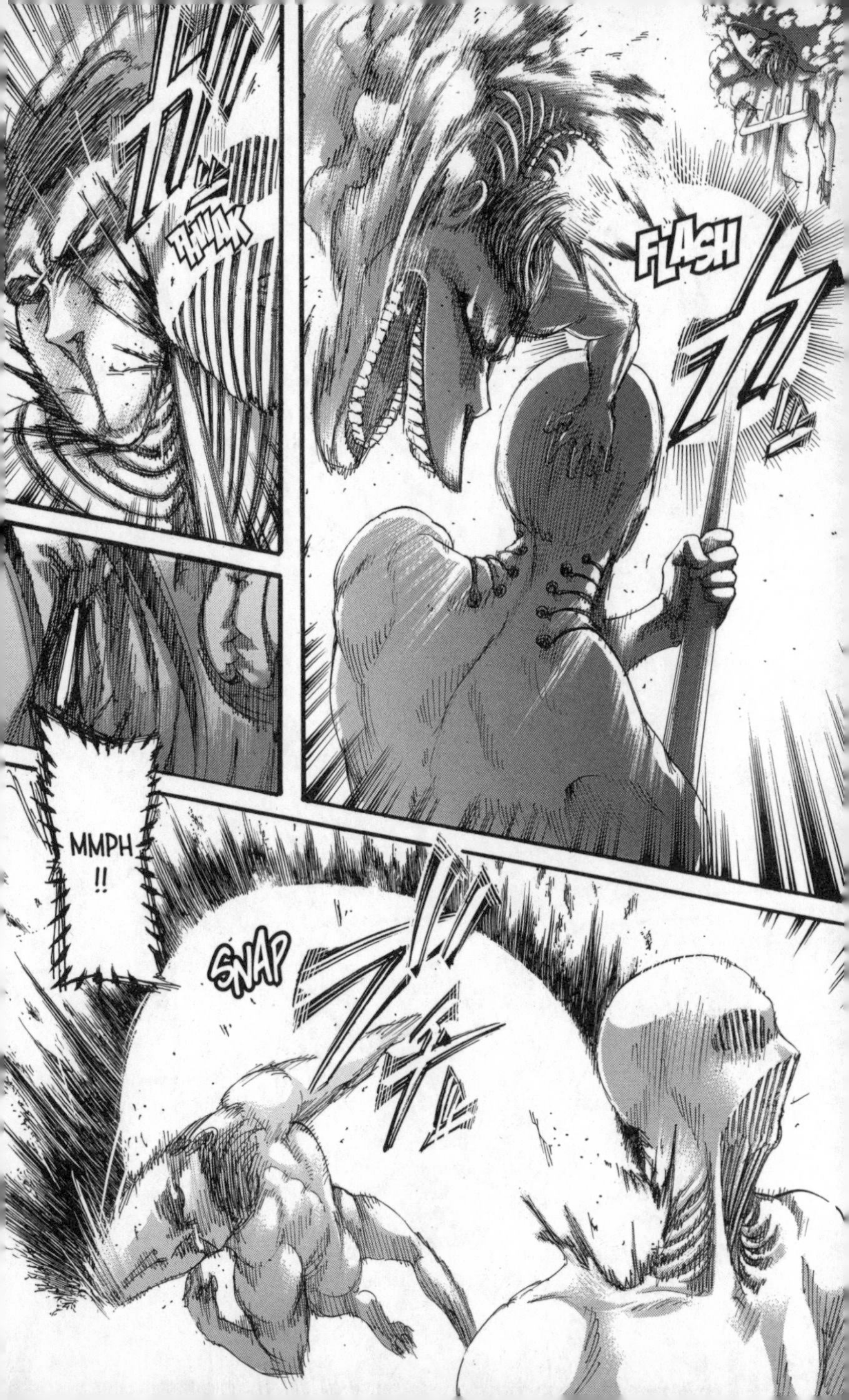
FLASH
THWAK
MMPH !!
SNAP

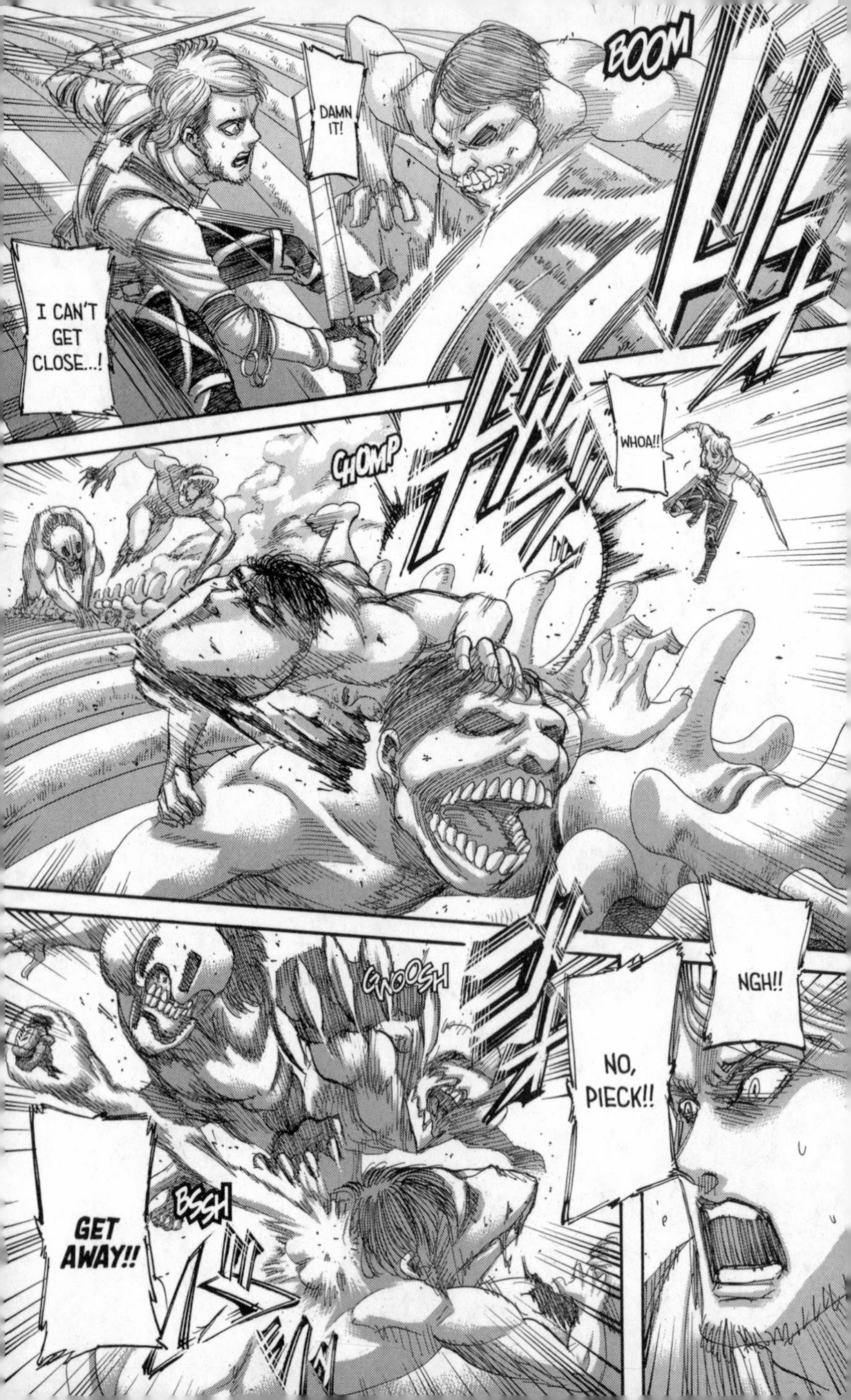
BOOM
DAMN IT!
I CAN'T GET CLOSE...!
WHOA!!
CHOMP
NGH!!
NO, PIECK!!
GNOOSH
BSSH
GET AWAY!!

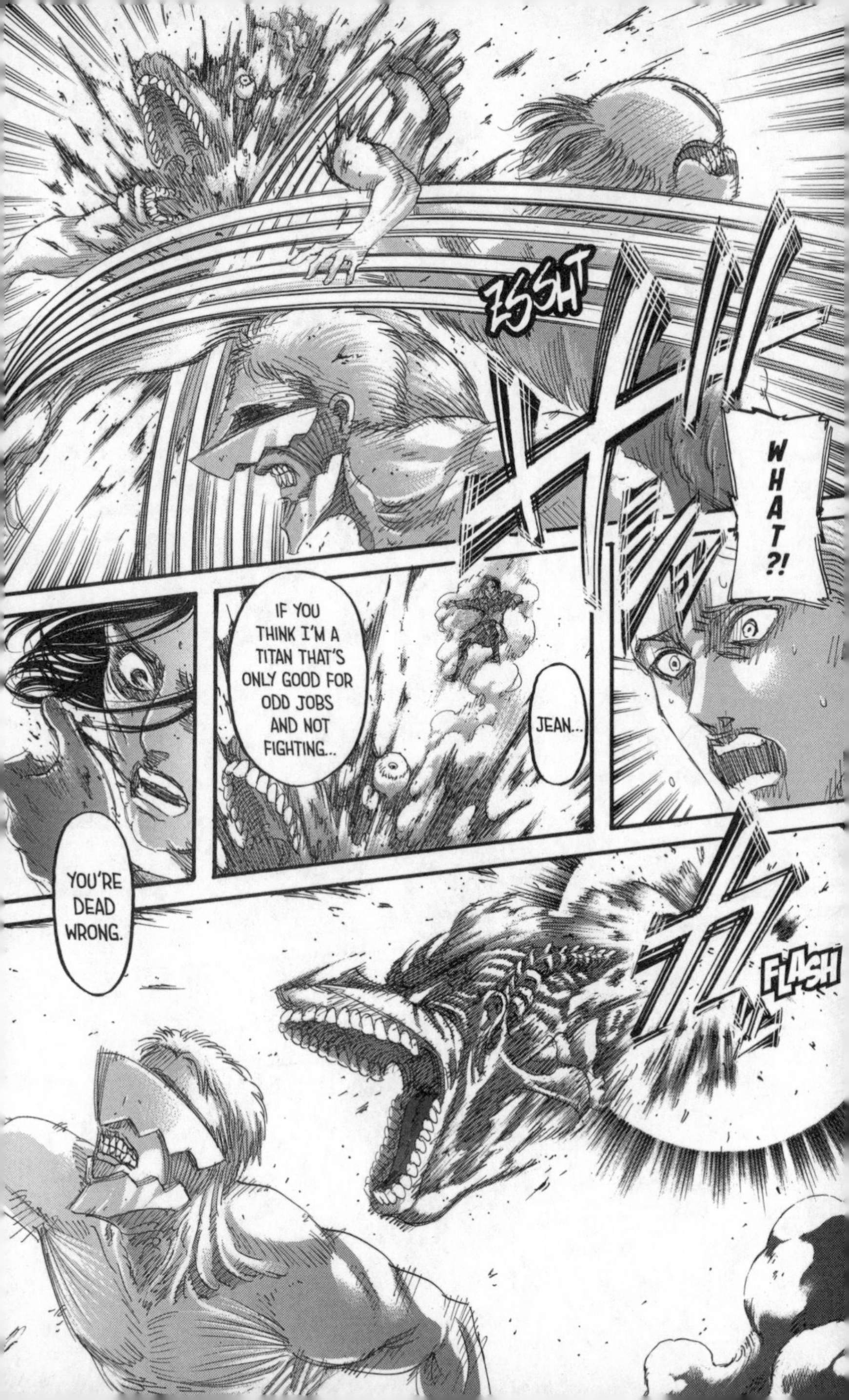
ZSSHT
WHAT?!
JEAN...
IF YOU THINK I'M A TITAN THAT'S ONLY GOOD FOR ODD JOBS AND NOT FIGHTING...
YOU'RE DEAD WRONG.
FLASH

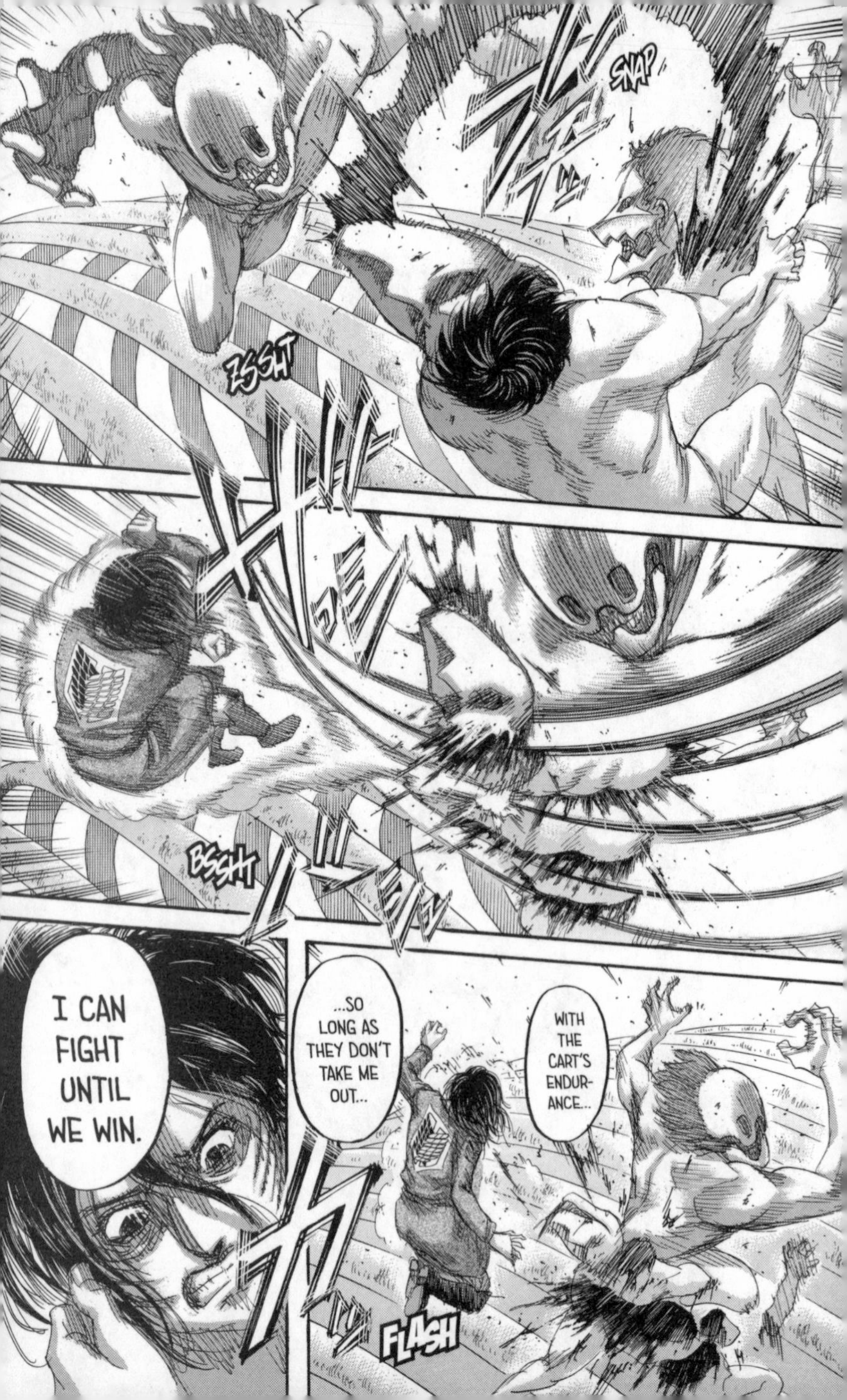
SNAP
ZSSHT
BSSHT
WITH THE CART'S ENDURANCE...
...SO LONG AS THEY DON'T TAKE ME OUT...
FLASH
I CAN FIGHT UNTIL WE WIN.

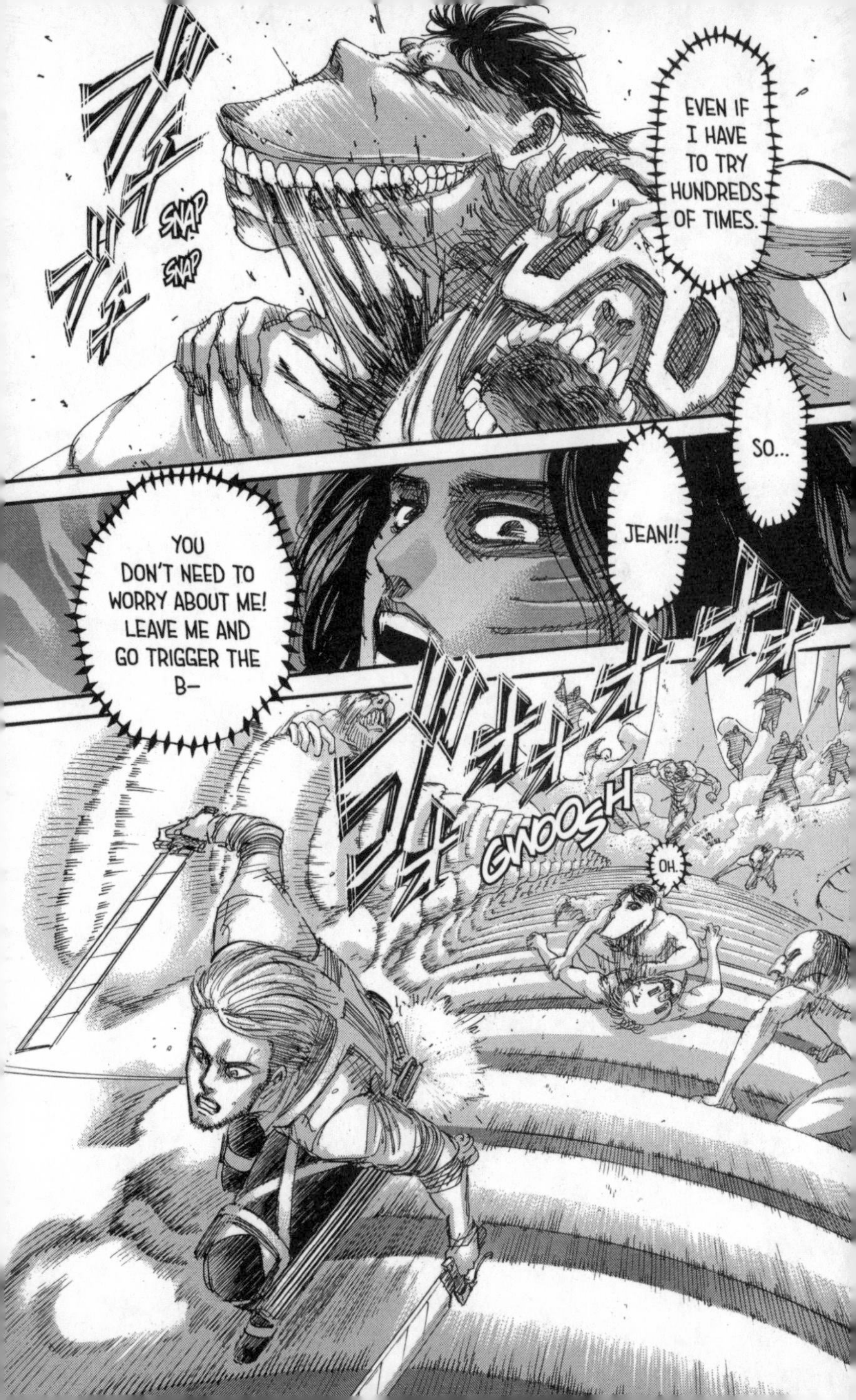
EVEN IF I HAVE TO TRY HUNDREDS OF TIMES.
SNAP
SNAP
SO...
JEAN!!
YOU DON'T NEED TO WORRY ABOUT ME! LEAVE ME AND GO TRIGGER THE B–
GWOOSH
OH.

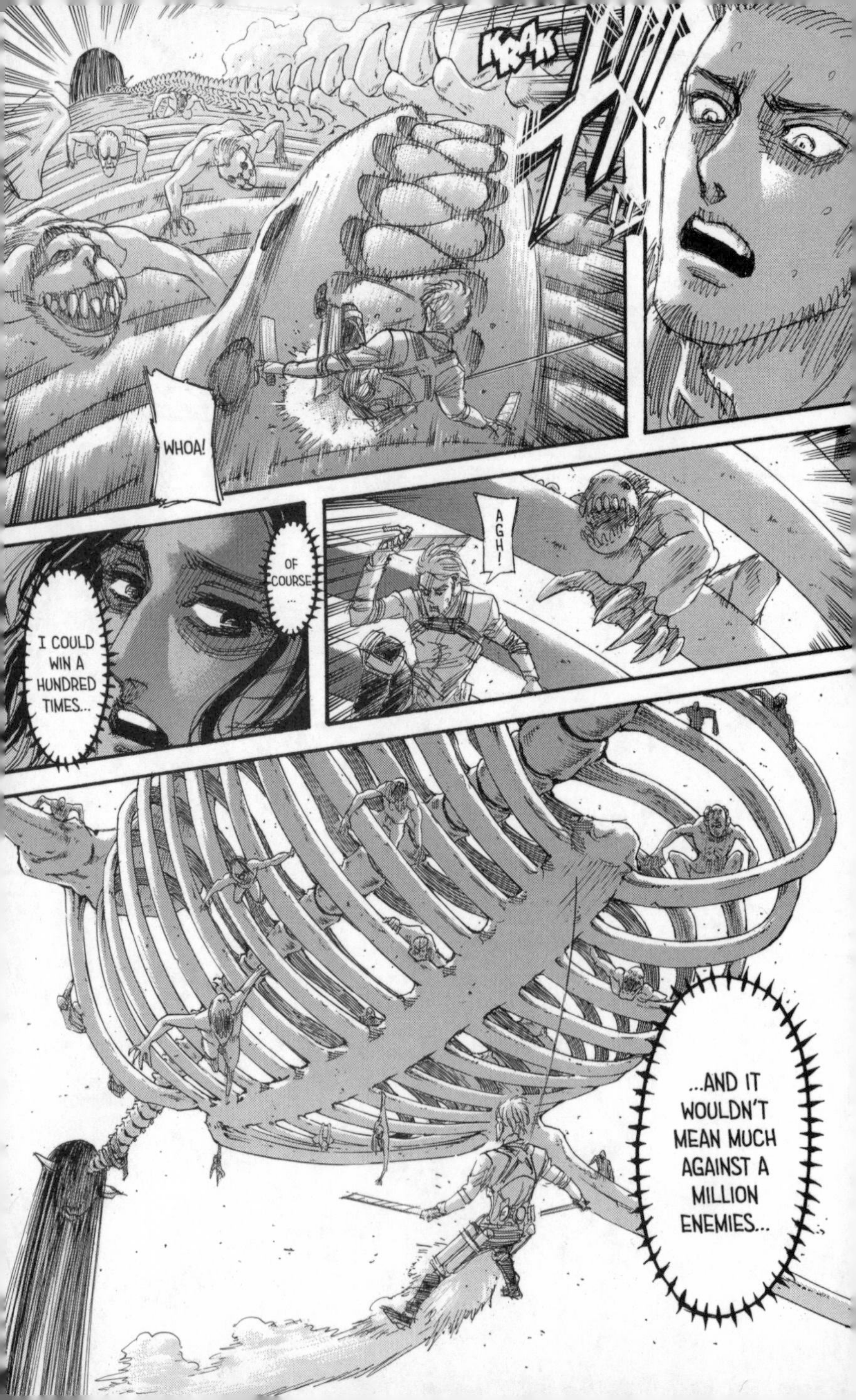
KRAK
WHOA!
AGH!
OF COURSE...
I COULD WIN A HUNDRED TIMES...
...AND IT WOULDN'T MEAN MUCH AGAINST A MILLION ENEMIES...

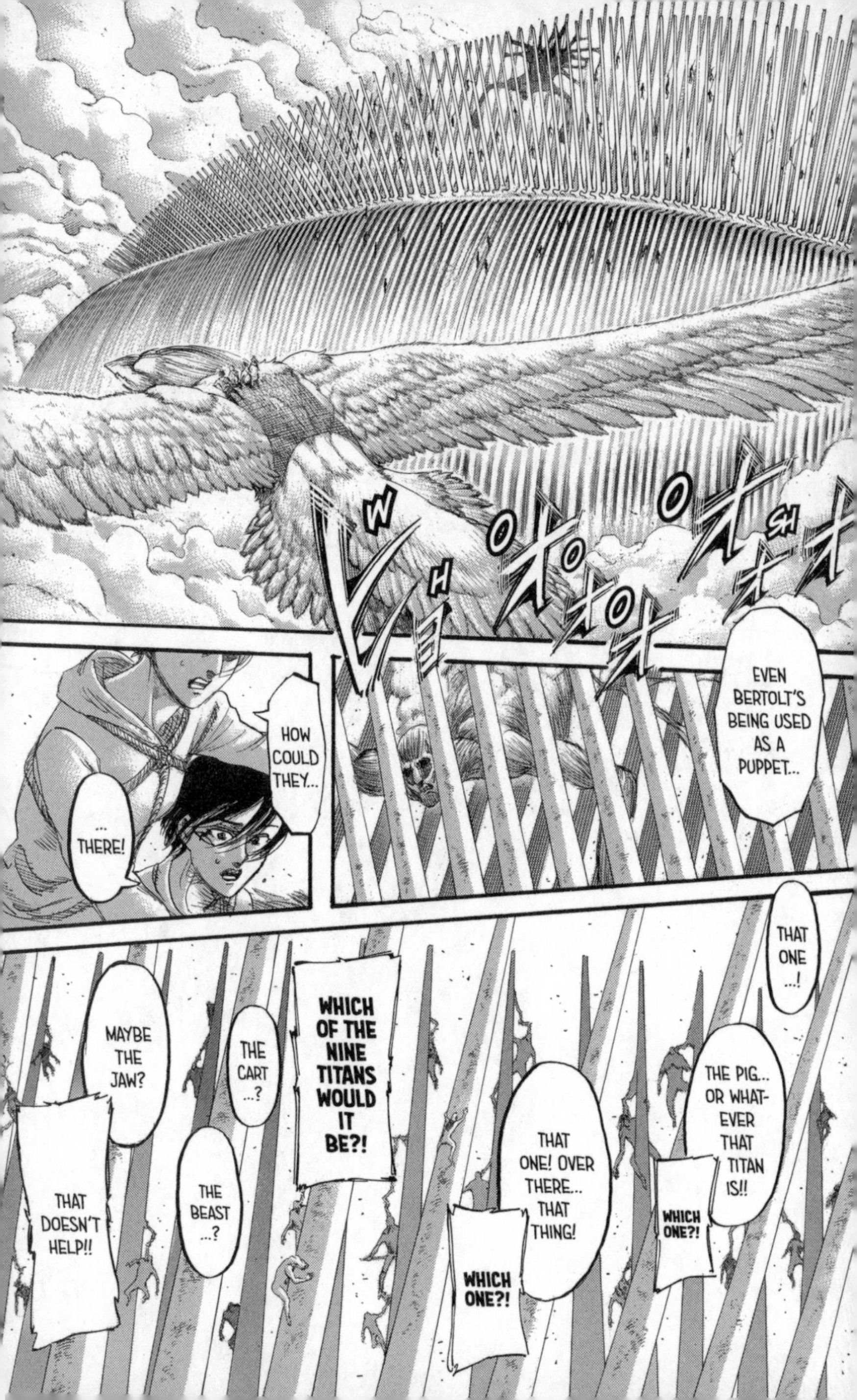
WHOOOOSH
EVEN BERTOLT'S BEING USED AS A PUPPET...
HOW COULD THEY...
...THERE!
THAT ONE ...!
THE PIG... OR WHATEVER THAT TITAN IS!!
WHICH ONE?!
THAT ONE! OVER THERE... THAT THING!
WHICH ONE?!
WHICH OF THE NINE TITANS WOULD IT BE?!
THE CART ...?
THE BEAST ...?
MAYBE THE JAW?
THAT DOESN'T HELP!!

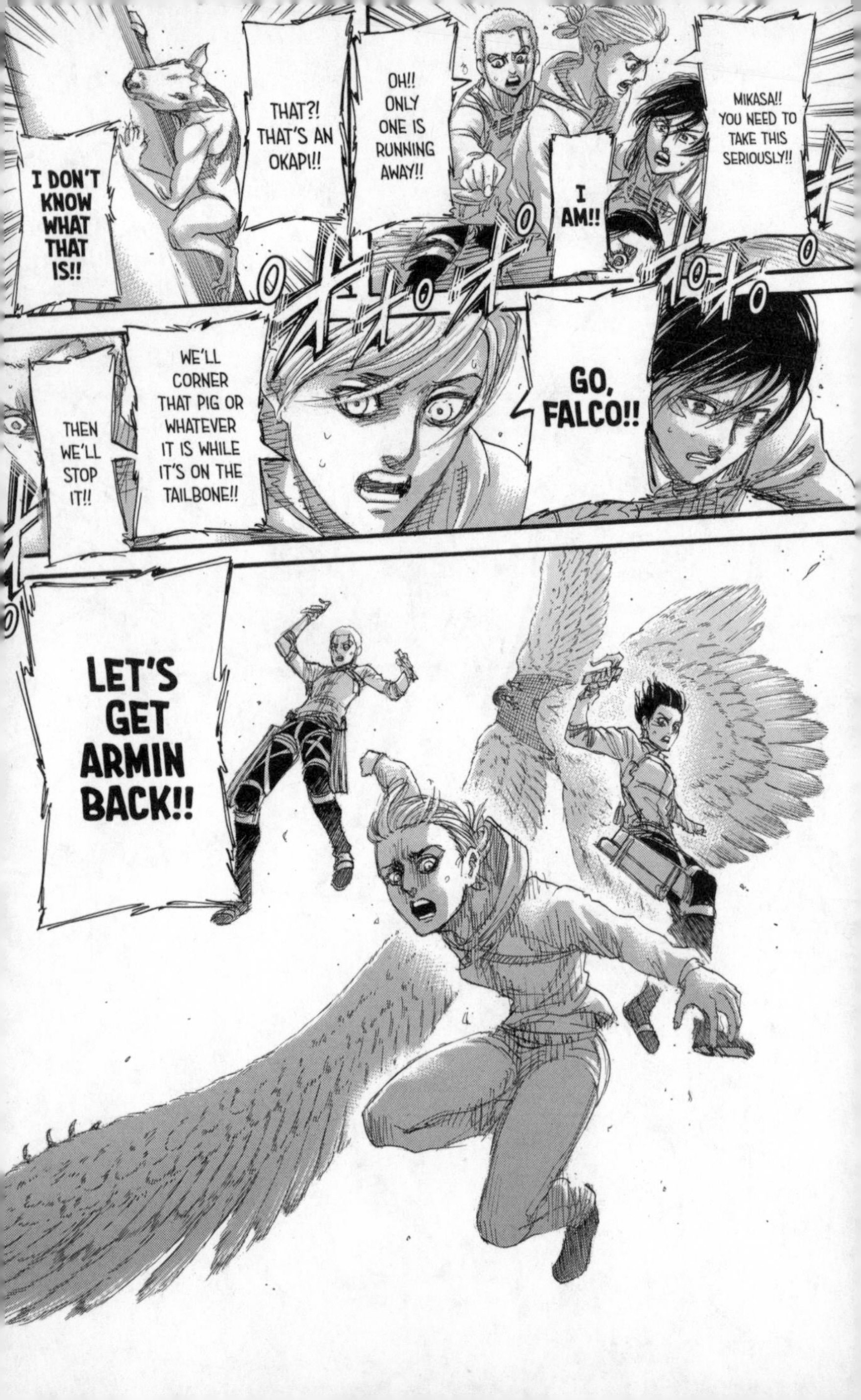

MIKASA!! YOU NEED TO TAKE THIS SERIOUSLY!!
I AM!!
OH!! ONLY ONE IS RUNNING AWAY!!
THAT?! THAT'S AN OKAPI!!
I DON'T KNOW WHAT THAT IS!!
GO, FALCO!!
WE'LL CORNER THAT PIG OR WHATEVER IT IS WHILE IT'S ON THE TAILBONE!!
THEN WE'LL STOP IT!!
LET'S GET ARMIN BACK!!

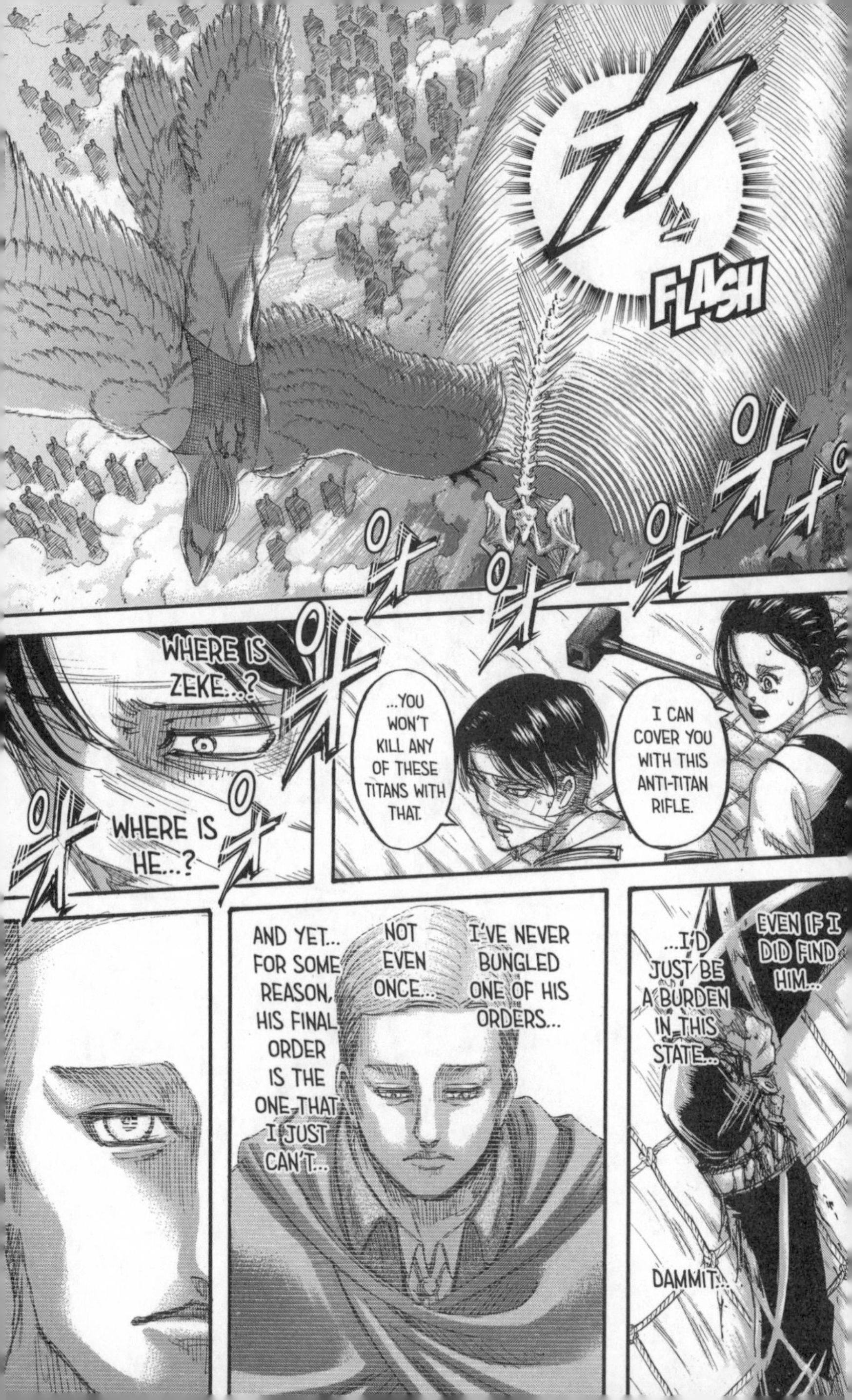
FLASH
I CAN COVER YOU WITH THIS ANTI-TITAN RIFLE.
...YOU WON'T KILL ANY OF THESE TITANS WITH THAT.
WHERE IS ZEKE...?
WHERE IS HE...?
EVEN IF I DID FIND HIM...
...I'D JUST BE A BURDEN IN THIS STATE...
DAMMIT...
I'VE NEVER BUNGLED ONE OF HIS ORDERS...
NOT EVEN ONCE...
AND YET... FOR SOME REASON, HIS FINAL ORDER IS THE ONE THAT I JUST CAN'T...

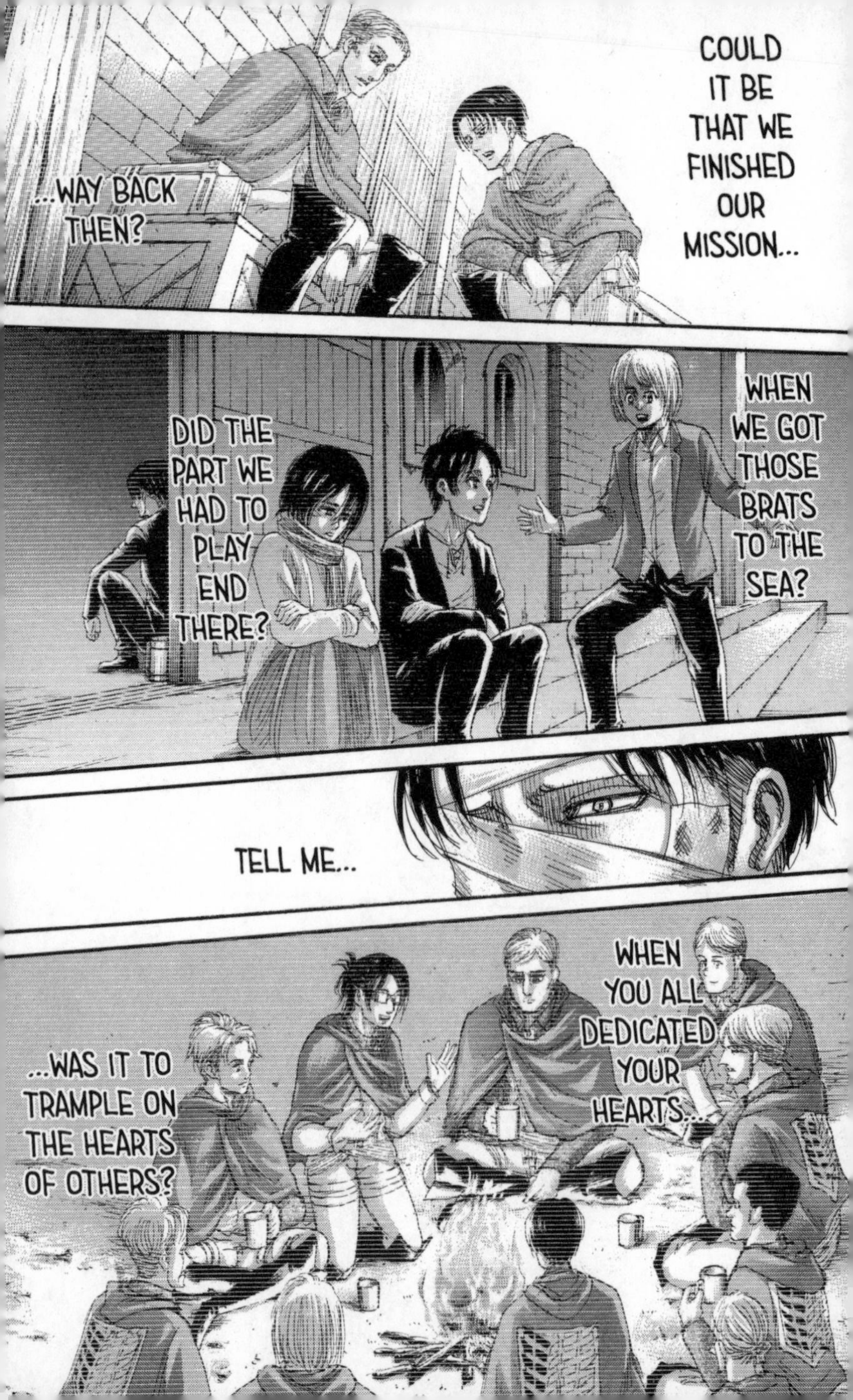
COULD IT BE THAT WE FINISHED OUR MISSION...
...WAY BACK THEN?
WHEN WE GOT THOSE BRATS TO THE SEA?
DID THE PART WE HAD TO PLAY END THERE?
TELL ME...
WHEN YOU ALL DEDICATED YOUR HEARTS...
...WAS IT TO TRAMPLE ON THE HEARTS OF OTHERS?

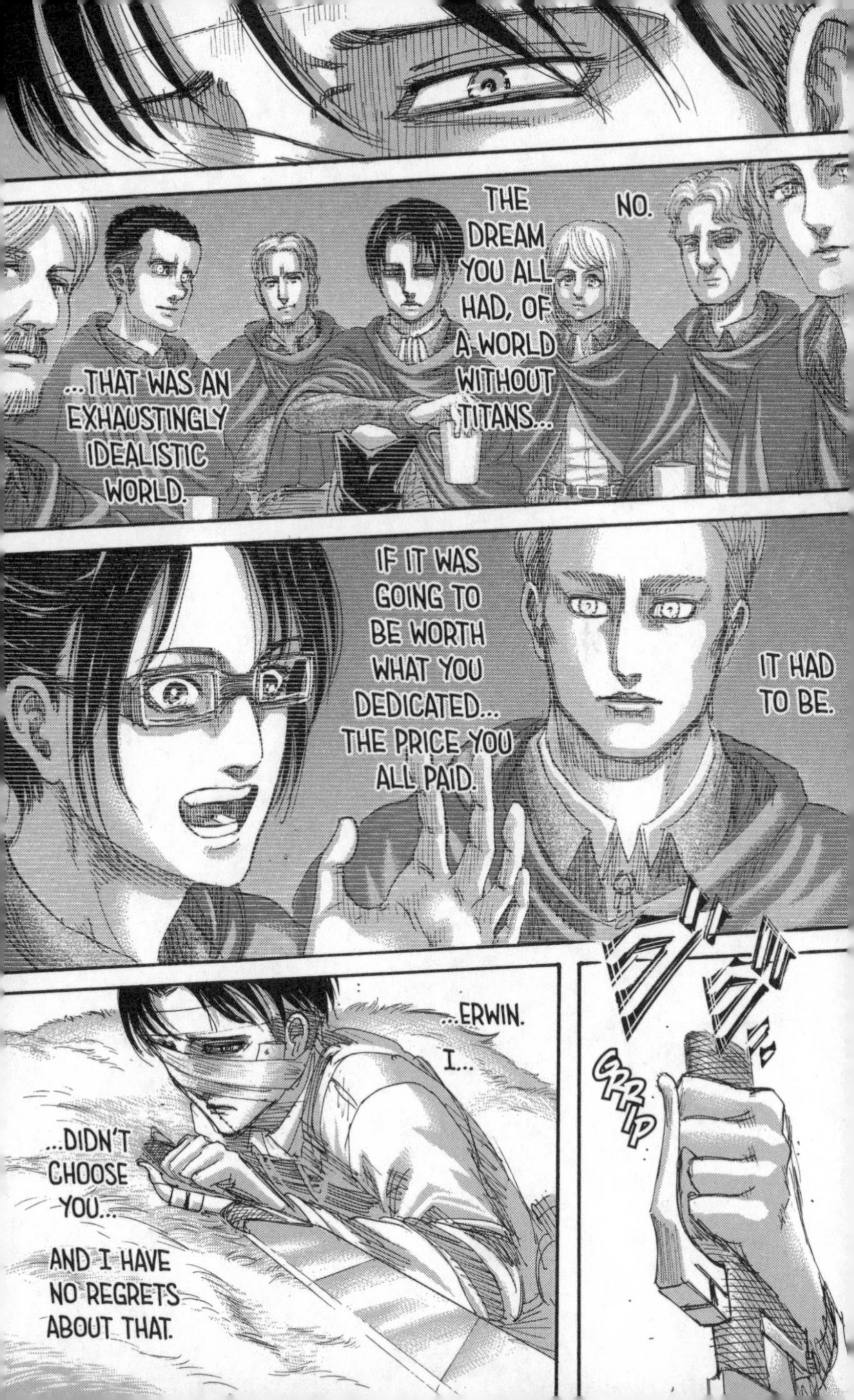
NO.
THE DREAM YOU ALL HAD, OF A WORLD WITHOUT TITANS...
...THAT WAS AN EXHAUSTINGLY IDEALISTIC WORLD.
IF IT WAS GOING TO BE WORTH WHAT YOU DEDICATED... THE PRICE YOU ALL PAID.
IT HAD TO BE.
GRRIP
...ERWIN.
I...
...DIDN'T CHOOSE YOU...
AND I HAVE NO REGRETS ABOUT THAT.

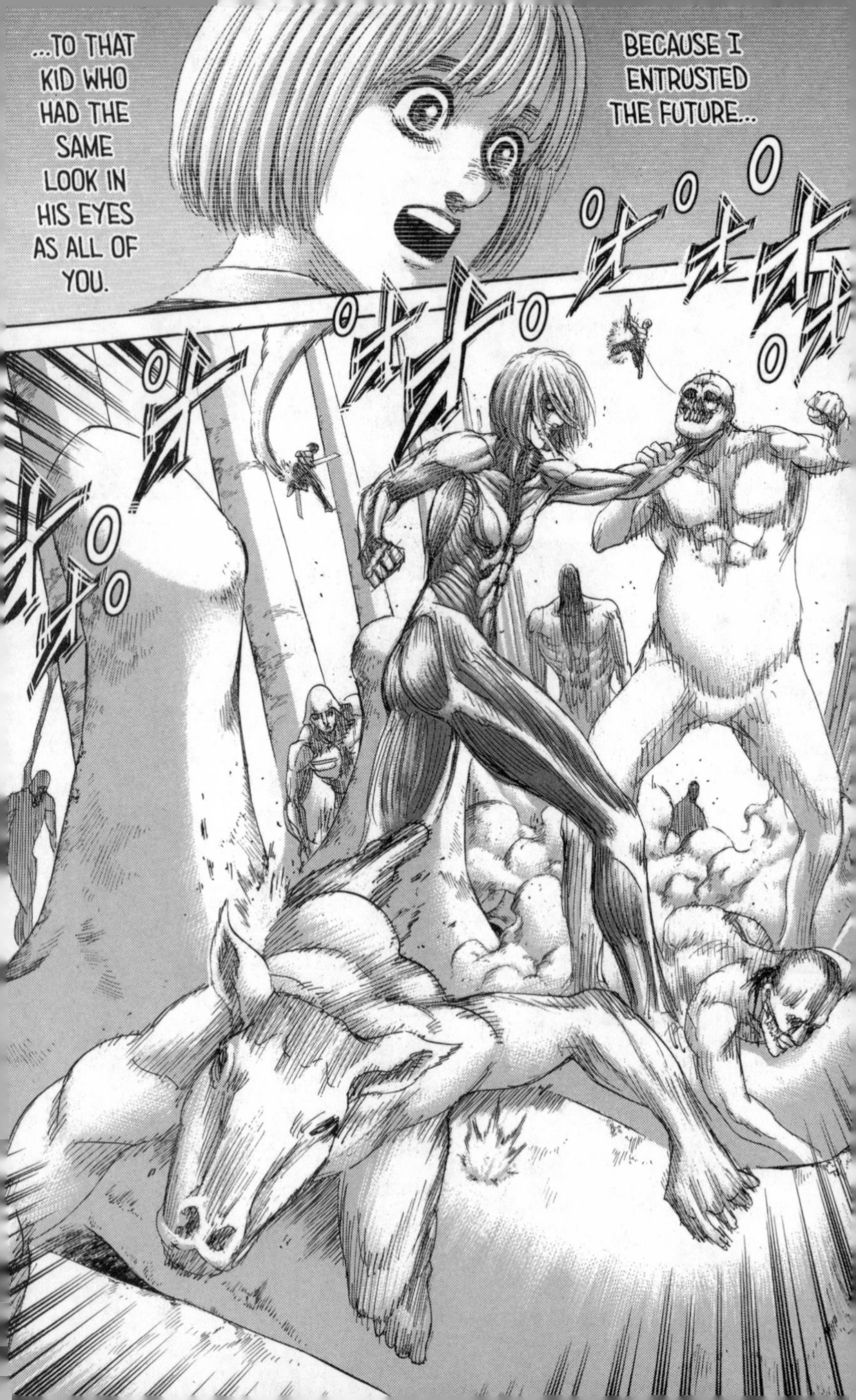
BECAUSE I ENTRUSTED THE FUTURE...
...TO THAT KID WHO HAD THE SAME LOOK IN HIS EYES AS ALL OF YOU.

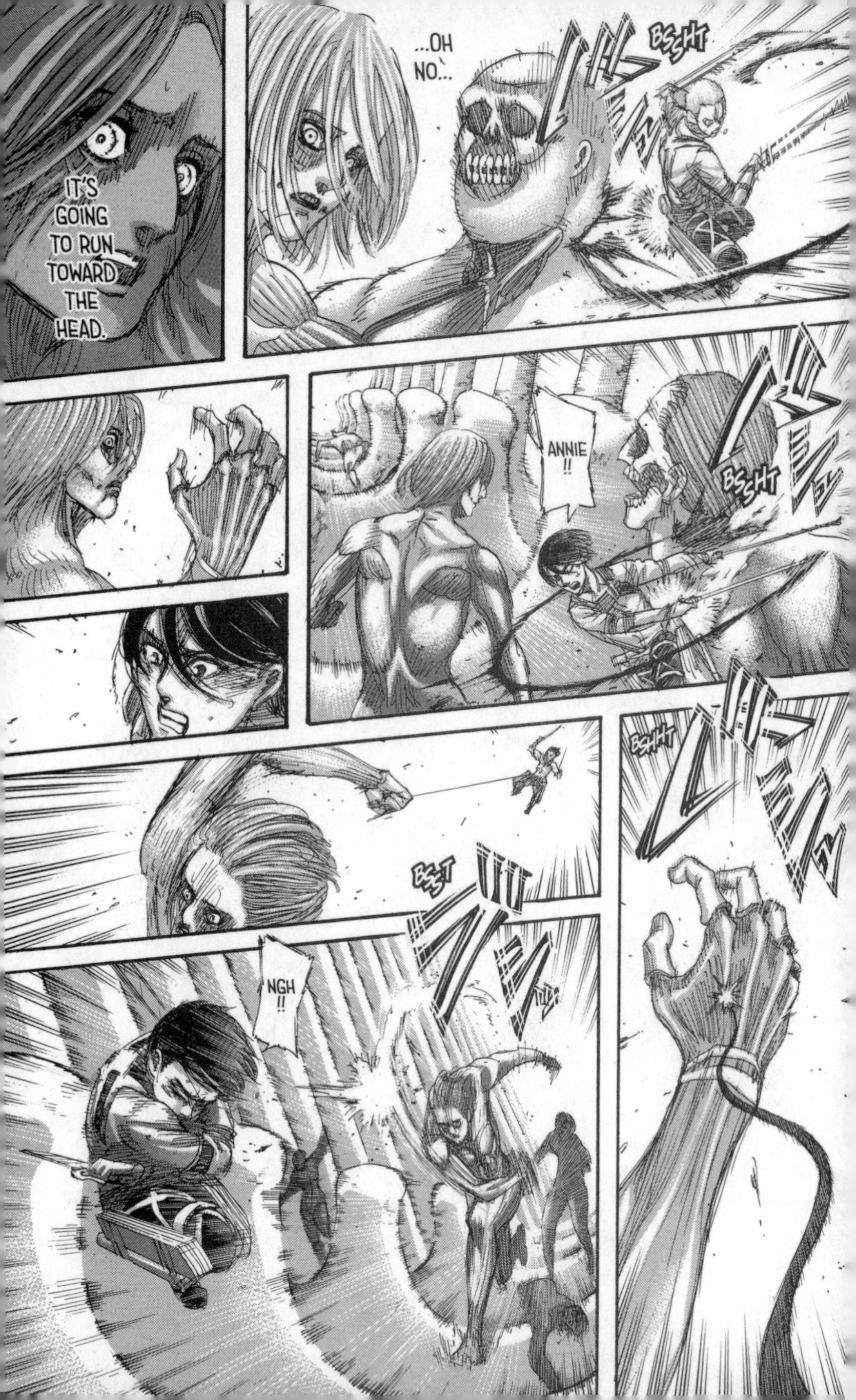
...OH NO...
BSSHT
IT'S GOING TO RUN TOWARD THE HEAD.
ANNIE!!
BSSHT
BSHHT
BSST
NGH!!

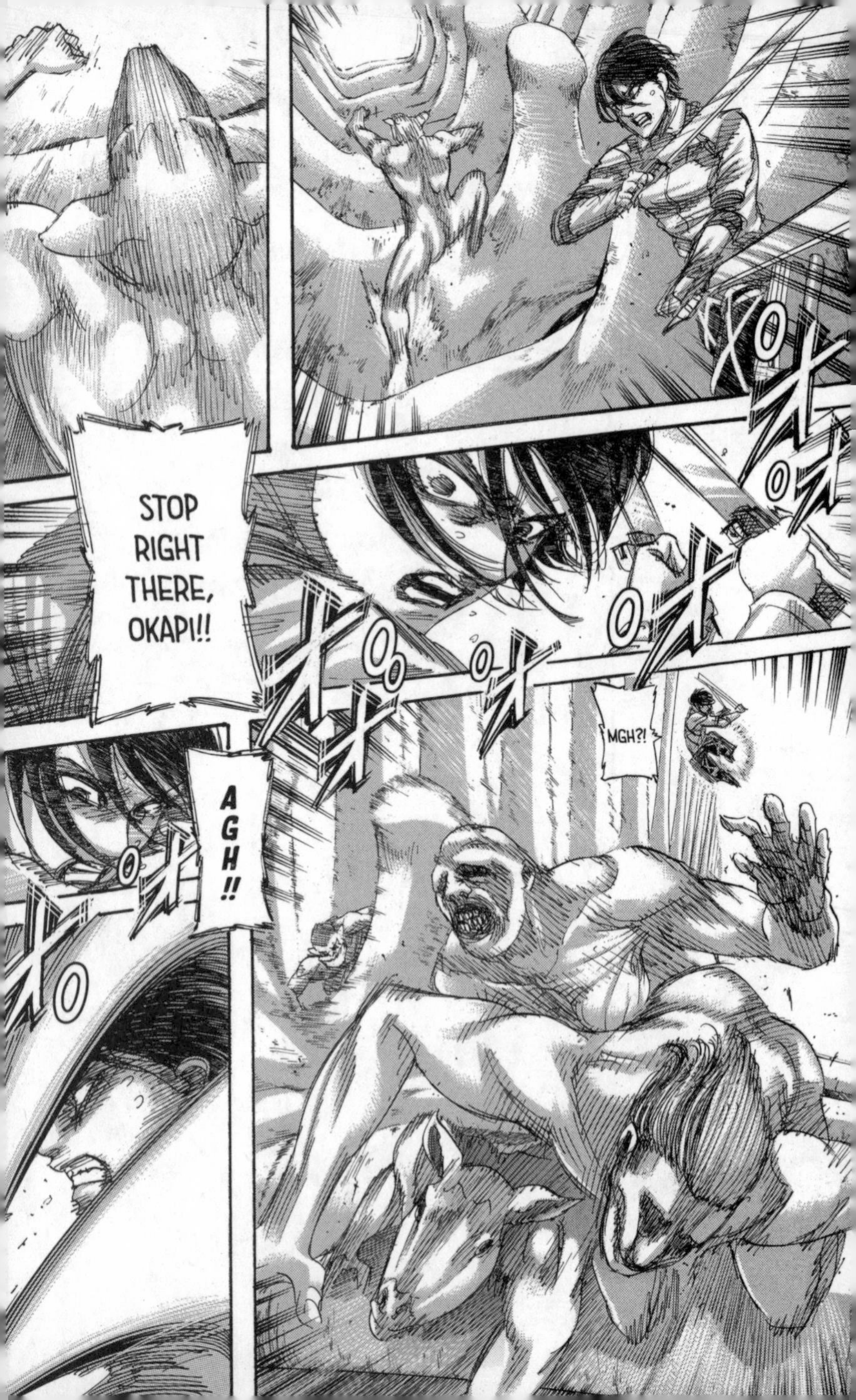
STOP RIGHT THERE, OKAPI!!
MGH?!
AGH!!

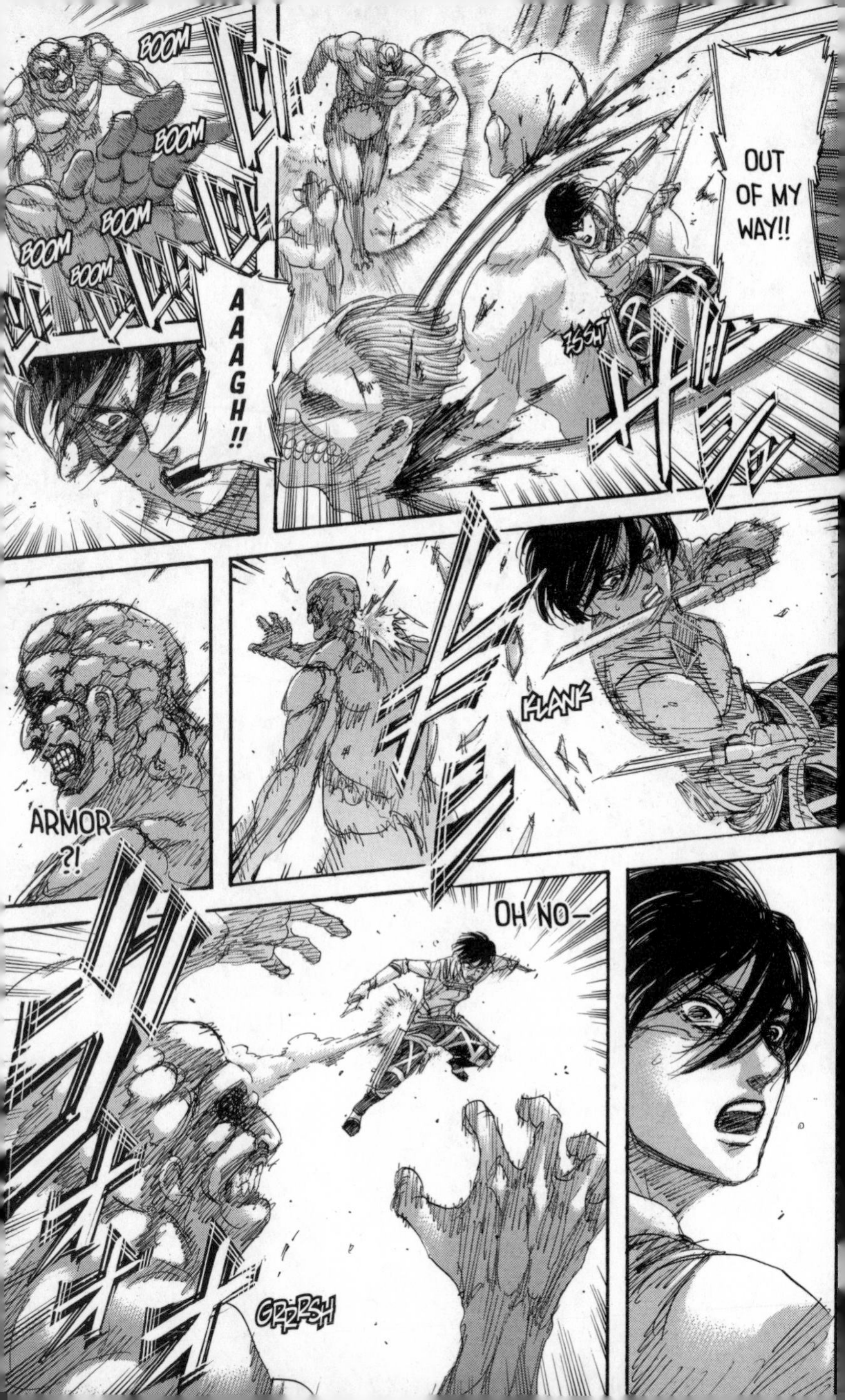
OUT OF MY WAY!!
ZSSHT
BOOM
BOOM
BOOM
BOOM
BOOM
AAAAGH!!
KLANK
ARMOR ?!
OH NO–
GRRRSH

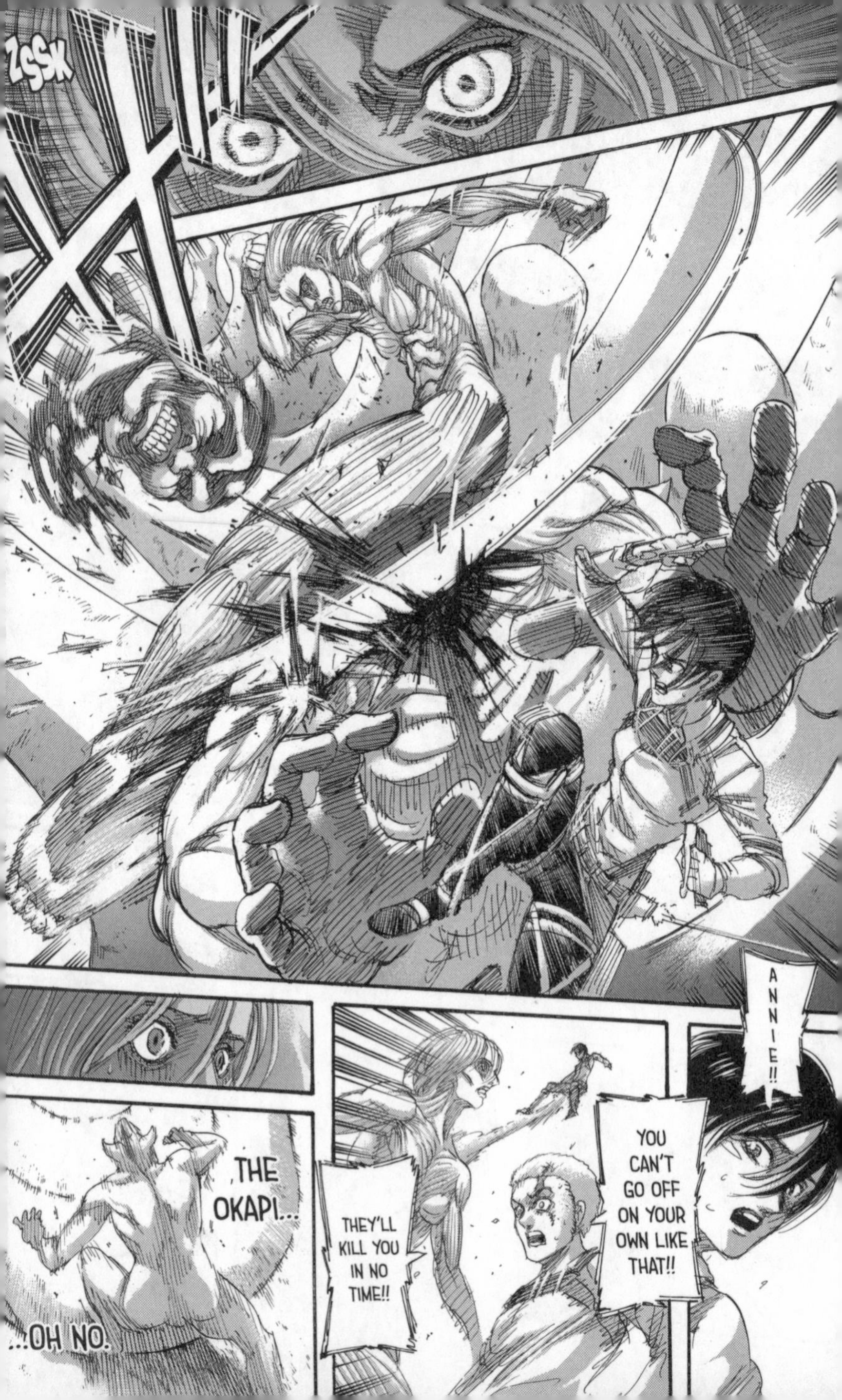
ZSSK
ANNIE!!
YOU CAN'T GO OFF ON YOUR OWN LIKE THAT!!
THEY'LL KILL YOU IN NO TIME!!
THE OKAPI...
...OH NO.

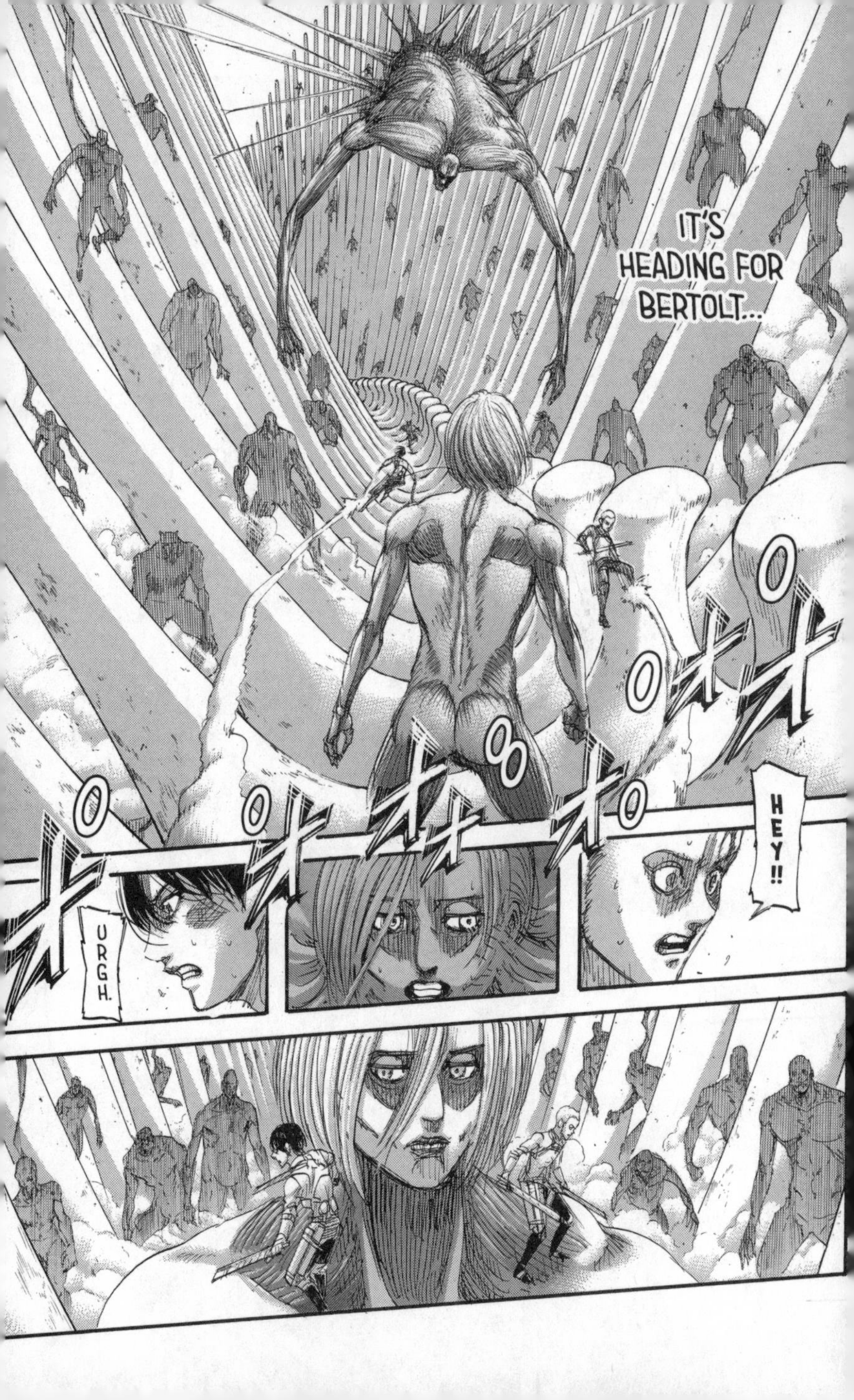
IT'S HEADING FOR BERTOLT...
HEY!!
URGH.

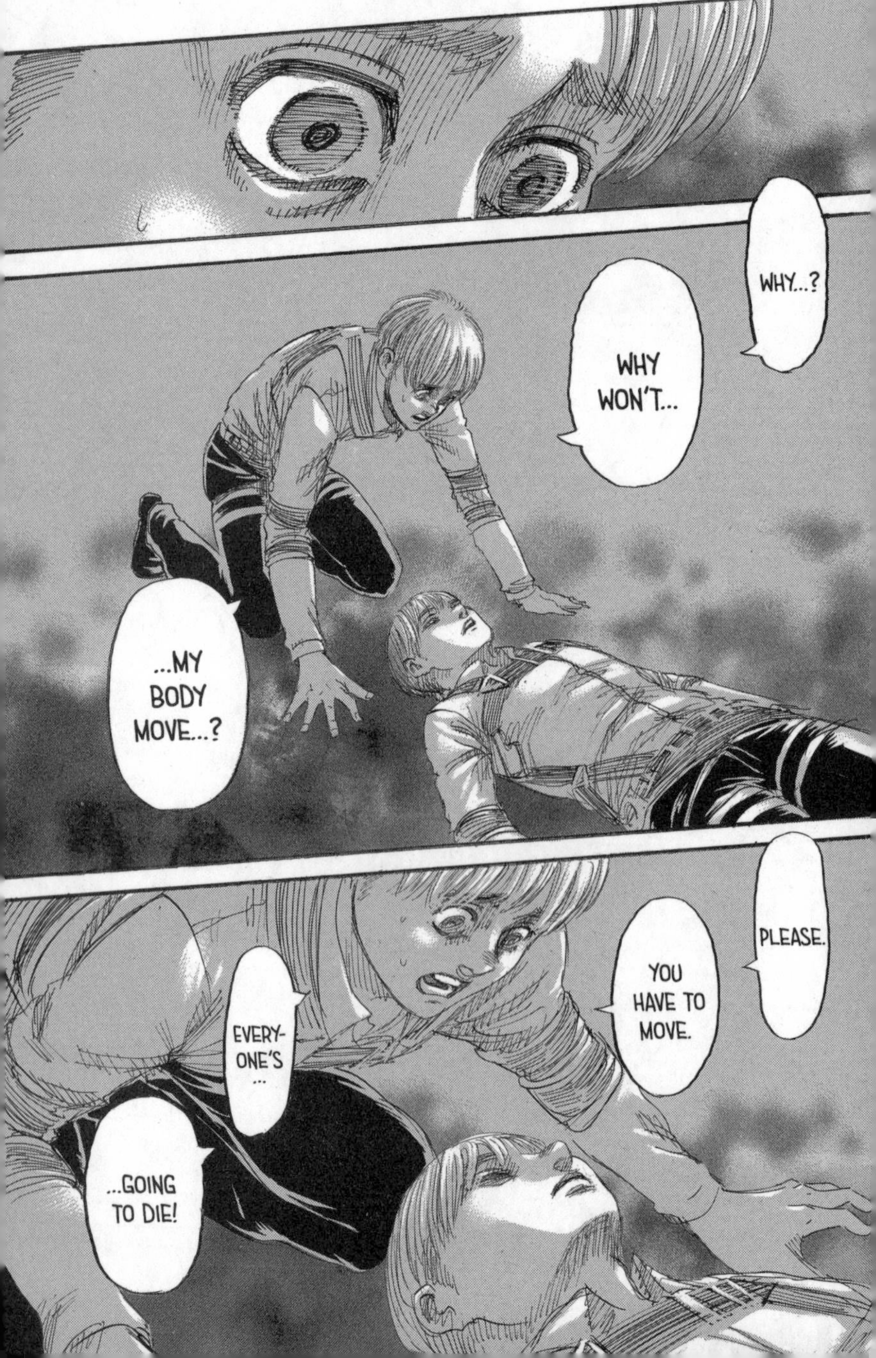
WHY...?
WHY WON'T...
...MY BODY MOVE...?
PLEASE.
YOU HAVE TO MOVE.
EVERY-ONE'S...
...GOING TO DIE!

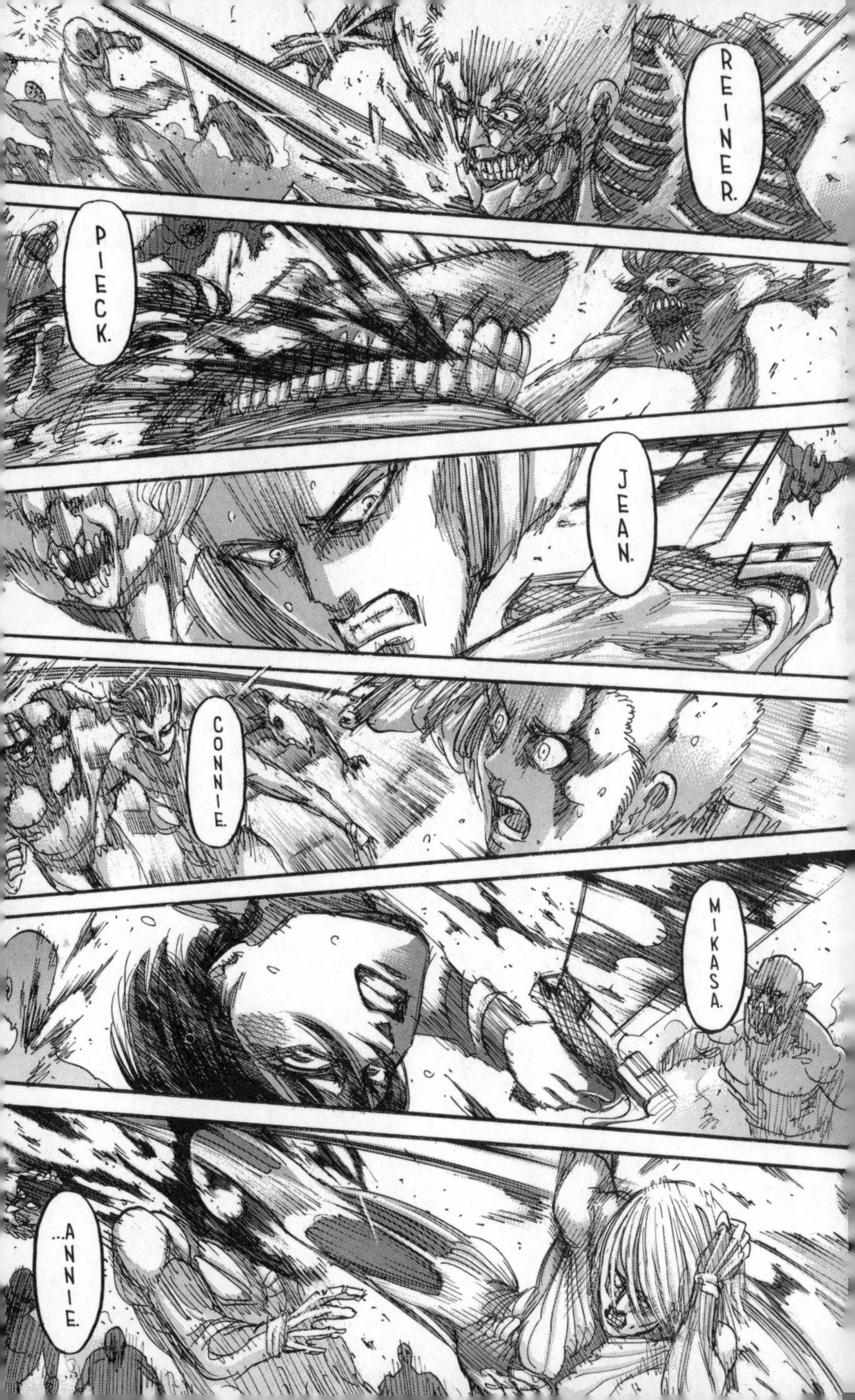
REINER.
PIECK.
JEAN.
CONNIE.
MIKASA.
...ANNIE.

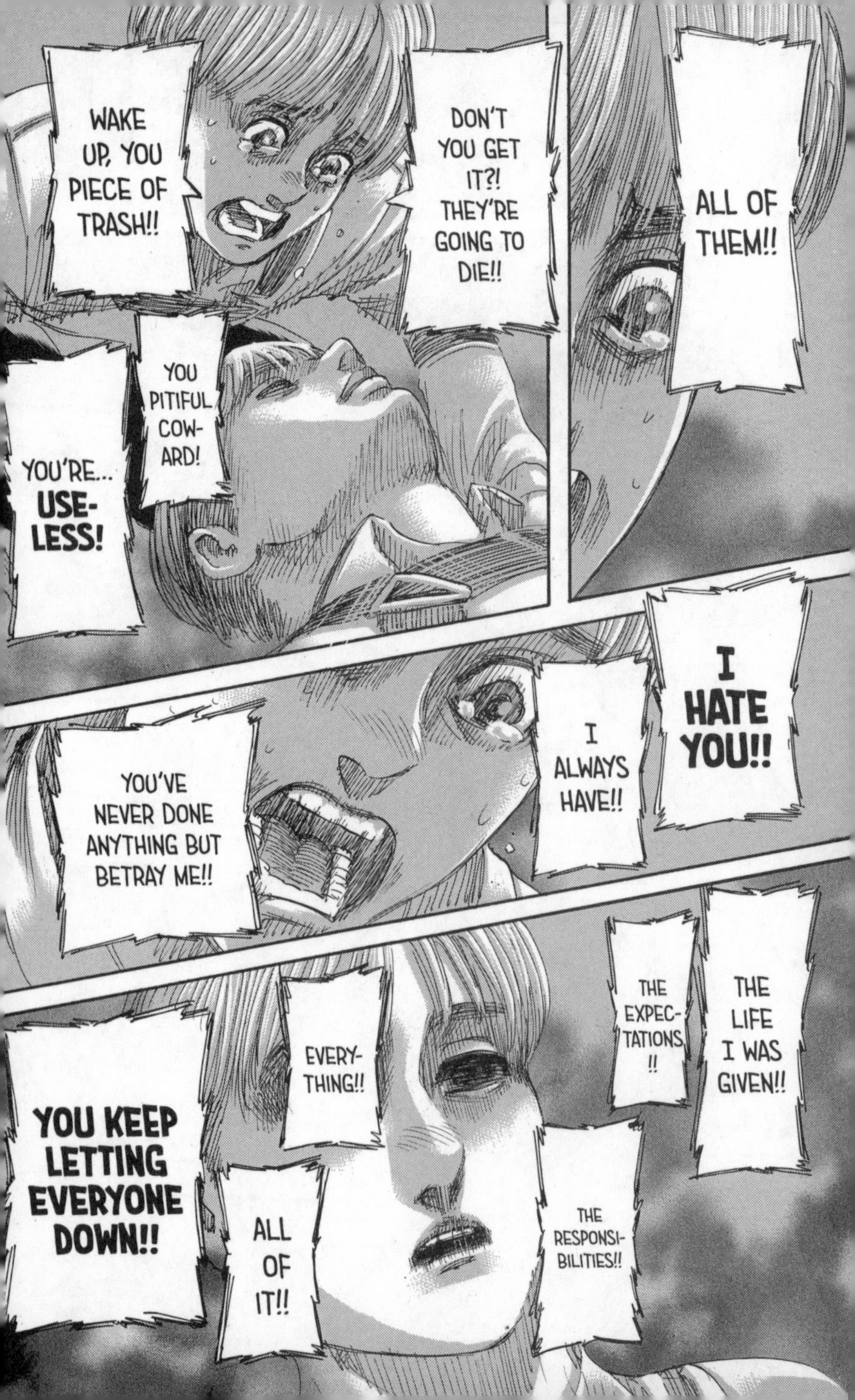
ALL OF THEM!!
DON'T YOU GET IT?! THEY'RE GOING TO DIE!!
WAKE UP, YOU PIECE OF TRASH!!
YOU PITIFUL COW-ARD!
YOU'RE... USE-LESS!
I HATE YOU!!
I ALWAYS HAVE!!
YOU'VE NEVER DONE ANYTHING BUT BETRAY ME!!
THE LIFE I WAS GIVEN!!
THE EXPEC-TATIONS!!
THE RESPONSI-BILITIES!!
EVERY-THING!!
ALL OF IT!!
YOU KEEP LETTING EVERYONE DOWN!!

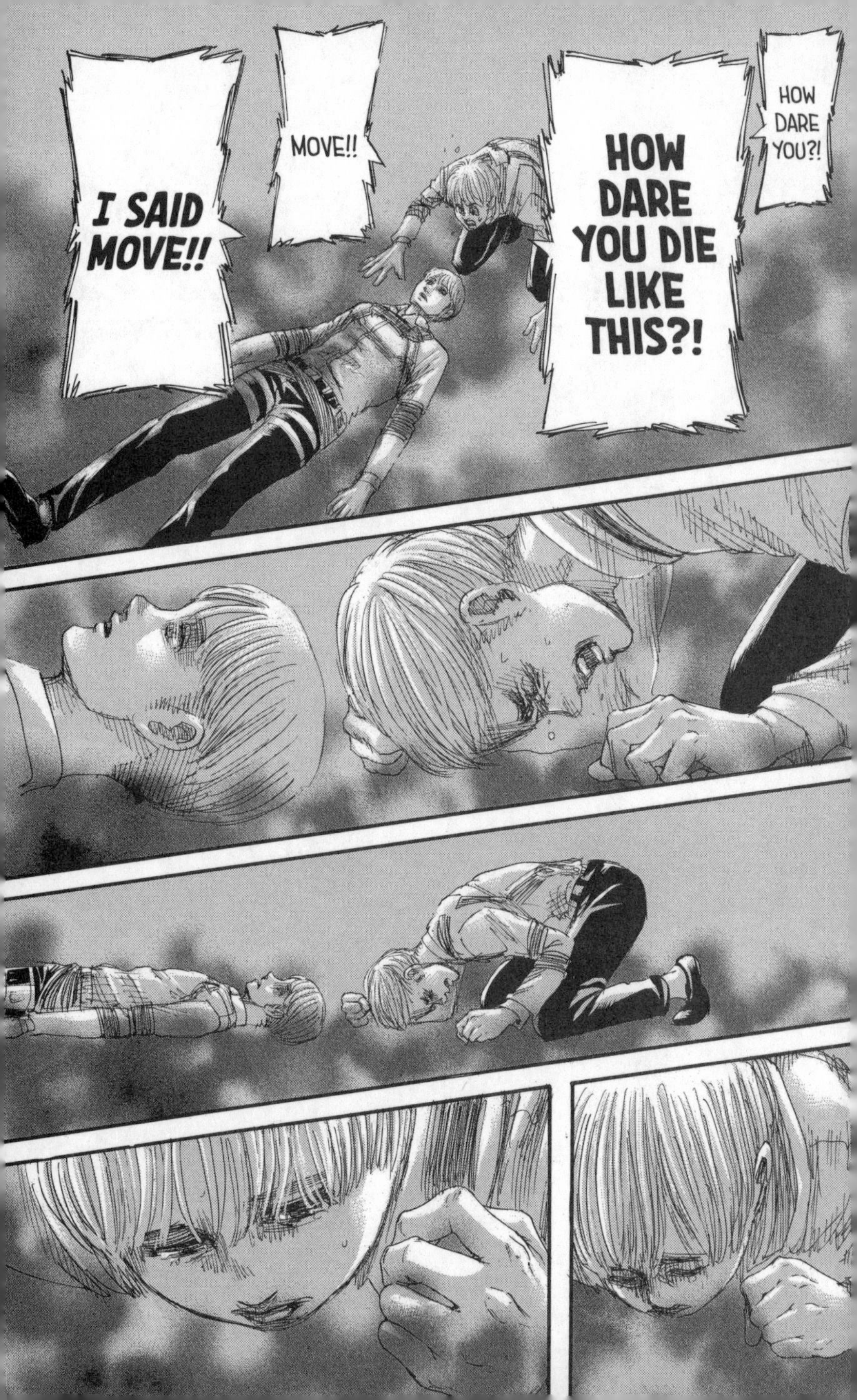
HOW DARE YOU?!
HOW DARE YOU DIE LIKE THIS?!
MOVE!!
I SAID MOVE!!

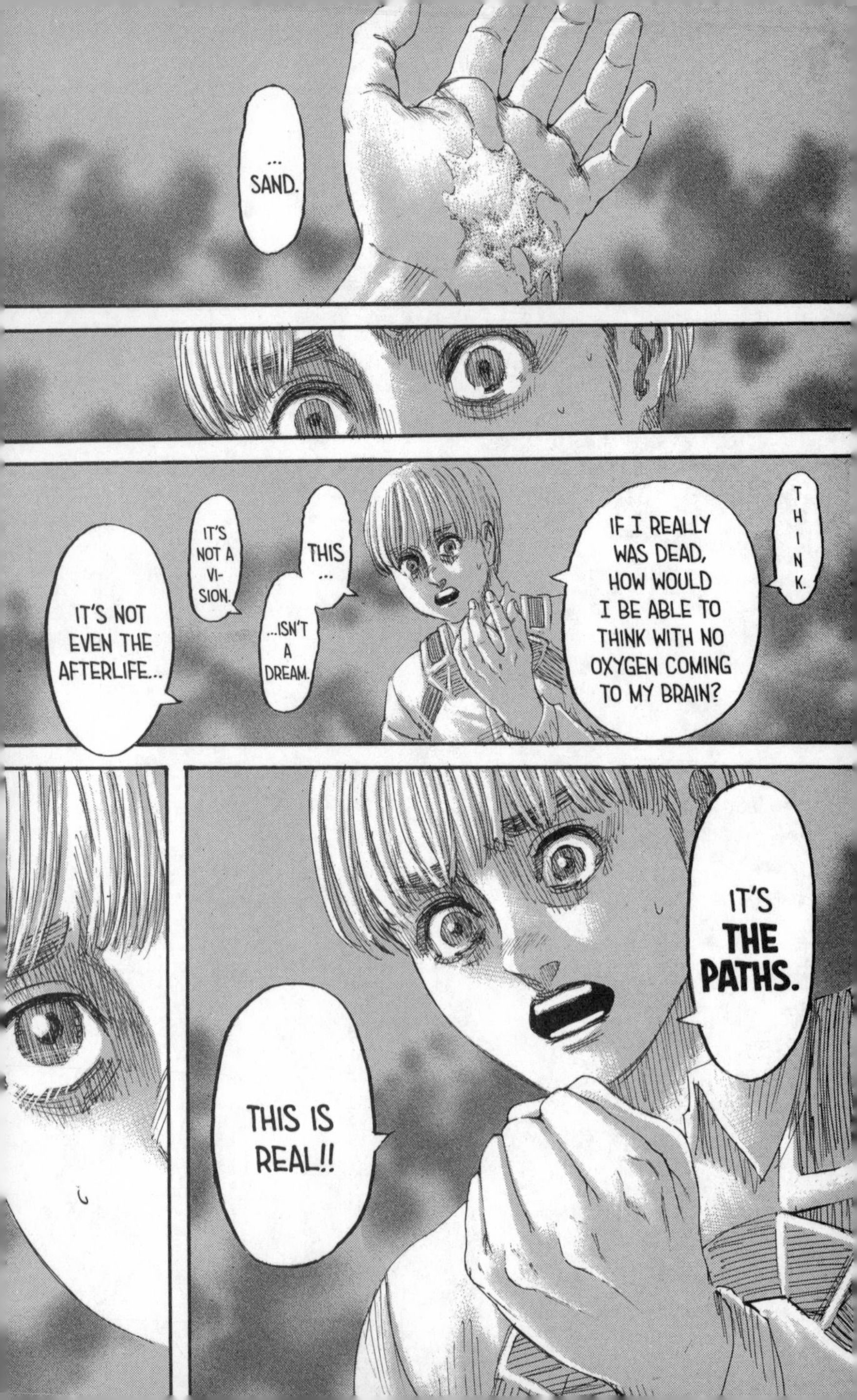
... SAND.
T H I N K.
IF I REALLY WAS DEAD, HOW WOULD I BE ABLE TO THINK WITH NO OXYGEN COMING TO MY BRAIN?
THIS ...
...ISN'T A DREAM.
IT'S NOT A VI- SION.
IT'S NOT EVEN THE AFTERLIFE...
IT'S THE PATHS.
THIS IS REAL!!

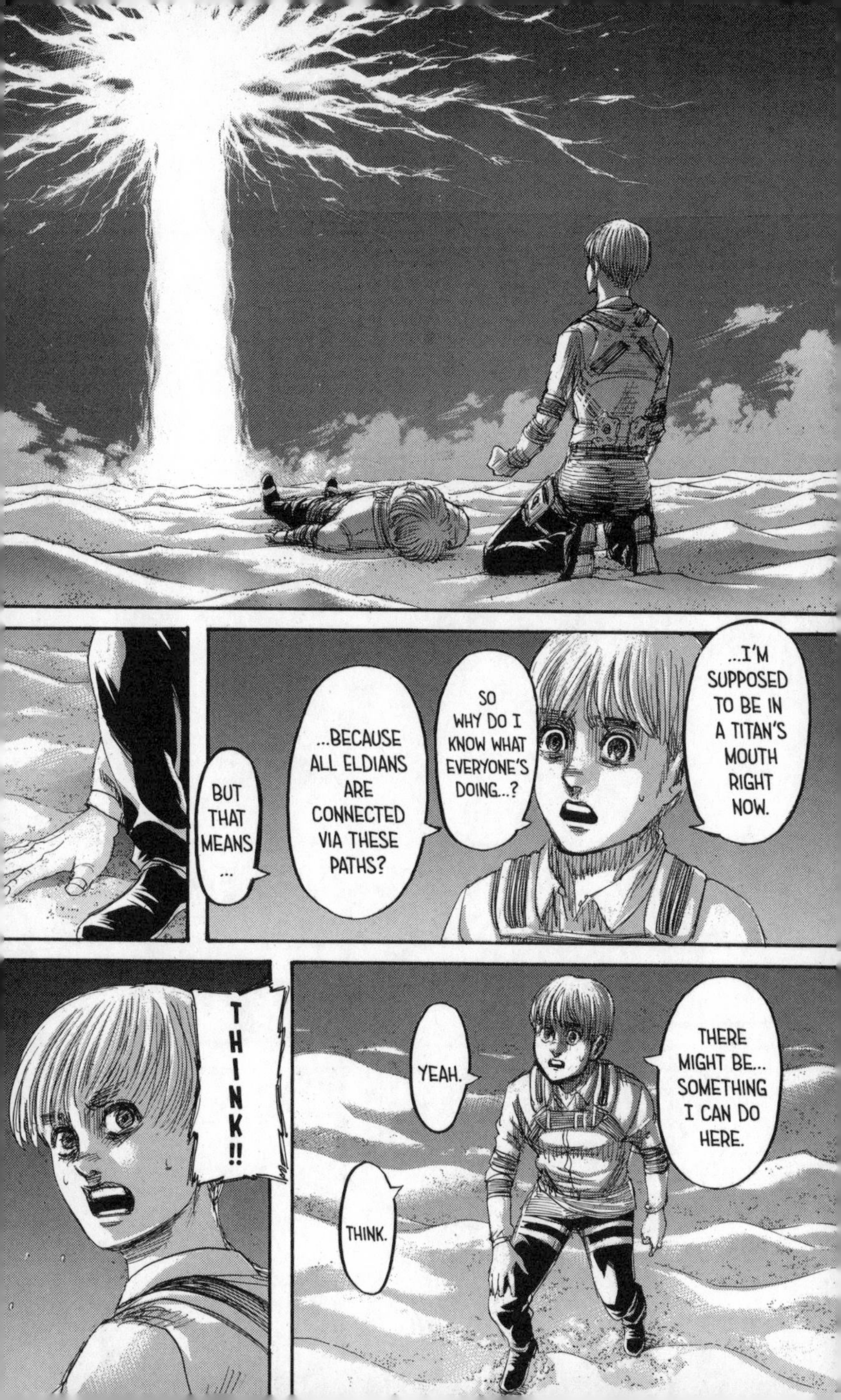

...I'M SUPPOSED TO BE IN A TITAN'S MOUTH RIGHT NOW.
SO WHY DO I KNOW WHAT EVERYONE'S DOING...?
...BECAUSE ALL ELDIANS ARE CONNECTED VIA THESE PATHS?
BUT THAT MEANS ...
THERE MIGHT BE... SOMETHING I CAN DO HERE.
YEAH.
THINK.
THINK!!

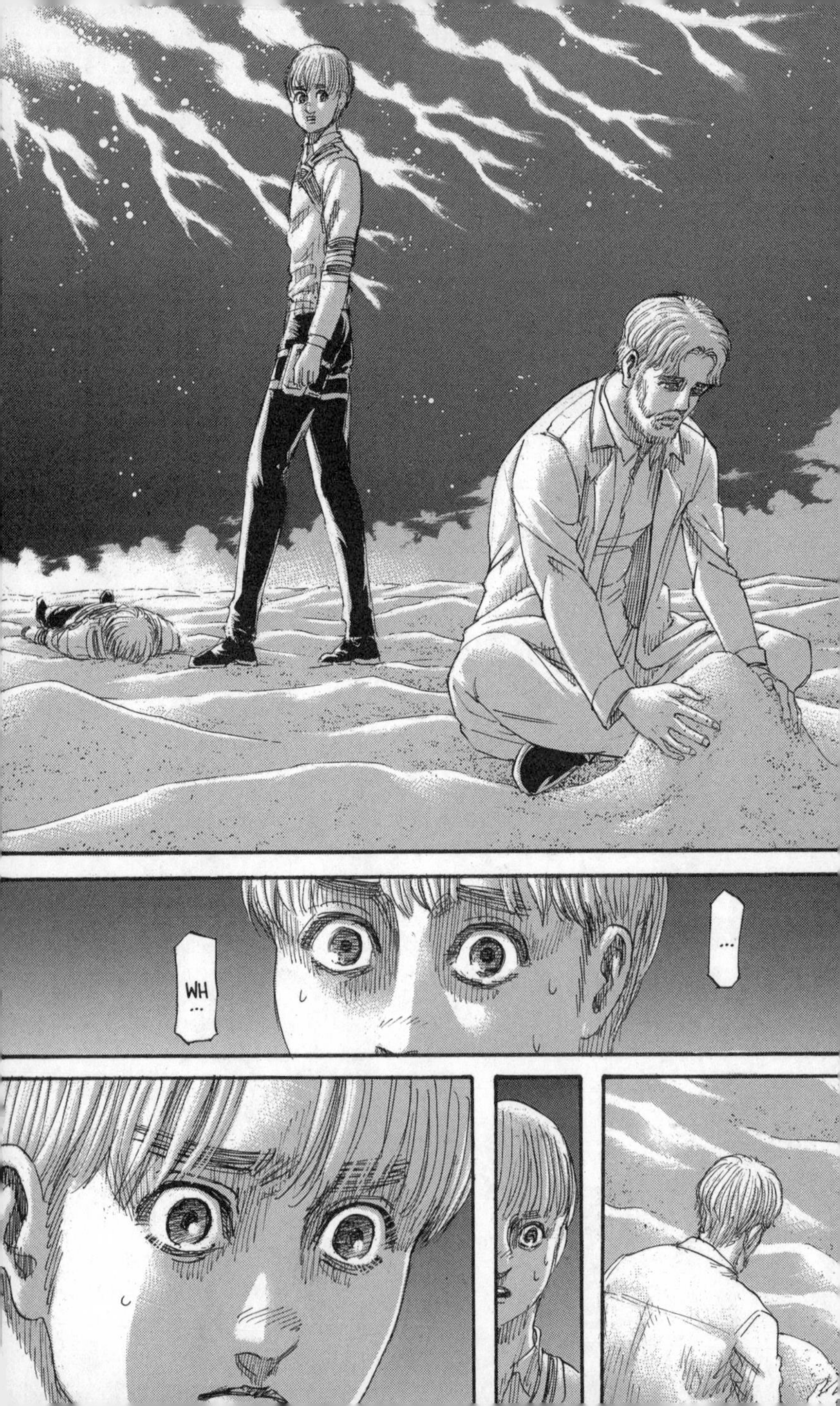
...
WH
...

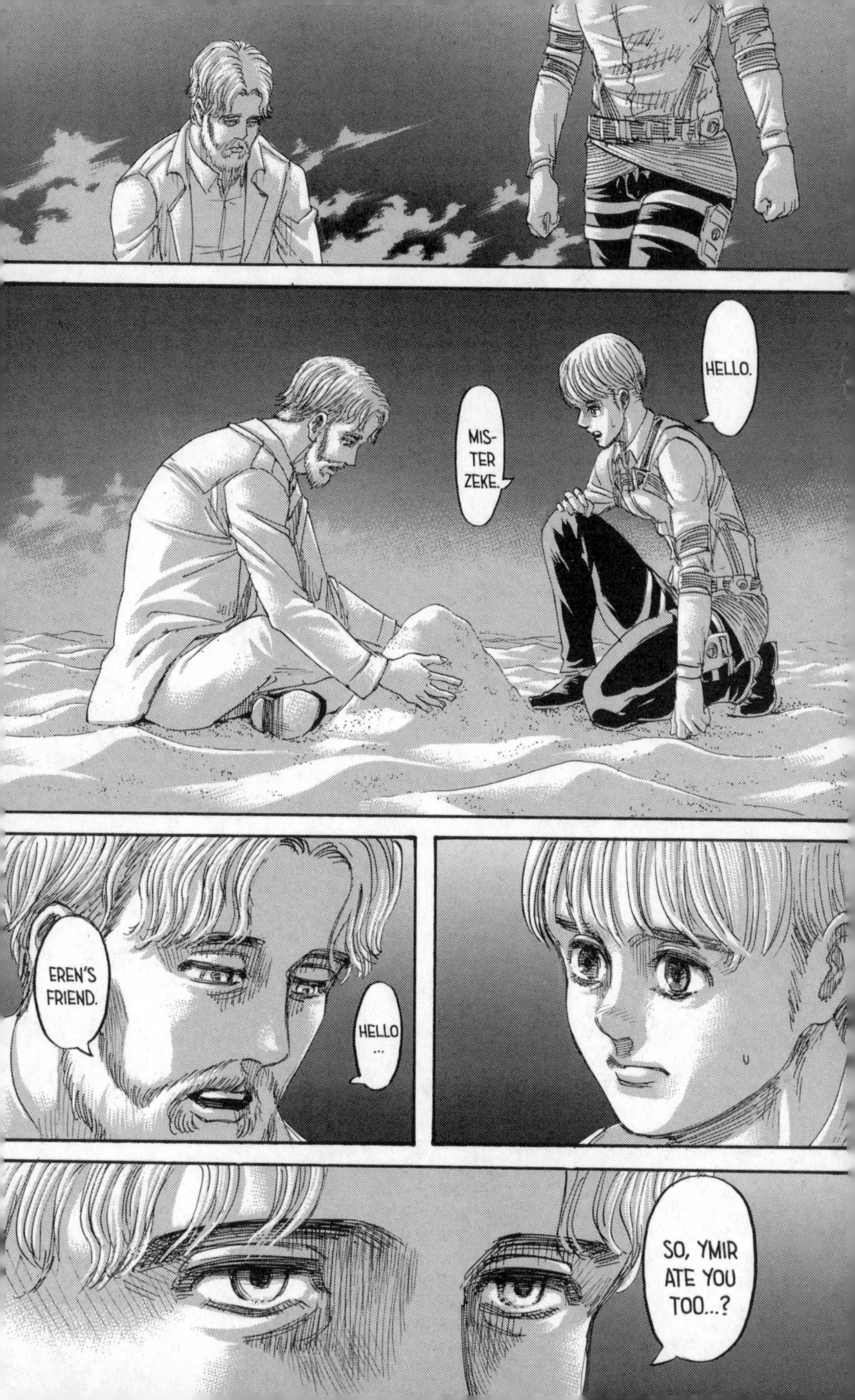
HELLO.
MISTER ZEKE.
HELLO...
EREN'S FRIEND.
SO, YMIR ATE YOU TOO...?

ATTACK on TITAN

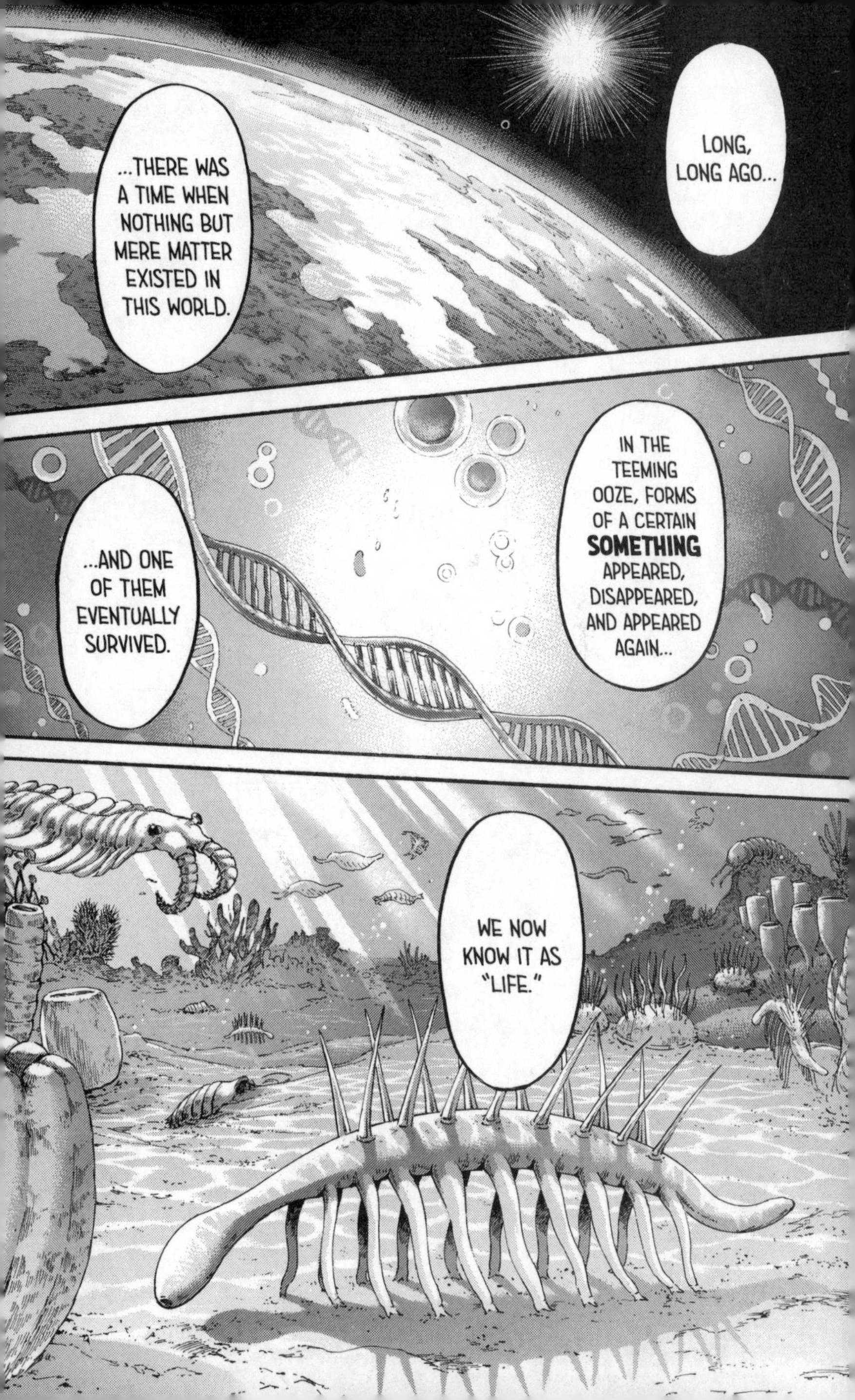
LONG, LONG AGO...
...THERE WAS A TIME WHEN NOTHING BUT MERE MATTER EXISTED IN THIS WORLD.
IN THE TEEMING OOZE, FORMS OF A CERTAIN **SOMETHING** APPEARED, DISAPPEARED, AND APPEARED AGAIN...
...AND ONE OF THEM EVENTUALLY SURVIVED.
WE NOW KNOW IT AS "LIFE."

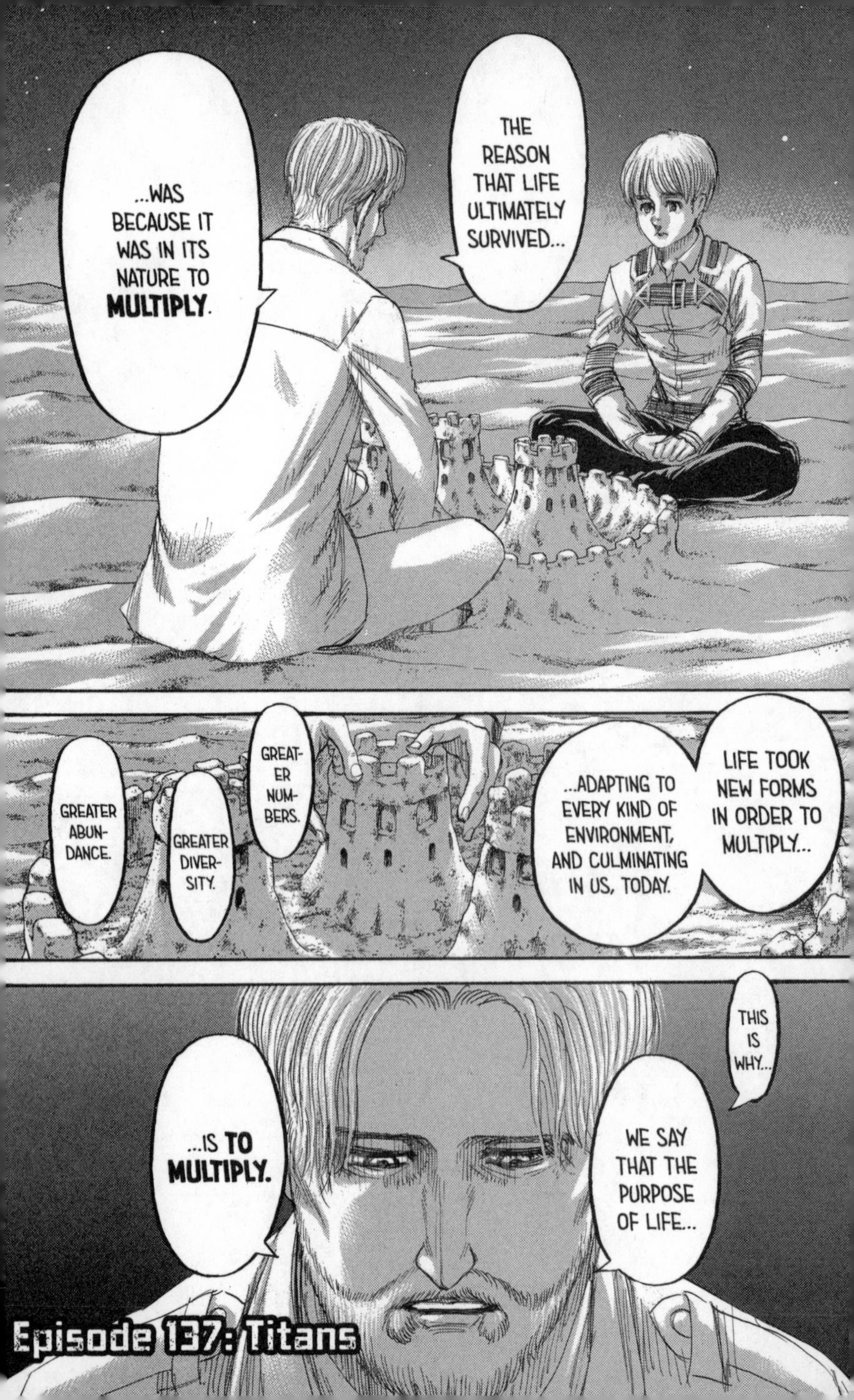
THE REASON THAT LIFE ULTIMATELY SURVIVED...
...WAS BECAUSE IT WAS IN ITS NATURE TO **MULTIPLY**.
LIFE TOOK NEW FORMS IN ORDER TO MULTIPLY...
...ADAPTING TO EVERY KIND OF ENVIRONMENT, AND CULMINATING IN US, TODAY.
GREATER NUMBERS.
GREATER DIVERSITY.
GREATER ABUNDANCE.
THIS IS WHY...
WE SAY THAT THE PURPOSE OF LIFE...
...IS **TO MULTIPLY.**
Episode 137: Titans

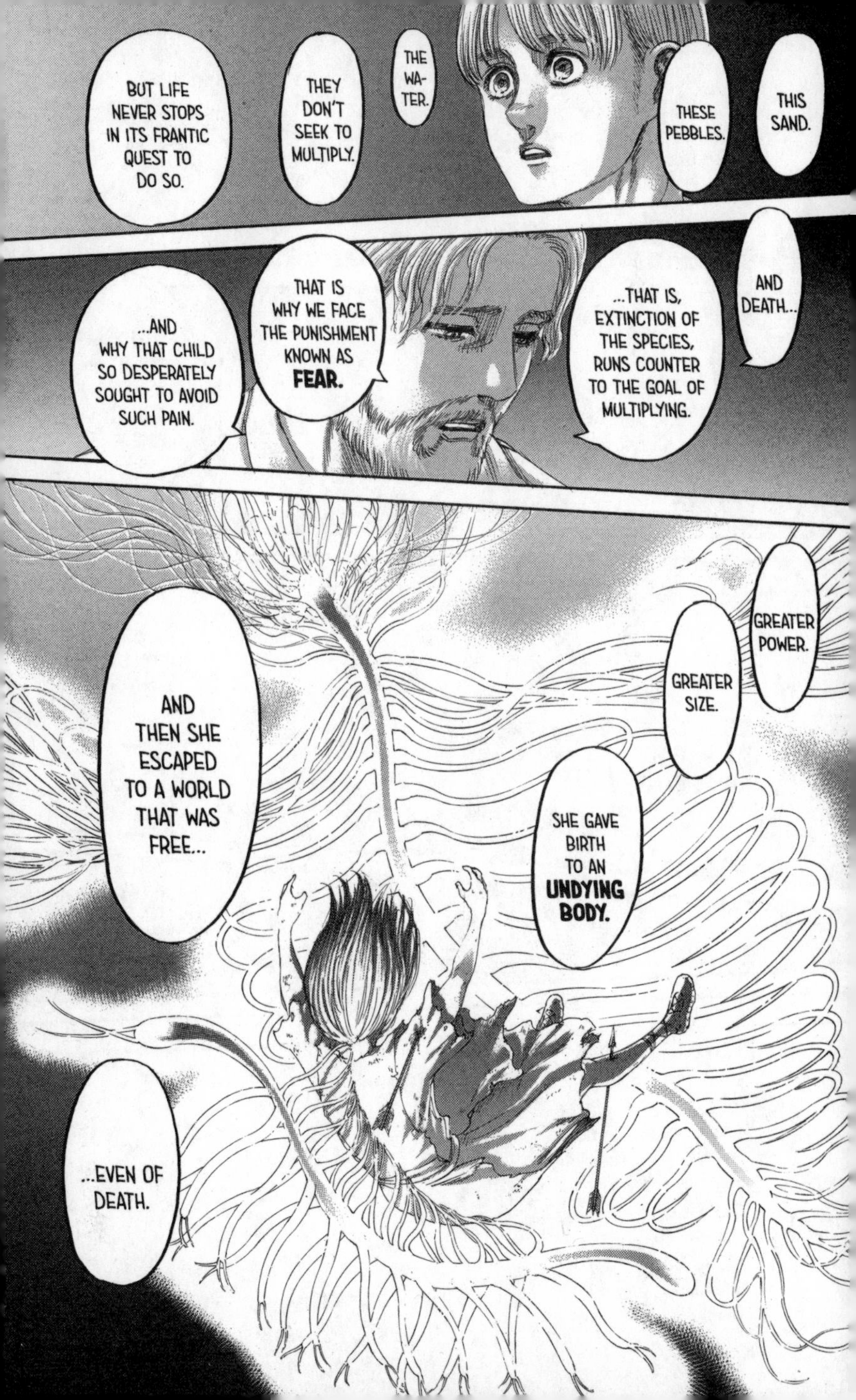
THIS SAND.
THESE PEBBLES.
THE WA-TER.
THEY DON'T SEEK TO MULTIPLY.
BUT LIFE NEVER STOPS IN ITS FRANTIC QUEST TO DO SO.
AND DEATH...
...THAT IS, EXTINCTION OF THE SPECIES, RUNS COUNTER TO THE GOAL OF MULTIPLYING.
THAT IS WHY WE FACE THE PUNISHMENT KNOWN AS **FEAR.**
...AND WHY THAT CHILD SO DESPERATELY SOUGHT TO AVOID SUCH PAIN.
GREATER POWER.
GREATER SIZE.
SHE GAVE BIRTH TO AN **UNDYING BODY.**
AND THEN SHE ESCAPED TO A WORLD THAT WAS FREE...
...EVEN OF DEATH.

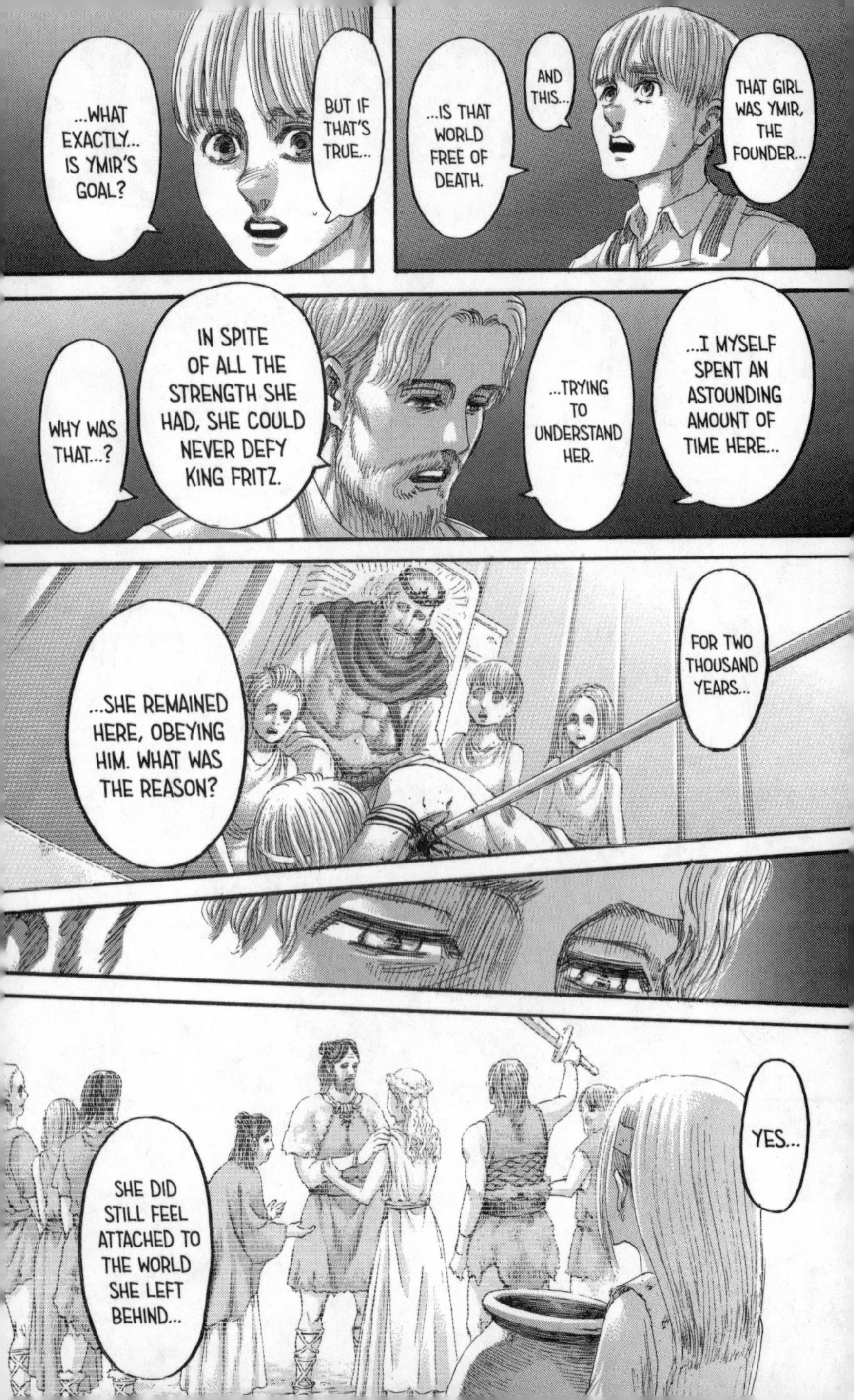
THAT GIRL WAS YMIR, THE FOUNDER...
AND THIS...
...IS THAT WORLD FREE OF DEATH.
BUT IF THAT'S TRUE...
...WHAT EXACTLY... IS YMIR'S GOAL?
...I MYSELF SPENT AN ASTOUNDING AMOUNT OF TIME HERE...
...TRYING TO UNDERSTAND HER.
IN SPITE OF ALL THE STRENGTH SHE HAD, SHE COULD NEVER DEFY KING FRITZ.
WHY WAS THAT...?
FOR TWO THOUSAND YEARS...
...SHE REMAINED HERE, OBEYING HIM. WHAT WAS THE REASON?
YES...
SHE DID STILL FEEL ATTACHED TO THE WORLD SHE LEFT BEHIND...

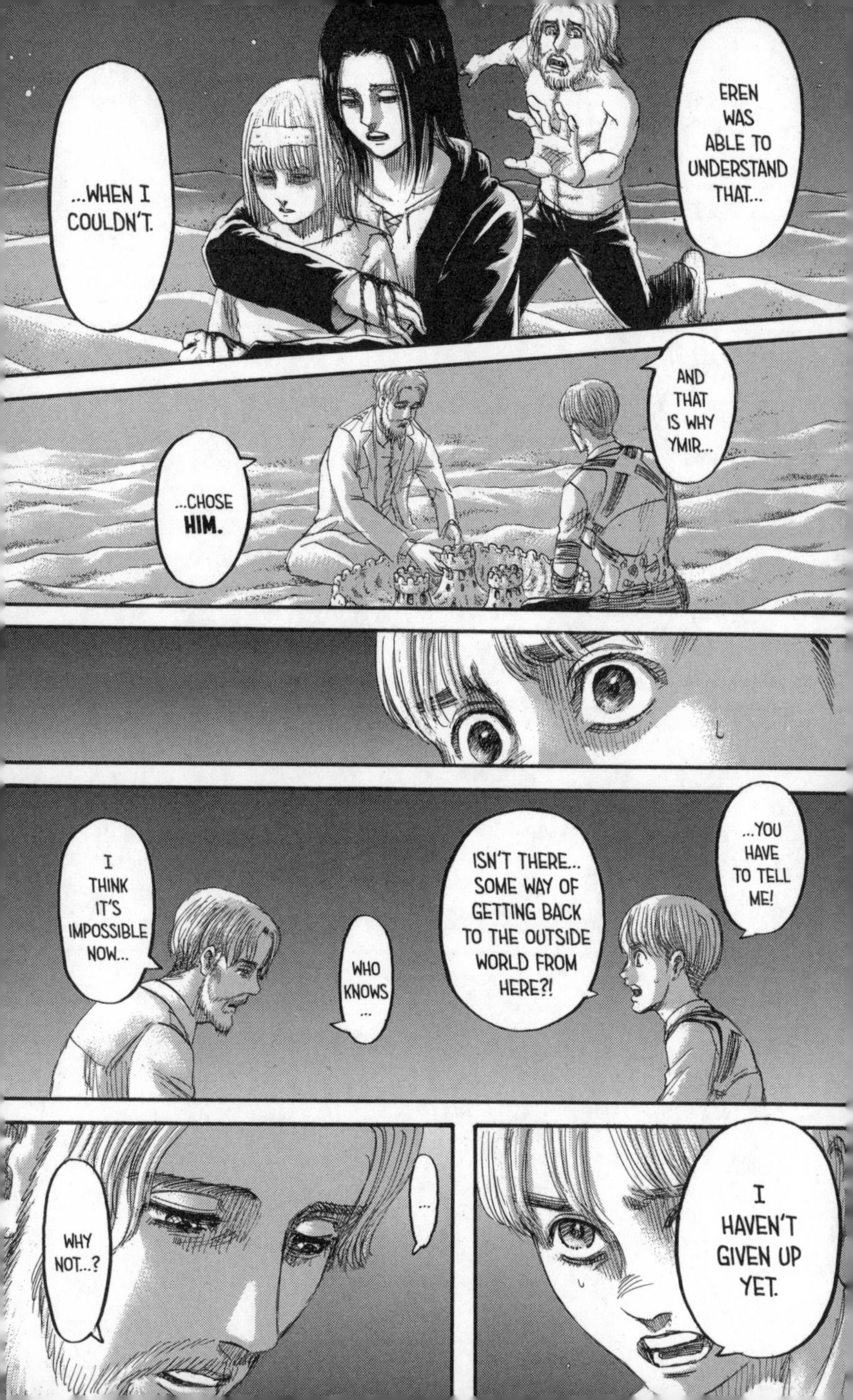
EREN WAS ABLE TO UNDERSTAND THAT...
...WHEN I COULDN'T.
AND THAT IS WHY YMIR...
...CHOSE **HIM.**
ISN'T THERE... SOME WAY OF GETTING BACK TO THE OUTSIDE WORLD FROM HERE?!
...YOU HAVE TO TELL ME!
WHO KNOWS ...
I THINK IT'S IMPOSSIBLE NOW...
I HAVEN'T GIVEN UP YET.
...
WHY NOT...?

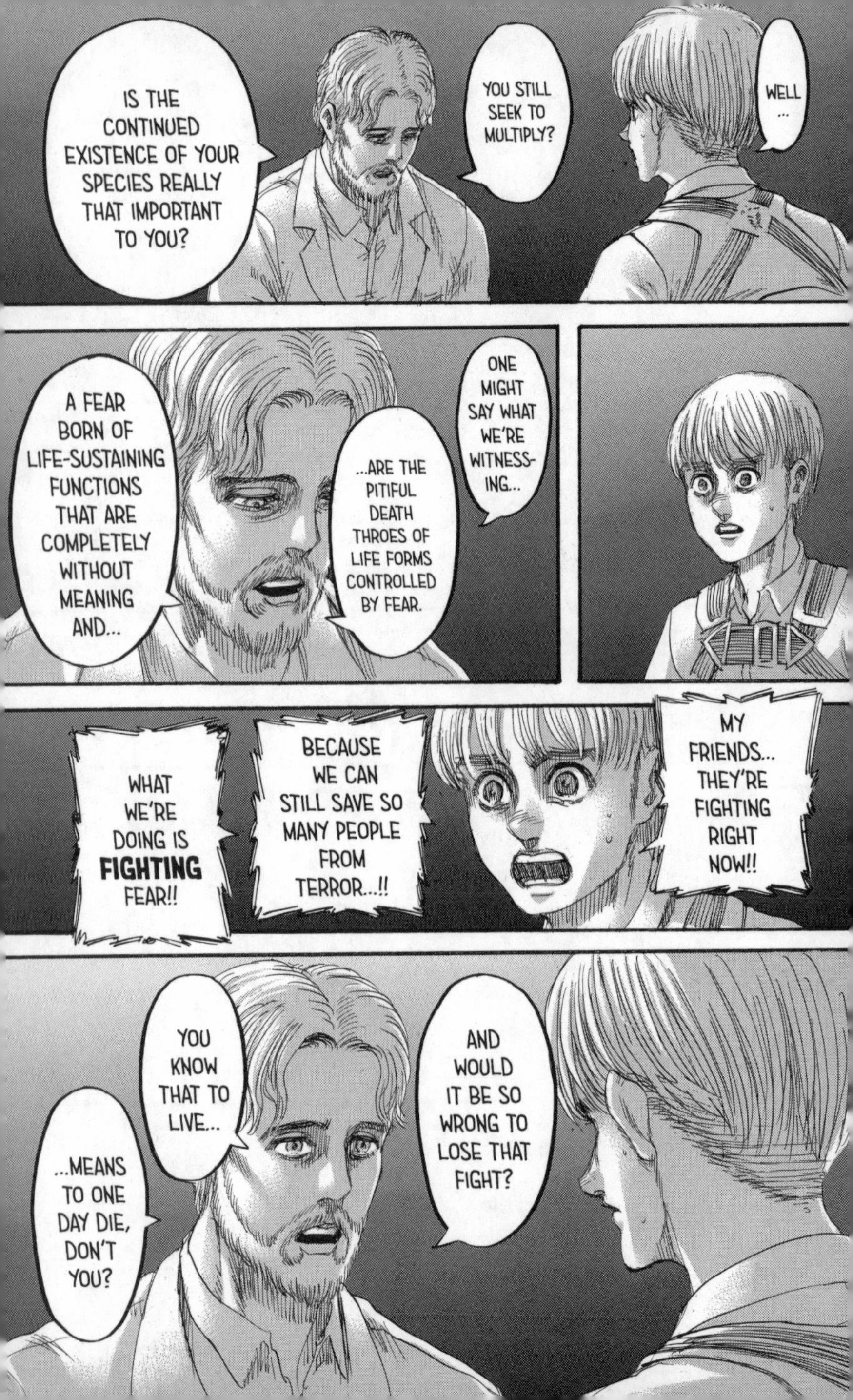
WELL ...
YOU STILL SEEK TO MULTIPLY?
IS THE CONTINUED EXISTENCE OF YOUR SPECIES REALLY THAT IMPORTANT TO YOU?
ONE MIGHT SAY WHAT WE'RE WITNESS-ING...
...ARE THE PITIFUL DEATH THROES OF LIFE FORMS CONTROLLED BY FEAR.
A FEAR BORN OF LIFE-SUSTAINING FUNCTIONS THAT ARE COMPLETELY WITHOUT MEANING AND...
MY FRIENDS... THEY'RE FIGHTING RIGHT NOW!!
BECAUSE WE CAN STILL SAVE SO MANY PEOPLE FROM TERROR...!!
WHAT WE'RE DOING IS **FIGHTING** FEAR!!
AND WOULD IT BE SO WRONG TO LOSE THAT FIGHT?
YOU KNOW THAT TO LIVE...
...MEANS TO ONE DAY DIE, DON'T YOU?

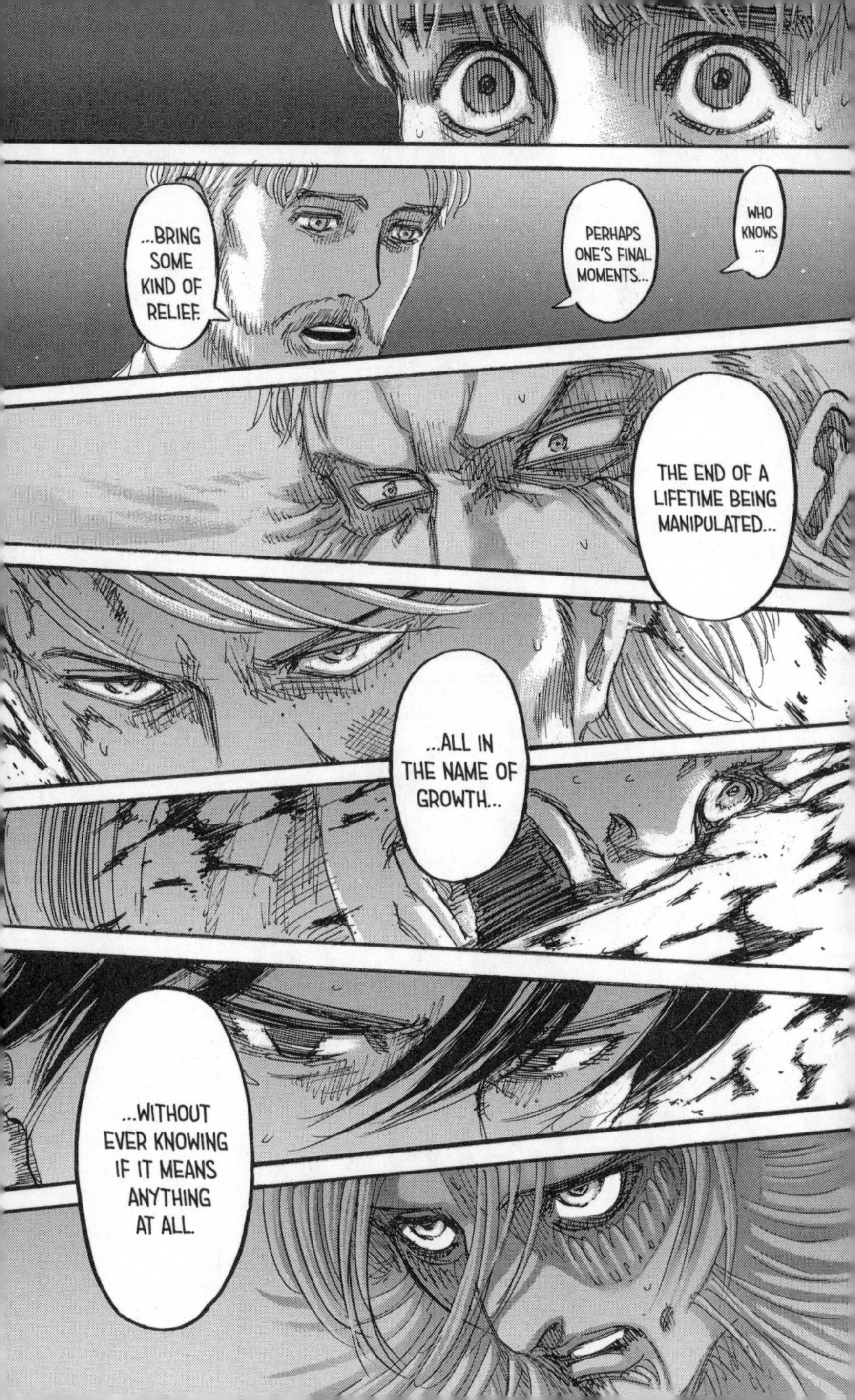
WHO KNOWS...
PERHAPS ONE'S FINAL MOMENTS...
...BRING SOME KIND OF RELIEF.
THE END OF A LIFETIME BEING MANIPULATED...
...ALL IN THE NAME OF GROWTH...
...WITHOUT EVER KNOWING IF IT MEANS ANYTHING AT ALL.

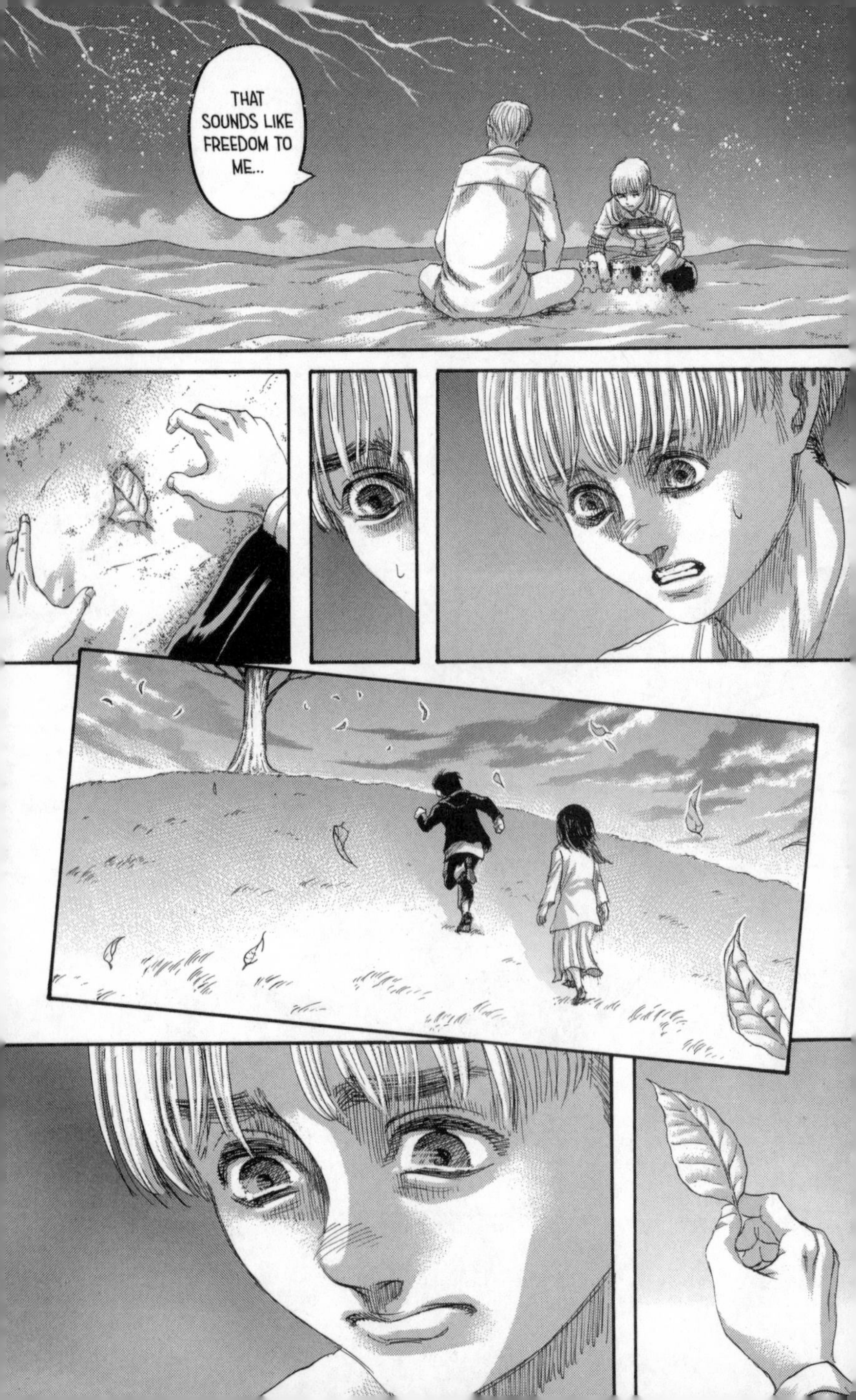
THAT SOUNDS LIKE FREEDOM TO ME...

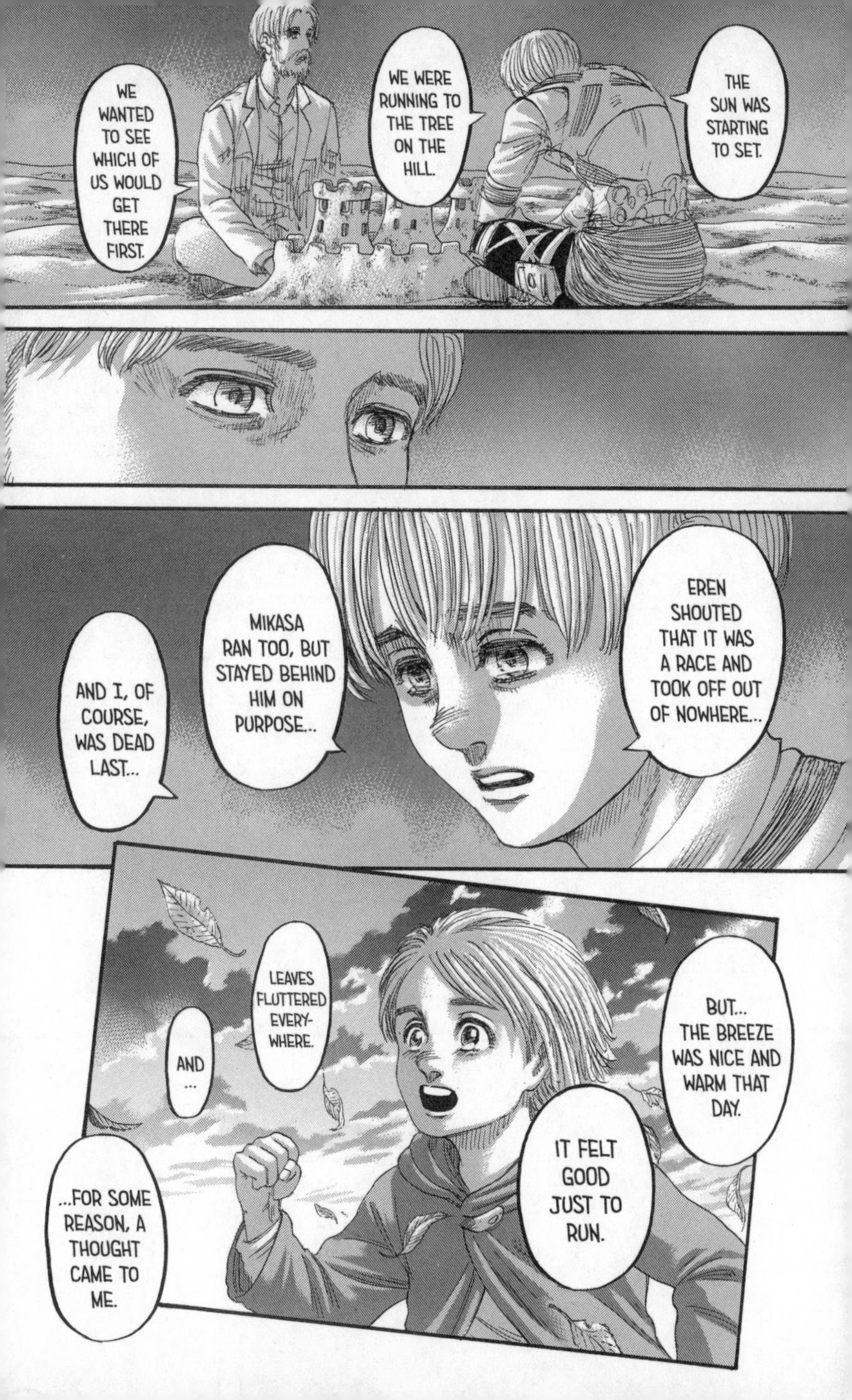
THE SUN WAS STARTING TO SET.
WE WERE RUNNING TO THE TREE ON THE HILL.
WE WANTED TO SEE WHICH OF US WOULD GET THERE FIRST.
EREN SHOUTED THAT IT WAS A RACE AND TOOK OFF OUT OF NOWHERE...
MIKASA RAN TOO, BUT STAYED BEHIND HIM ON PURPOSE...
AND I, OF COURSE, WAS DEAD LAST...
BUT... THE BREEZE WAS NICE AND WARM THAT DAY.
IT FELT GOOD JUST TO RUN.
LEAVES FLUTTERED EVERY-WHERE.
AND ...
...FOR SOME REASON, A THOUGHT CAME TO ME.

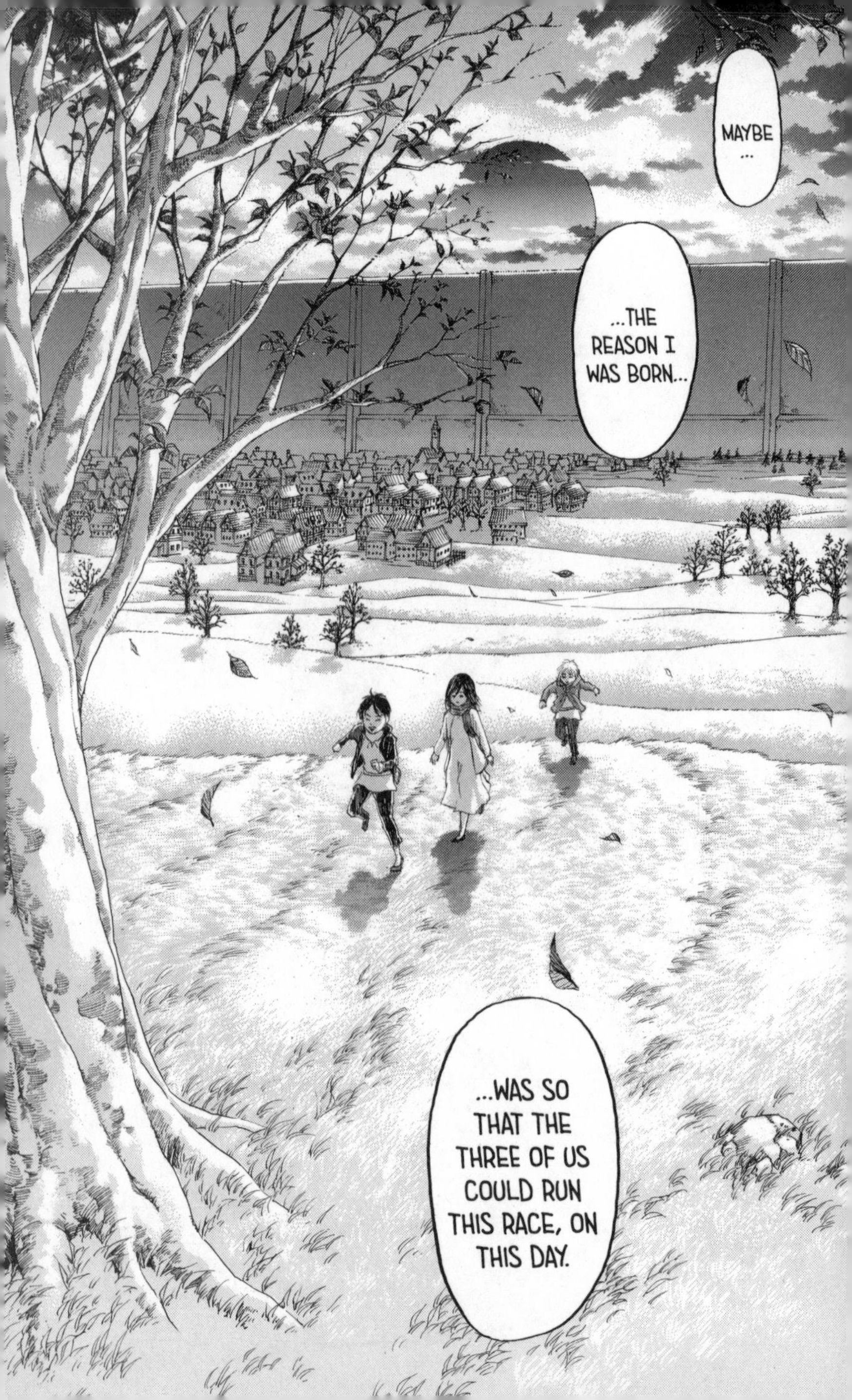
MAYBE ...
...THE REASON I WAS BORN...
...WAS SO THAT THE THREE OF US COULD RUN THIS RACE, ON THIS DAY.

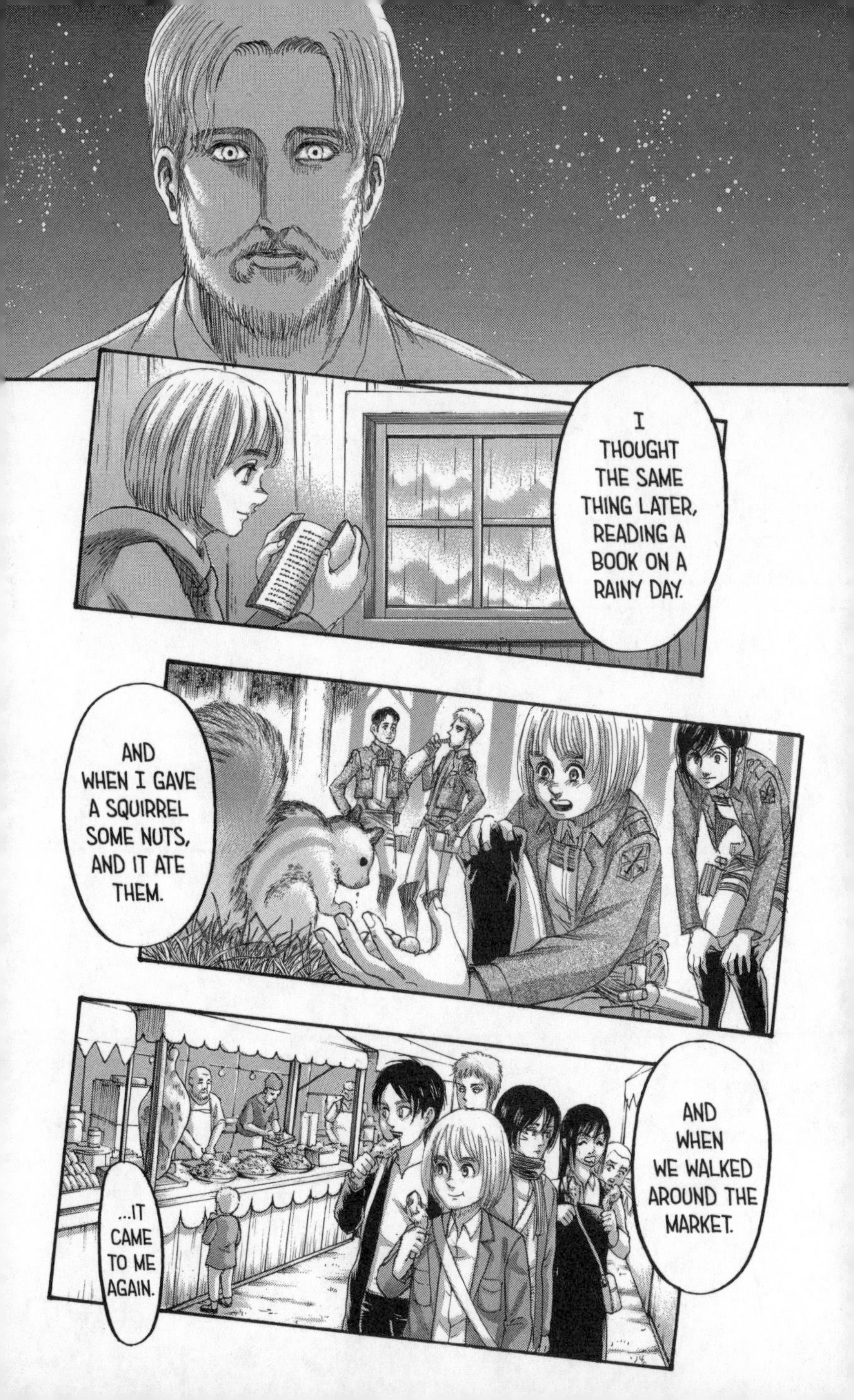
I THOUGHT THE SAME THING LATER, READING A BOOK ON A RAINY DAY.
AND WHEN I GAVE A SQUIRREL SOME NUTS, AND IT ATE THEM.
AND WHEN WE WALKED AROUND THE MARKET.
...IT CAME TO ME AGAIN.

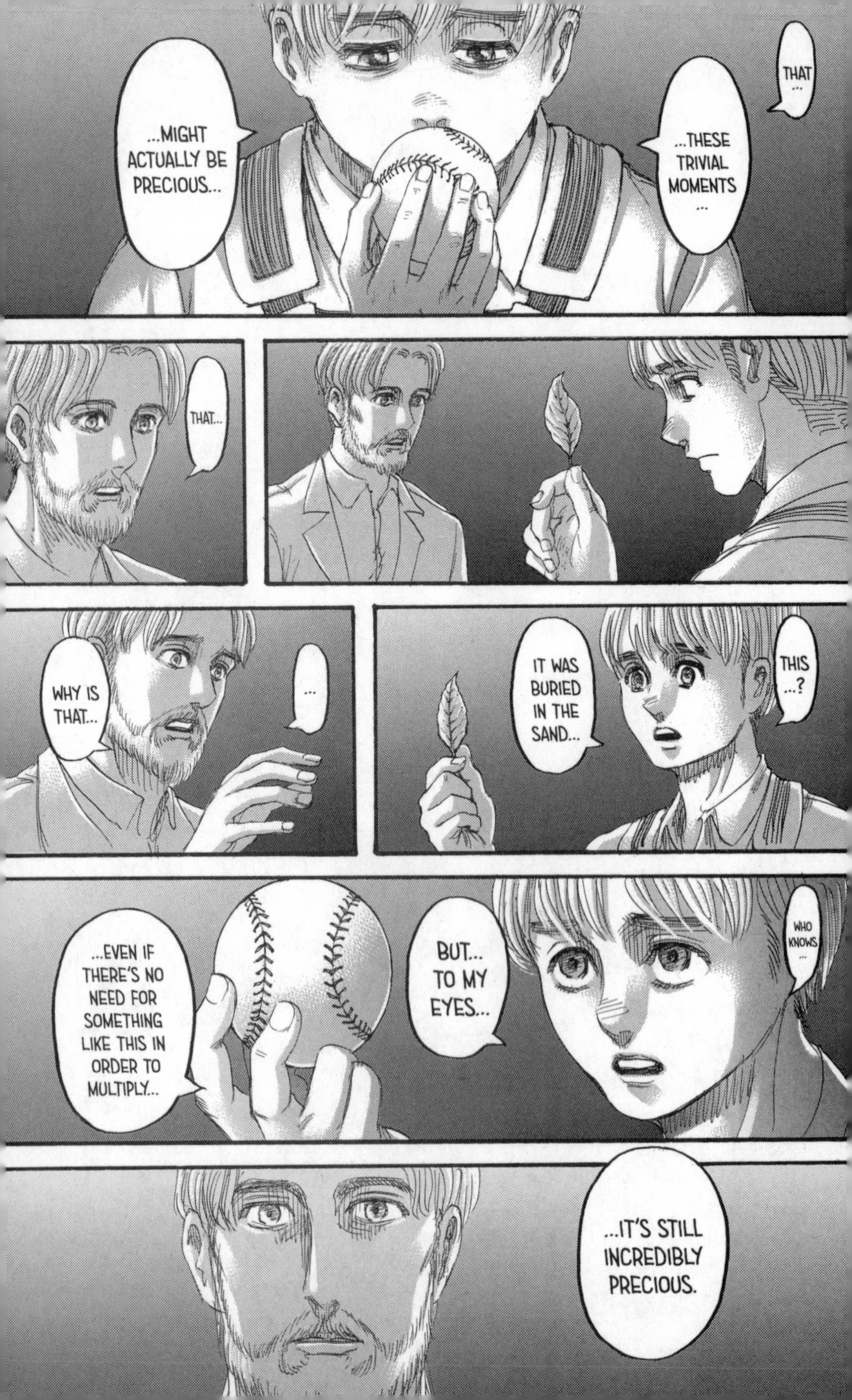
THAT ...
...THESE TRIVIAL MOMENTS ...
...MIGHT ACTUALLY BE PRECIOUS...
THAT...
THIS ...?
IT WAS BURIED IN THE SAND...
...
WHY IS THAT...
WHO KNOWS ...
BUT... TO MY EYES...
...EVEN IF THERE'S NO NEED FOR SOMETHING LIKE THIS IN ORDER TO MULTIPLY...
...IT'S STILL INCREDIBLY PRECIOUS.

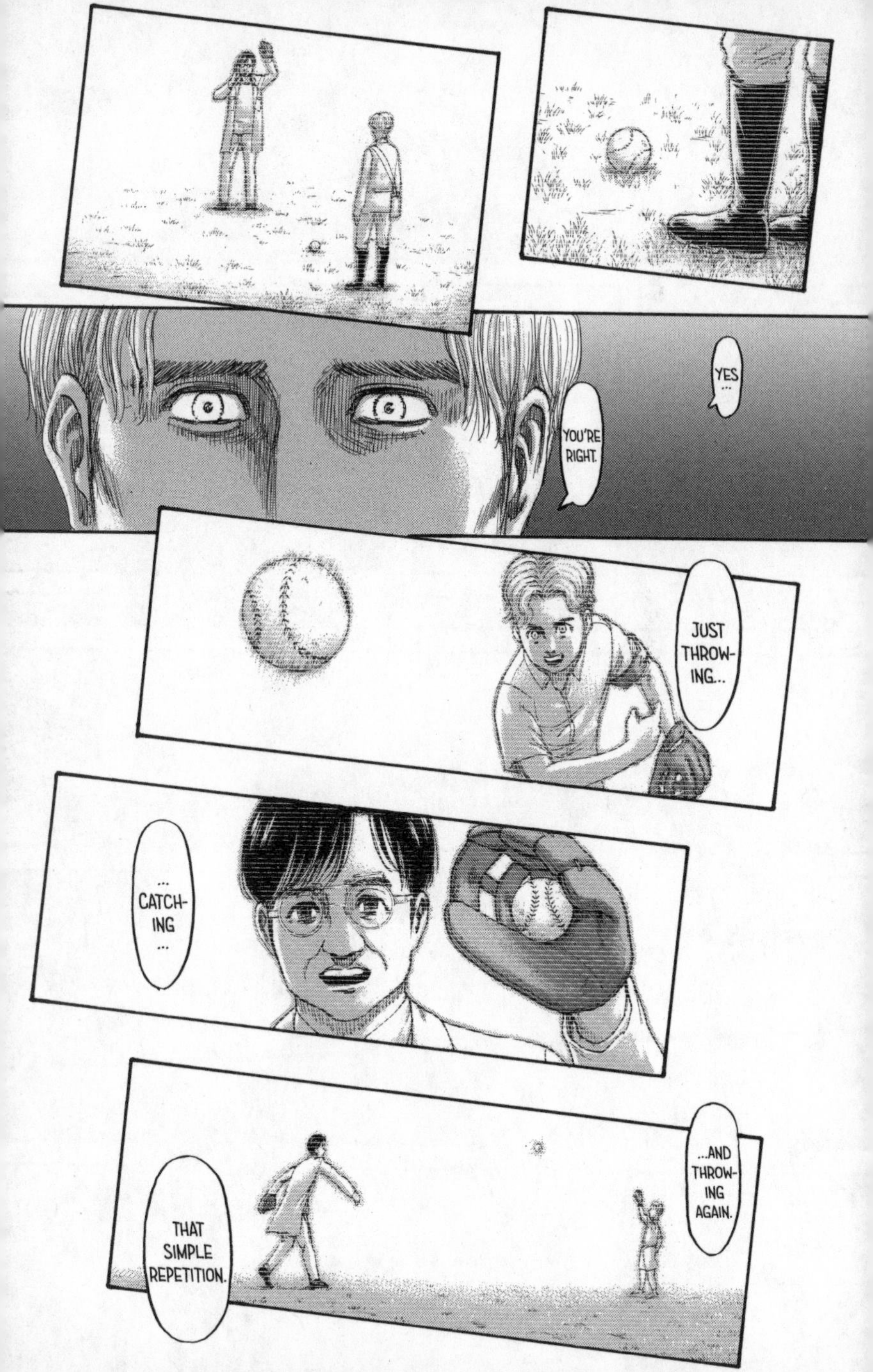
YES ...
YOU'RE RIGHT.
JUST THROWING...
... CATCHING ...
...AND THROWING AGAIN.
THAT SIMPLE REPETITION.

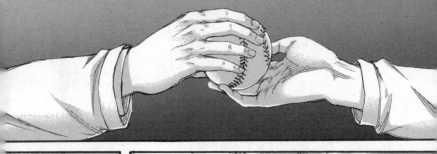

YOU'RE RIGHT...

BUT...

IT DOESN'T MEAN A THING...

I...

...WOULD HAVE BEEN HAPPY PLAYING CATCH FOREVER.

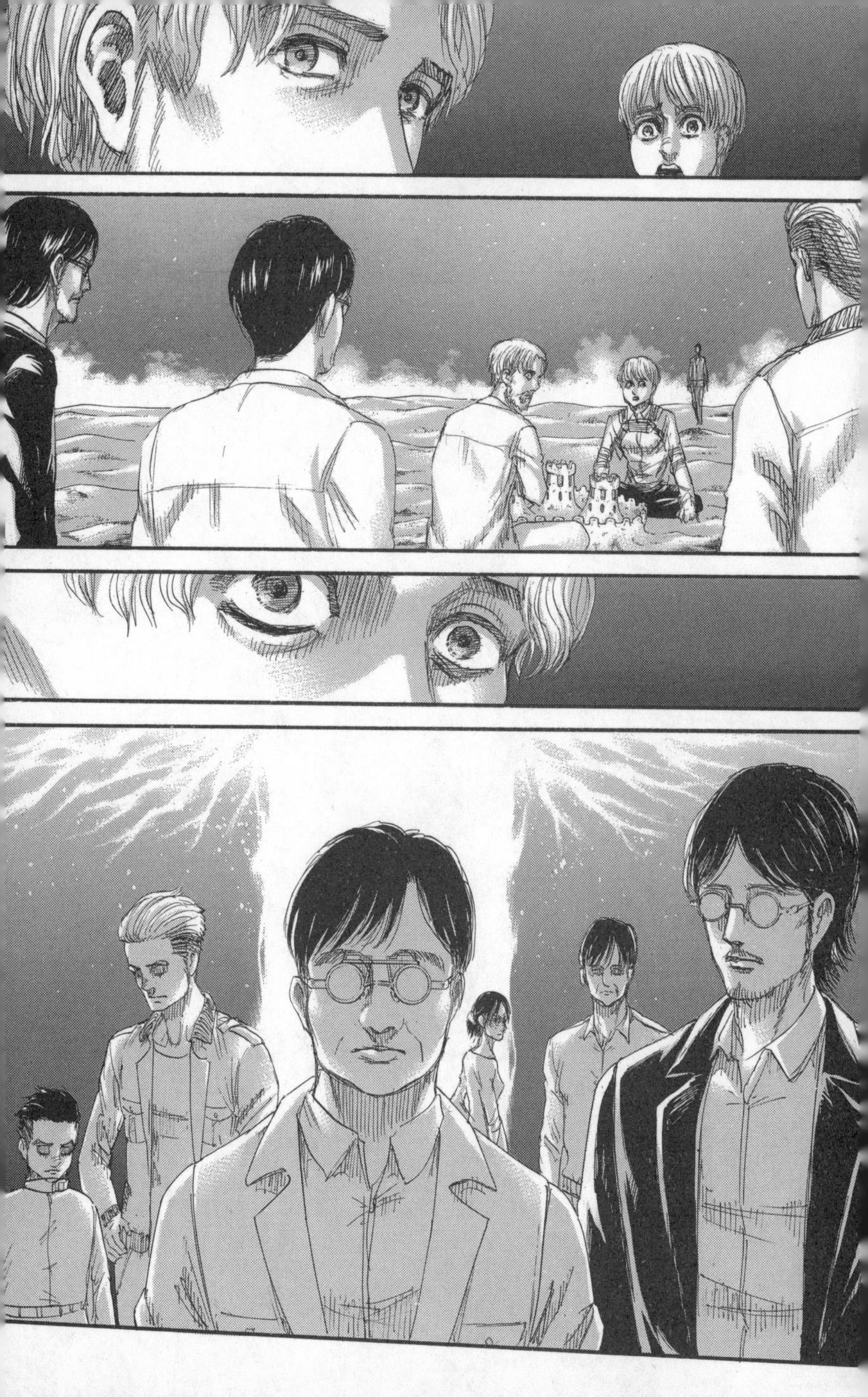

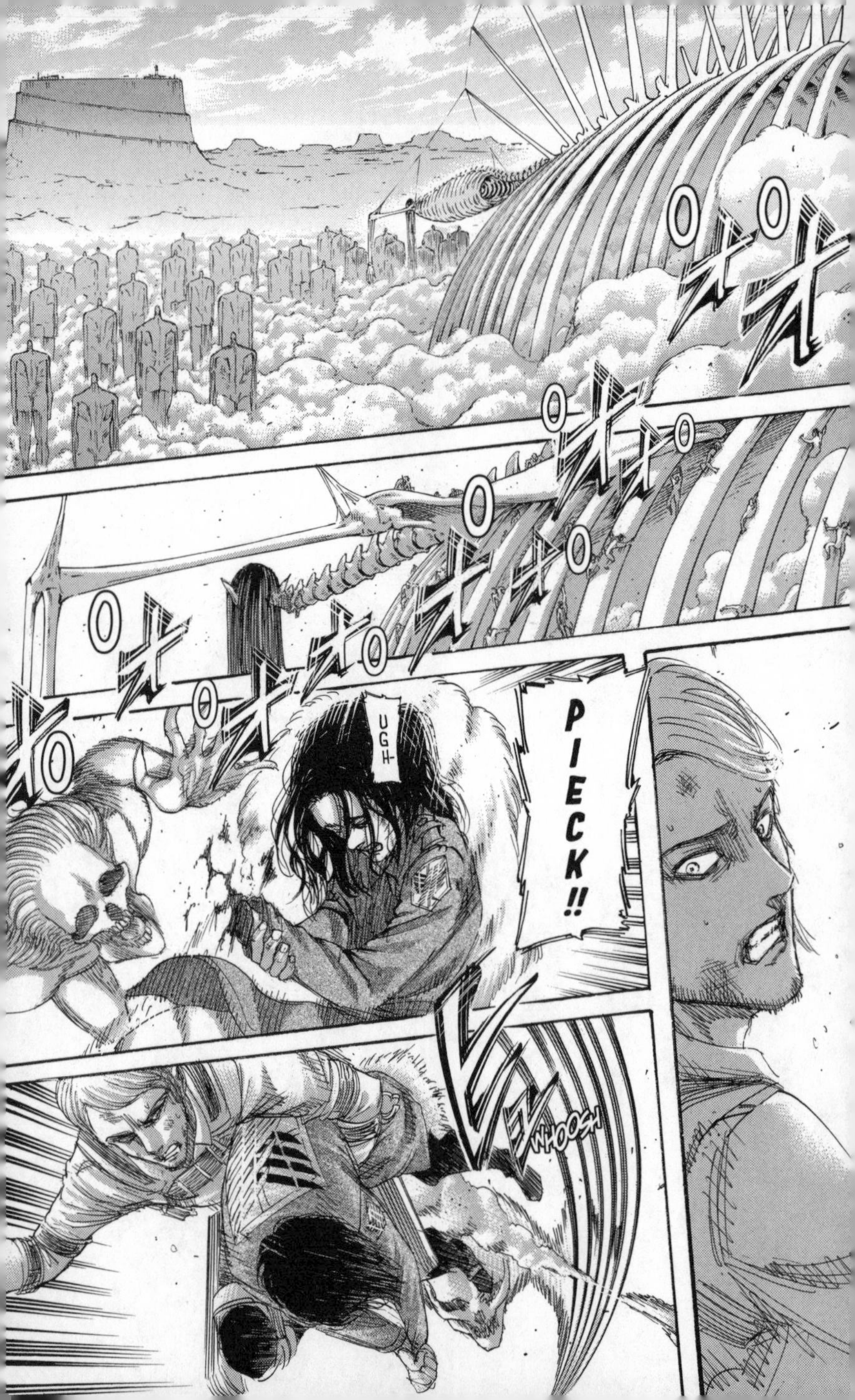
PIECK!!
UGH-
WHOOSH

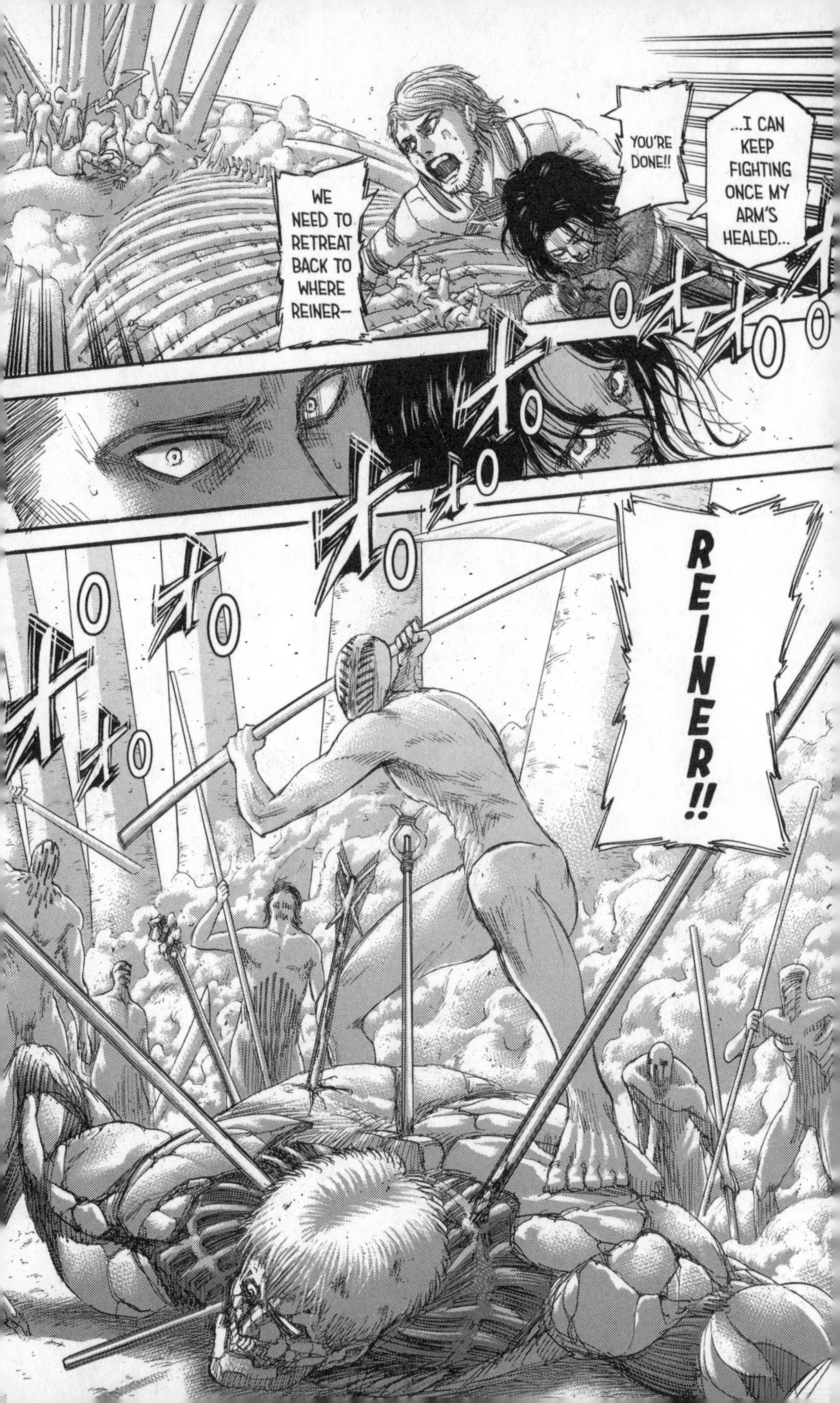
...I CAN KEEP FIGHTING ONCE MY ARM'S HEALED...
YOU'RE DONE!!
WE NEED TO RETREAT BACK TO WHERE REINER—
REINER!!

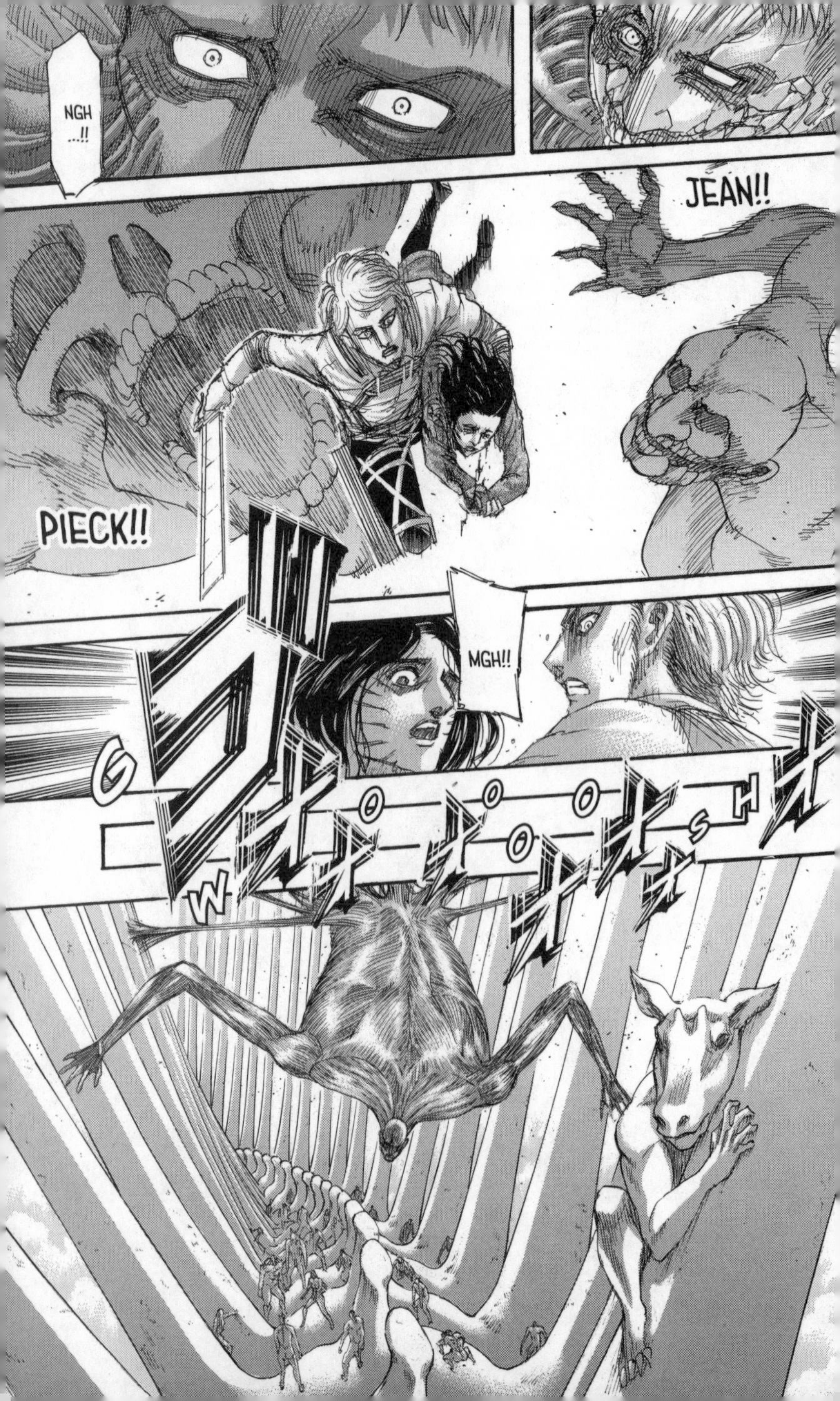
NGH ...!!
JEAN!!
PIECK!!
MGH!!
GWOOOOSH

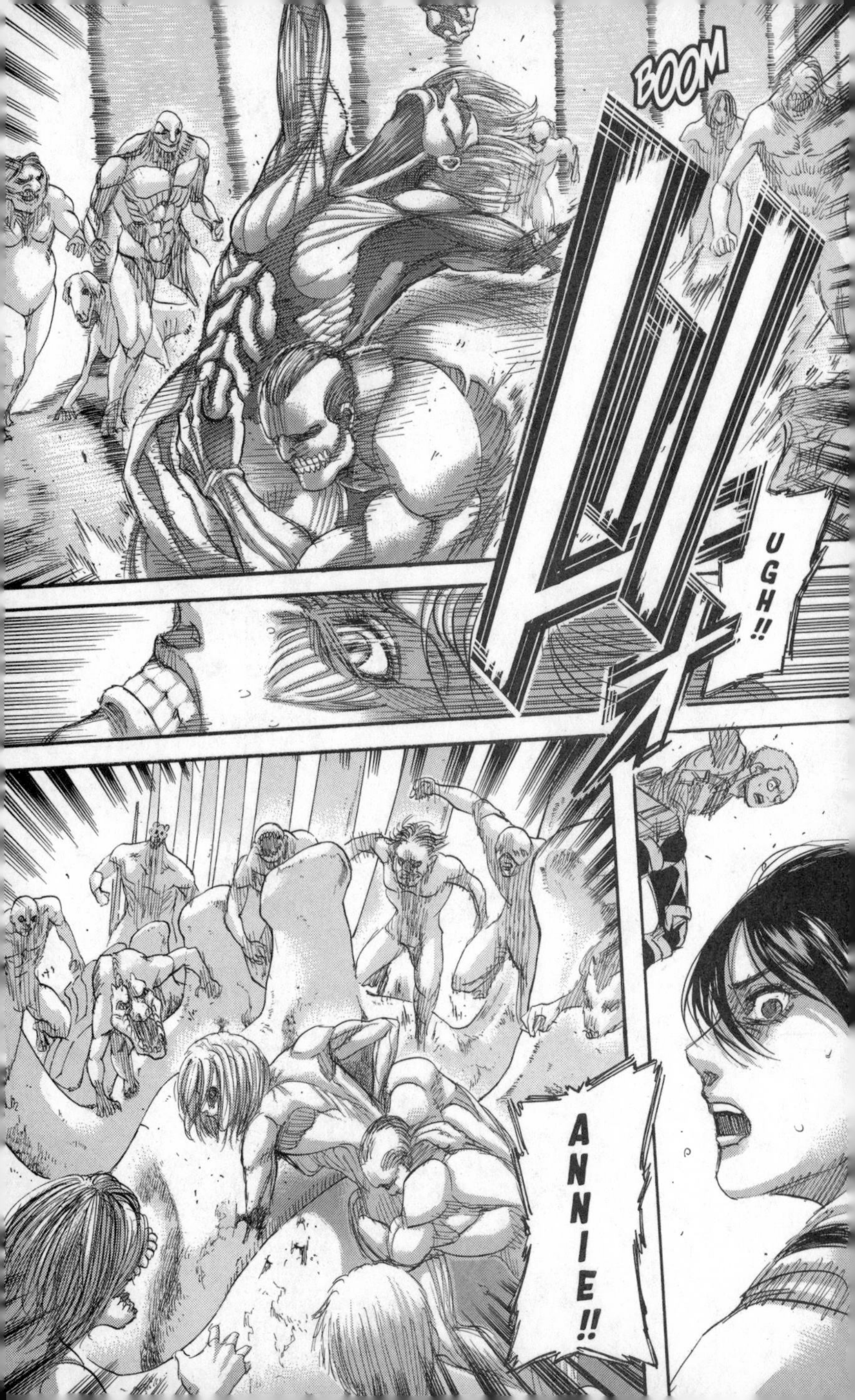
BOOM
UGH!!
ANNIE!!

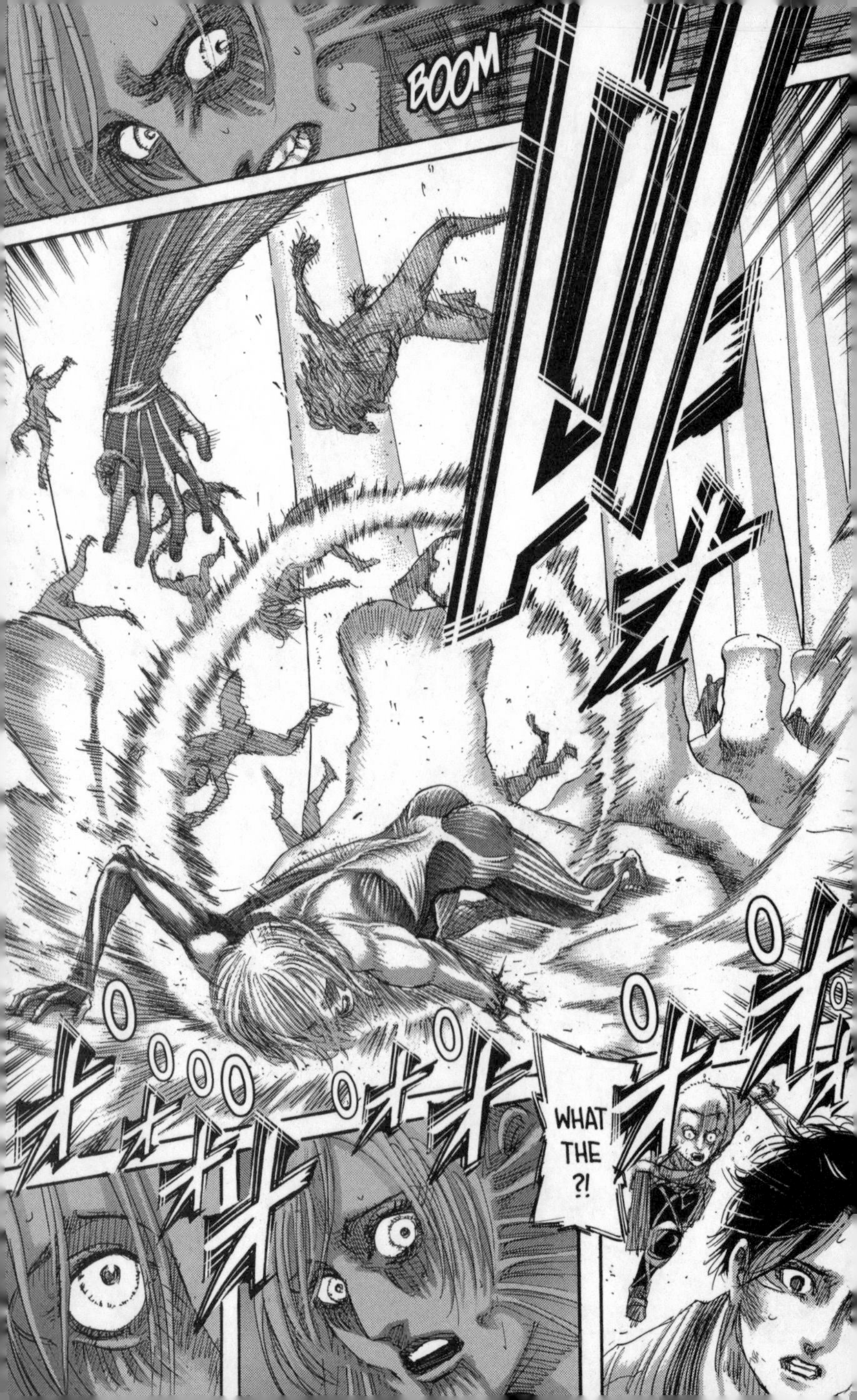
BOOM
WHAT THE ?!

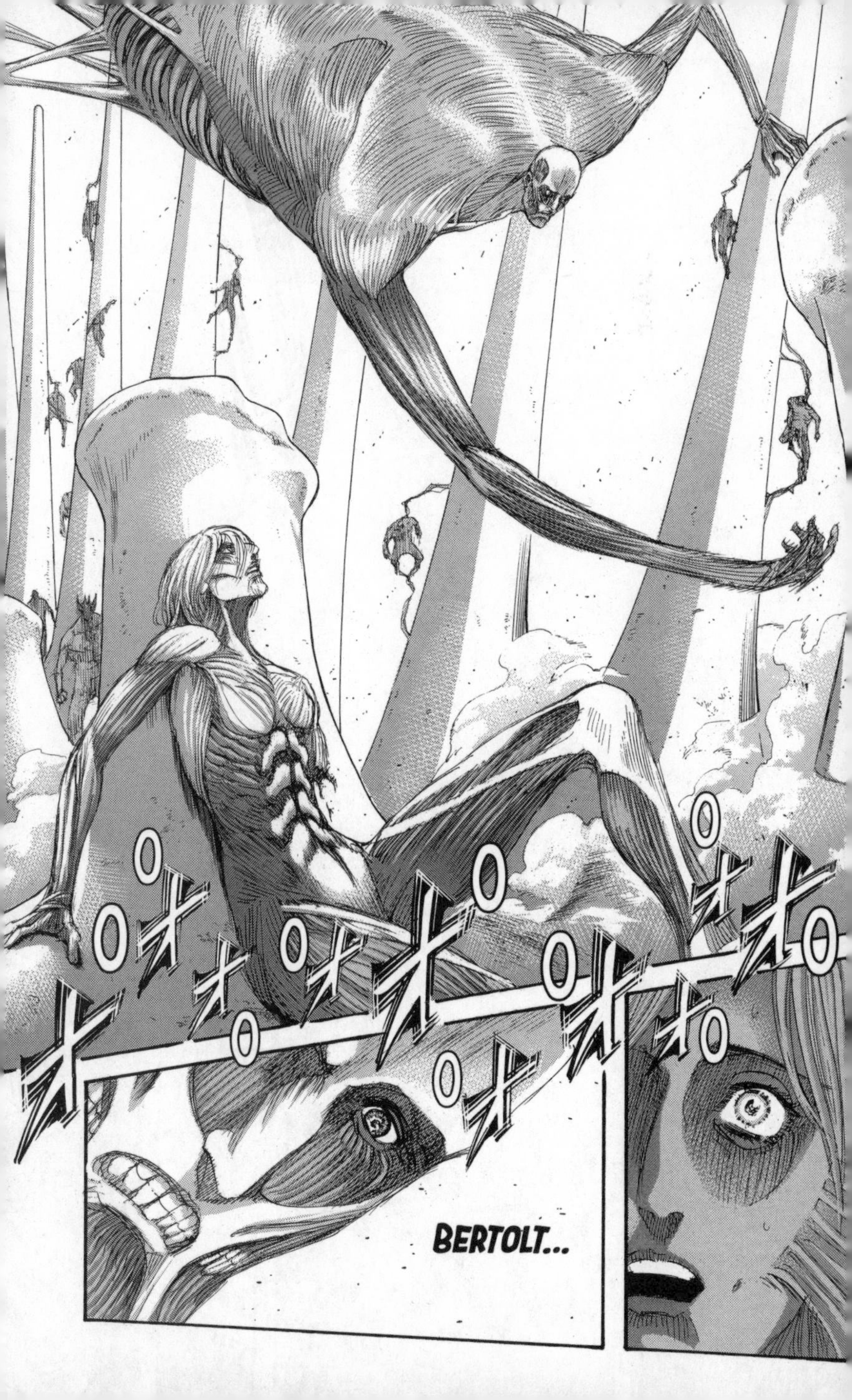
BERTOLT...

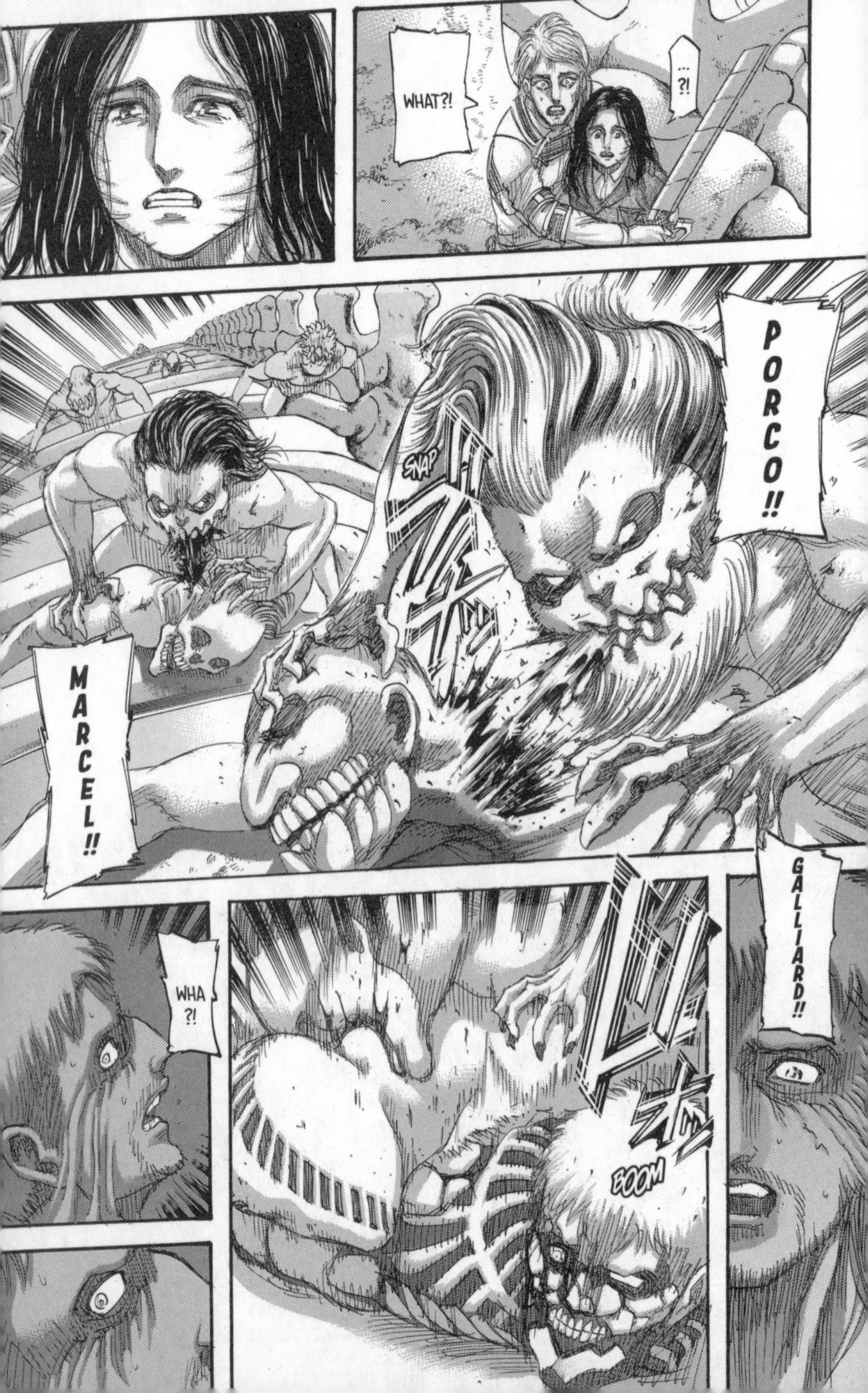
...?!
WHAT?!
PORCO!!
SNAP
MARCEL!!
GALLIARD!!
BOOM
WHA ?!

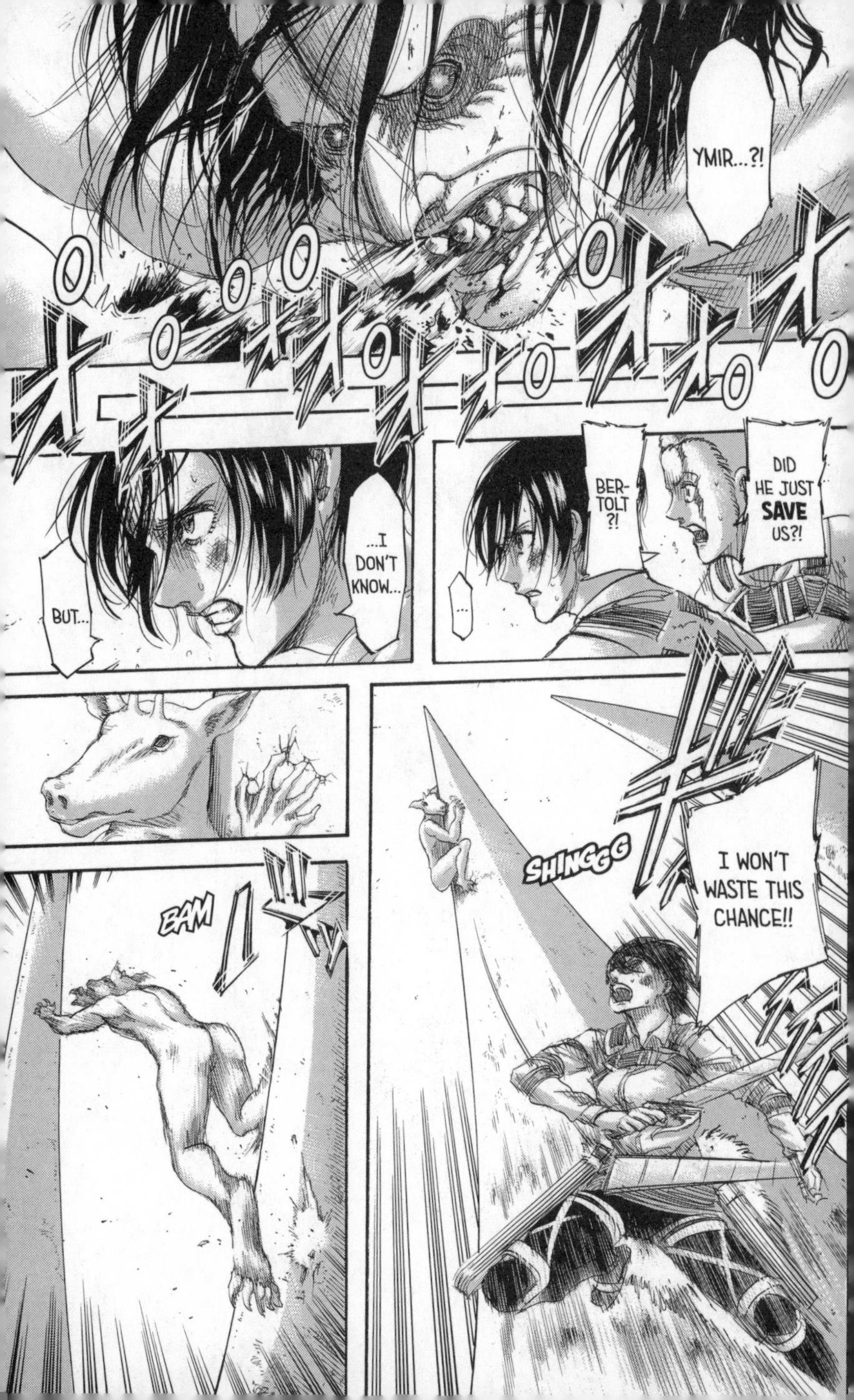
YMIR...?!
DID HE JUST SAVE US?!
BER-TOLT?!
...
...I DON'T KNOW...
BUT...
SHINGGG
I WON'T WASTE THIS CHANCE!!
BAM

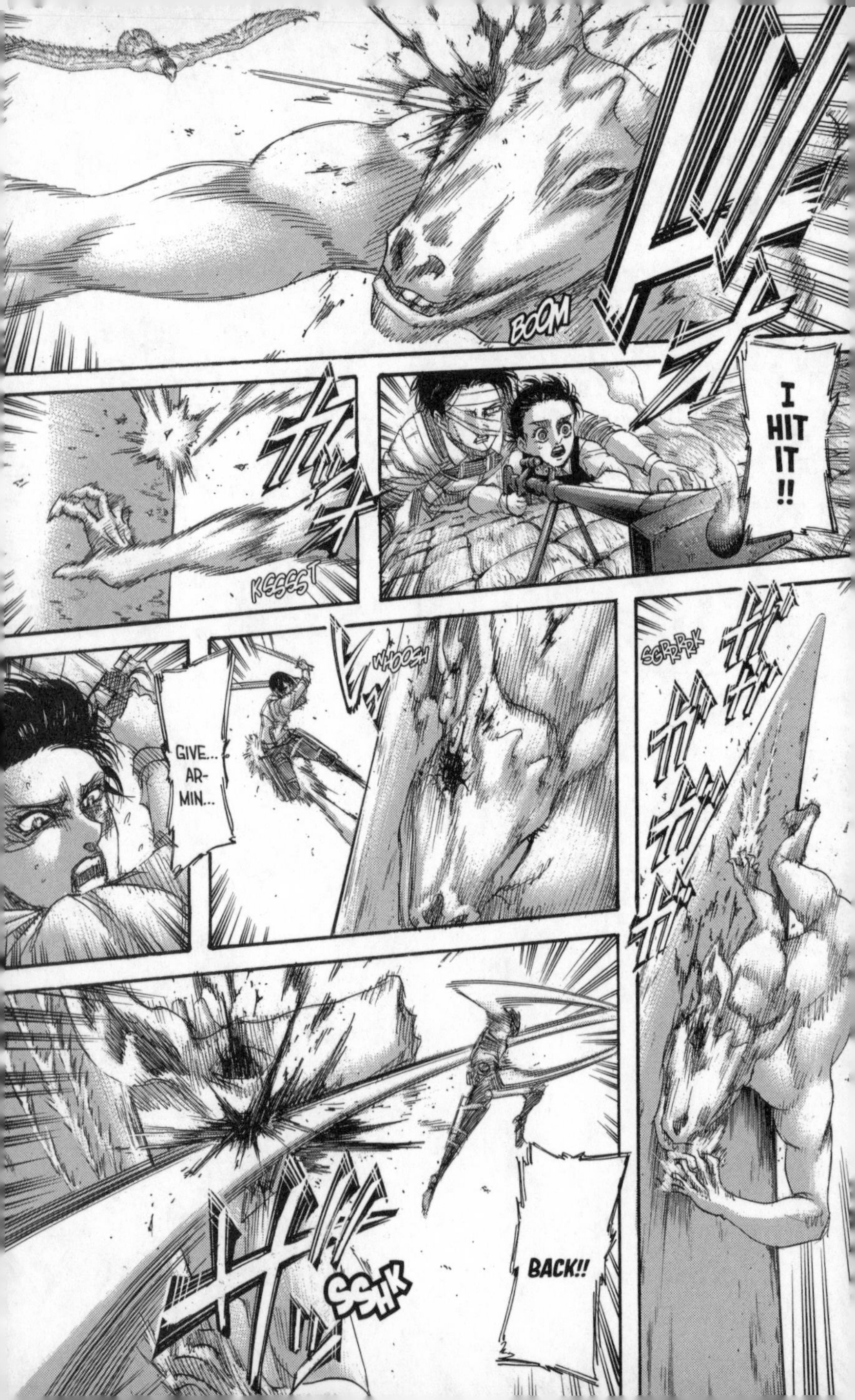
BOOM
I HIT IT!!
KSSSST
SCRRRK
WHOOSH
GIVE... AR-MIN...
BACK!!
SSHK

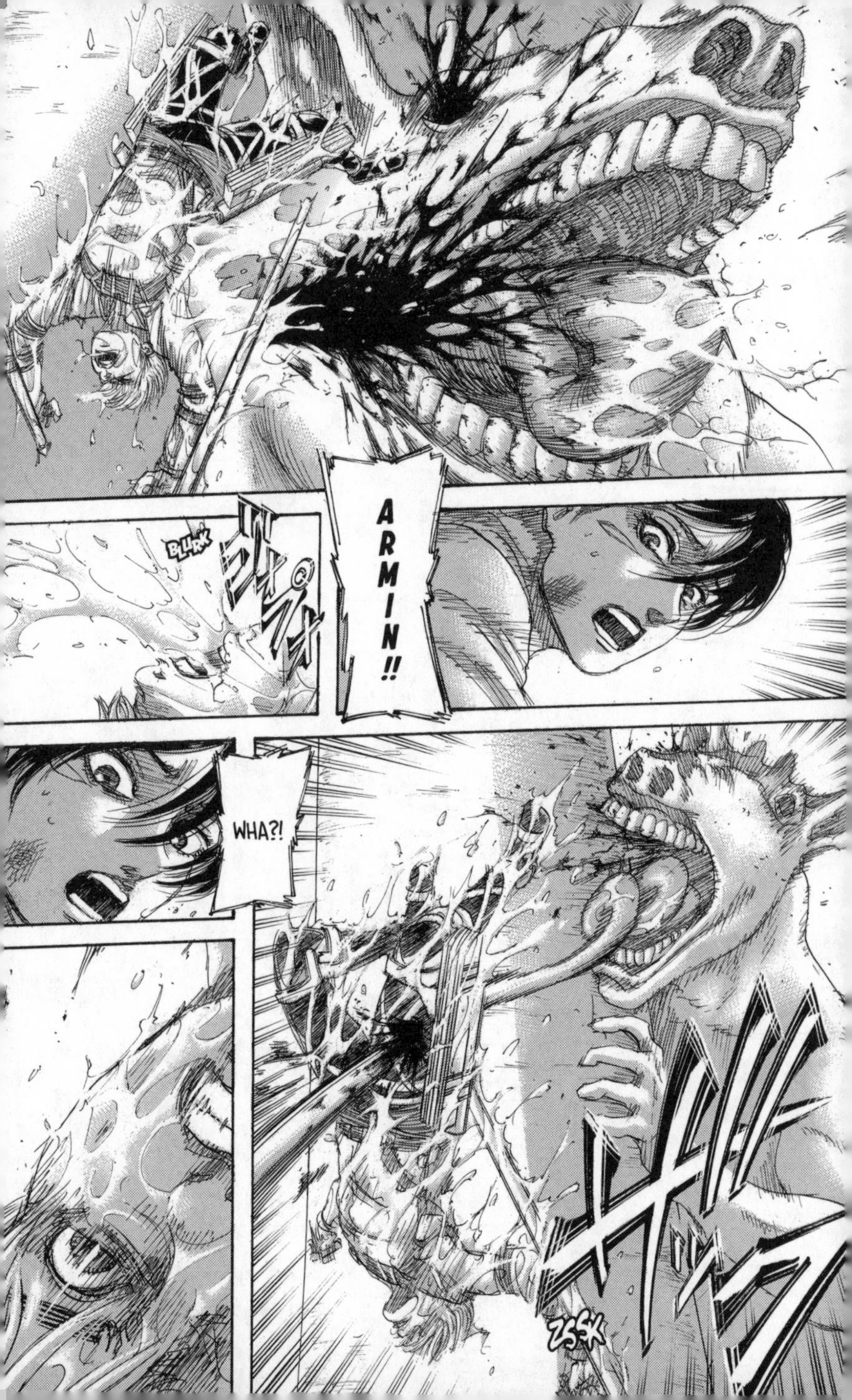
ARMIN!!
BLURK
ZSSK
WHA?!

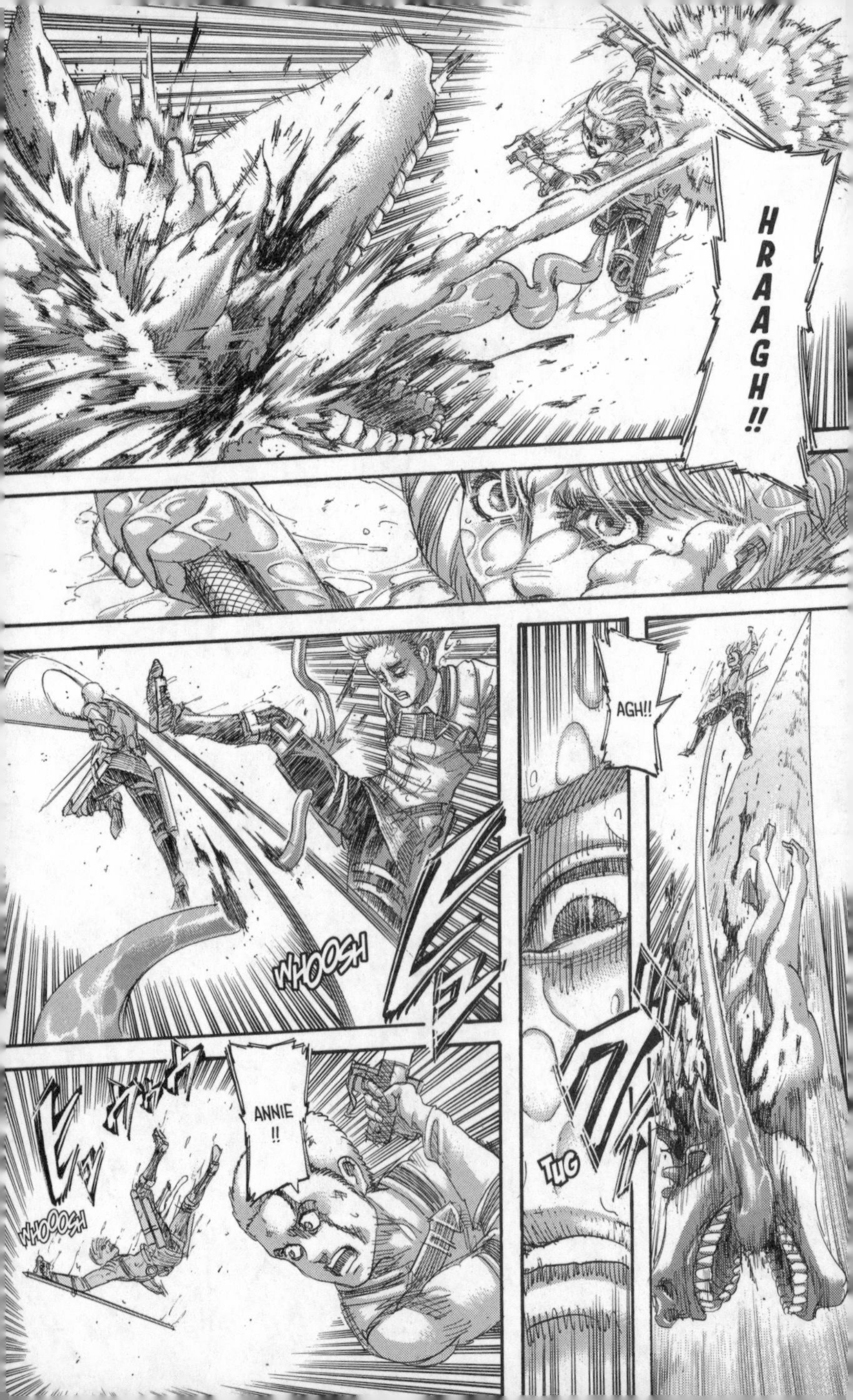
HRAAGH!!
AGH!!
WHOOSH
TUG
ANNIE!!
WHOOOSH

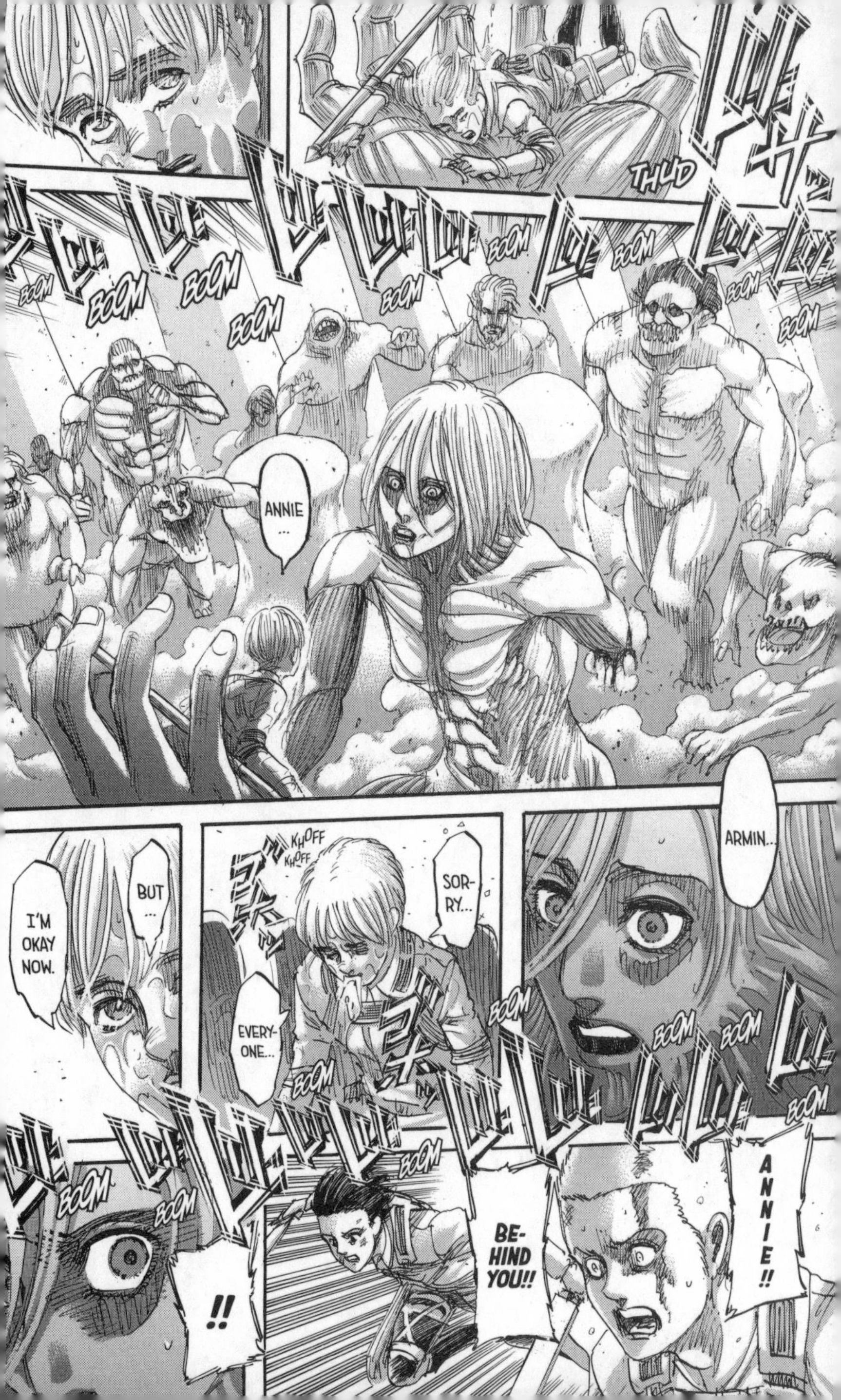
THUD
BOOM
BOOM
BOOM
BOOM
BOOM
BOOM
BOOM
BOOM
BOOM
BOOM
ANNIE ...
ARMIN...
SORRY...
EVERYONE...
KHOFF KHOFF
BUT ...
I'M OKAY NOW.
BOOM
BOOM
BOOM
ANNIE!!
BE-HIND YOU!!
!!

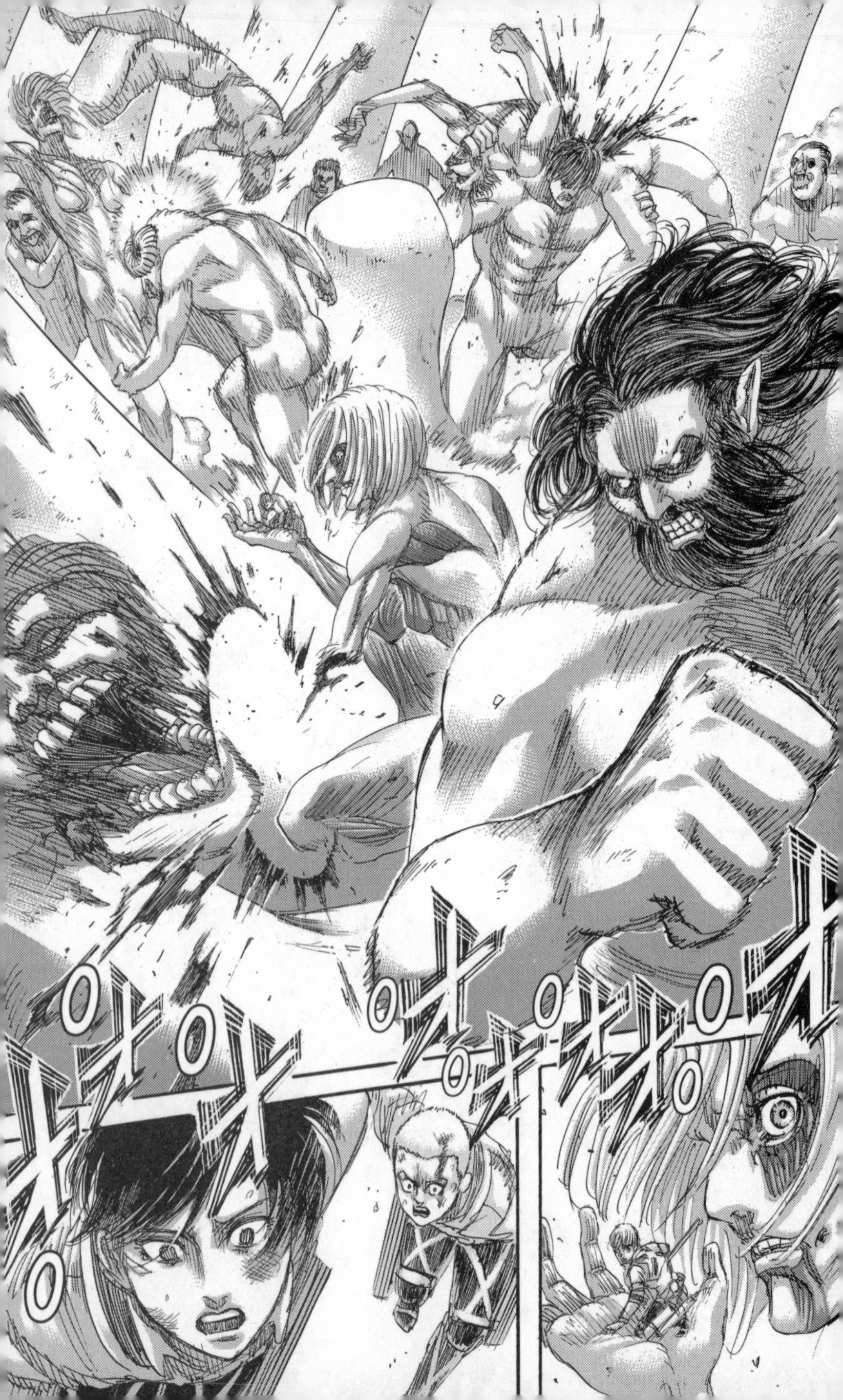
ドオドオ
ドオ
ドオオ

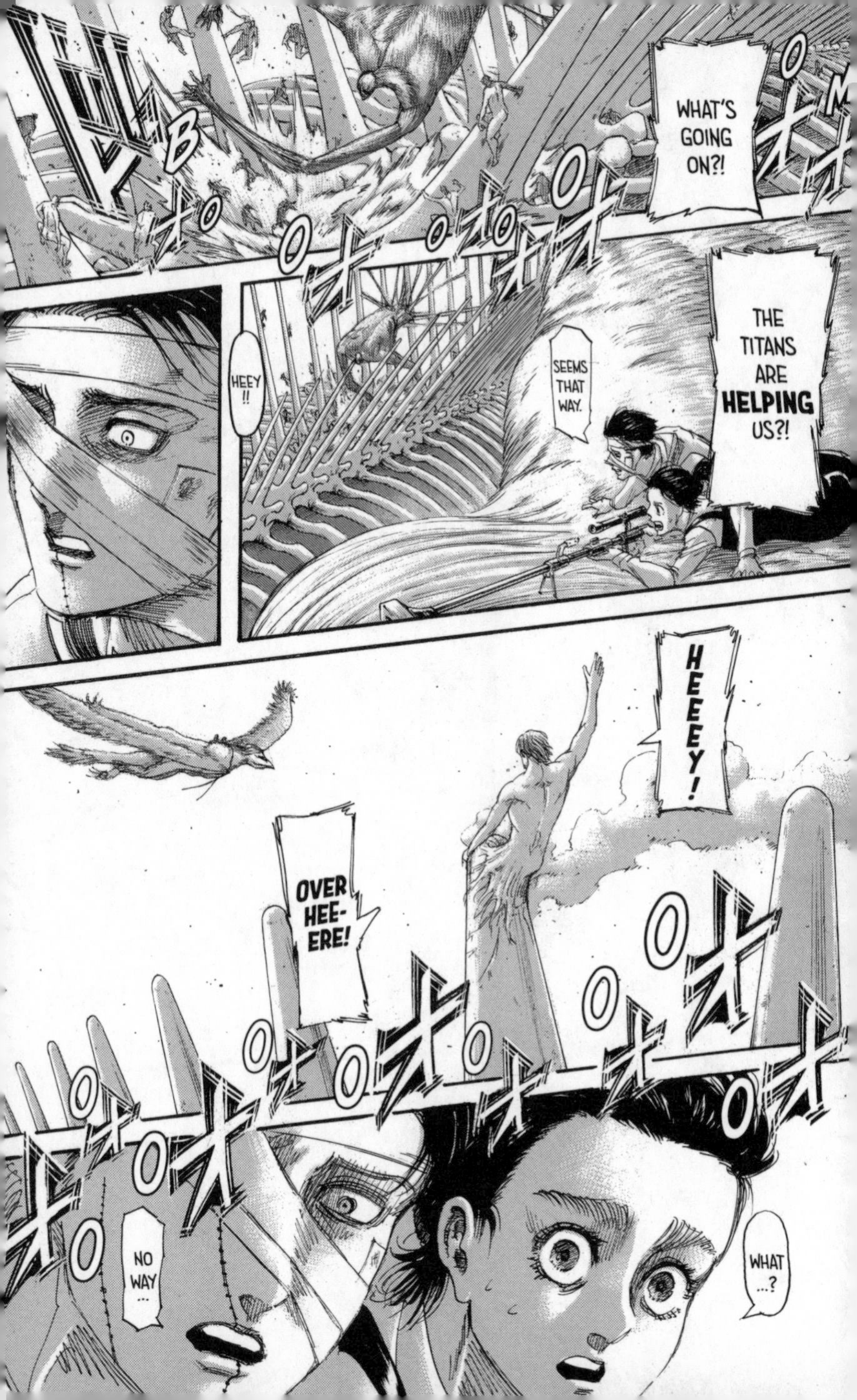
WHAT'S GOING ON?!
THE TITANS ARE HELPING US?!
SEEMS THAT WAY.
HEEY!!
HEEEEY!
OVER HEE-ERE!
WHAT ...?
NO WAY ...

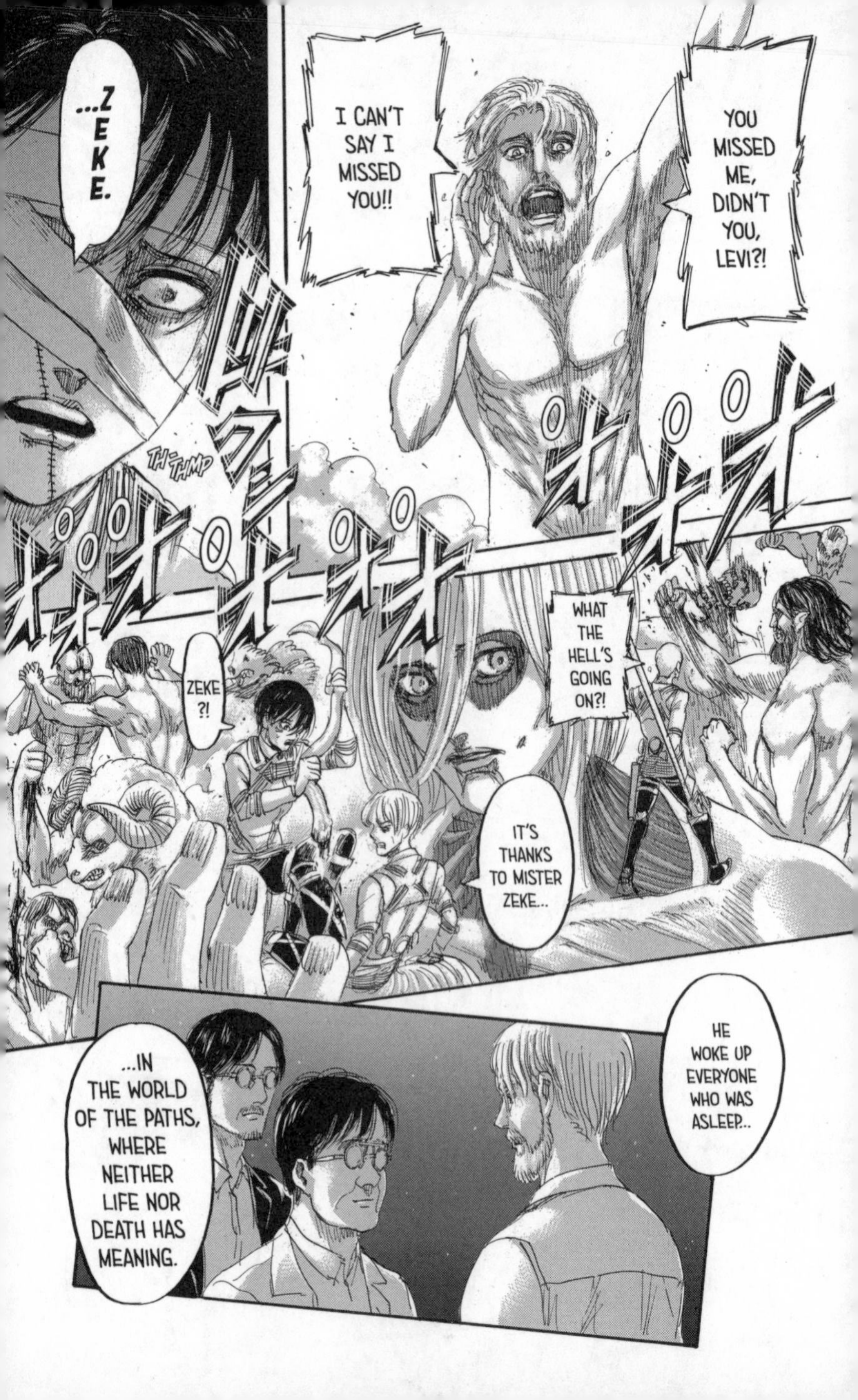
YOU MISSED ME, DIDN'T YOU, LEVI?!
I CAN'T SAY I MISSED YOU!!
...ZEKE.
TH-THMP
WHAT THE HELL'S GOING ON?!
ZEKE ?!
IT'S THANKS TO MISTER ZEKE...
HE WOKE UP EVERYONE WHO WAS ASLEEP...
...IN THE WORLD OF THE PATHS, WHERE NEITHER LIFE NOR DEATH HAS MEANING.

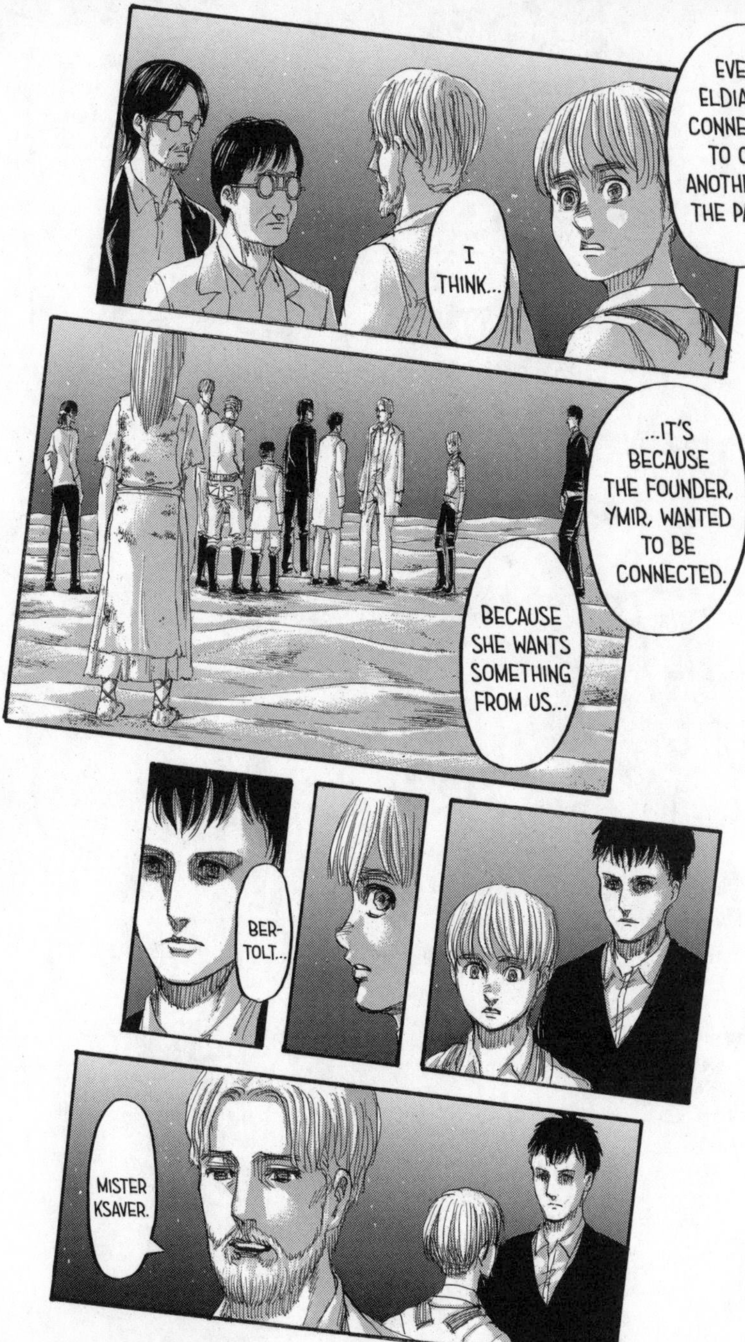
EVERY ELDIAN IS CONNECTED TO ONE ANOTHER BY THE PATHS.
I THINK...
...IT'S BECAUSE THE FOUNDER, YMIR, WANTED TO BE CONNECTED.
BECAUSE SHE WANTS SOMETHING FROM US...
BER-TOLT...
MISTER KSAVER.

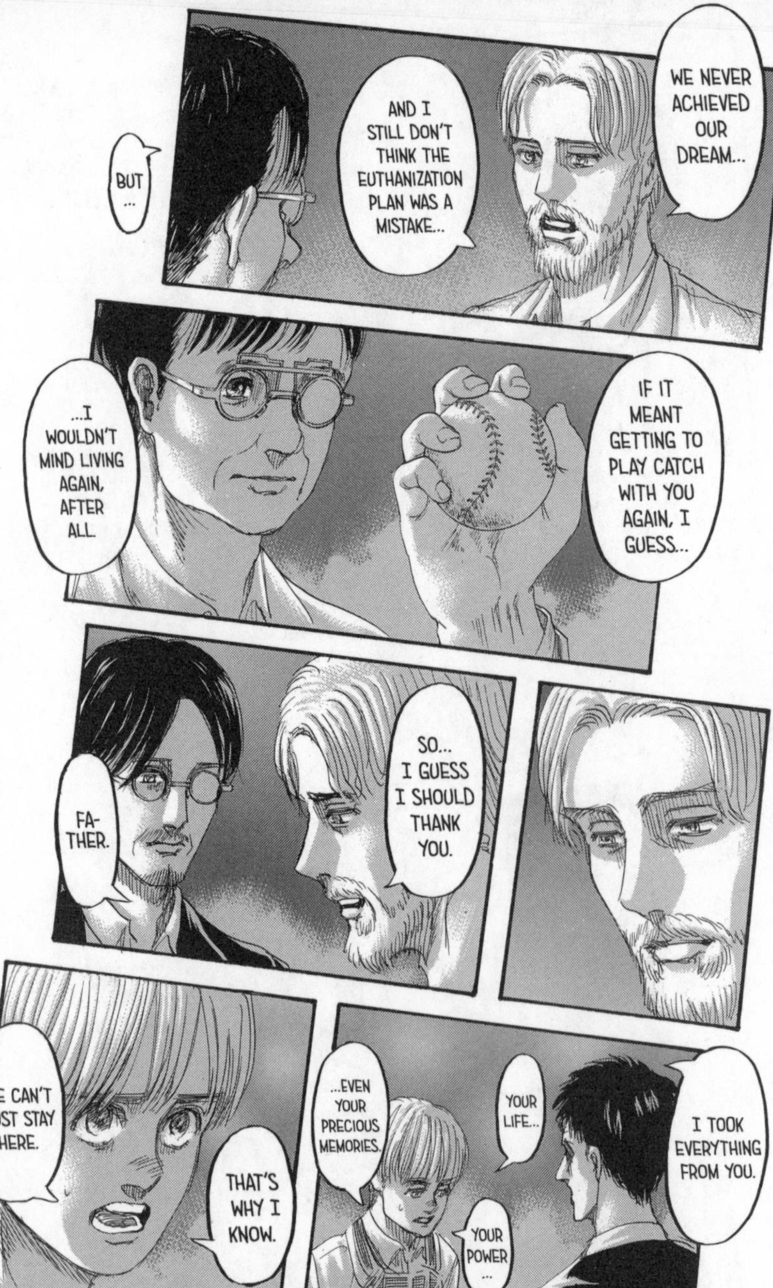
WE NEVER ACHIEVED OUR DREAM...
AND I STILL DON'T THINK THE EUTHANIZATION PLAN WAS A MISTAKE...
BUT ...
IF IT MEANT GETTING TO PLAY CATCH WITH YOU AGAIN, I GUESS...
...I WOULDN'T MIND LIVING AGAIN, AFTER ALL.
SO... I GUESS I SHOULD THANK YOU.
FA-THER.
I TOOK EVERYTHING FROM YOU.
YOUR LIFE...
YOUR POWER ...
...EVEN YOUR PRECIOUS MEMORIES.
THAT'S WHY I KNOW.
WE CAN'T JUST STAY HERE.

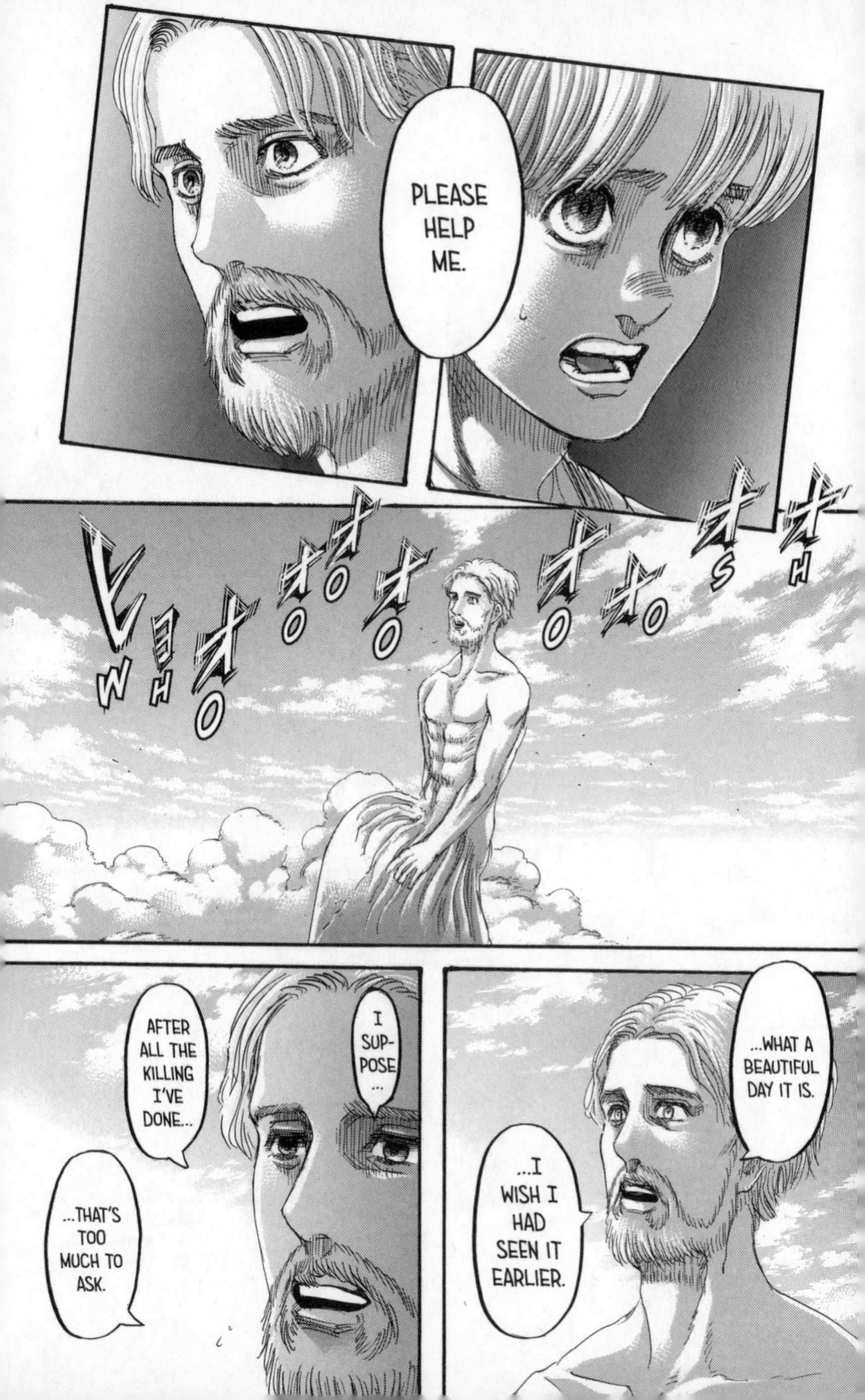
PLEASE HELP ME.
WHOOOOOOOSH
...WHAT A BEAUTIFUL DAY IT IS.
...I WISH I HAD SEEN IT EARLIER.
I SUPPOSE...
AFTER ALL THE KILLING I'VE DONE...
...THAT'S TOO MUCH TO ASK.

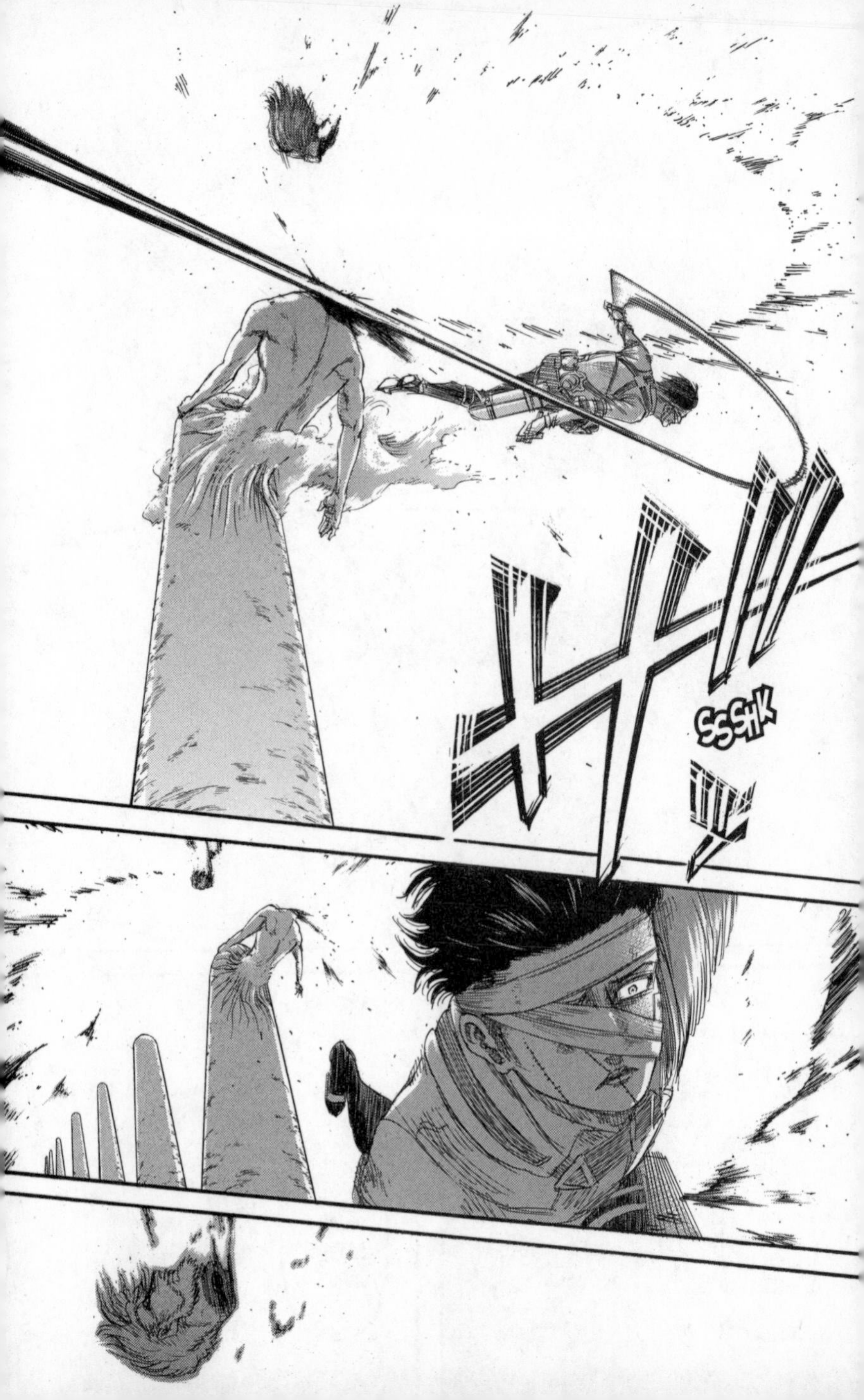
SSSHK

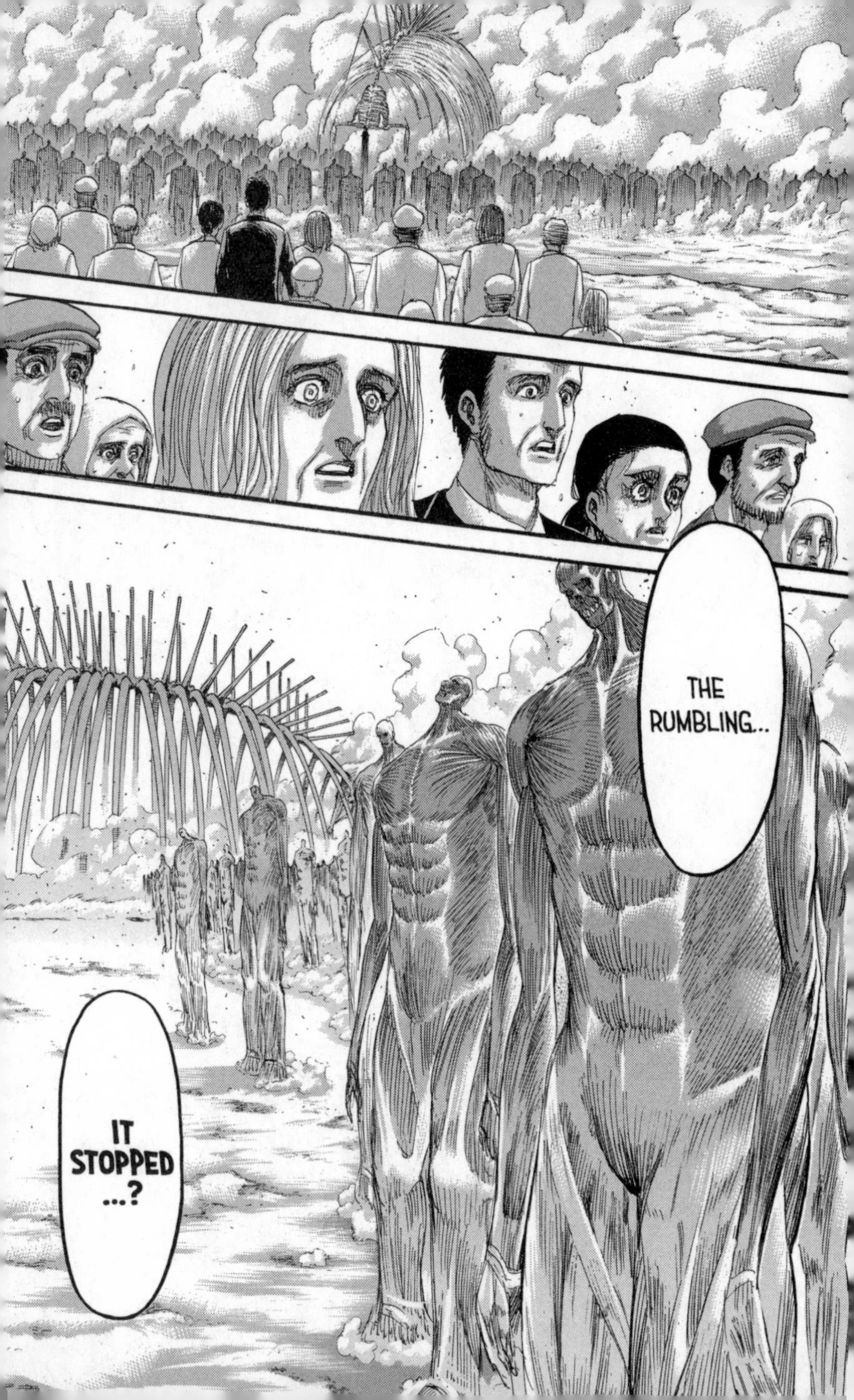
THE RUMBLING...
IT STOPPED ...?

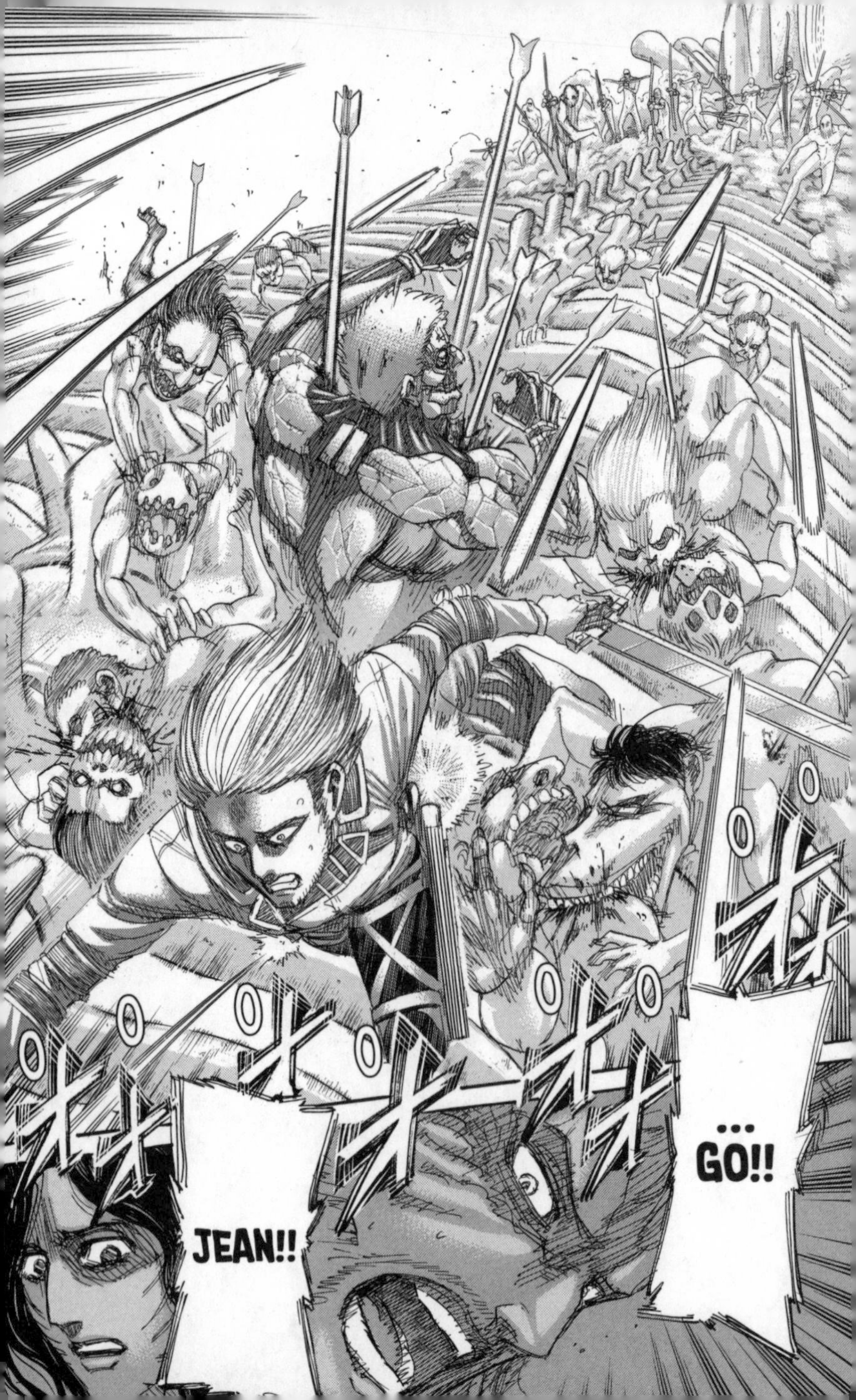
...GO!!
JEAN!!

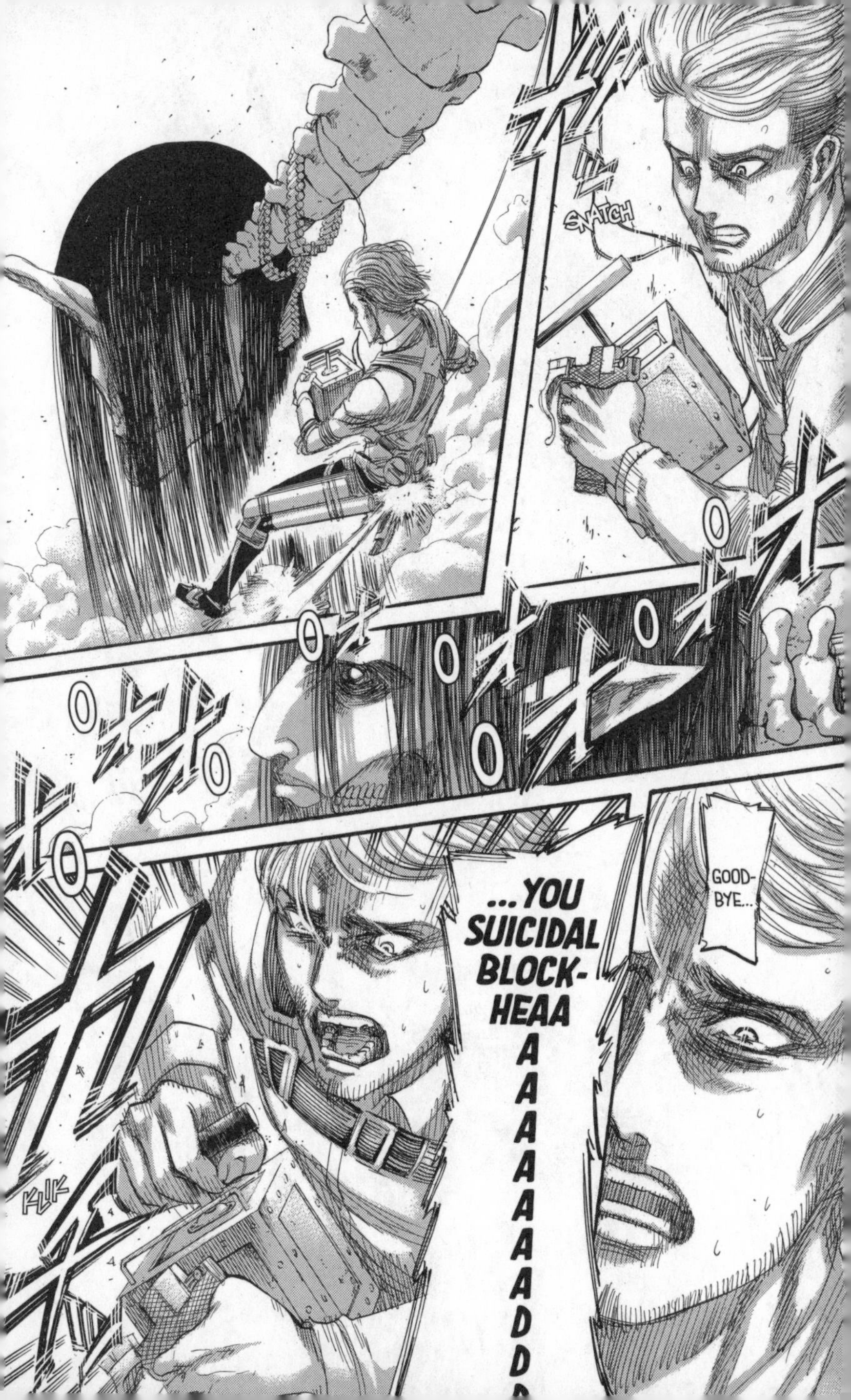
SNATCH
GOOD-BYE...
...YOU SUICIDAL BLOCK-HEAAAAAAAAADDD
KLIK

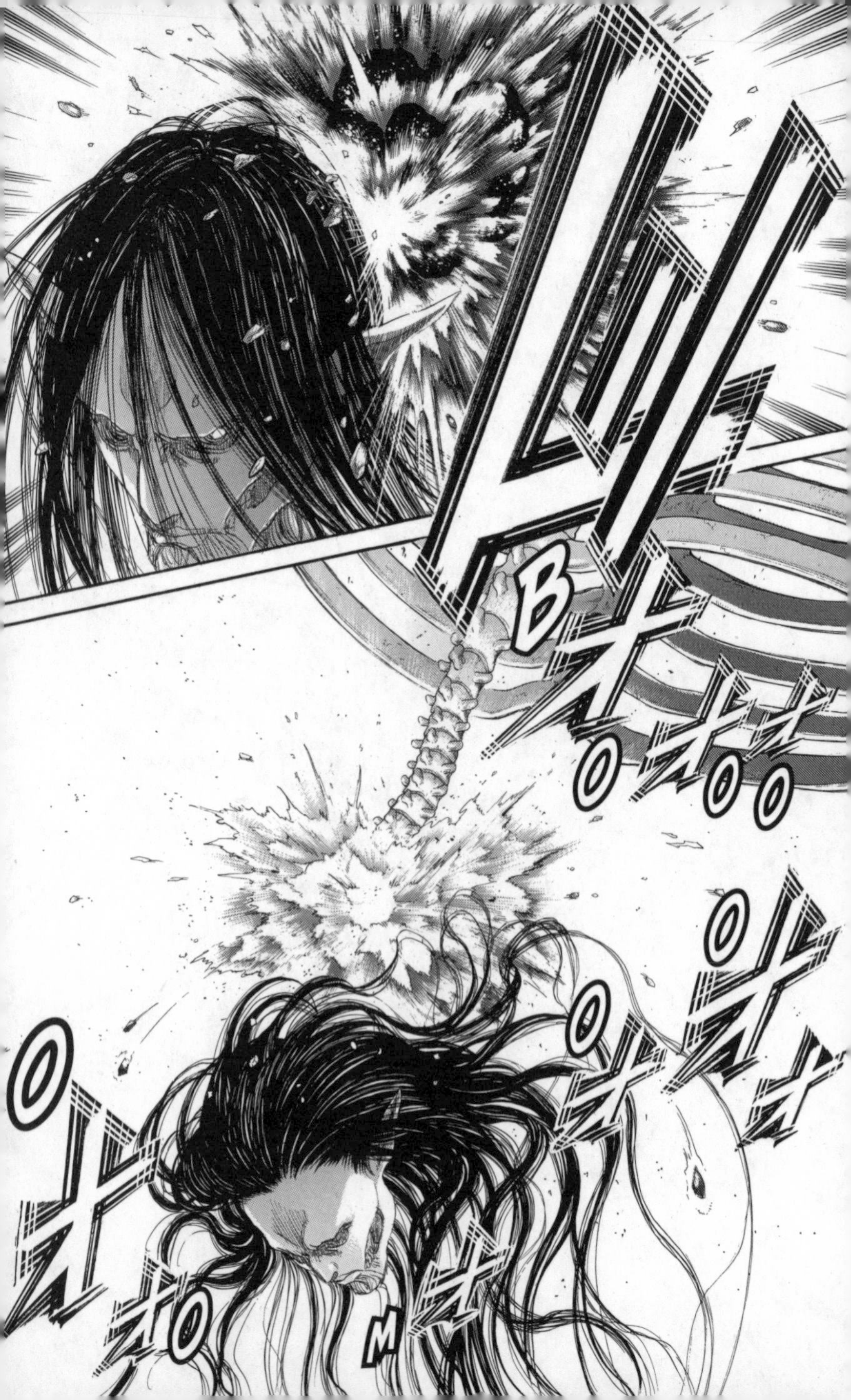
BOOM

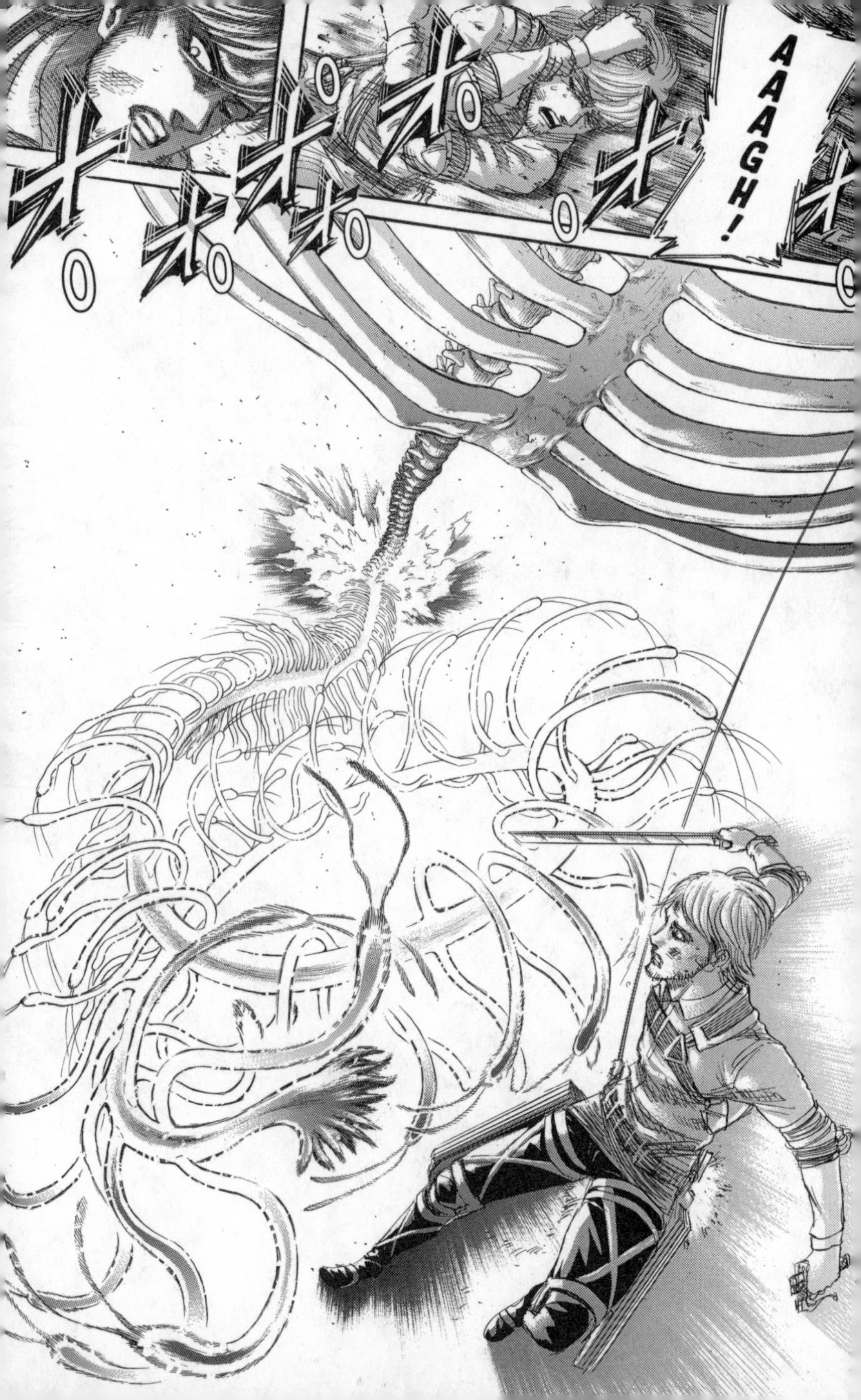
AAAGH!

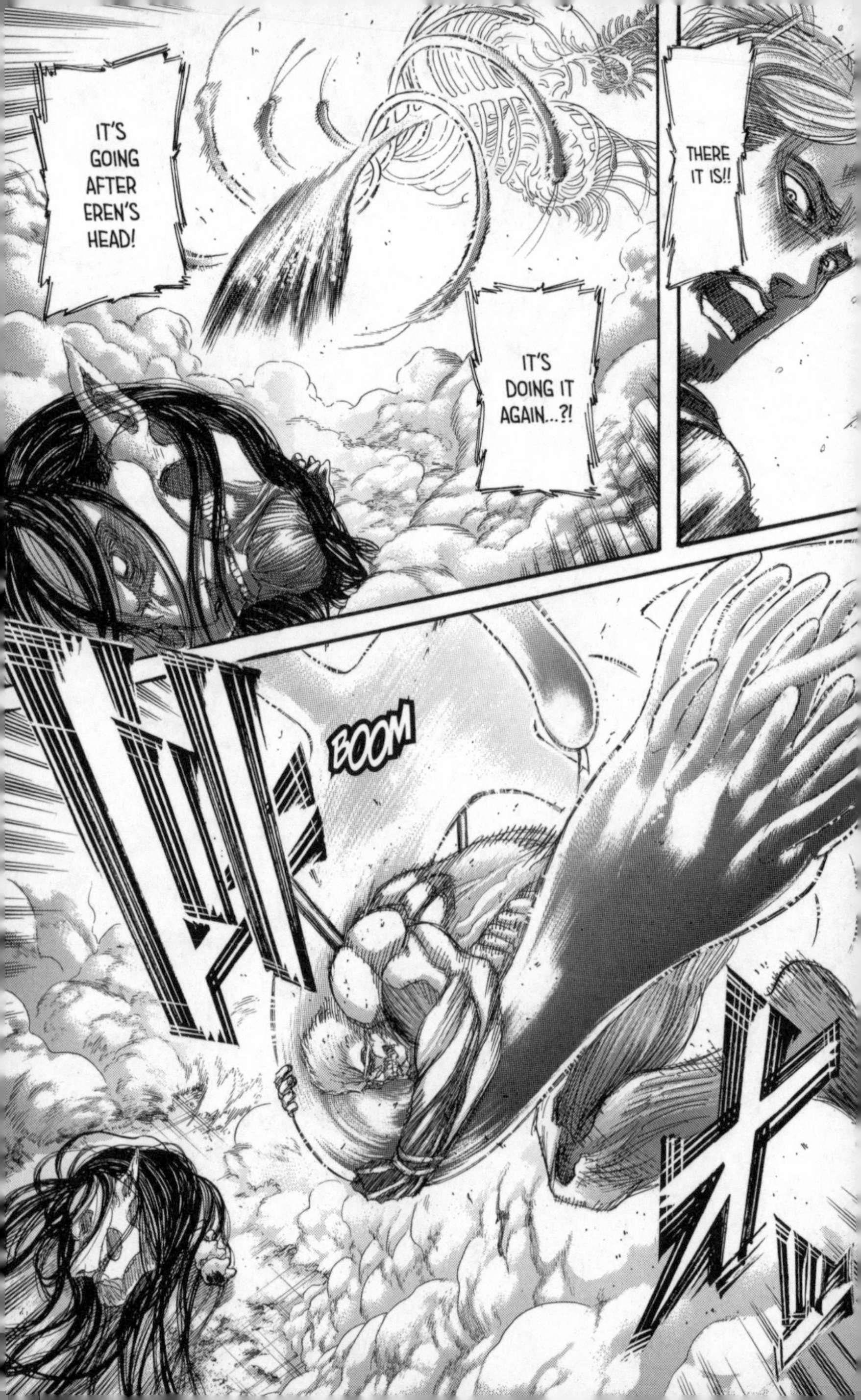
THERE IT IS!!
IT'S GOING AFTER EREN'S HEAD!
IT'S DOING IT AGAIN...?!
BOOM

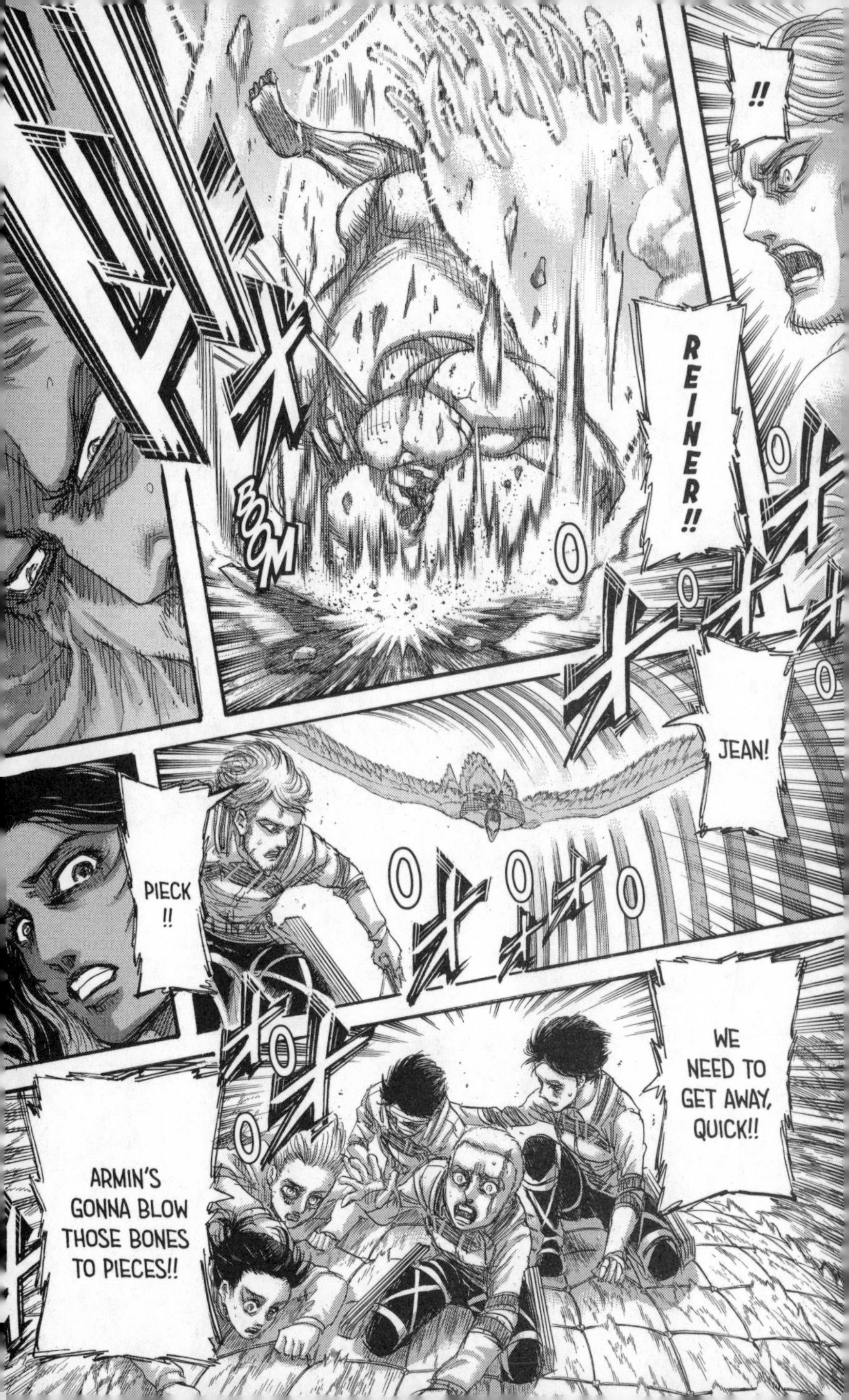
!!
REINER!!
BOOM
JEAN!
PIECK !!
WE NEED TO GET AWAY, QUICK!!
ARMIN'S GONNA BLOW THOSE BONES TO PIECES!!

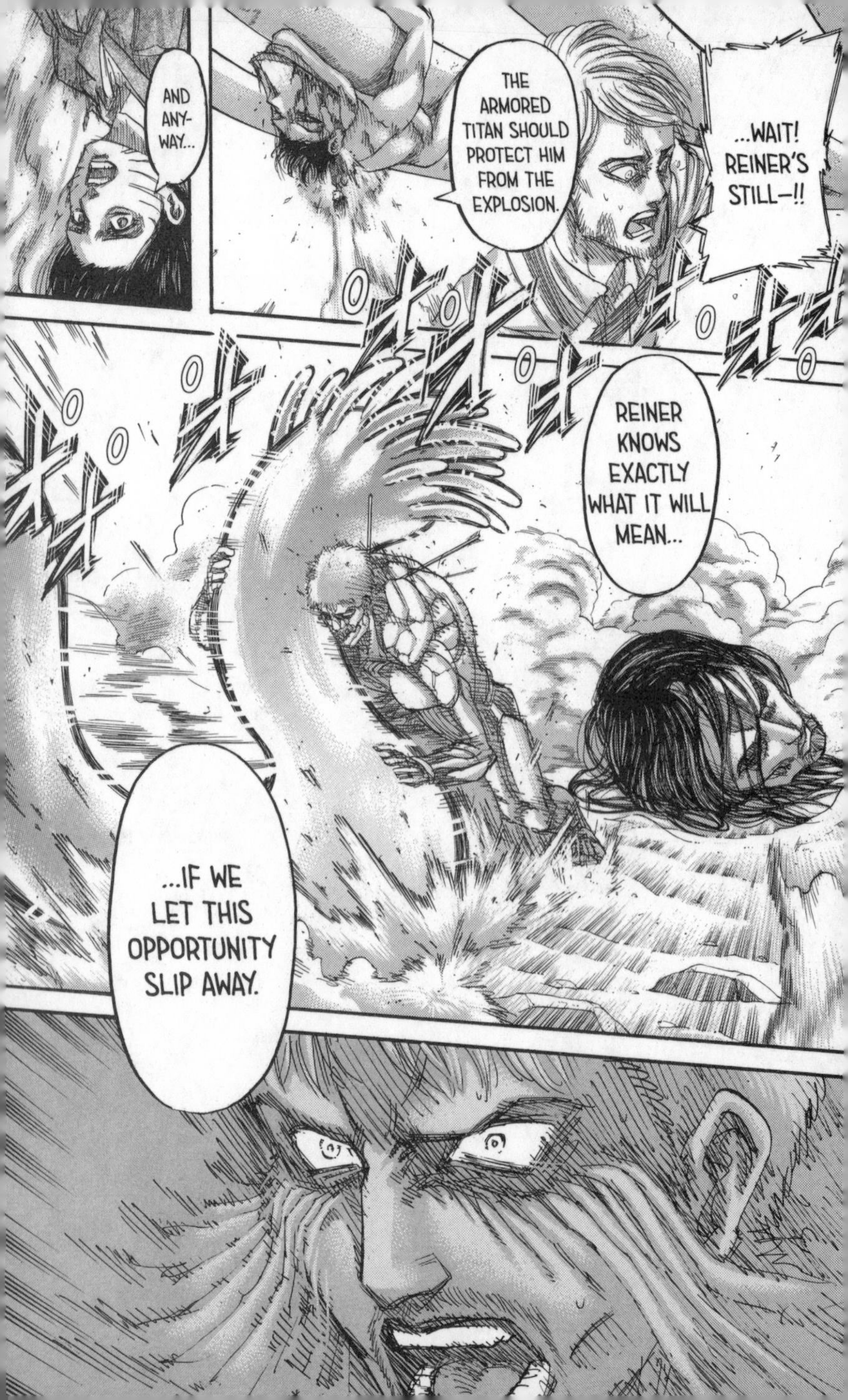
...WAIT! REINER'S STILL—!!
THE ARMORED TITAN SHOULD PROTECT HIM FROM THE EXPLOSION.
AND ANY-WAY...
REINER KNOWS EXACTLY WHAT IT WILL MEAN...
...IF WE LET THIS OPPORTUNITY SLIP AWAY.

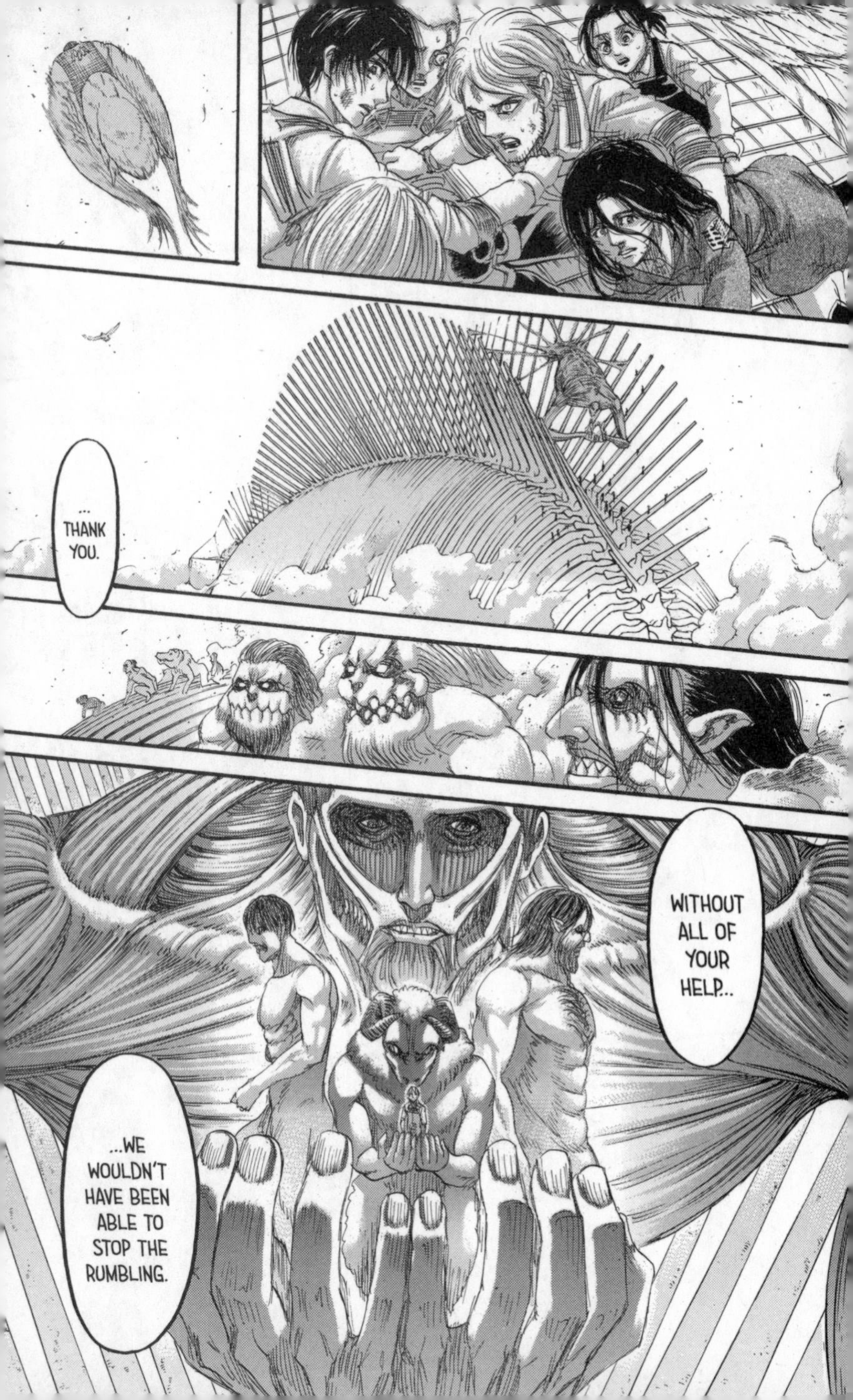

...THANK YOU.
WITHOUT ALL OF YOUR HELP...
...WE WOULDN'T HAVE BEEN ABLE TO STOP THE RUMBLING.

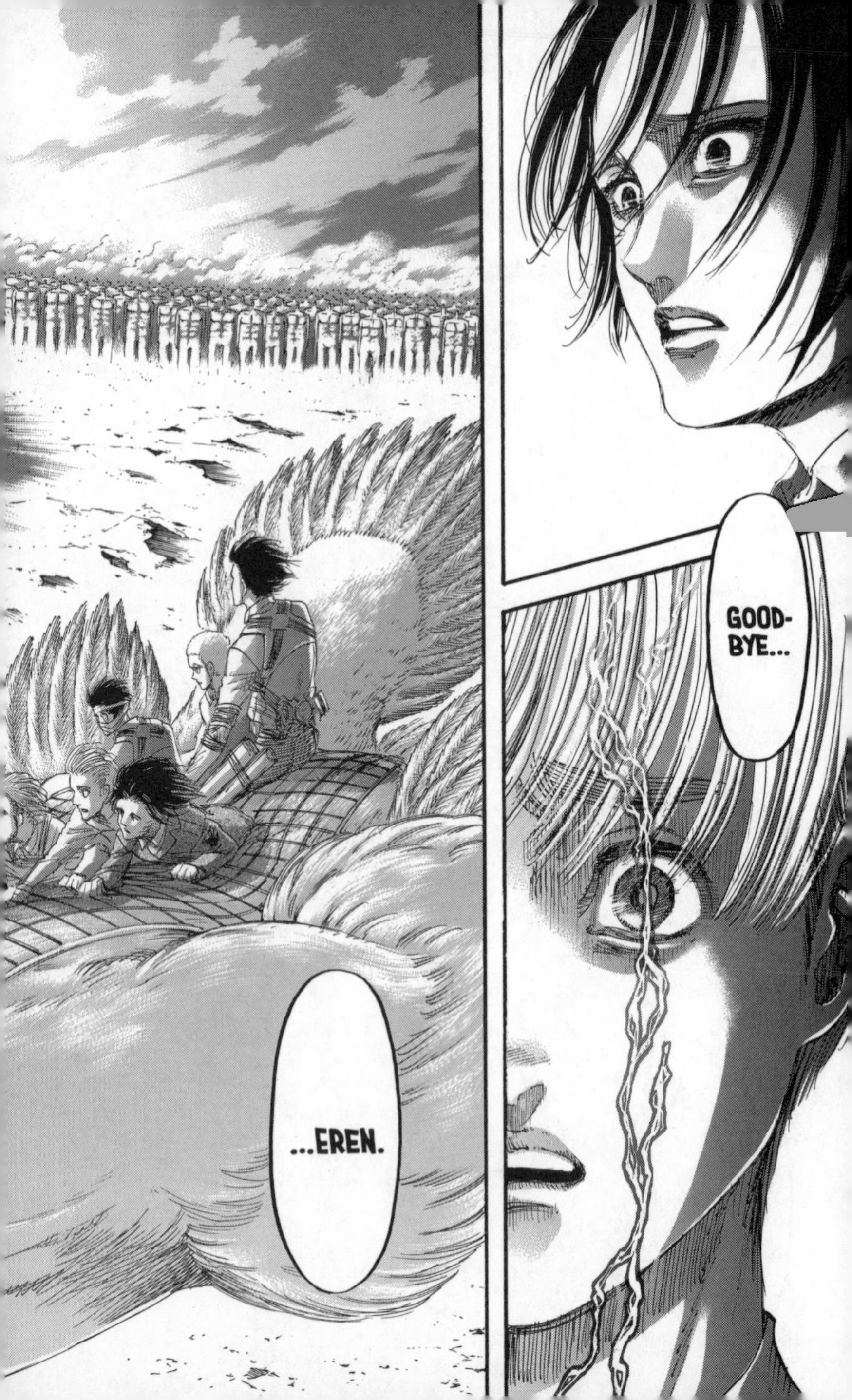
GOOD-BYE...
...EREN.

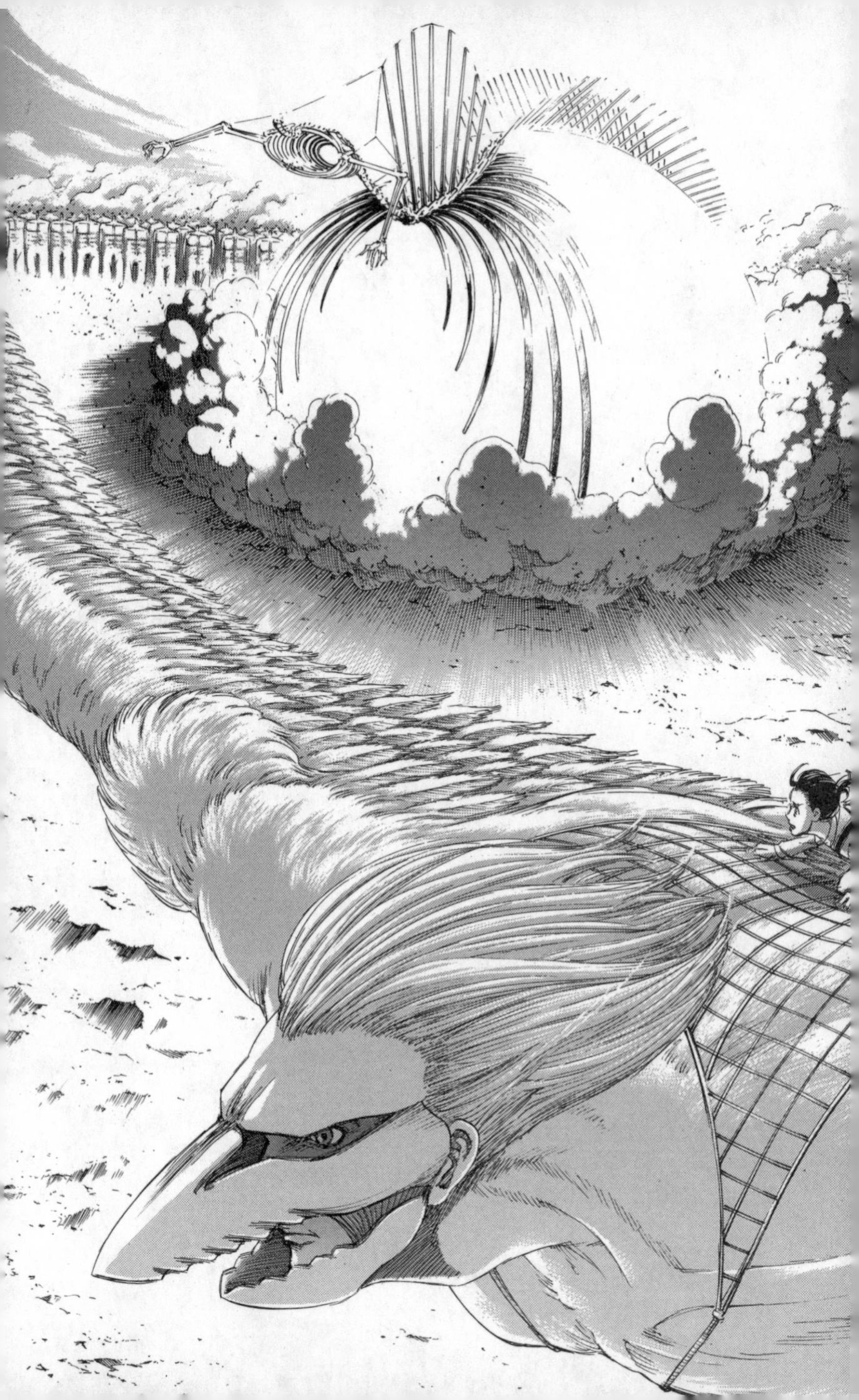

ATTACK on TITAN

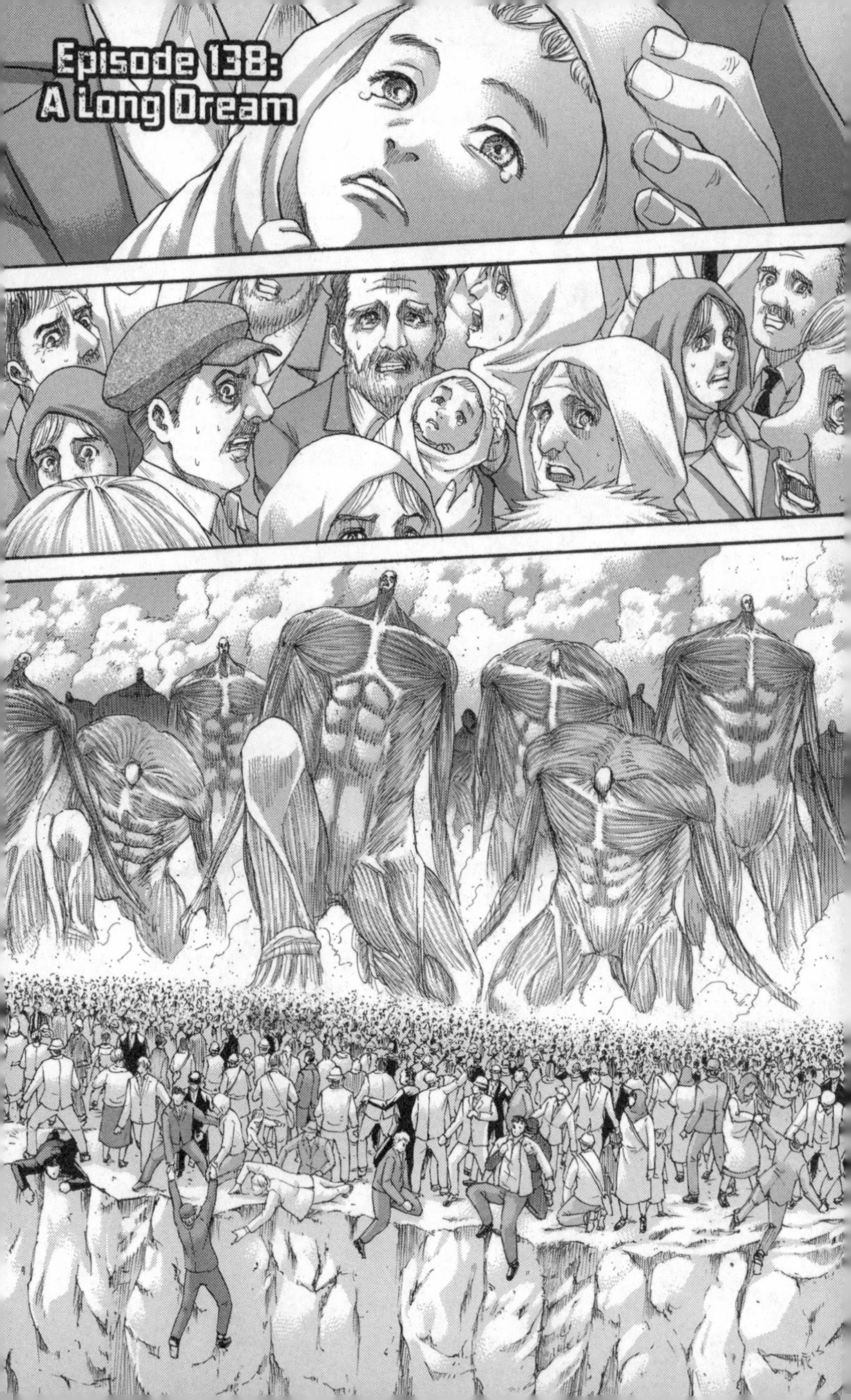
Episode 138:
A Long Dream

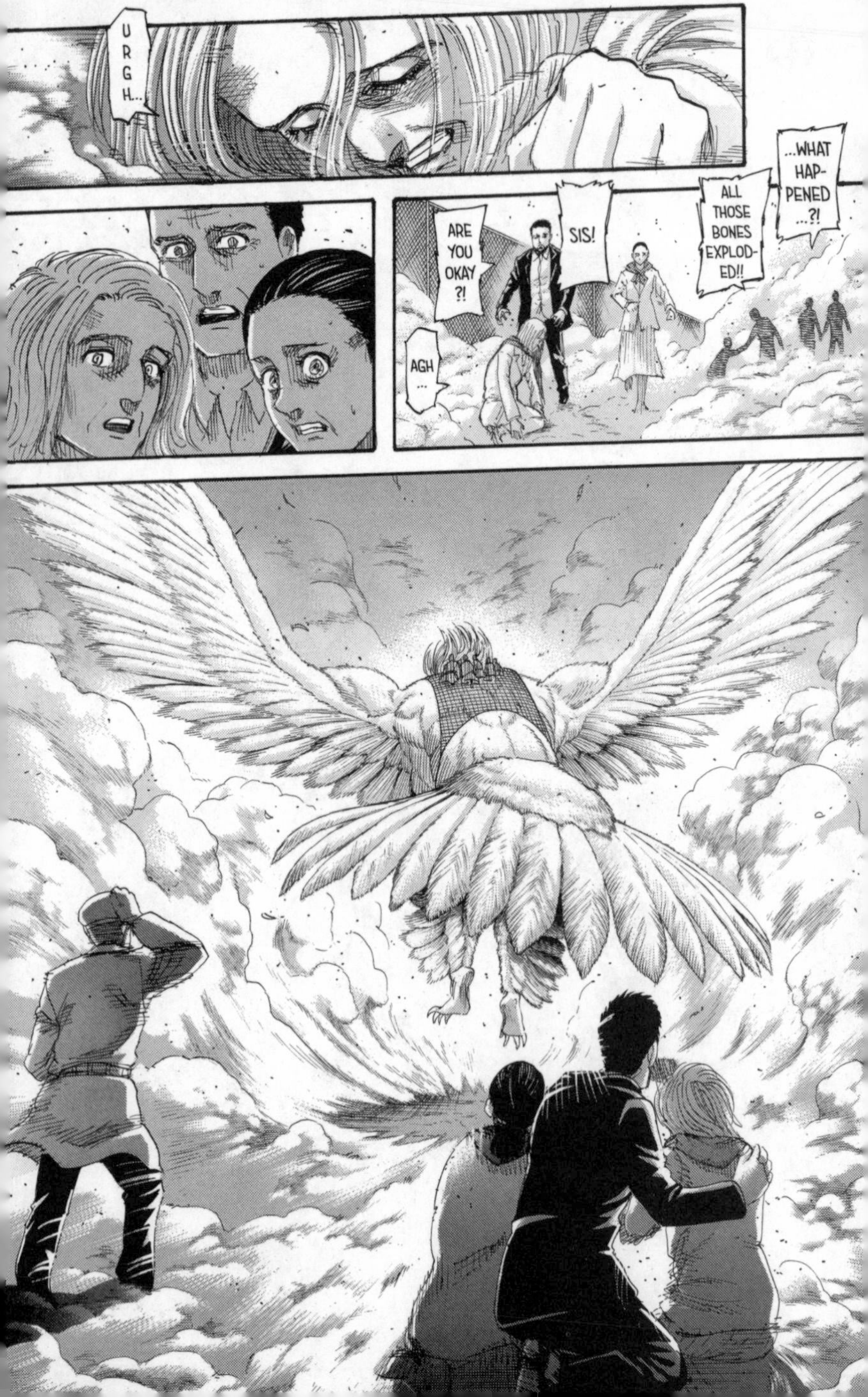
URGH...
...WHAT HAPPENED ...?!
ALL THOSE BONES EXPLODED!!
SIS!
ARE YOU OKAY ?!
AGH ...

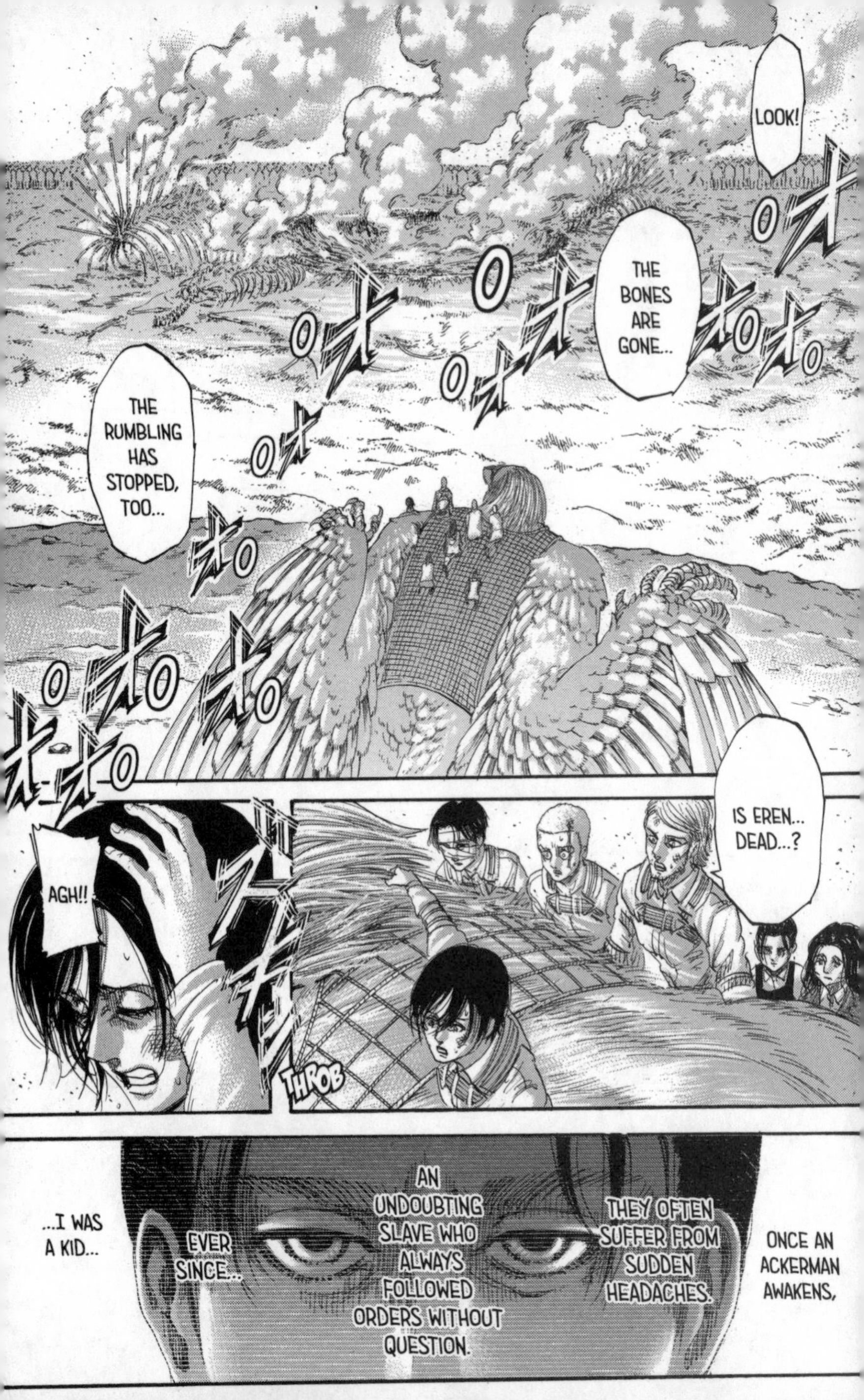
LOOK!
THE BONES ARE GONE...
THE RUMBLING HAS STOPPED, TOO...
IS EREN... DEAD...?
THROB
AGH!!
ONCE AN ACKERMAN AWAKENS,
THEY OFTEN SUFFER FROM SUDDEN HEADACHES.
AN UNDOUBTING SLAVE WHO ALWAYS FOLLOWED ORDERS WITHOUT QUESTION.
EVER SINCE...
...I WAS A KID...

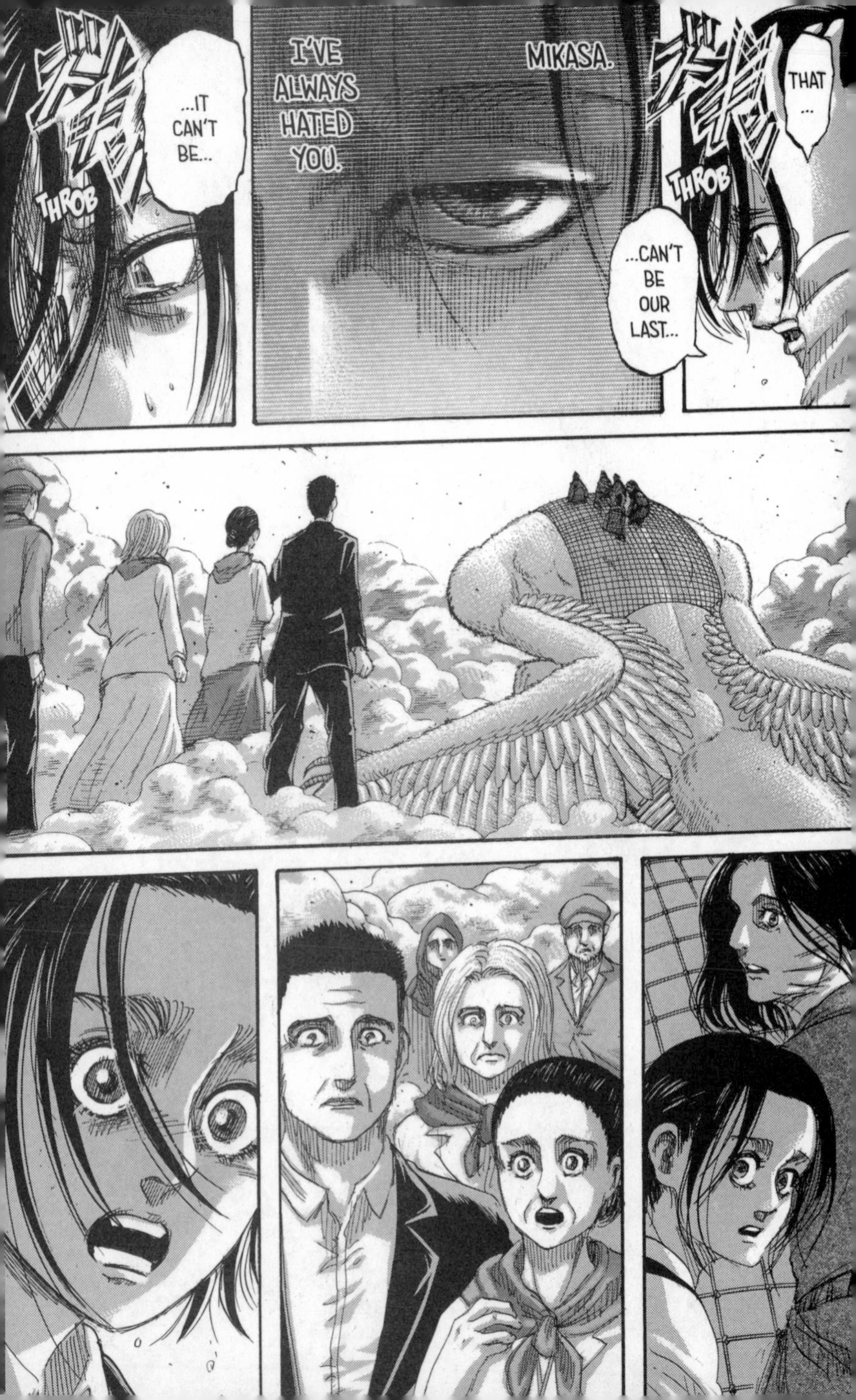
THAT ...
THROB
...CAN'T BE OUR LAST...
MIKASA.
I'VE ALWAYS HATED YOU.
...IT CAN'T BE...
THROB

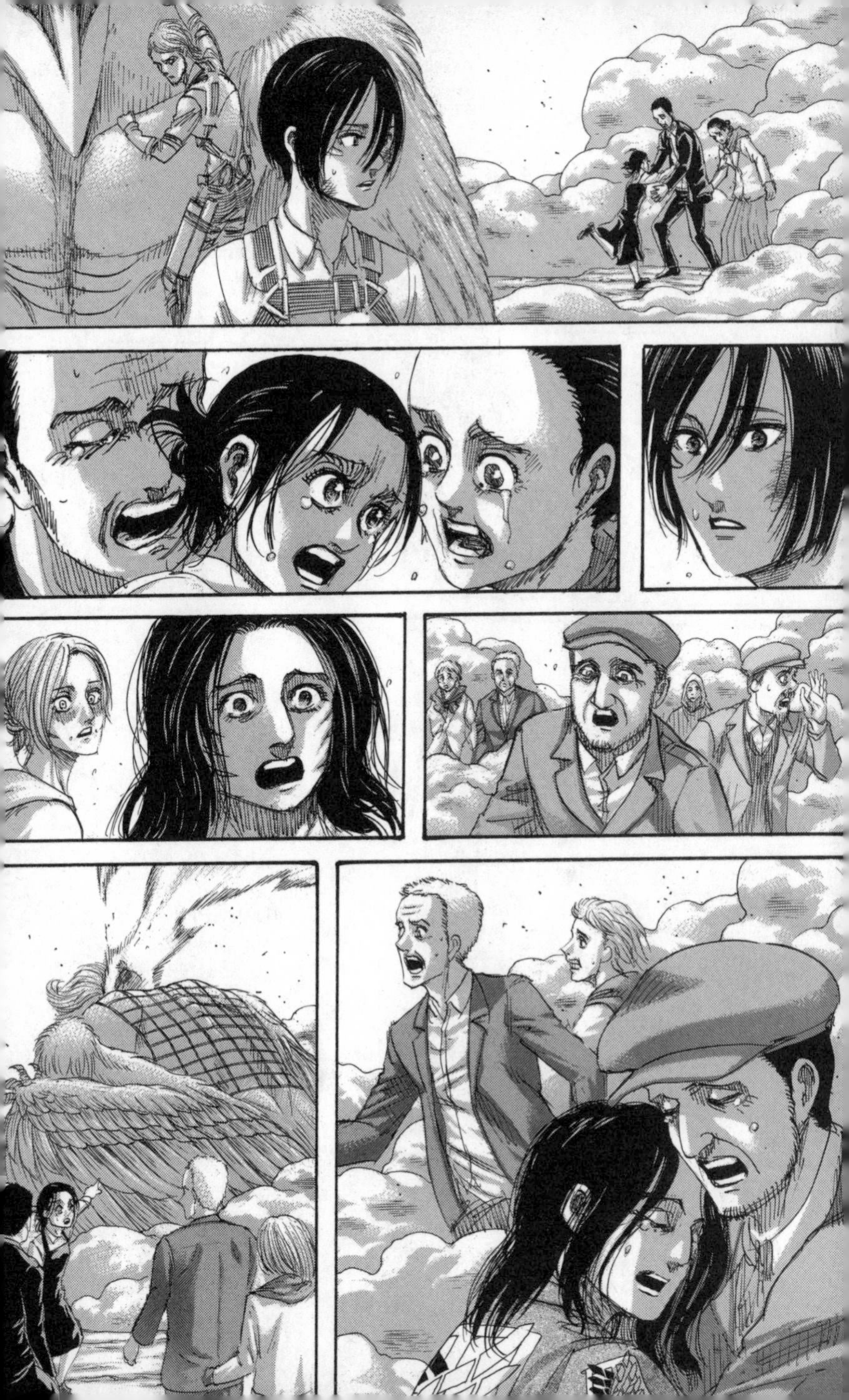

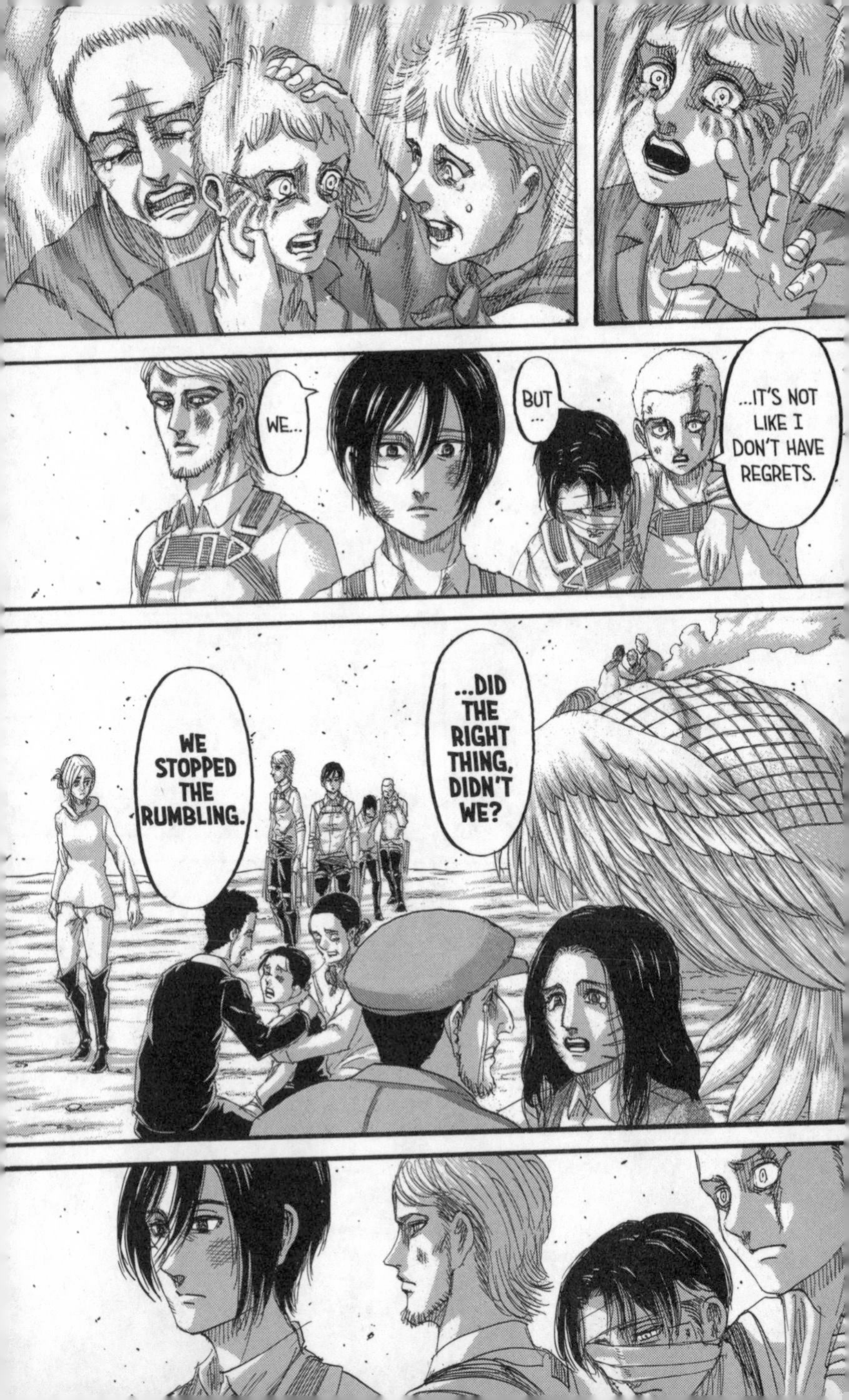
...IT'S NOT LIKE I DON'T HAVE REGRETS.
BUT ...
WE...
...DID THE RIGHT THING, DIDN'T WE?
WE STOPPED THE RUMBLING.

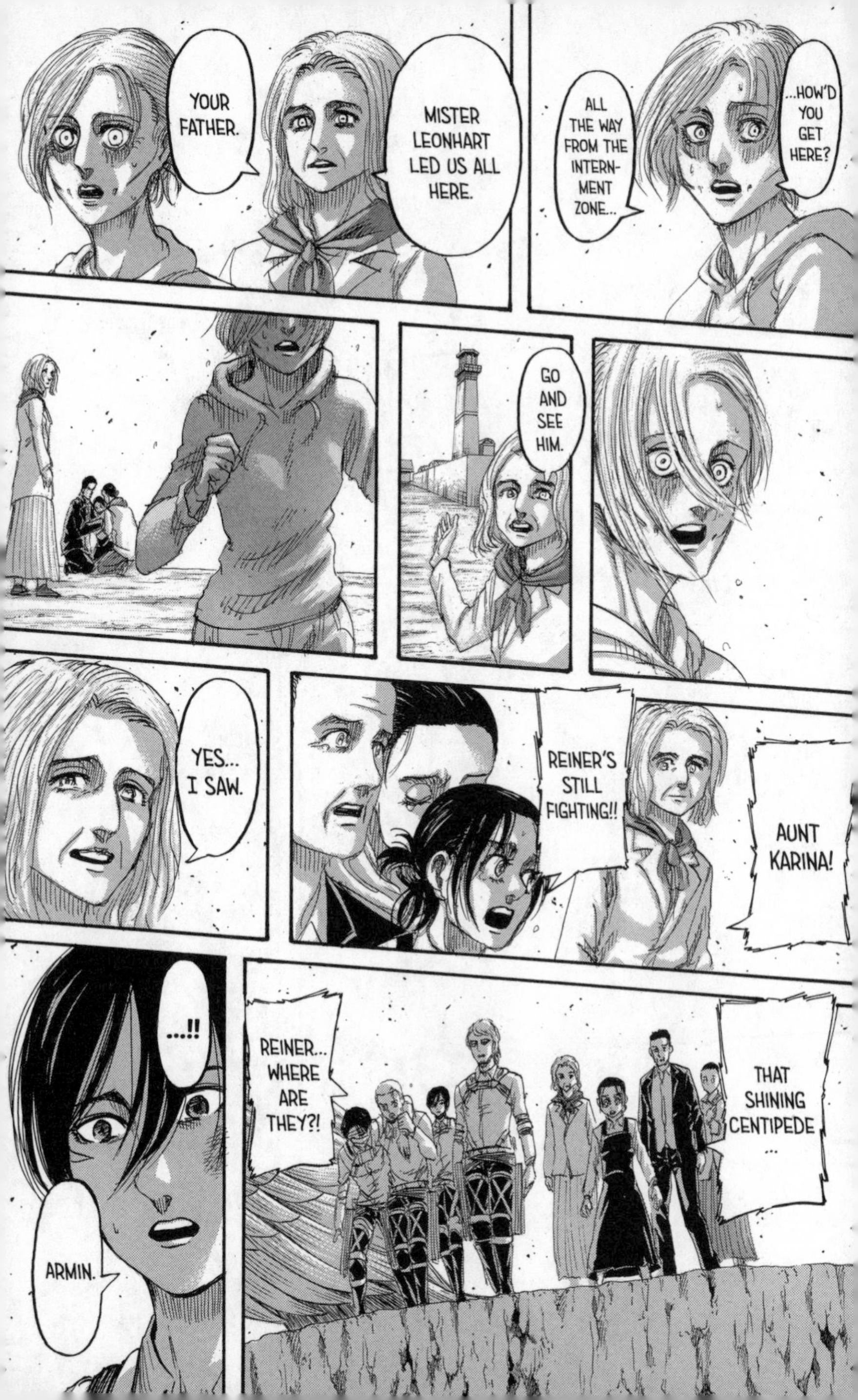
...HOW'D YOU GET HERE?
ALL THE WAY FROM THE INTERN-MENT ZONE...
MISTER LEONHART LED US ALL HERE.
YOUR FATHER.
GO AND SEE HIM.
AUNT KARINA!
REINER'S STILL FIGHTING!!
YES... I SAW.
THAT SHINING CENTIPEDE ...
REINER... WHERE ARE THEY?!
...!!
ARMIN.

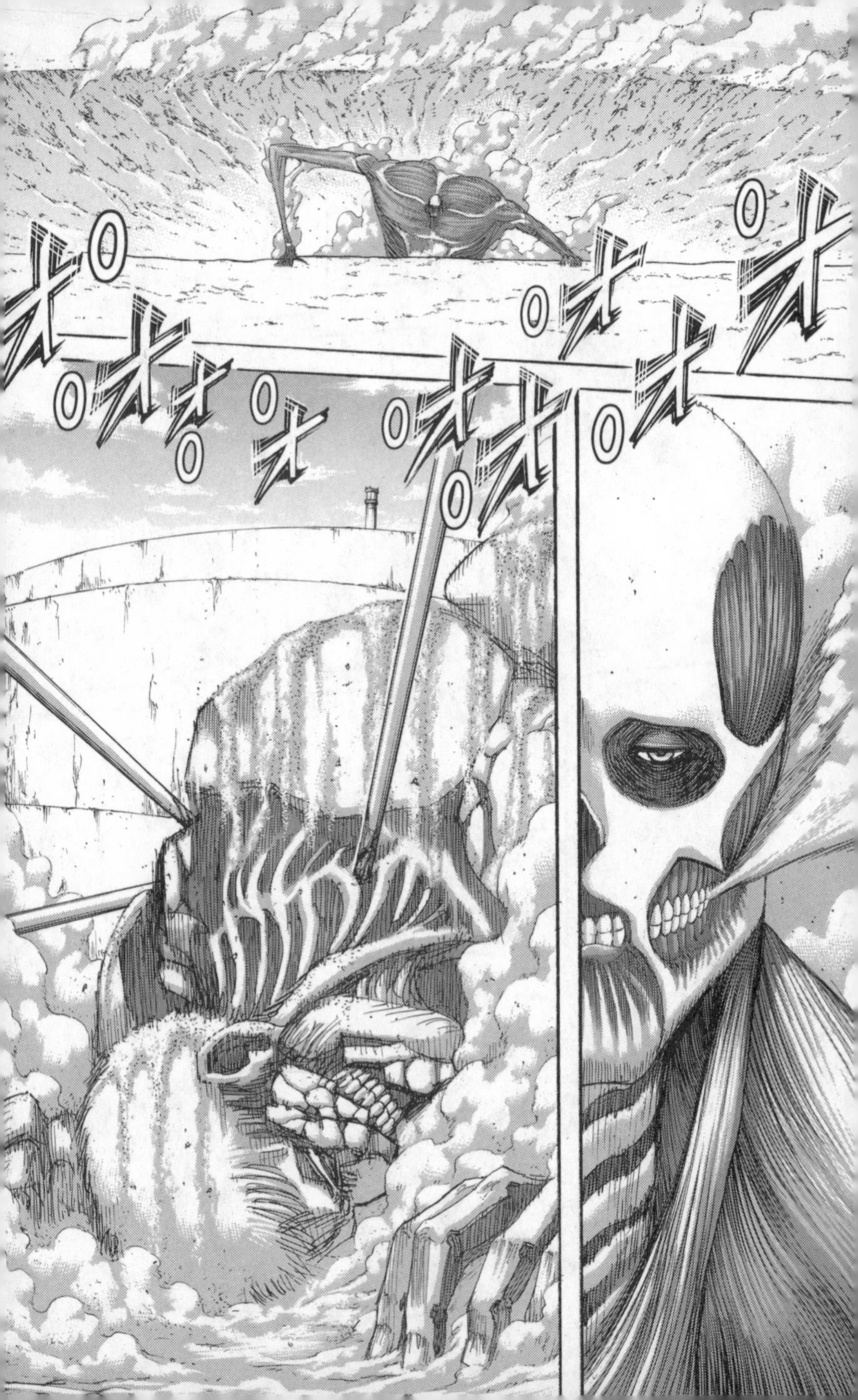
オ゜オ゜オ゜オ゜オ゜オ゜オ゜オ゜オ゜

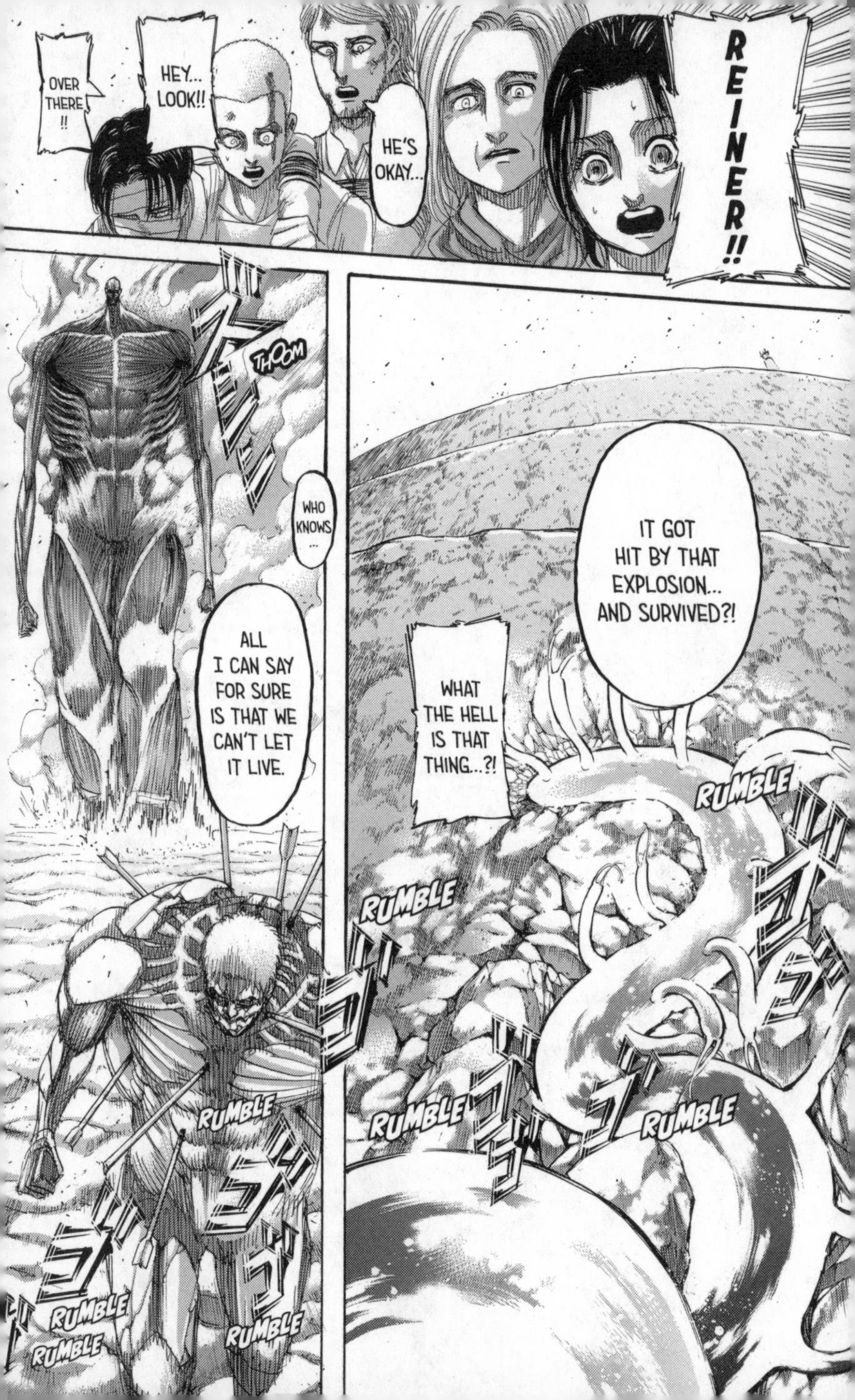
REINER!!
HE'S OKAY...
HEY... LOOK!!
OVER THERE!!
IT GOT HIT BY THAT EXPLOSION... AND SURVIVED?!
WHAT THE HELL IS THAT THING...?!
RUMBLE
RUMBLE
RUMBLE
RUMBLE
THOOM
WHO KNOWS...
ALL I CAN SAY FOR SURE IS THAT WE CAN'T LET IT LIVE.
RUMBLE
RUMBLE
RUMBLE
RUMBLE

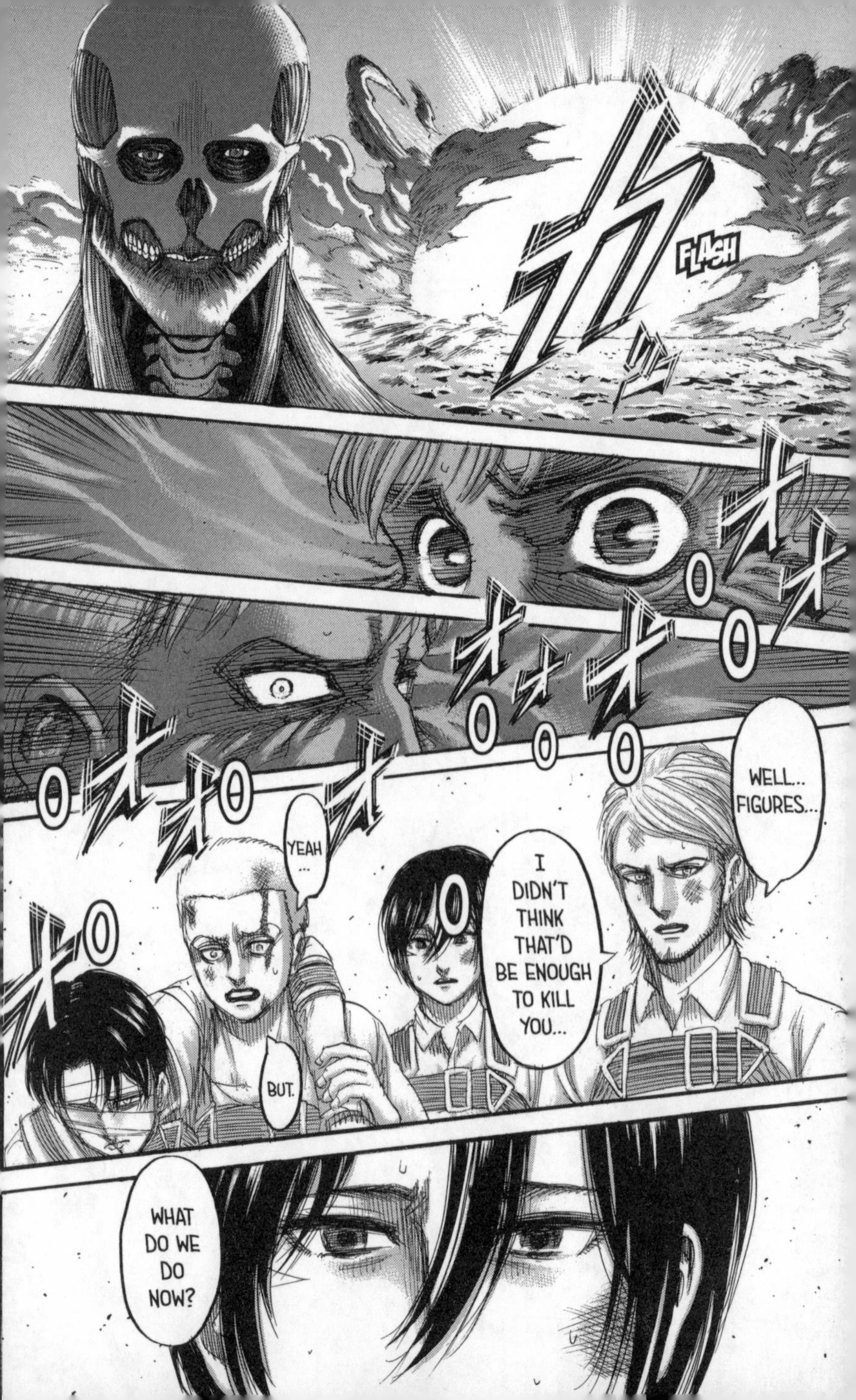
FLASH
WELL... FIGURES...
I DIDN'T THINK THAT'D BE ENOUGH TO KILL YOU...
YEAH ...
BUT.
WHAT DO WE DO NOW?

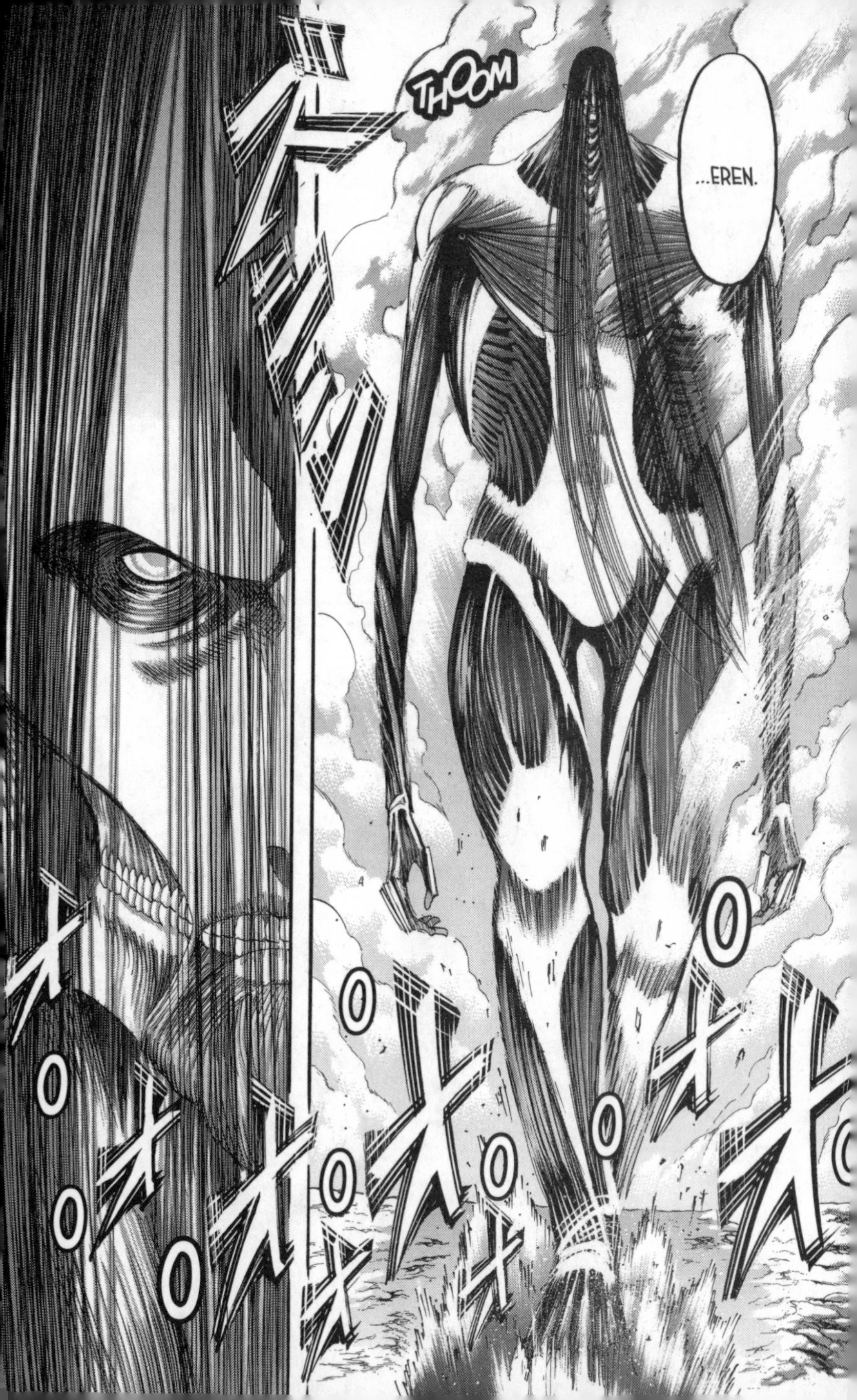
...EREN.
THOOM

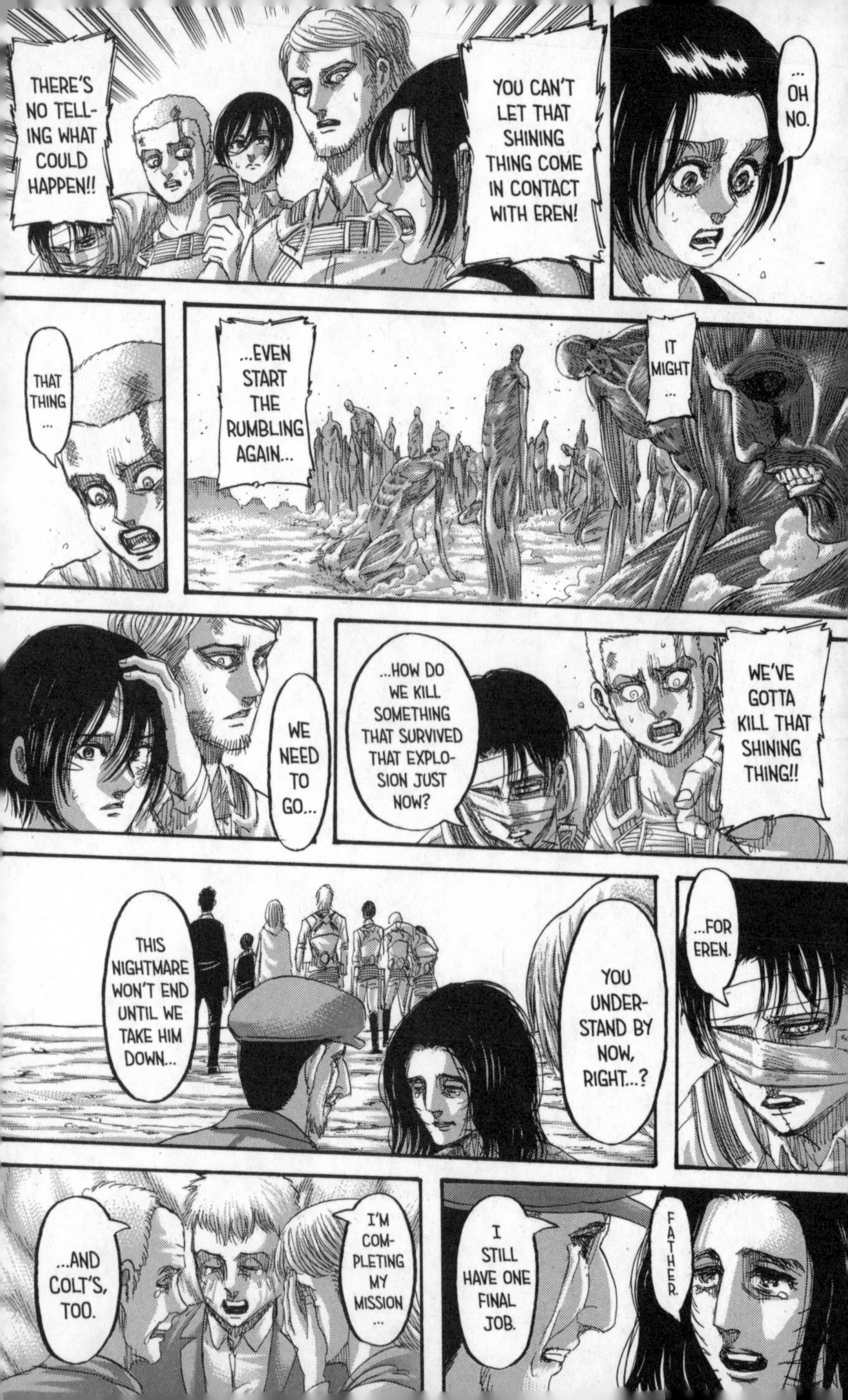
...OH NO.
YOU CAN'T LET THAT SHINING THING COME IN CONTACT WITH EREN!
THERE'S NO TELLING WHAT COULD HAPPEN!!
IT MIGHT...
...EVEN START THE RUMBLING AGAIN...
THAT THING...
WE'VE GOTTA KILL THAT SHINING THING!!
...HOW DO WE KILL SOMETHING THAT SURVIVED THAT EXPLOSION JUST NOW?
WE NEED TO GO...
...FOR EREN.
YOU UNDERSTAND BY NOW, RIGHT...?
THIS NIGHTMARE WON'T END UNTIL WE TAKE HIM DOWN...
FATHER.
I STILL HAVE ONE FINAL JOB.
I'M COMPLETING MY MISSION...
...AND COLT'S, TOO.

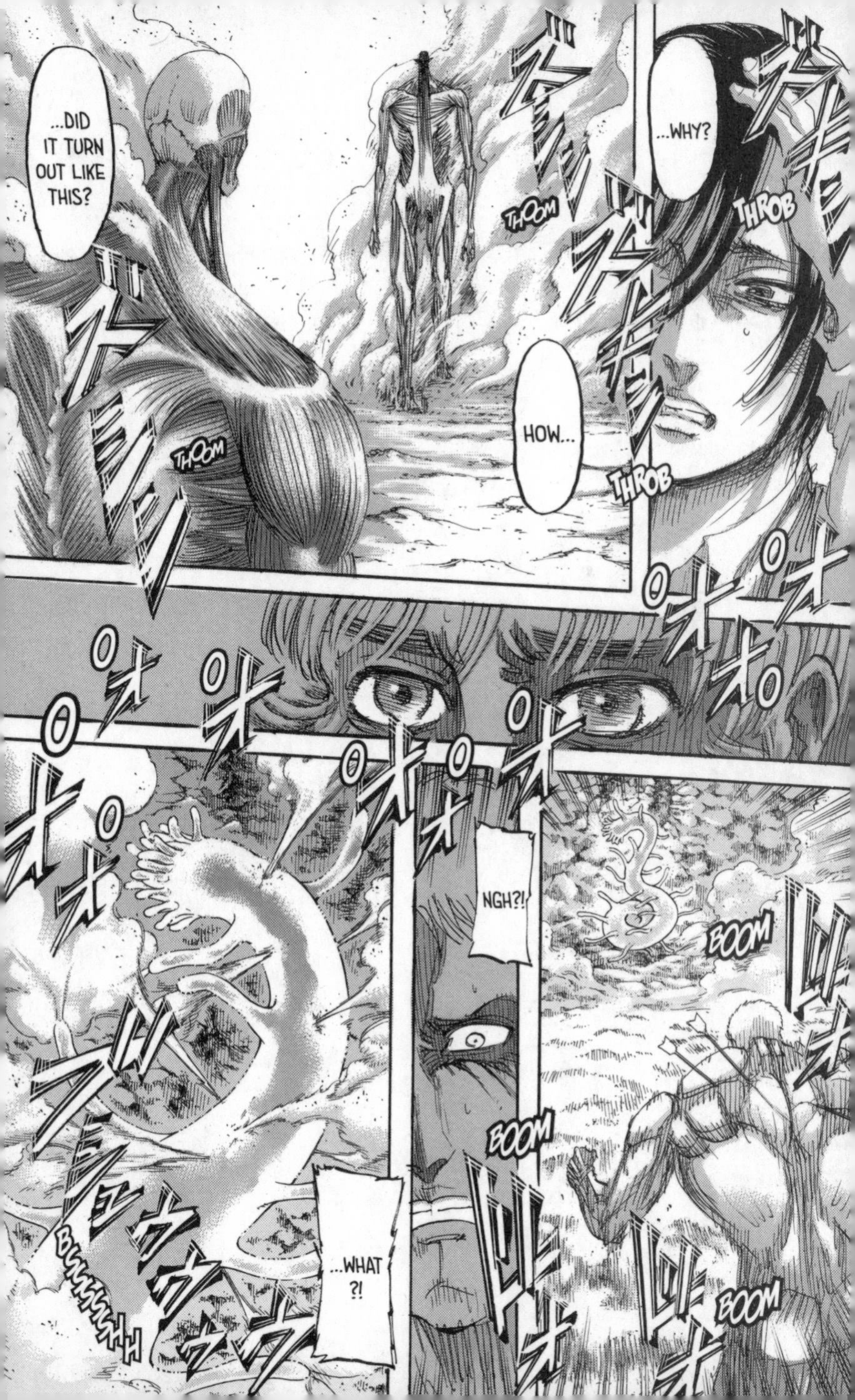
...WHY?
THROB
HOW...
THROB
THOOM
...DID IT TURN OUT LIKE THIS?
THOOM
BOOM
NGH?!
BOOM
...WHAT ?!
BOOM

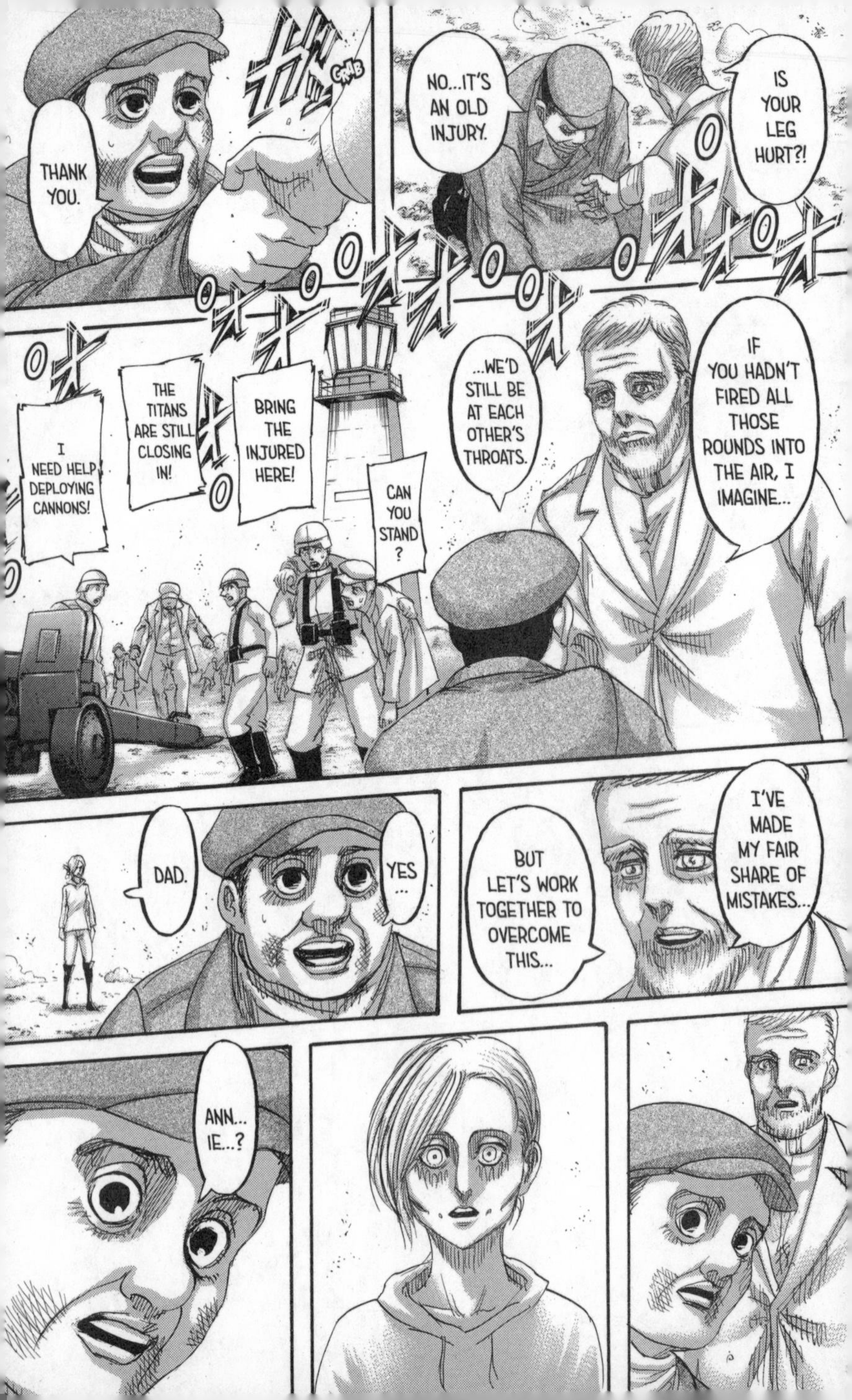
IS YOUR LEG HURT?!
NO...IT'S AN OLD INJURY.
GRAB
THANK YOU.
IF YOU HADN'T FIRED ALL THOSE ROUNDS INTO THE AIR, I IMAGINE...
...WE'D STILL BE AT EACH OTHER'S THROATS.
CAN YOU STAND?
BRING THE INJURED HERE!
THE TITANS ARE STILL CLOSING IN!
I NEED HELP DEPLOYING CANNONS!
I'VE MADE MY FAIR SHARE OF MISTAKES...
BUT LET'S WORK TOGETHER TO OVERCOME THIS...
YES...
DAD.
ANN... IE...?

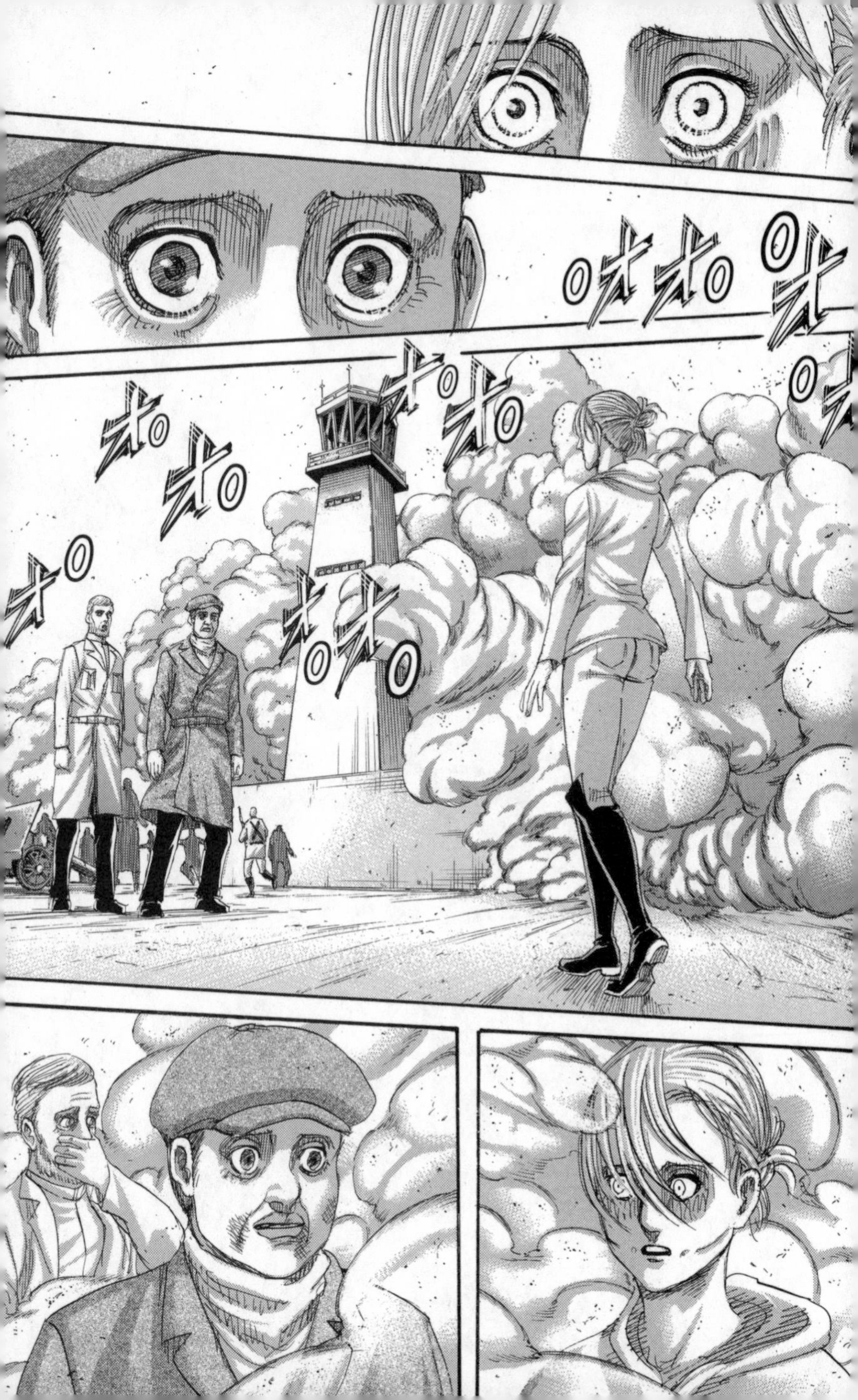
オオオオ
オオオオ
オオオ
オオオ
オオ

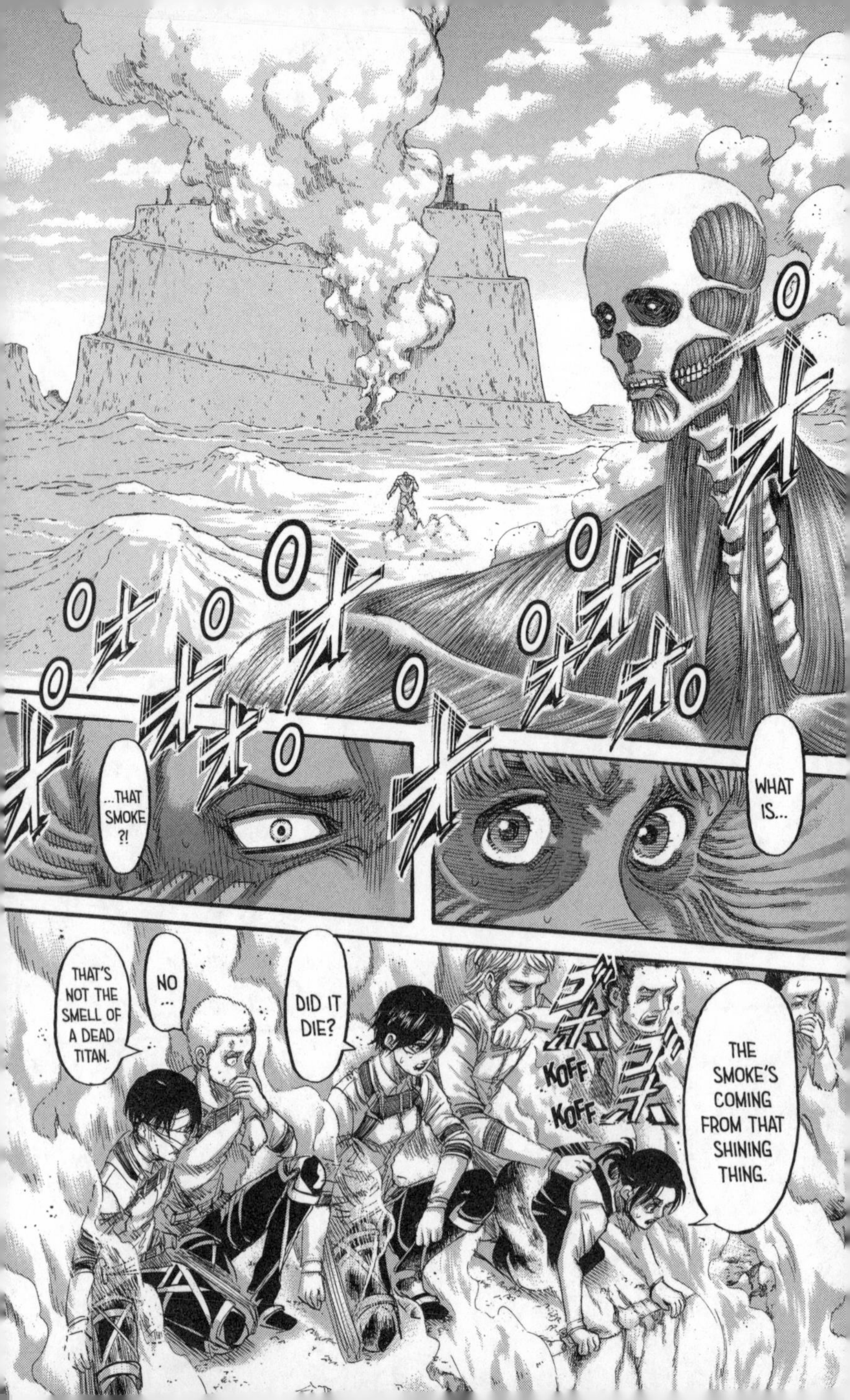
WHAT IS...
...THAT SMOKE ?!
THE SMOKE'S COMING FROM THAT SHINING THING.
KOFF
KOFF
DID IT DIE?
NO ...
THAT'S NOT THE SMELL OF A DEAD TITAN.

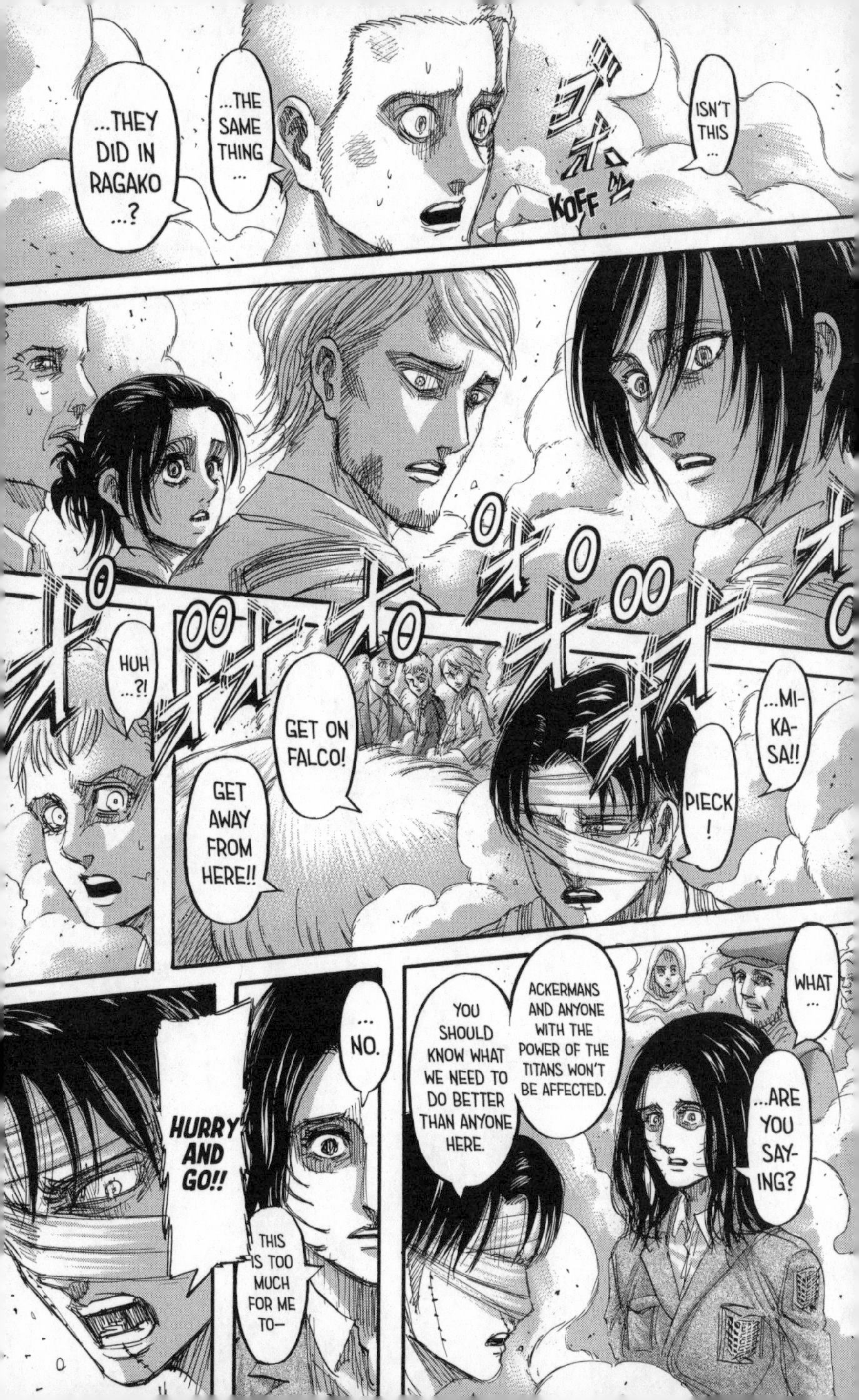
ISN'T THIS ...
KOFF
...THE SAME THING ...
...THEY DID IN RAGAKO ...?
...MI-KA-SA!!
PIECK!
GET ON FALCO!
GET AWAY FROM HERE!!
HUH ?!
WHAT ...
...ARE YOU SAY-ING?
ACKERMANS AND ANYONE WITH THE POWER OF THE TITANS WON'T BE AFFECTED.
YOU SHOULD KNOW WHAT WE NEED TO DO BETTER THAN ANYONE HERE.
... NO.
THIS IS TOO MUCH FOR ME TO—
HURRY AND GO!!

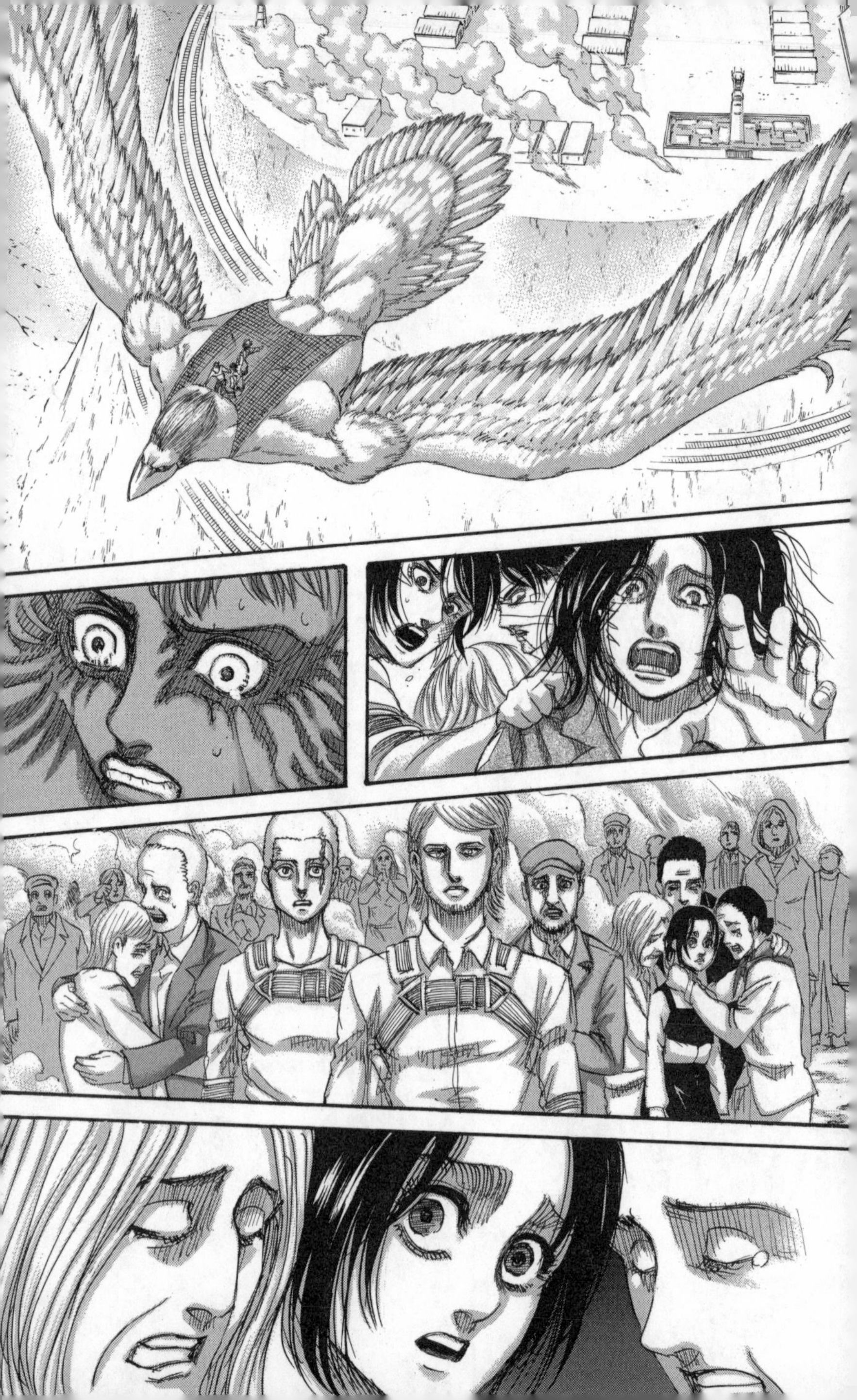

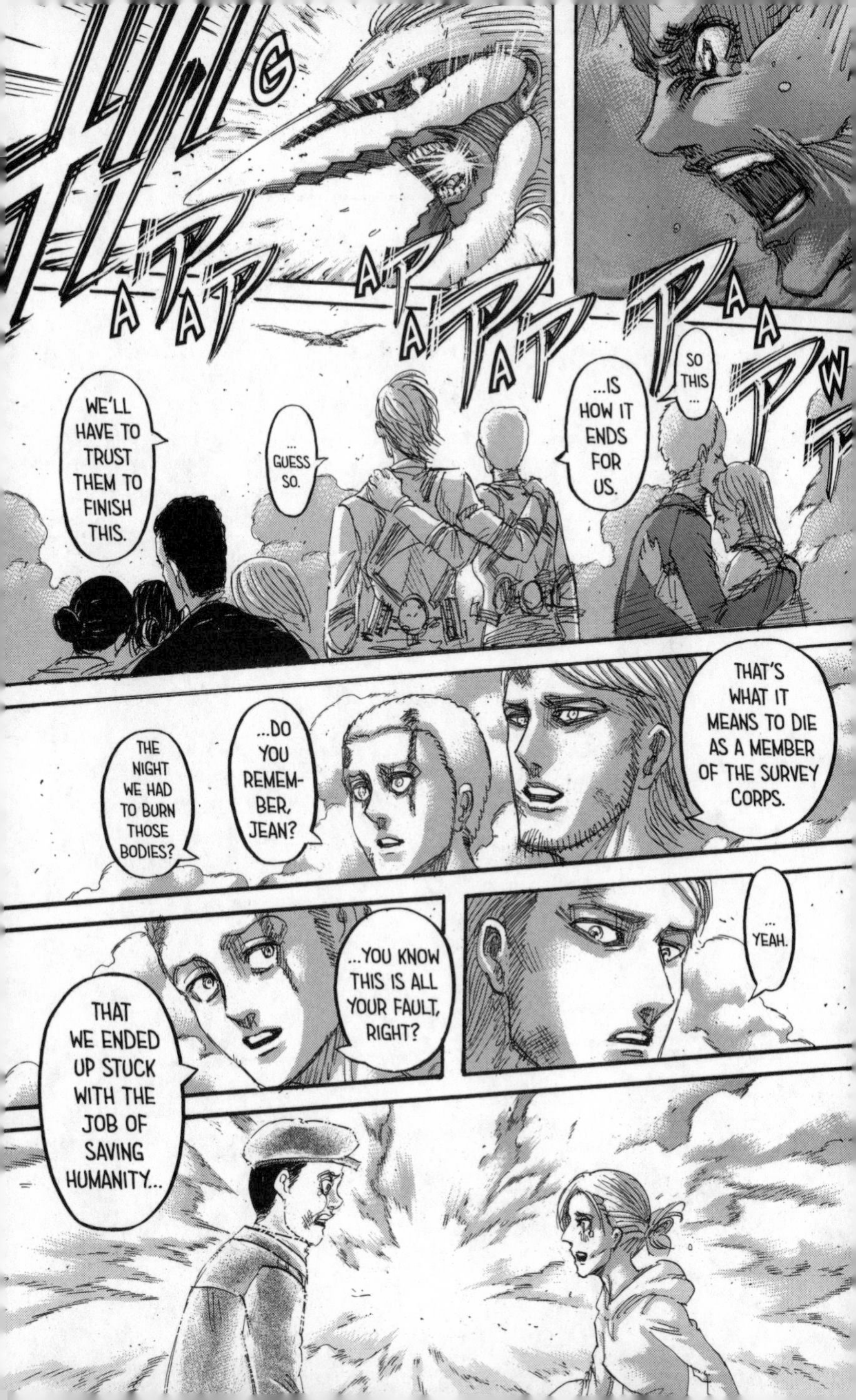
SO THIS...
...IS HOW IT ENDS FOR US.
...GUESS SO.
WE'LL HAVE TO TRUST THEM TO FINISH THIS.
THAT'S WHAT IT MEANS TO DIE AS A MEMBER OF THE SURVEY CORPS.
...DO YOU REMEMBER, JEAN?
THE NIGHT WE HAD TO BURN THOSE BODIES?
...YEAH.
...YOU KNOW THIS IS ALL YOUR FAULT, RIGHT?
THAT WE ENDED UP STUCK WITH THE JOB OF SAVING HUMANITY...

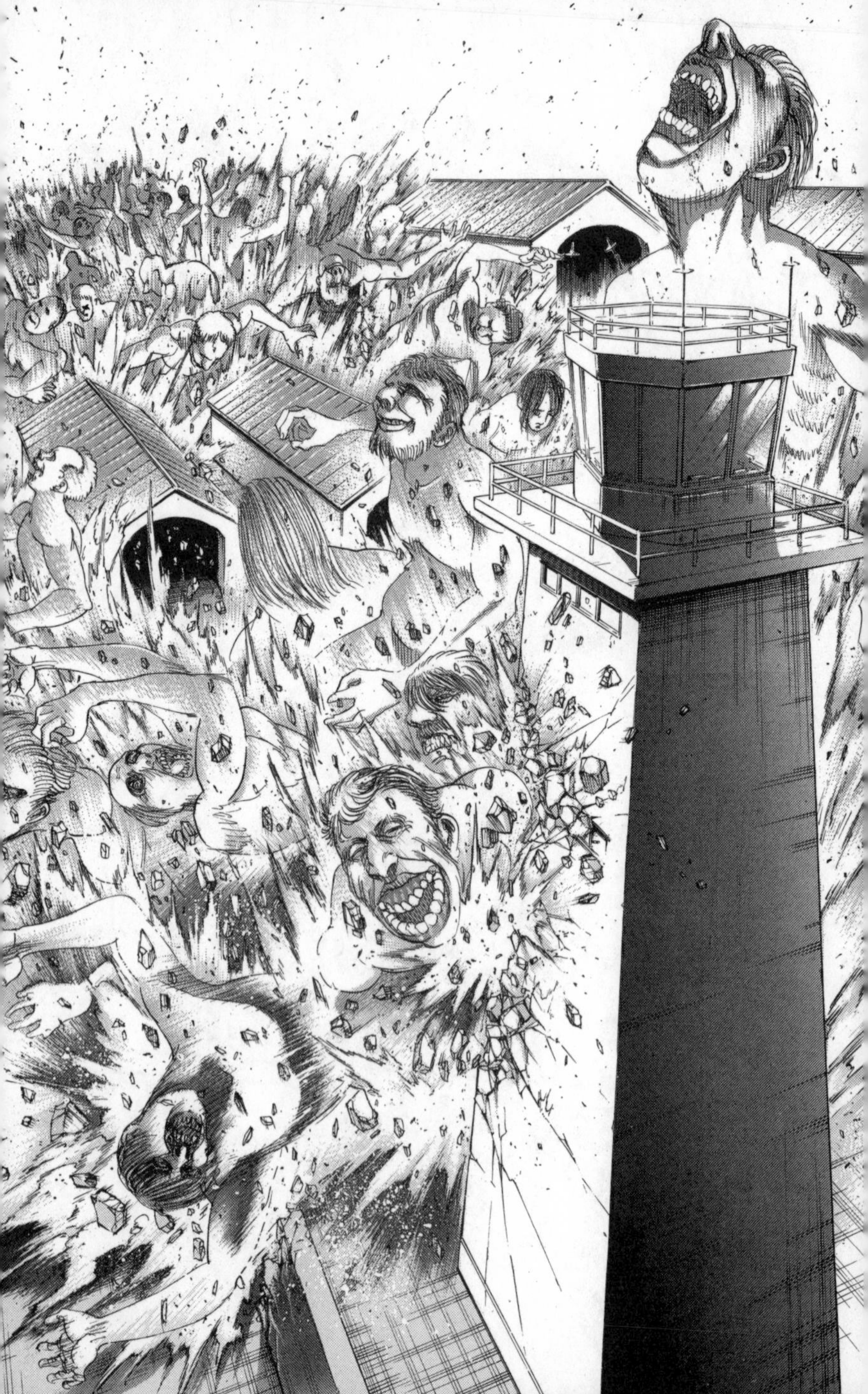

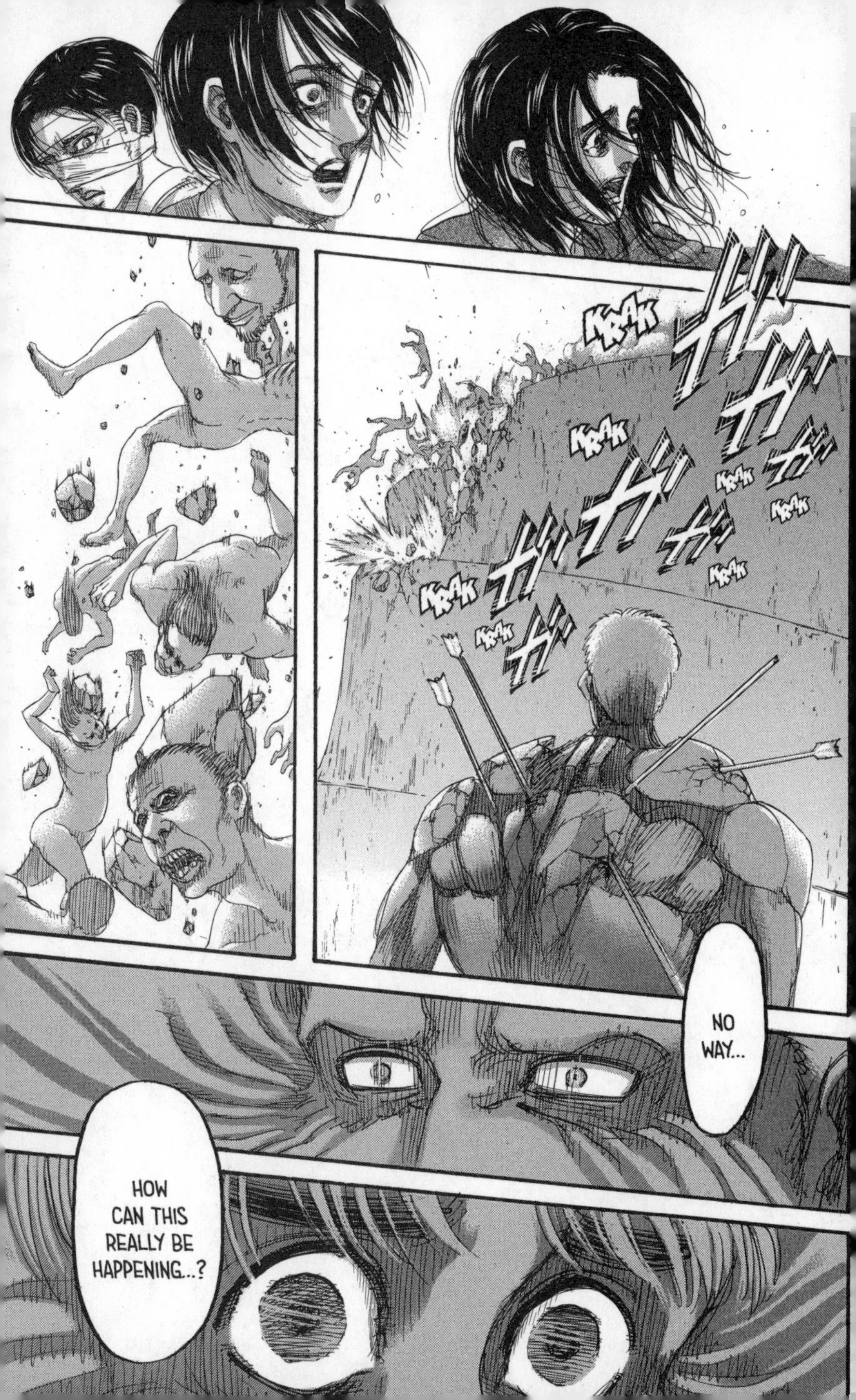
KRAK
KRAK
KRAK
KRAK
KRAK
KRAK
KRAK
NO WAY...
HOW CAN THIS REALLY BE HAPPENING...?

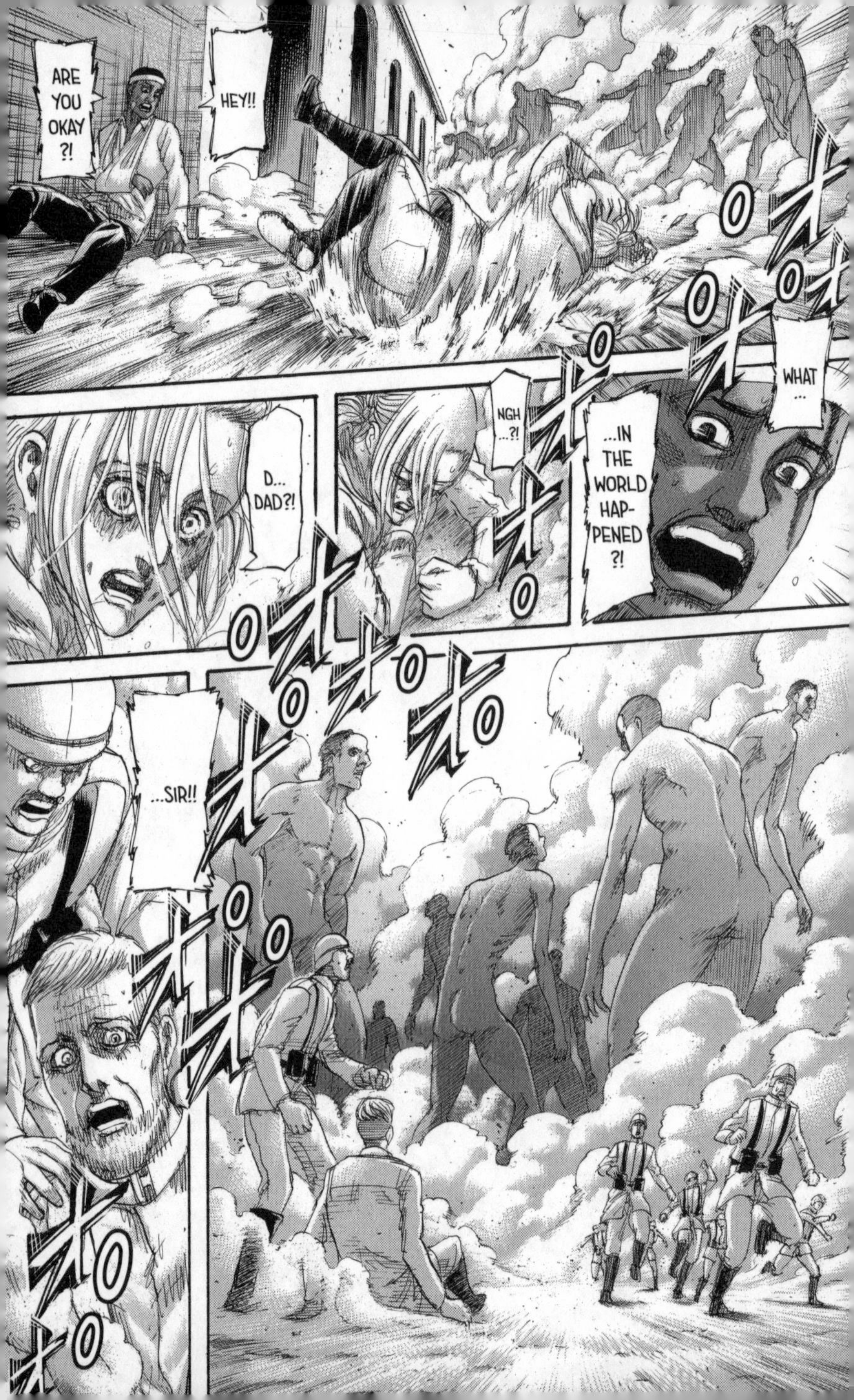
HEY!!
ARE YOU OKAY?!
WHAT...
...IN THE WORLD HAPPENED?!
NGH...?!
D... DAD?!
...SIR!!

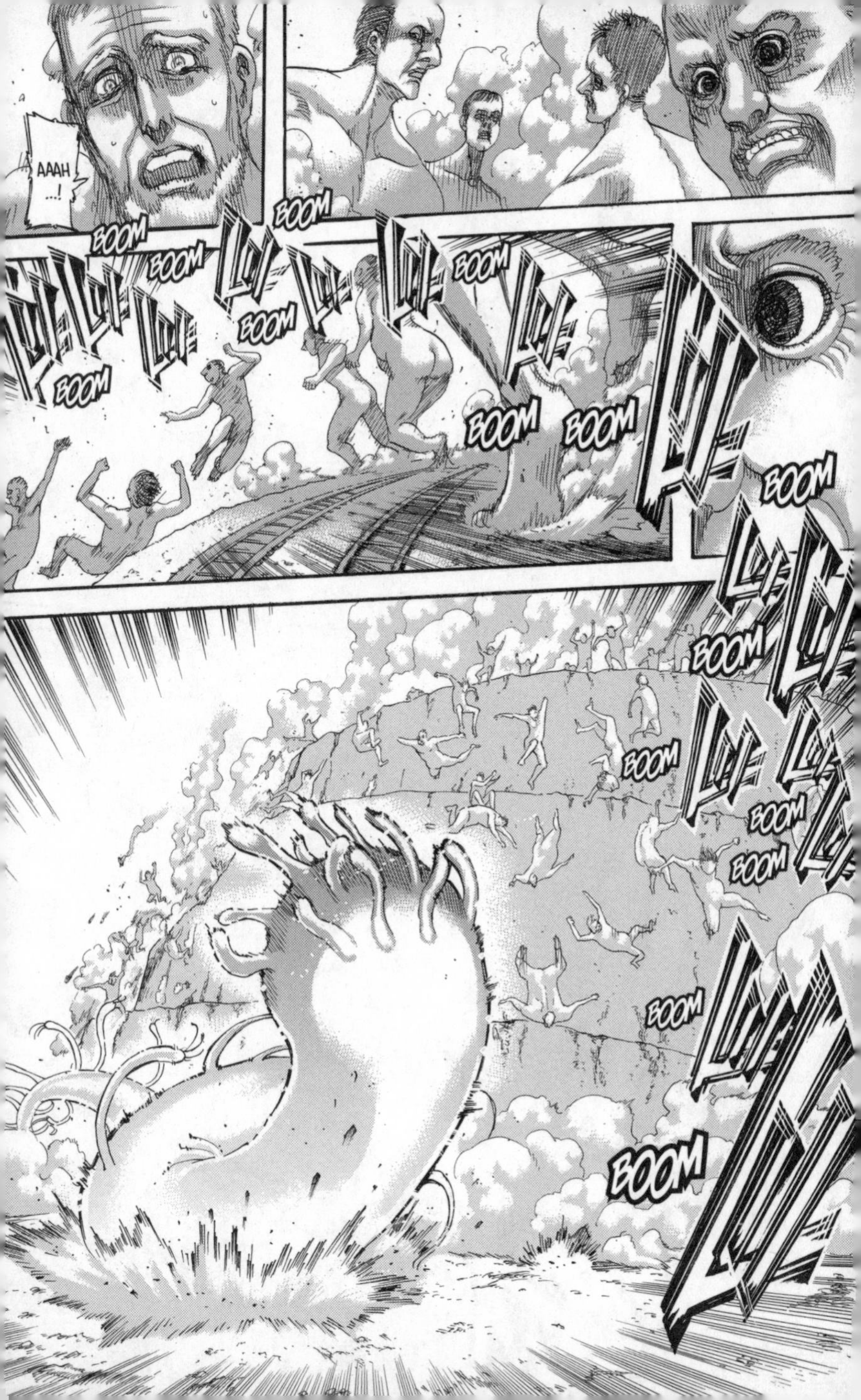
AAAH ...!
BOOM
BOOM
BOOM
BOOM
BOOM
BOOM
BOOM
BOOM
BOOM
BOOM
BOOM
BOOM
BOOM
BOOM
BOOM
BOOM
BOOM

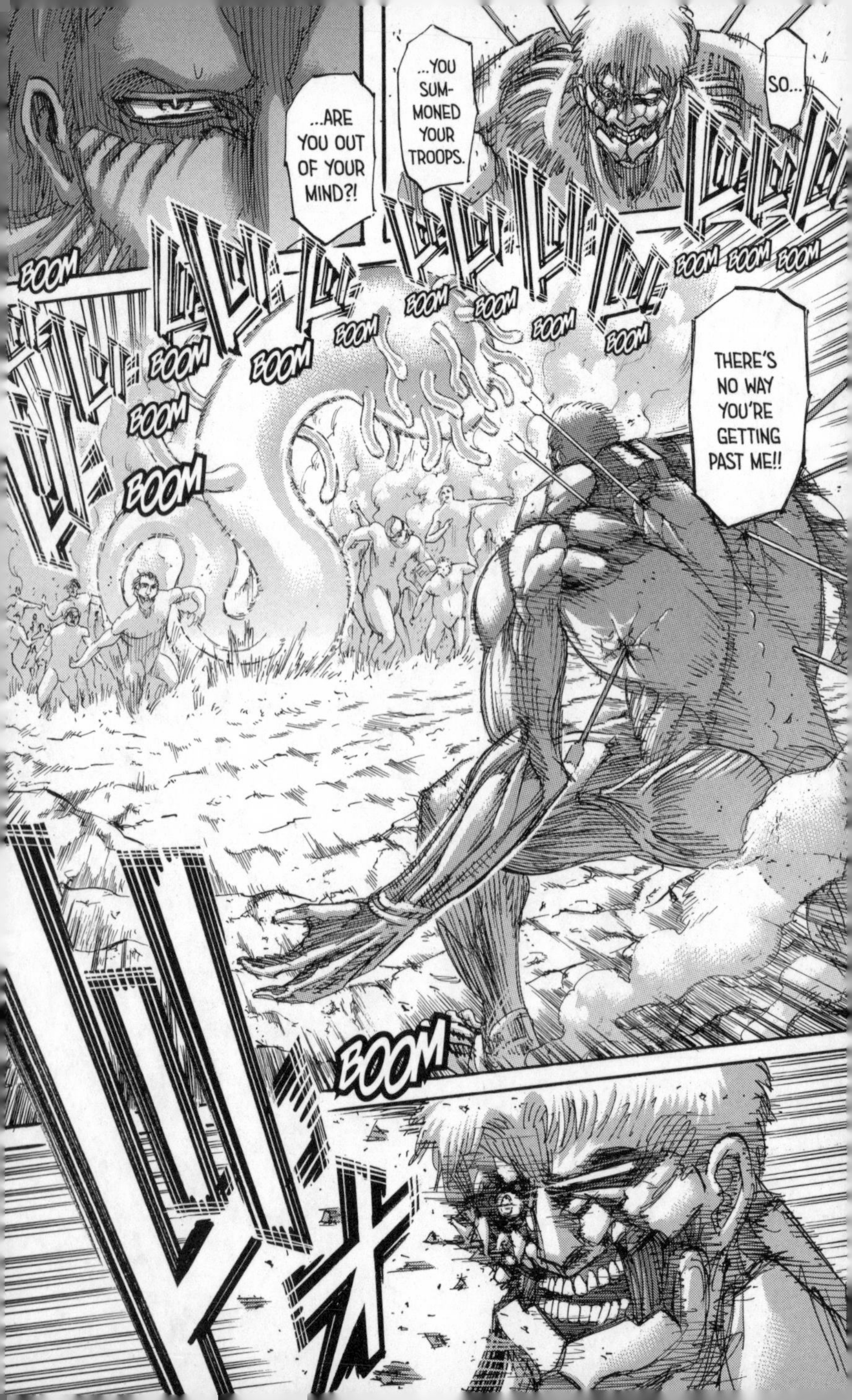
SO...
...YOU SUMMONED YOUR TROOPS.
...ARE YOU OUT OF YOUR MIND?!
BOOM BOOM BOOM
BOOM
BOOM
BOOM
BOOM
BOOM
BOOM
BOOM
BOOM
BOOM
BOOM
THERE'S NO WAY YOU'RE GETTING PAST ME!!
BOOM

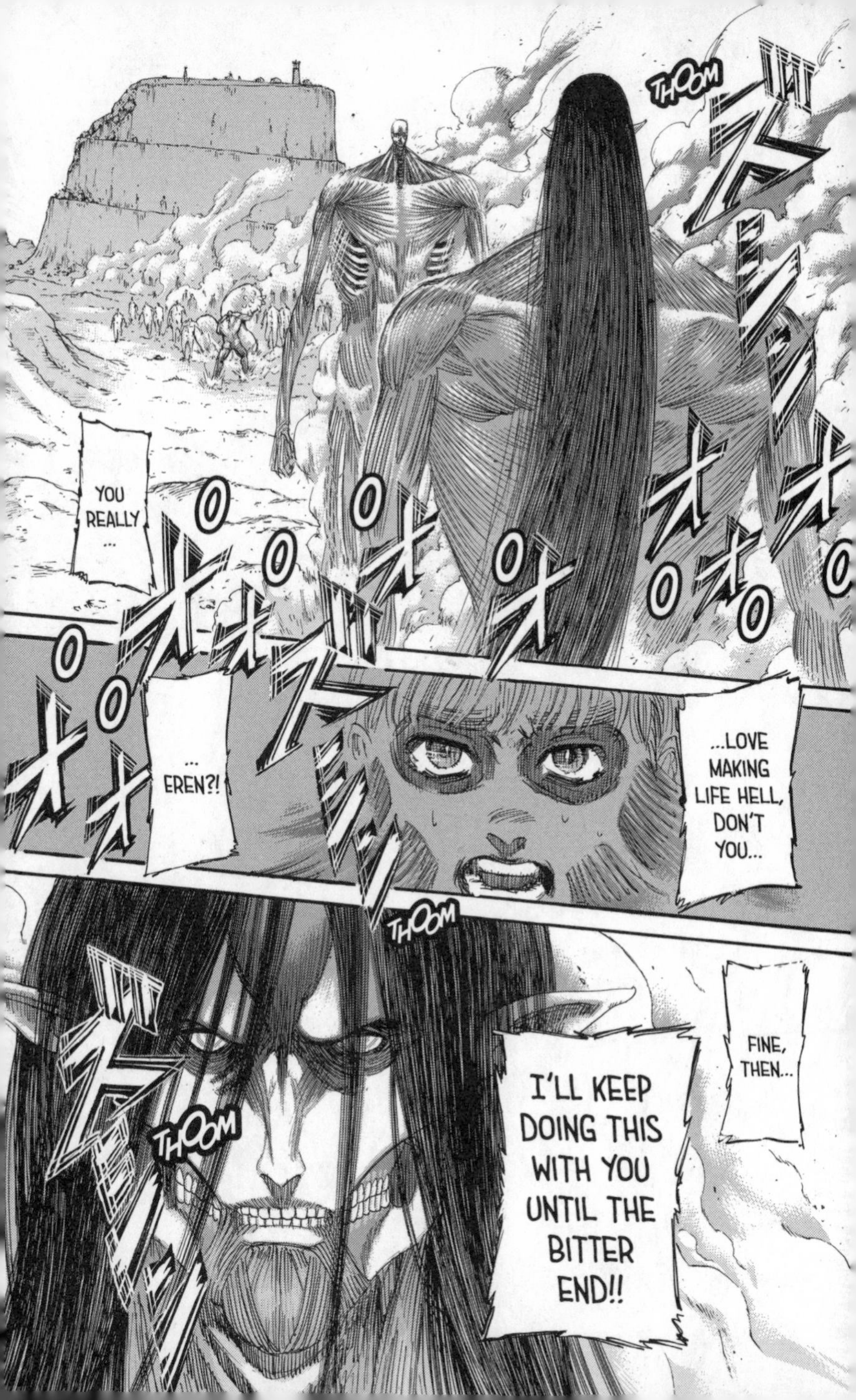
THOOM
YOU REALLY ...
...LOVE MAKING LIFE HELL, DON'T YOU...
... EREN?!
THOOM
FINE, THEN...
I'LL KEEP DOING THIS WITH YOU UNTIL THE BITTER END!!
THOOM

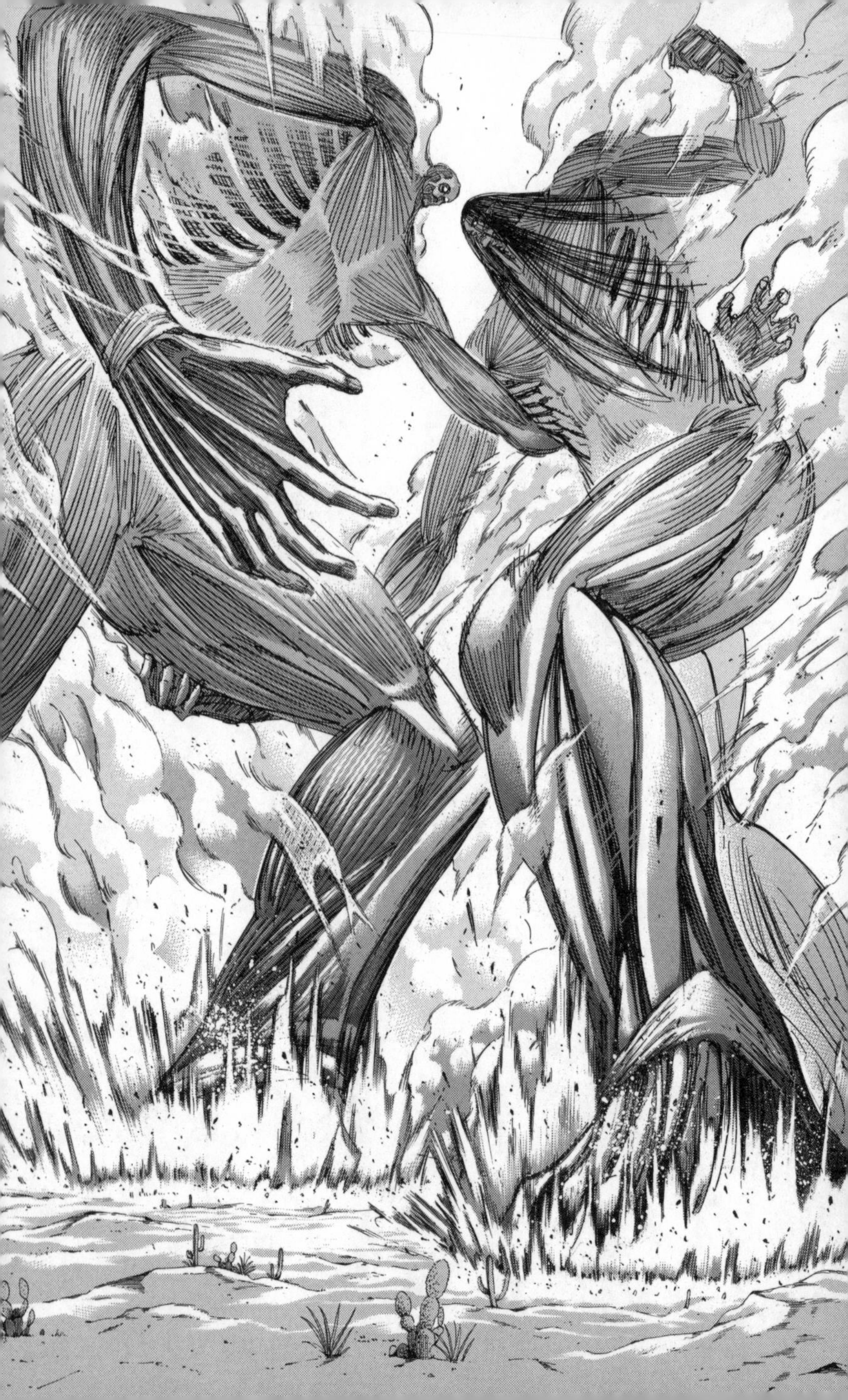

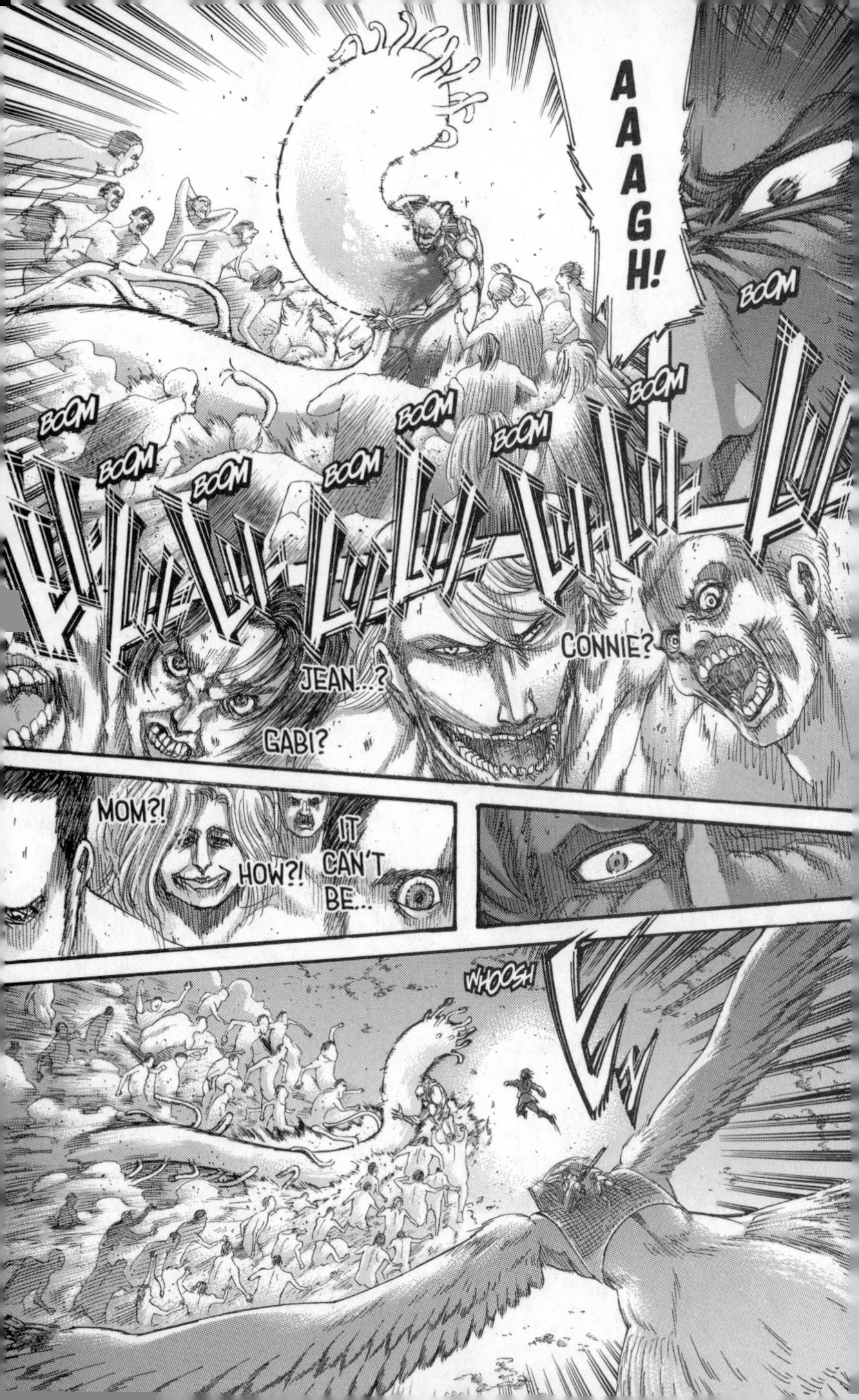
AAAGH!
BOOM
BOOM
BOOM
BOOM
BOOM
BOOM
BOOM
BOOM
CONNIE?
JEAN...?
GABI?
IT CAN'T BE...
HOW?!
MOM?!
WHOOSH

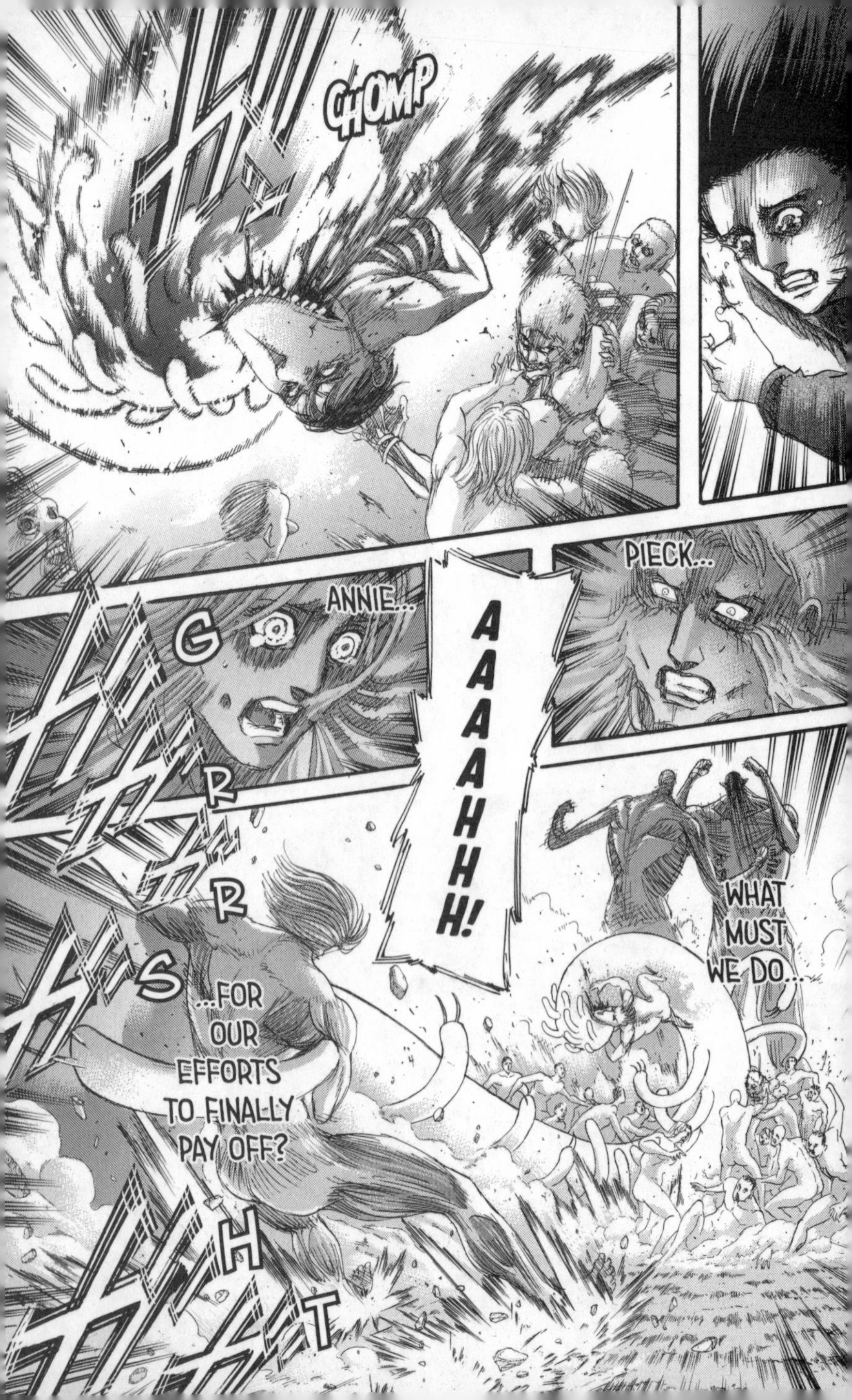
CHOMP
PIECK...
AAAAHHH!
ANNIE...
GRRSHHT
WHAT MUST WE DO...
...FOR OUR EFFORTS TO FINALLY PAY OFF?

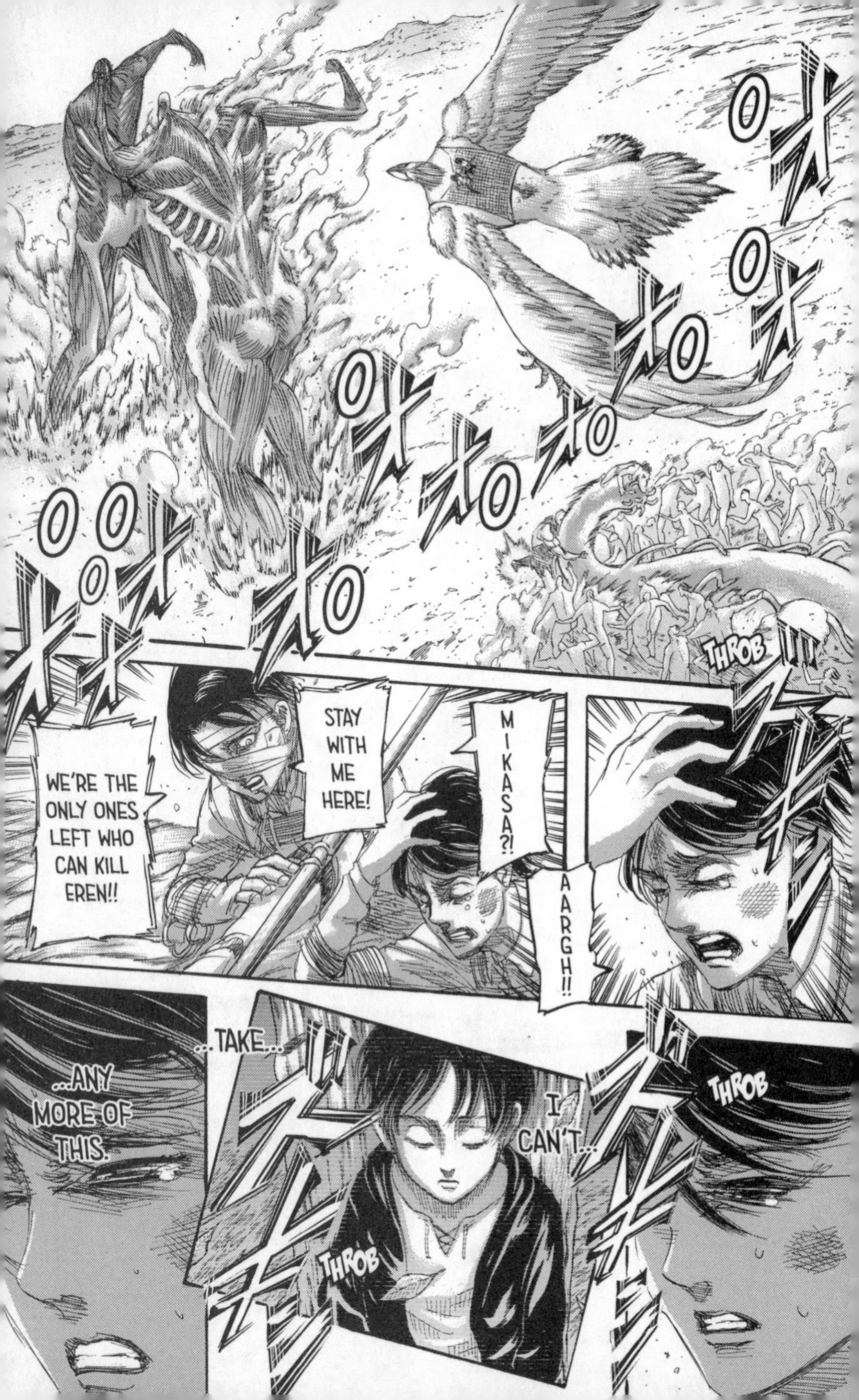
THROB
AARGH!!
MIKASA?!
STAY WITH ME HERE!
WE'RE THE ONLY ONES LEFT WHO CAN KILL EREN!!
THROB
I CAN'T...
...TAKE...
THROB
...ANY MORE OF THIS.

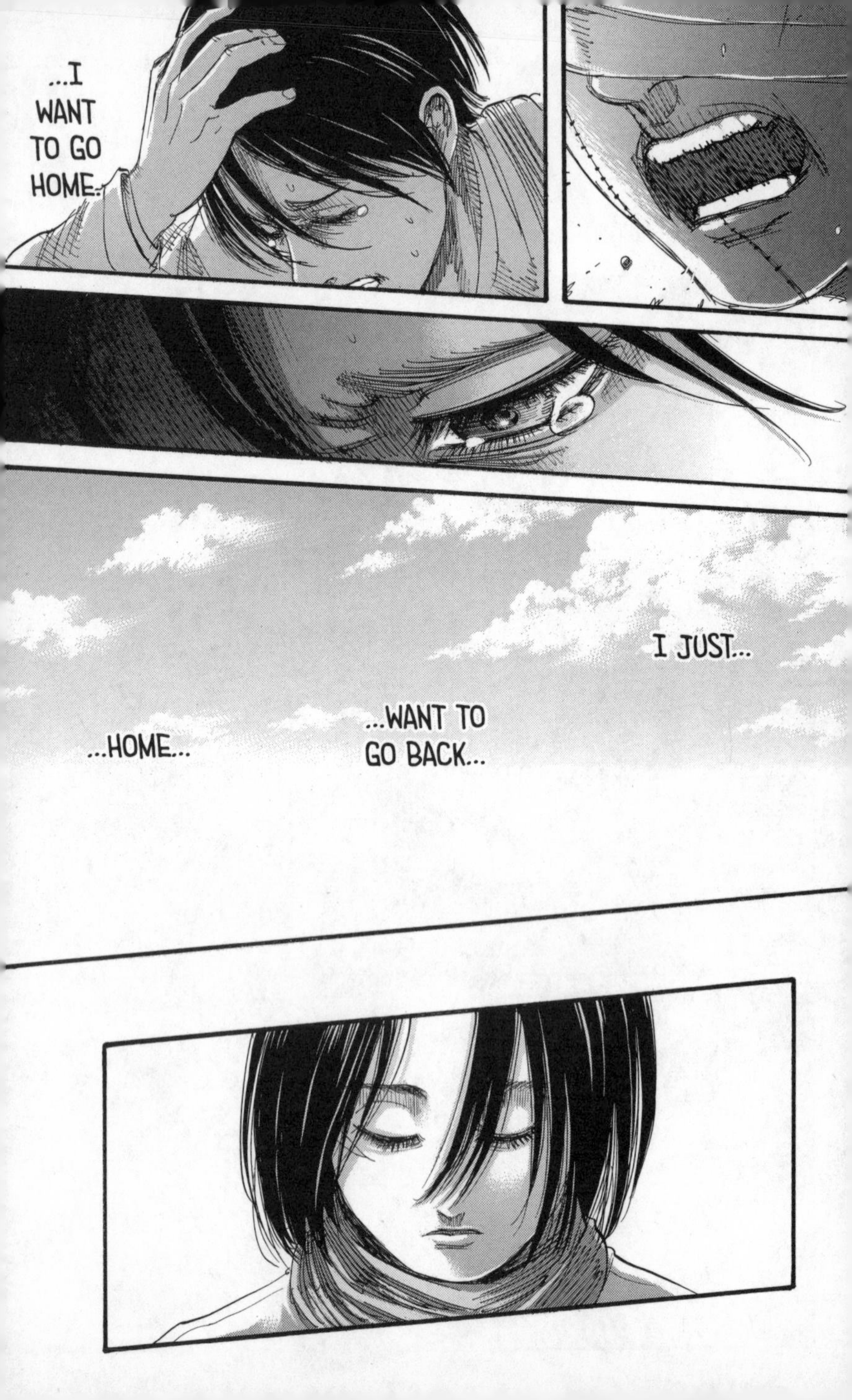
...I WANT TO GO HOME..
I JUST...
...WANT TO GO BACK...
...HOME...

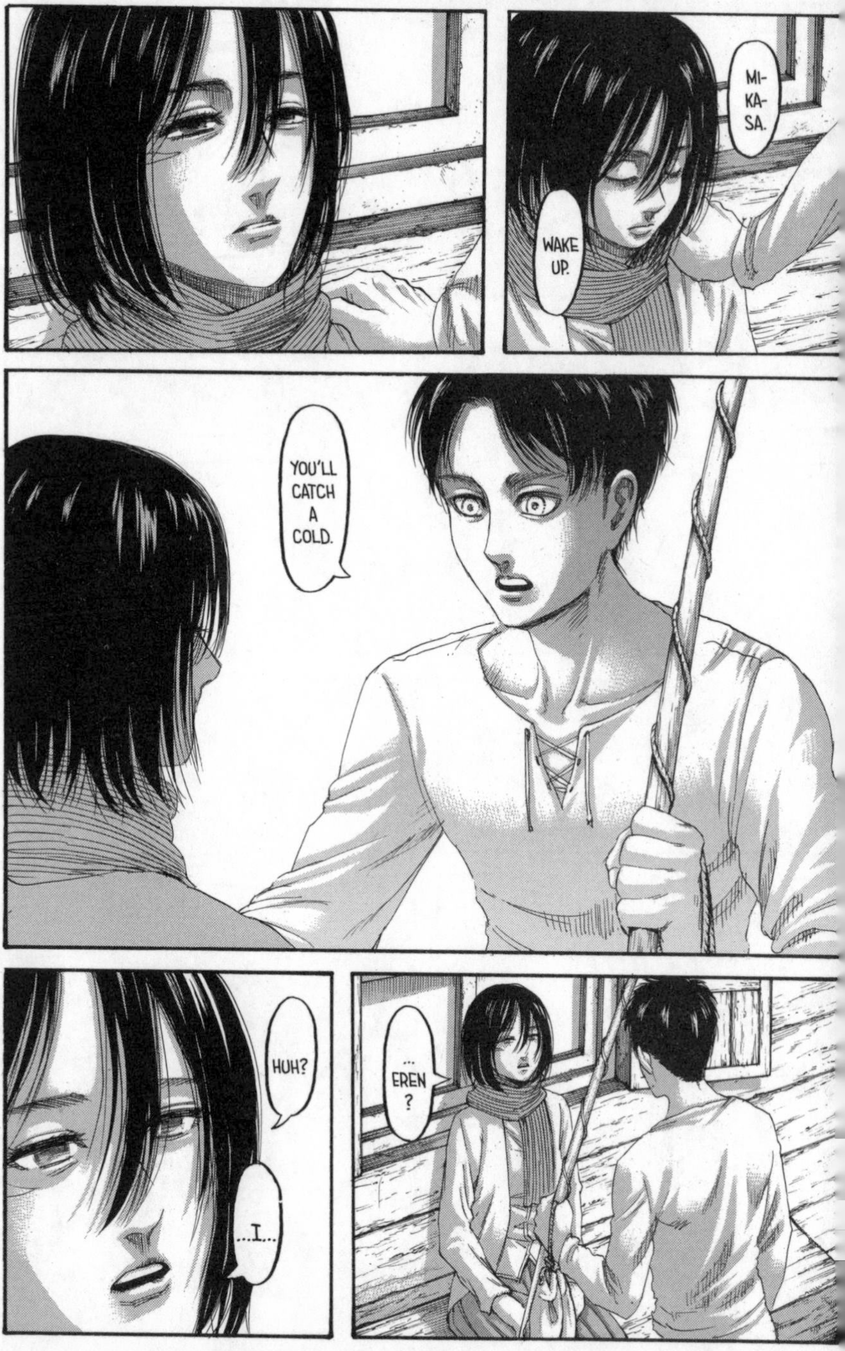
MI-KA-SA.
WAKE UP.
YOU'LL CATCH A COLD.
... EREN?
HUH?
...I...

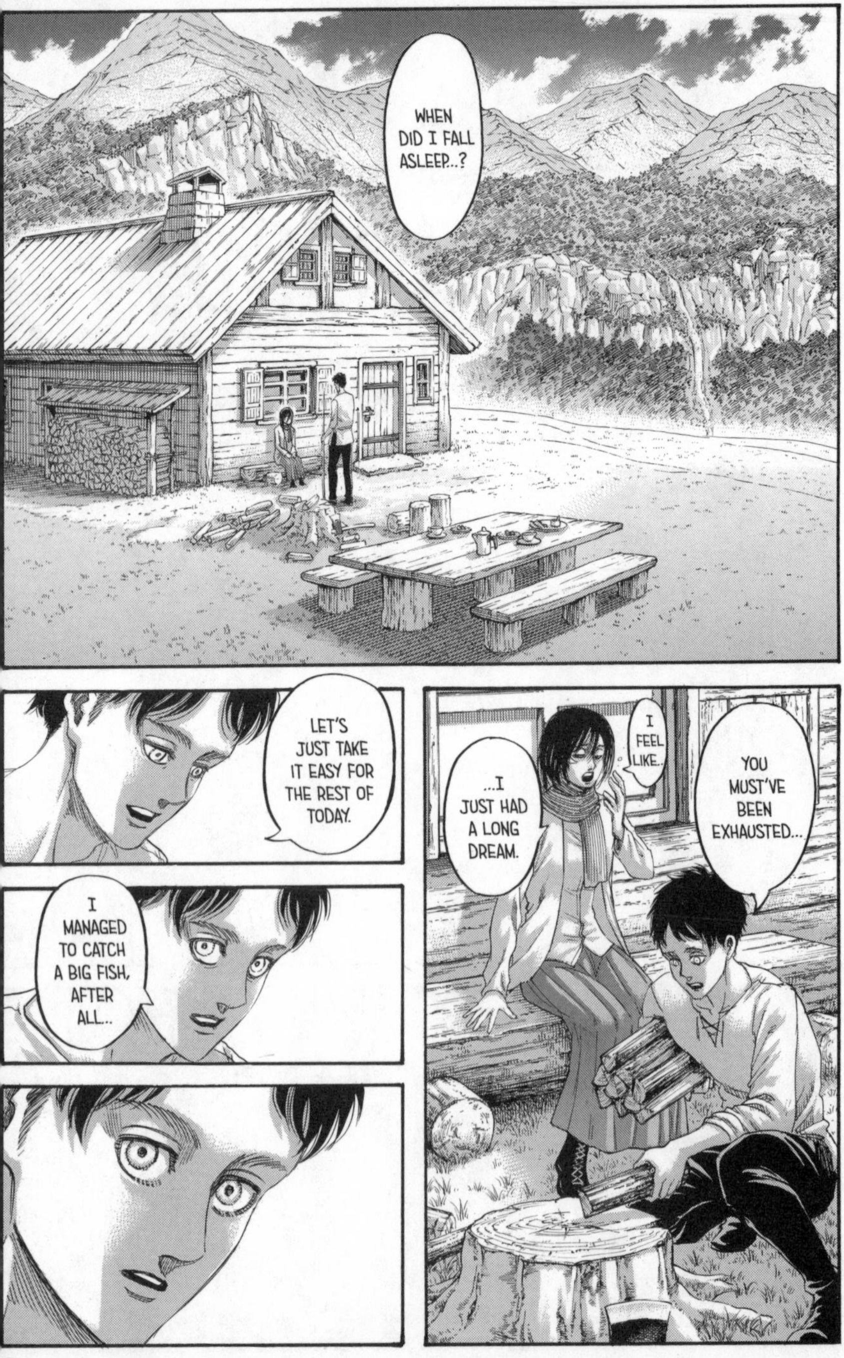
WHEN DID I FALL ASLEEP...?
I FEEL LIKE..
...I JUST HAD A LONG DREAM.
YOU MUST'VE BEEN EXHAUSTED...
LET'S JUST TAKE IT EASY FOR THE REST OF TODAY.
I MANAGED TO CATCH A BIG FISH, AFTER ALL...

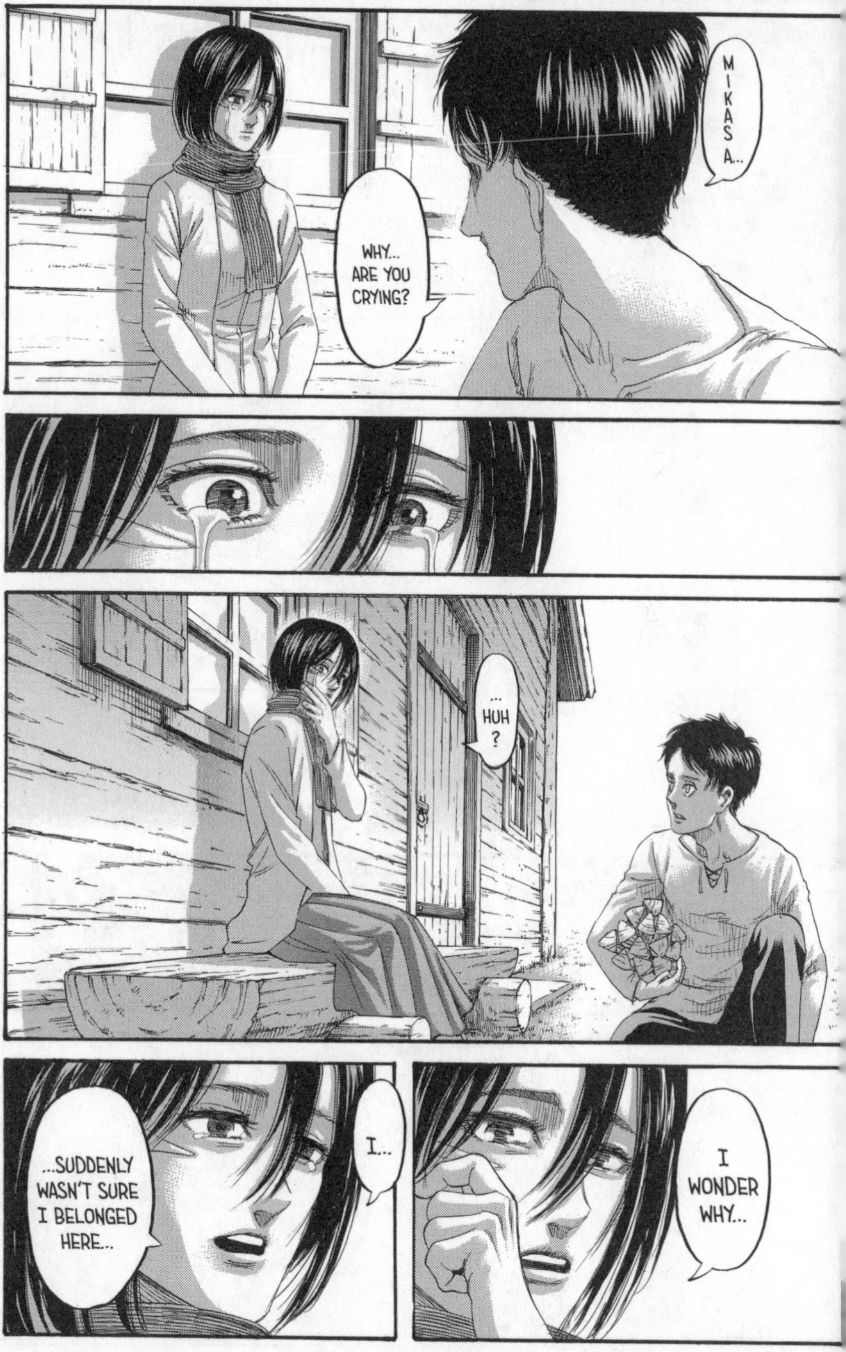
MIKASA...
WHY... ARE YOU CRYING?
...HUH?
I WONDER WHY...
I...
...SUDDENLY WASN'T SURE I BELONGED HERE...

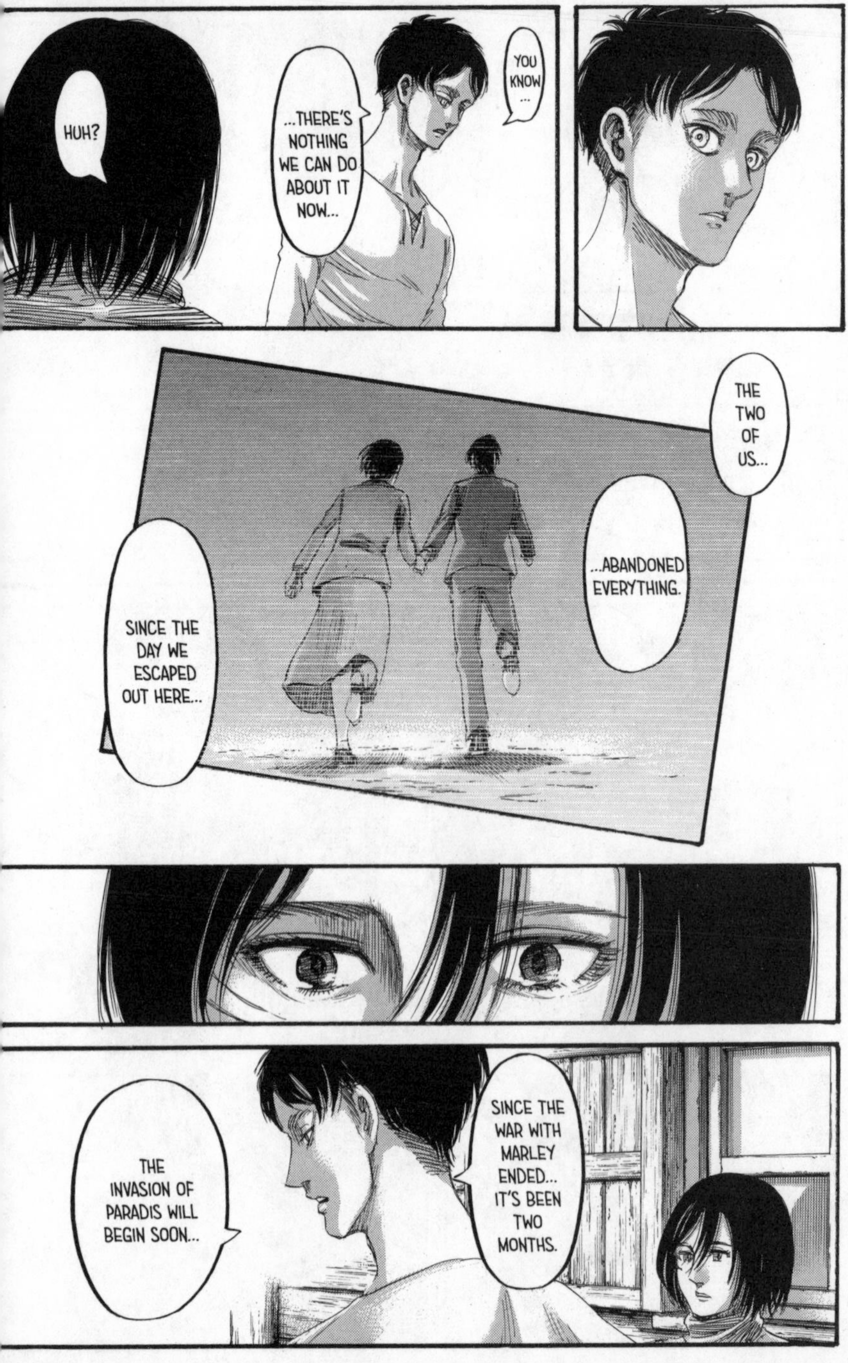
YOU KNOW...
...THERE'S NOTHING WE CAN DO ABOUT IT NOW...
HUH?
THE TWO OF US...
...ABANDONED EVERYTHING.
SINCE THE DAY WE ESCAPED OUT HERE...
SINCE THE WAR WITH MARLEY ENDED... IT'S BEEN TWO MONTHS.
THE INVASION OF PARADIS WILL BEGIN SOON...

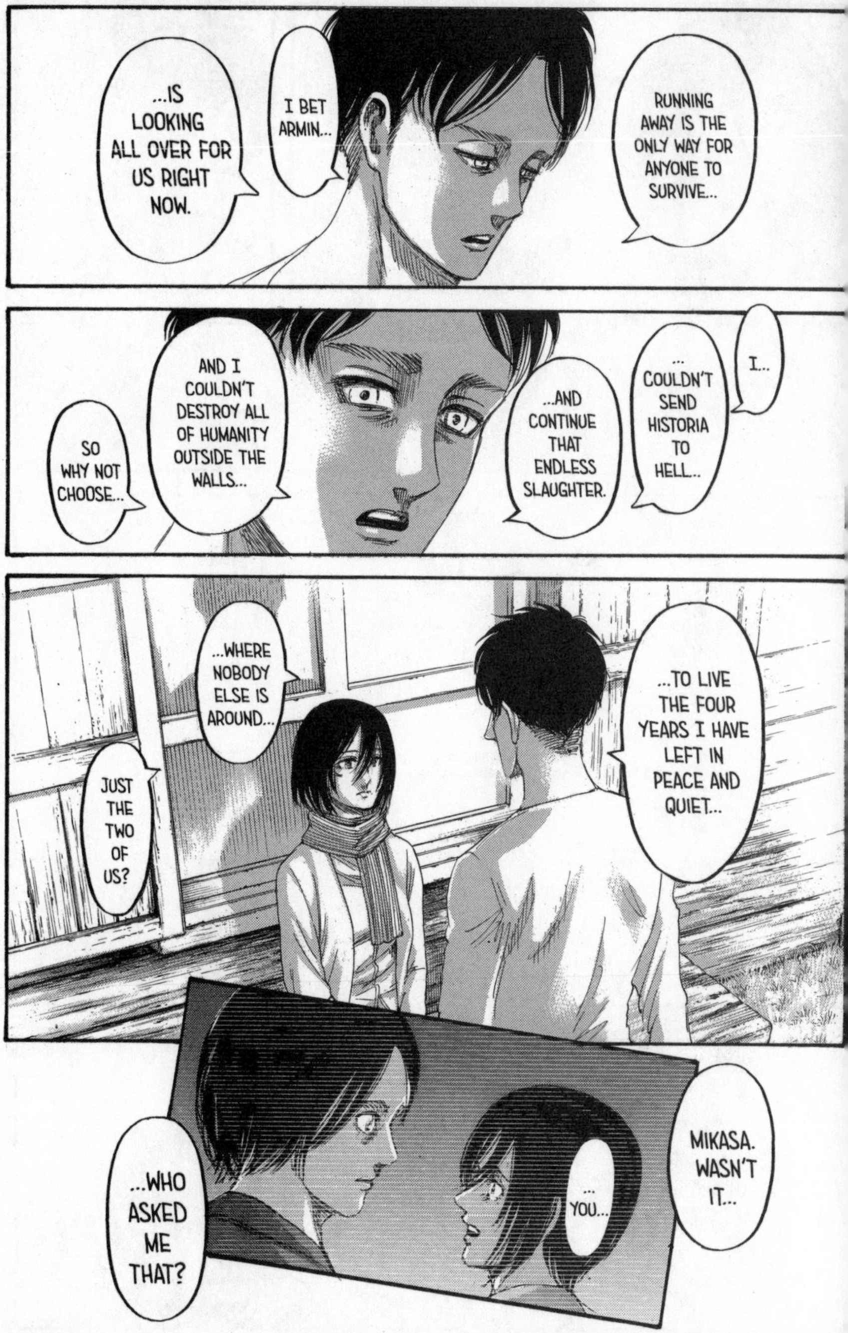
RUNNING AWAY IS THE ONLY WAY FOR ANYONE TO SURVIVE...
I BET ARMIN...
...IS LOOKING ALL OVER FOR US RIGHT NOW.
I...
... COULDN'T SEND HISTORIA TO HELL...
...AND CONTINUE THAT ENDLESS SLAUGHTER.
AND I COULDN'T DESTROY ALL OF HUMANITY OUTSIDE THE WALLS...
SO WHY NOT CHOOSE...
...TO LIVE THE FOUR YEARS I HAVE LEFT IN PEACE AND QUIET...
...WHERE NOBODY ELSE IS AROUND...
JUST THE TWO OF US?
MIKASA. WASN'T IT...
... YOU...
...WHO ASKED ME THAT?

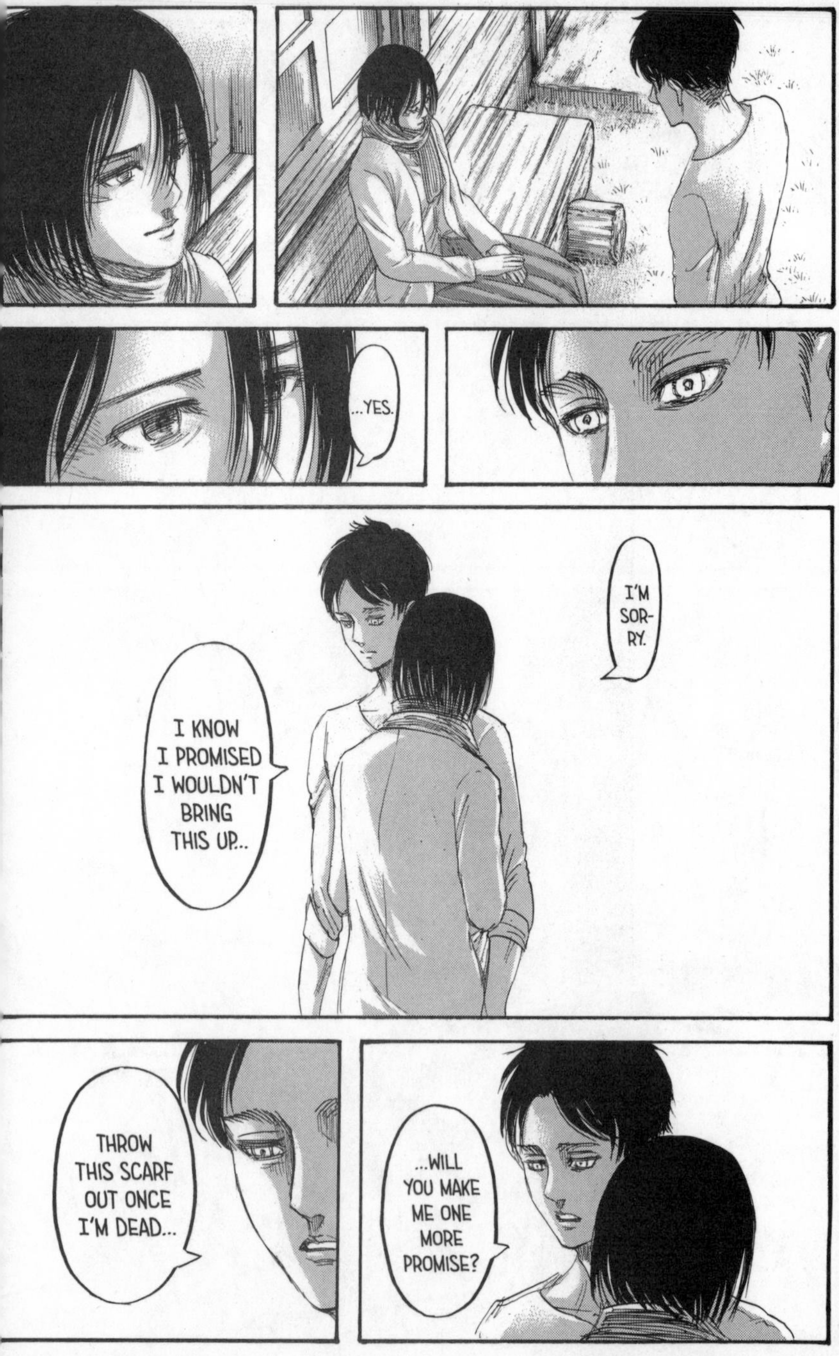
...YES.
I'M SOR-RY.
I KNOW I PROMISED I WOULDN'T BRING THIS UP...
...WILL YOU MAKE ME ONE MORE PROMISE?
THROW THIS SCARF OUT ONCE I'M DEAD...

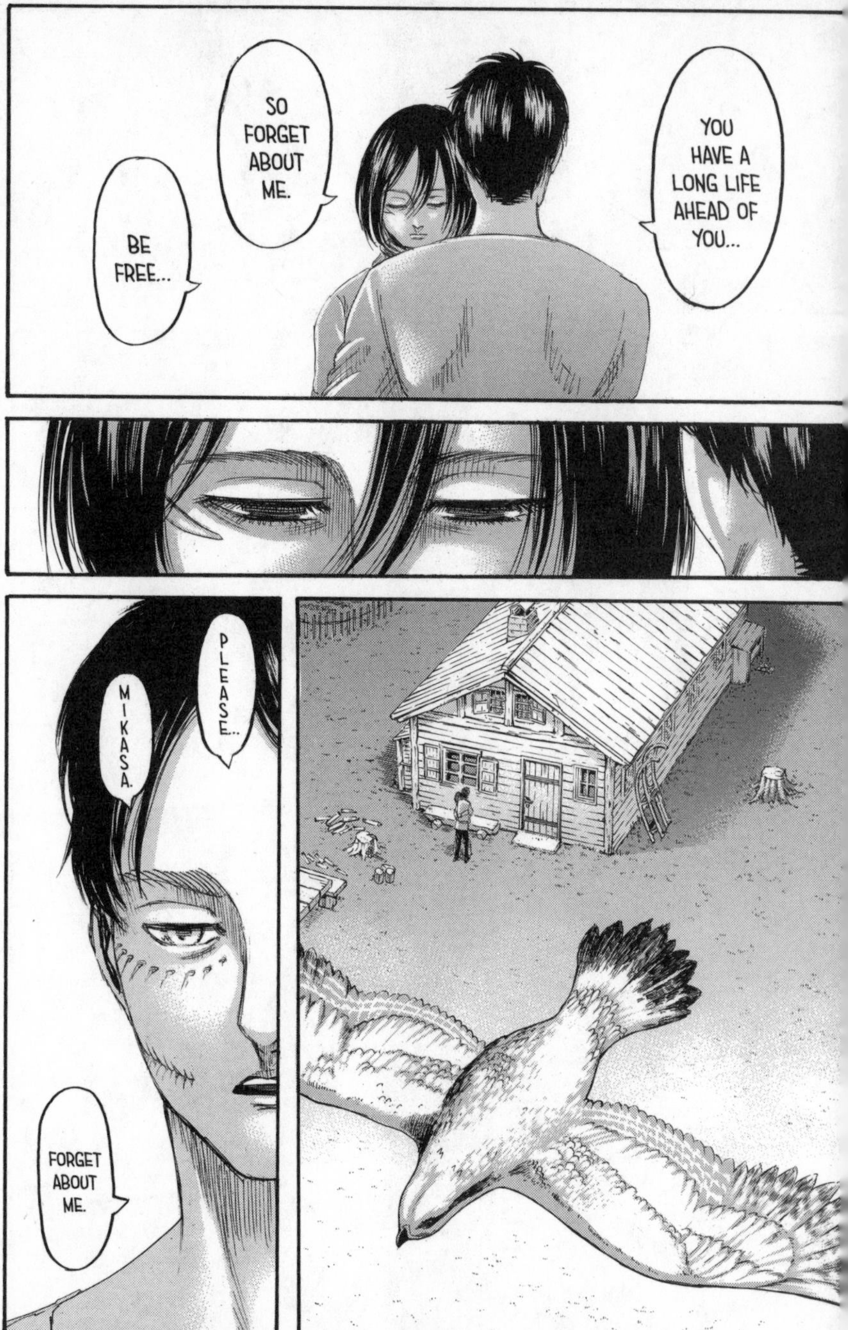
YOU HAVE A LONG LIFE AHEAD OF YOU...
SO FORGET ABOUT ME.
BE FREE...
PLEASE...
MIKASA.
FORGET ABOUT ME.

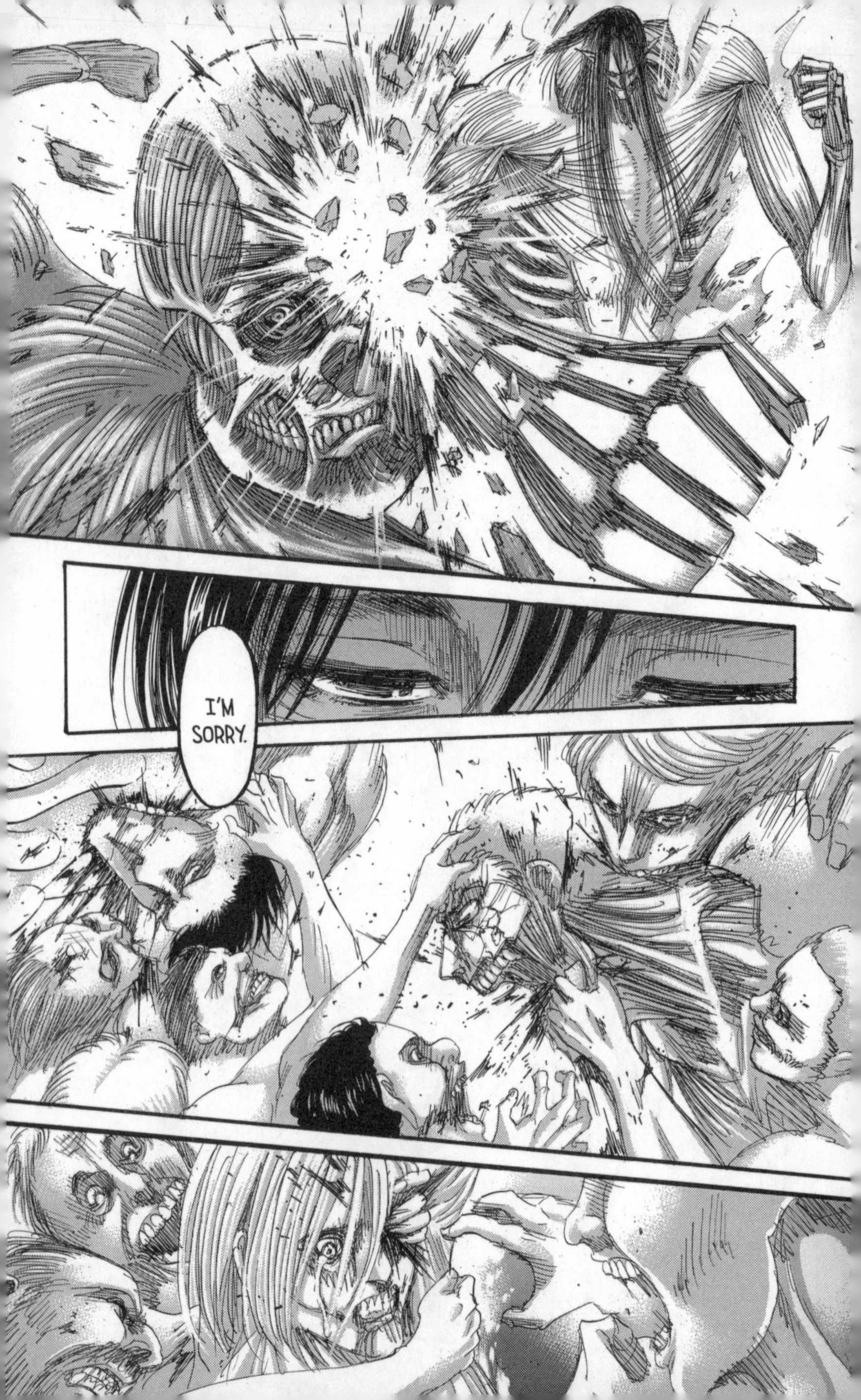
I'M SORRY.

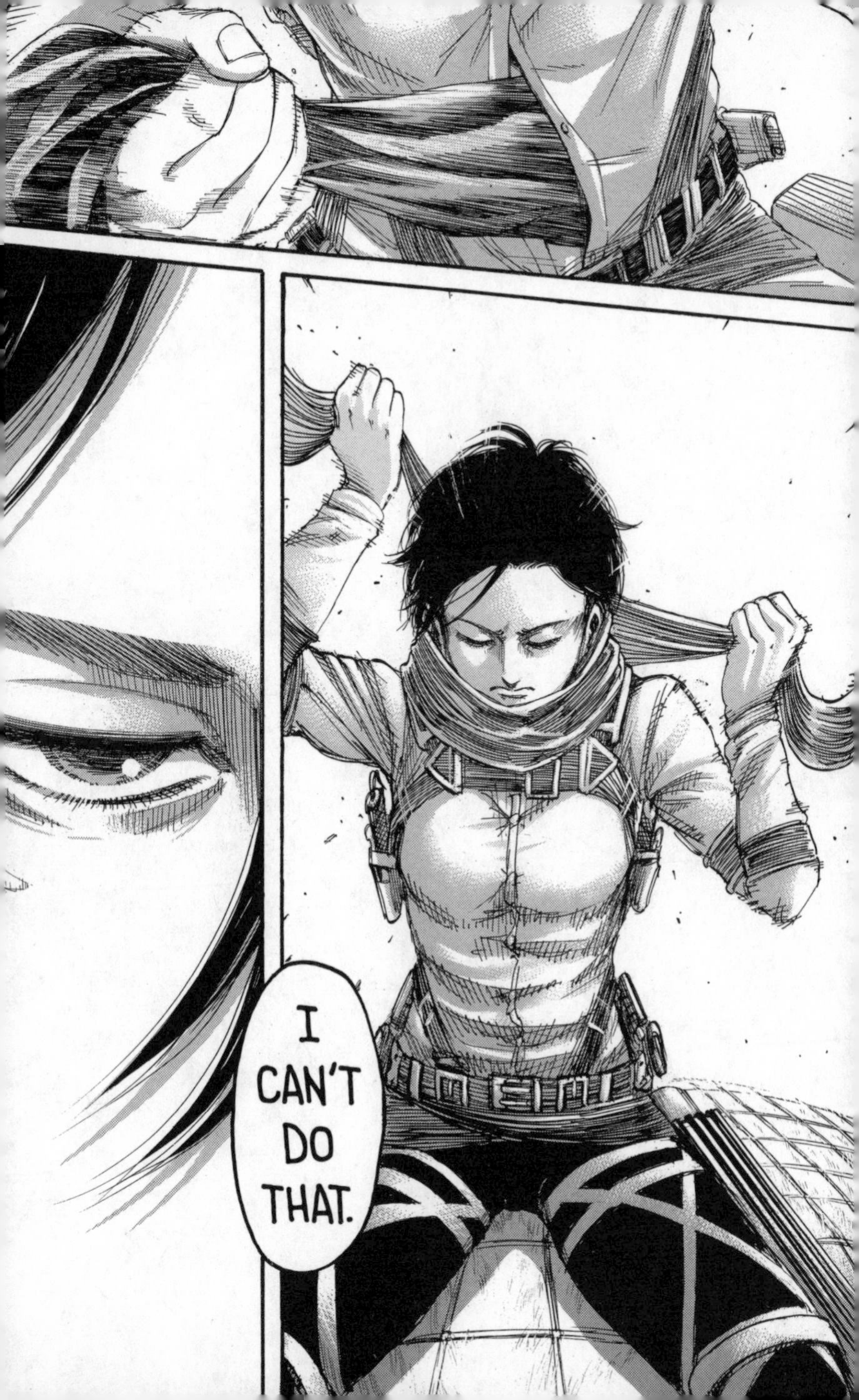
I CAN'T DO THAT.

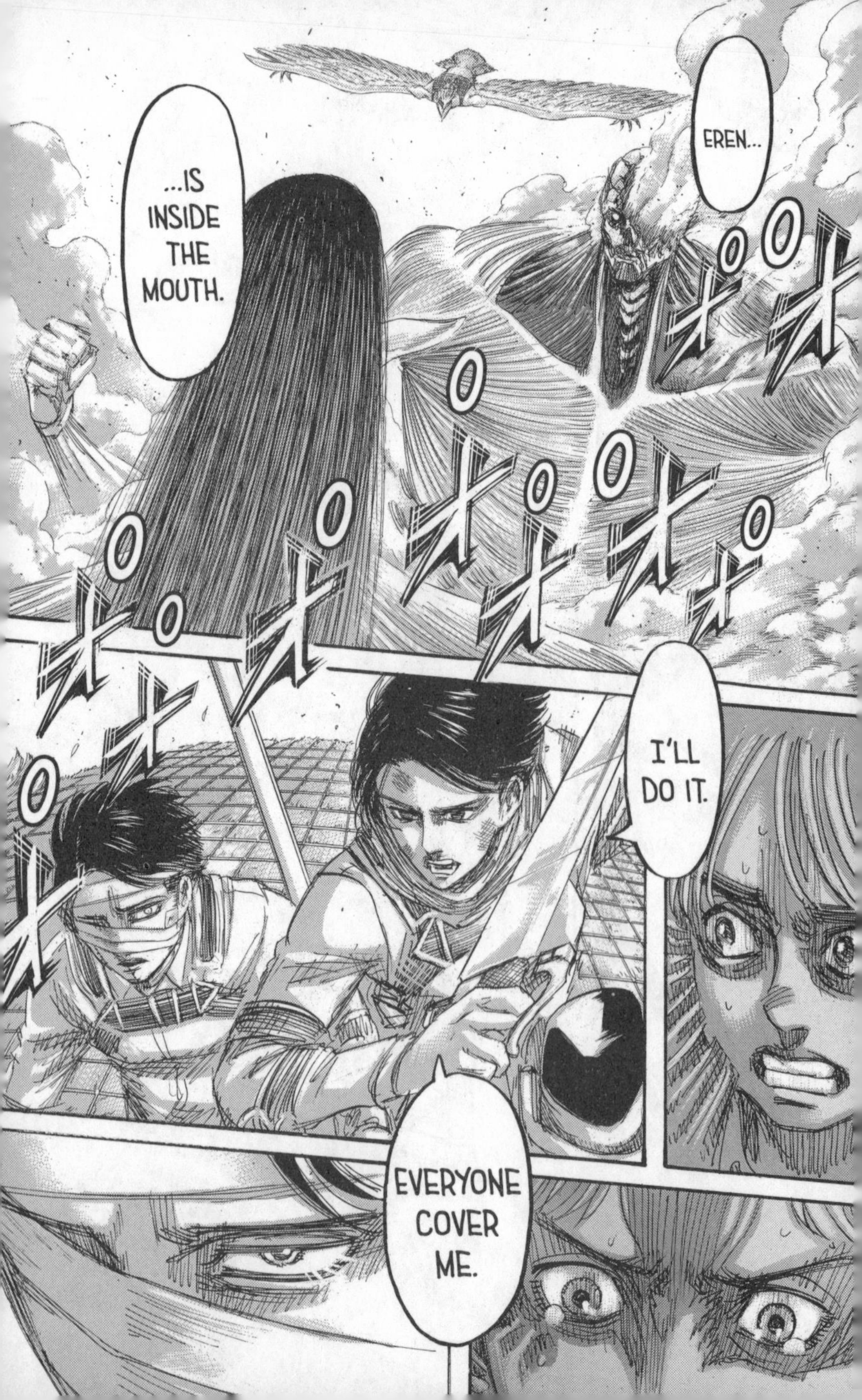
EREN...
...IS INSIDE THE MOUTH.
I'LL DO IT.
EVERYONE COVER ME.

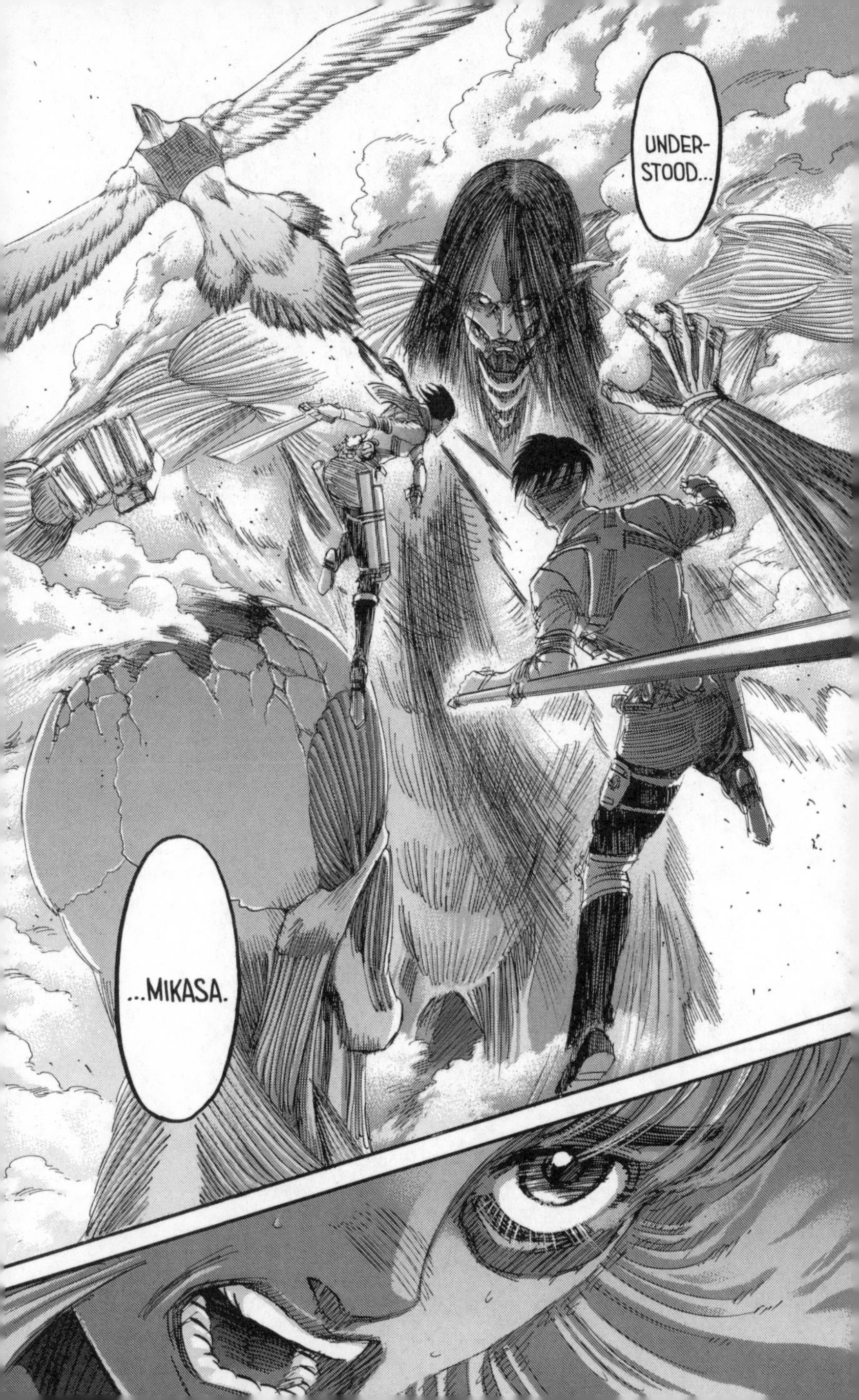
UNDER-STOOD...
...MIKASA.

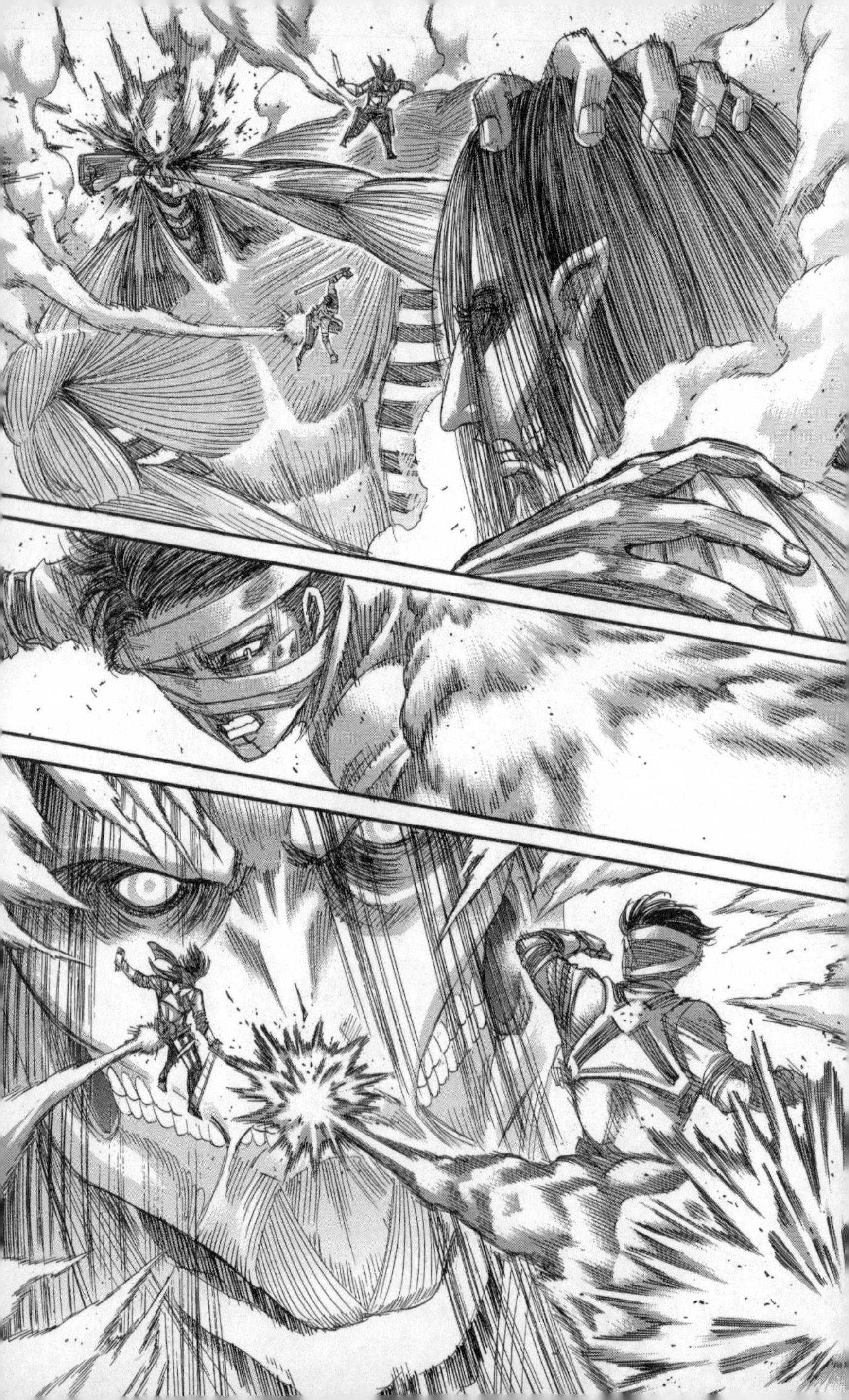

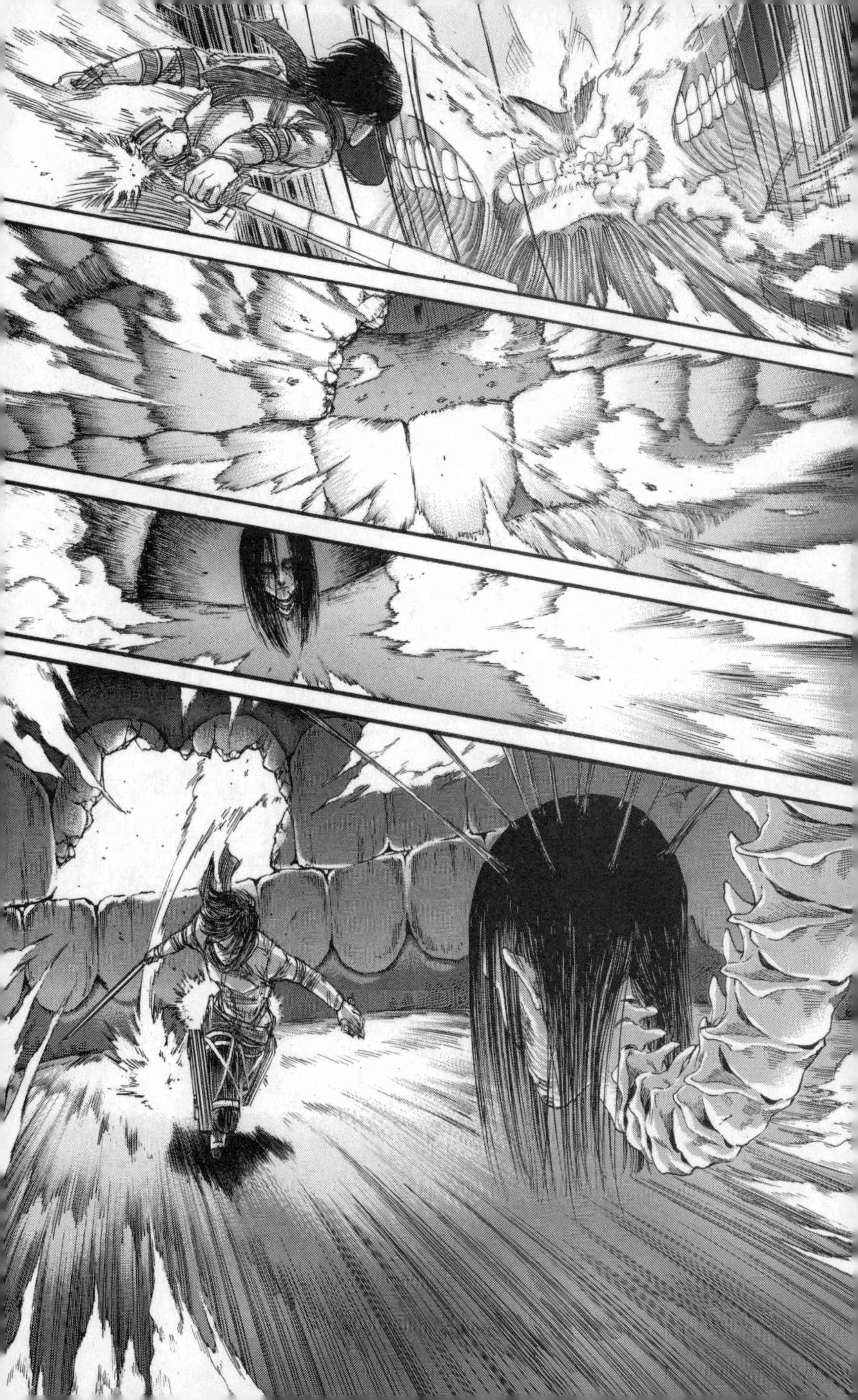

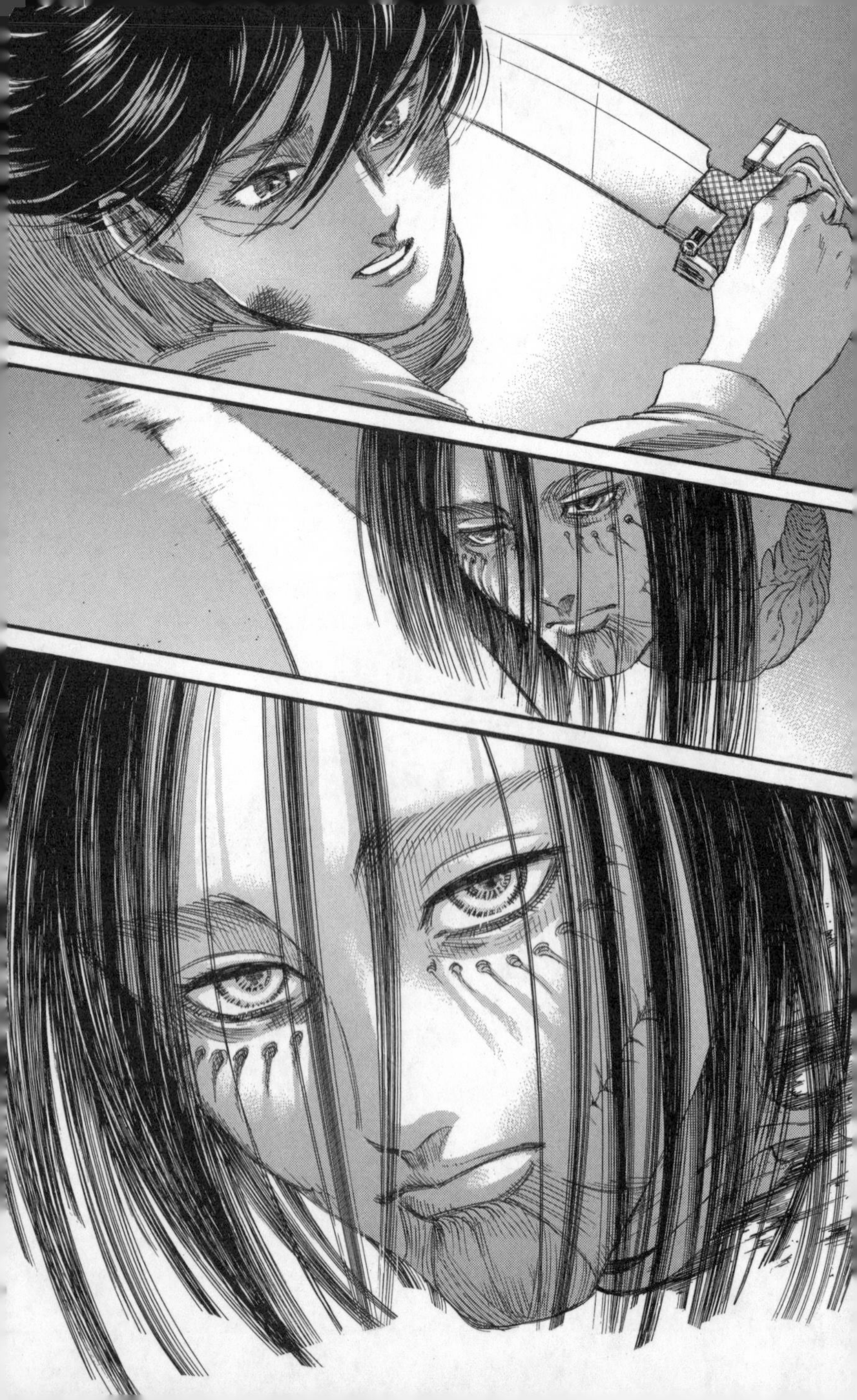

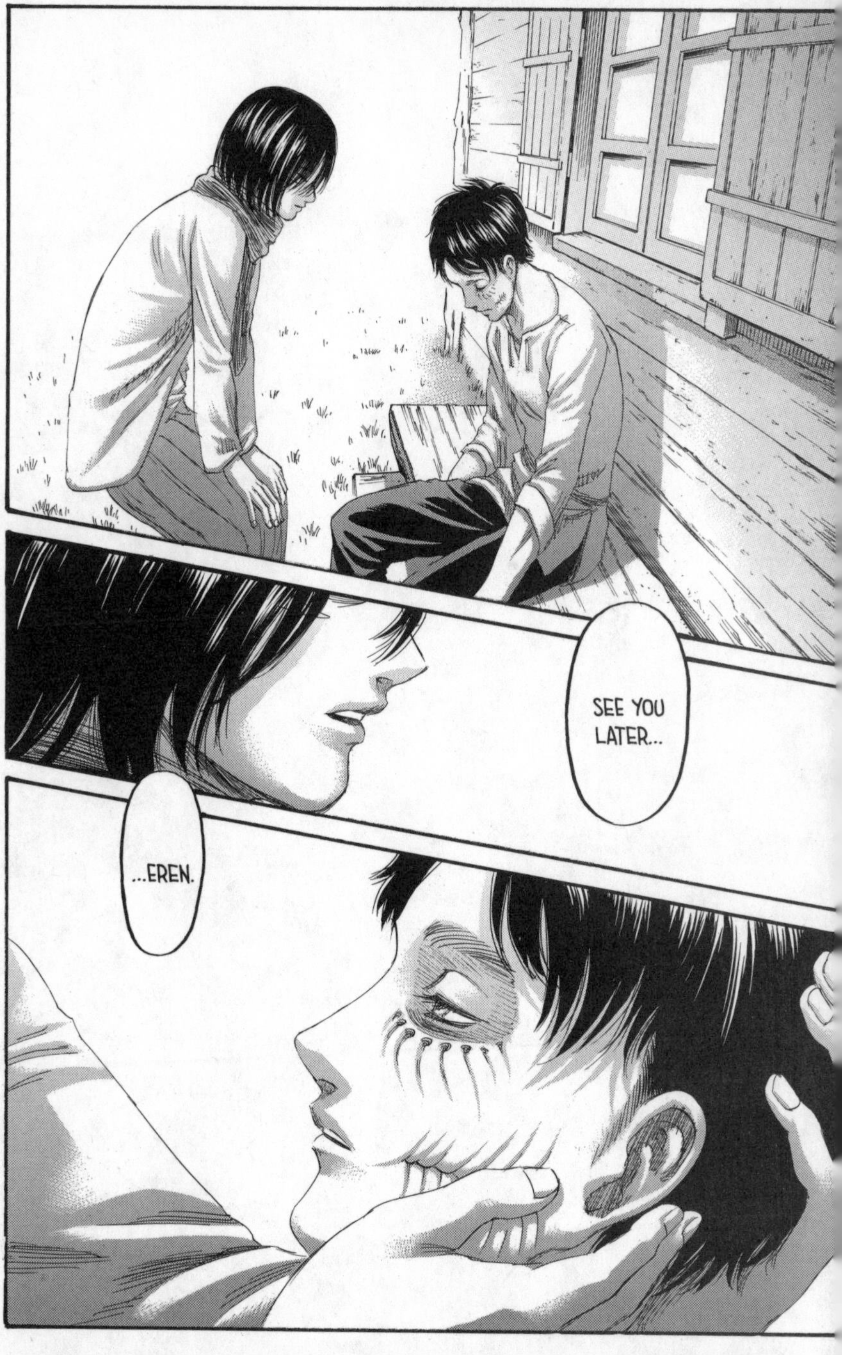
SEE YOU LATER...
...EREN.

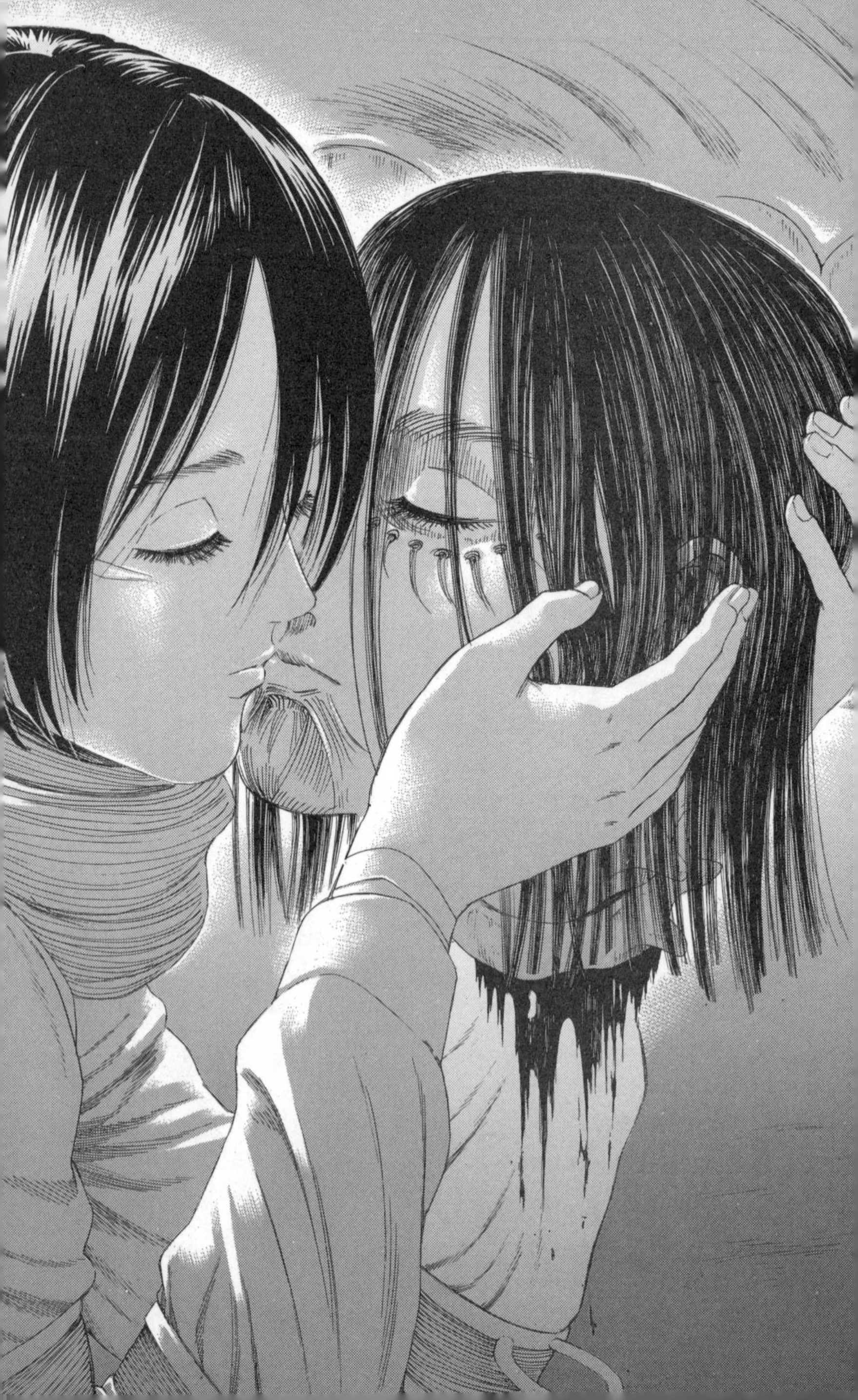

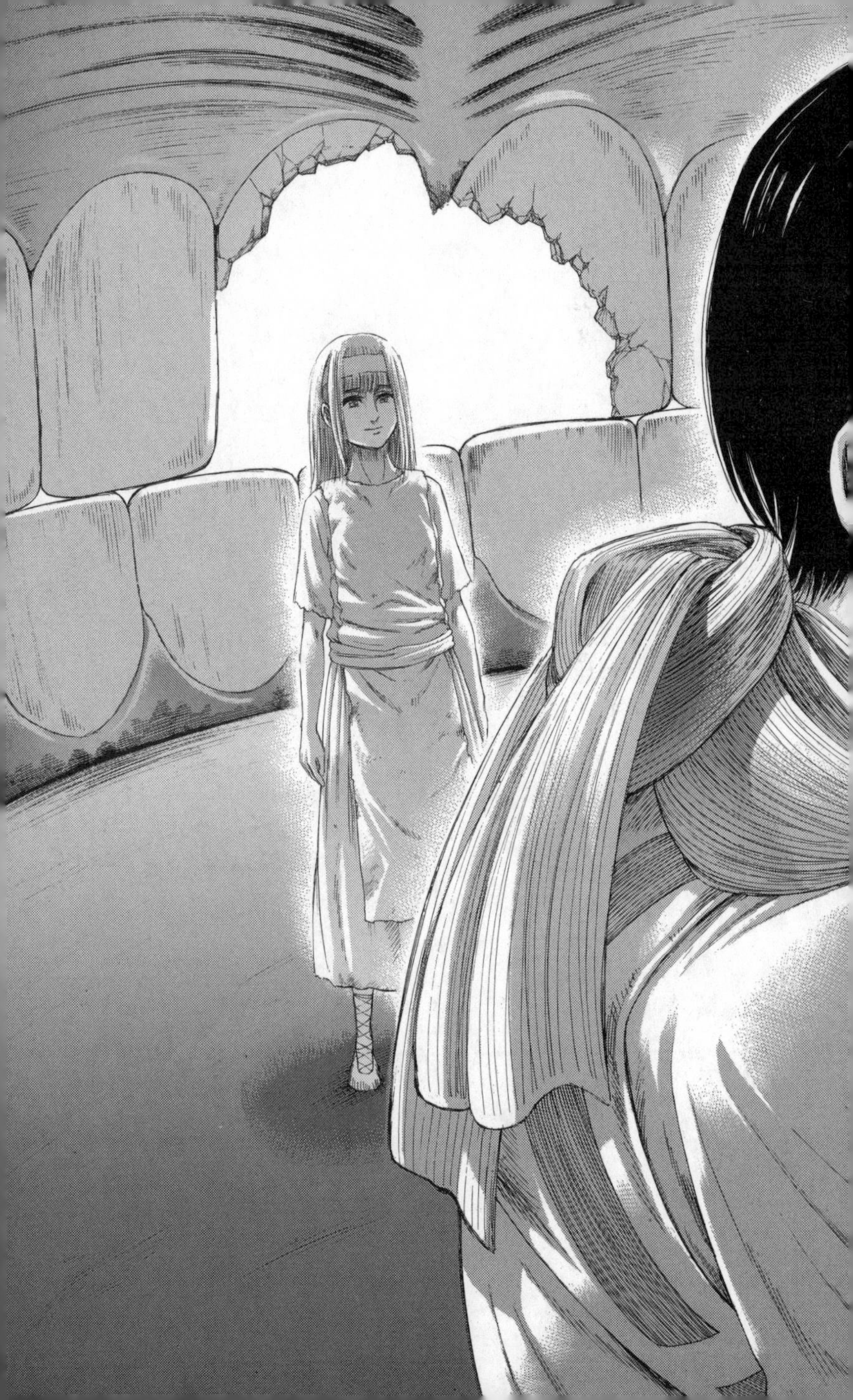

ATTACK on TITAN

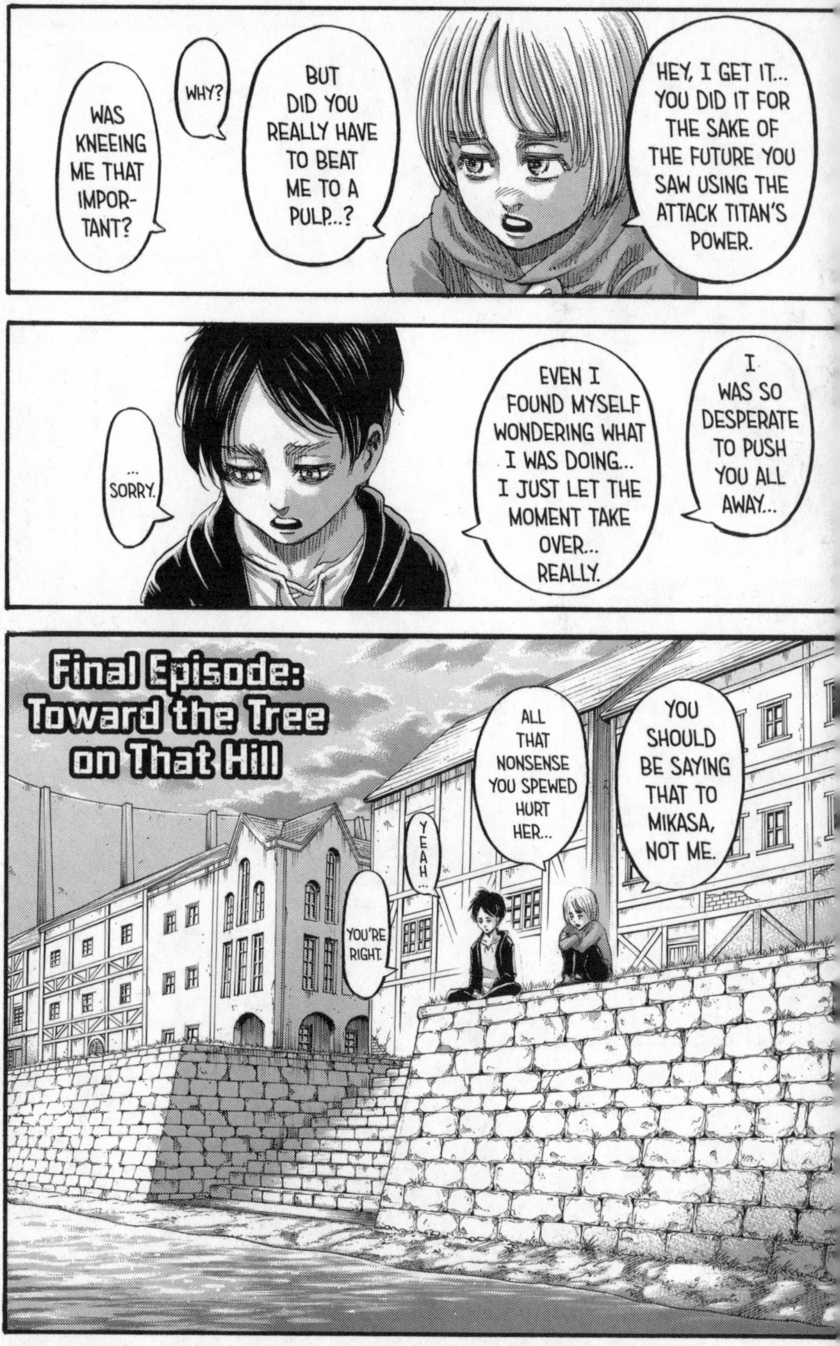
HEY, I GET IT... YOU DID IT FOR THE SAKE OF THE FUTURE YOU SAW USING THE ATTACK TITAN'S POWER.
BUT DID YOU REALLY HAVE TO BEAT ME TO A PULP...?
WHY?
WAS KNEEING ME THAT IMPOR-TANT?
I WAS SO DESPERATE TO PUSH YOU ALL AWAY...
EVEN I FOUND MYSELF WONDERING WHAT I WAS DOING... I JUST LET THE MOMENT TAKE OVER... REALLY.
...SORRY.
Final Episode: Toward the Tree on That Hill
YOU SHOULD BE SAYING THAT TO MIKASA, NOT ME.
ALL THAT NONSENSE YOU SPEWED HURT HER...
YEAH...
YOU'RE RIGHT.

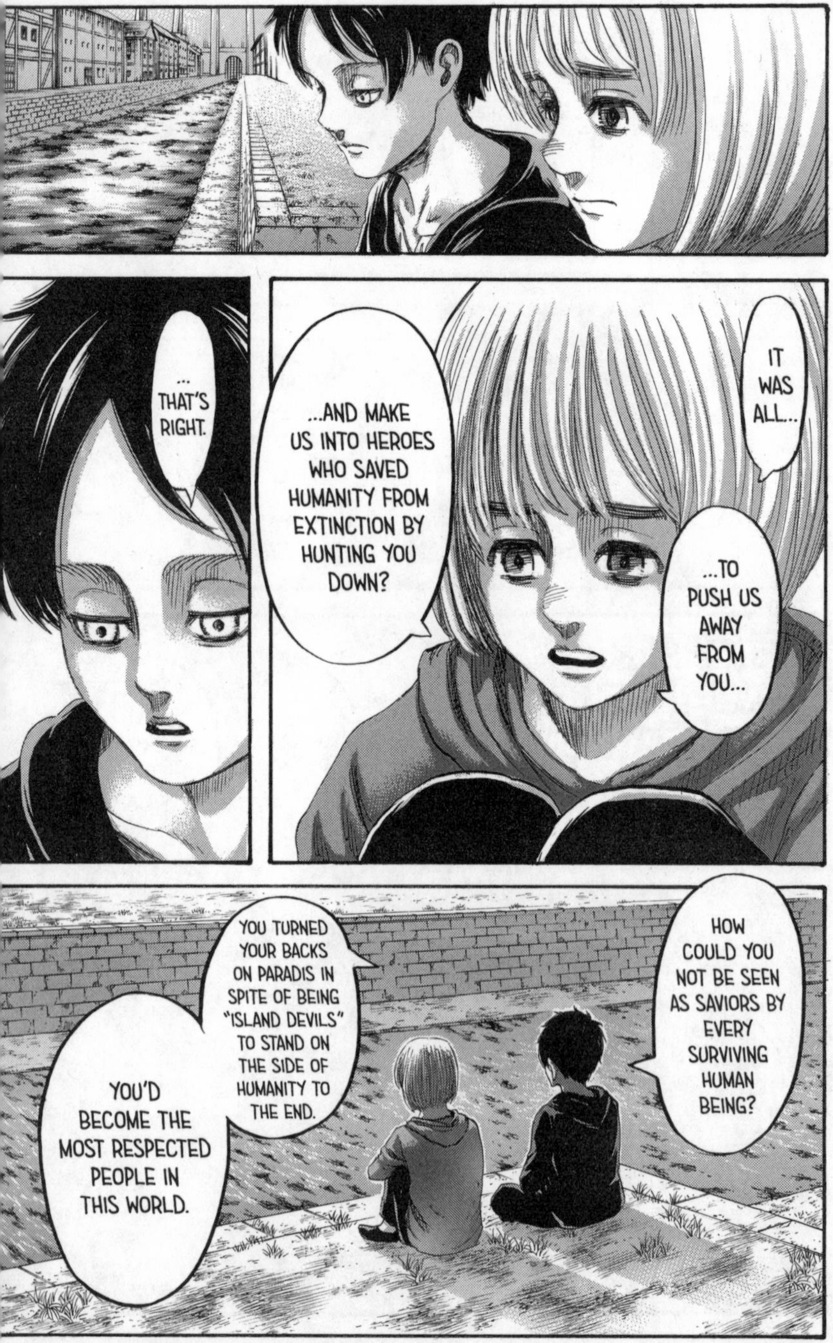
IT WAS ALL...
...TO PUSH US AWAY FROM YOU...
...AND MAKE US INTO HEROES WHO SAVED HUMANITY FROM EXTINCTION BY HUNTING YOU DOWN?
... THAT'S RIGHT.
HOW COULD YOU NOT BE SEEN AS SAVIORS BY EVERY SURVIVING HUMAN BEING?
YOU TURNED YOUR BACKS ON PARADIS IN SPITE OF BEING "ISLAND DEVILS" TO STAND ON THE SIDE OF HUMANITY TO THE END.
YOU'D BECOME THE MOST RESPECTED PEOPLE IN THIS WORLD.

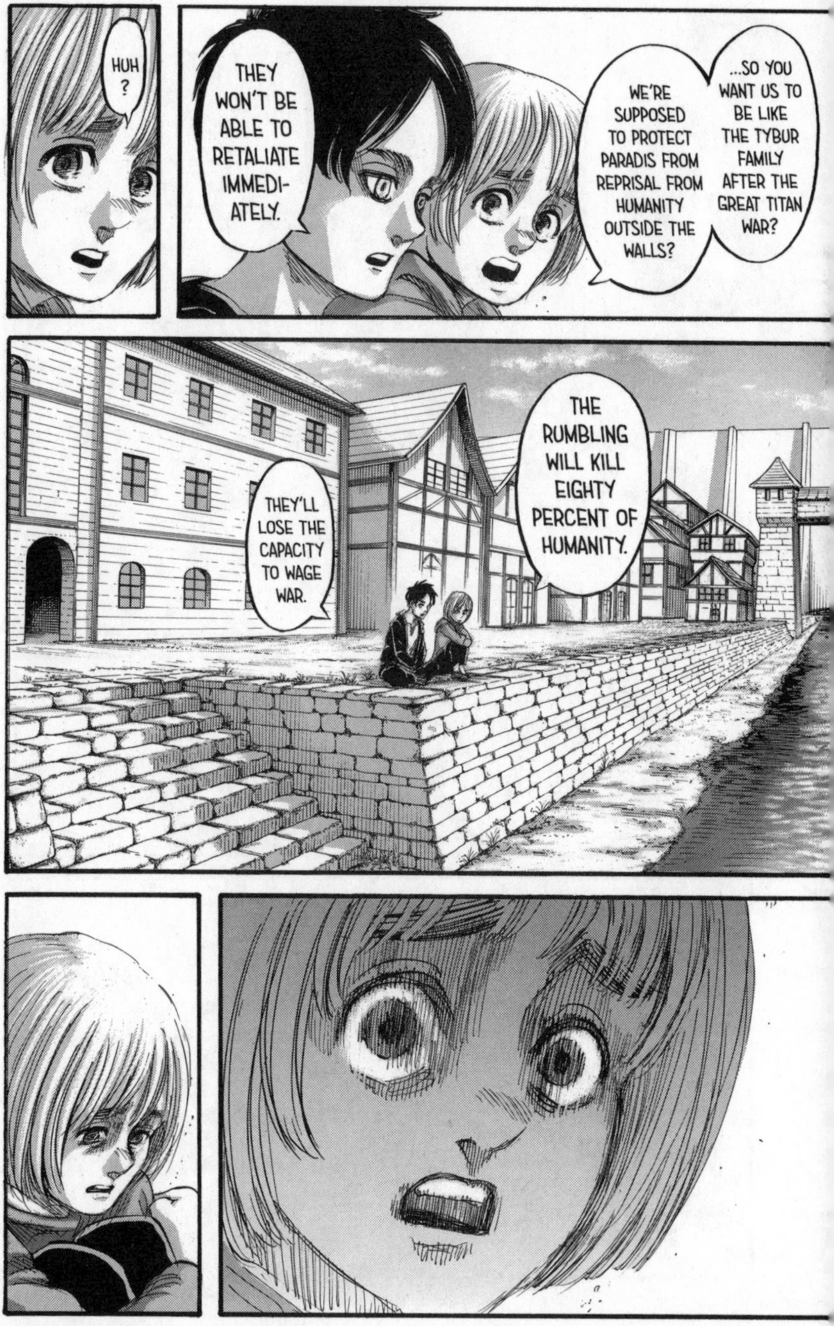
...SO YOU WANT US TO BE LIKE THE TYBUR FAMILY AFTER THE GREAT TITAN WAR?
WE'RE SUPPOSED TO PROTECT PARADIS FROM REPRISAL FROM HUMANITY OUTSIDE THE WALLS?
THEY WON'T BE ABLE TO RETALIATE IMMEDI-ATELY.
HUH?
THE RUMBLING WILL KILL EIGHTY PERCENT OF HUMANITY.
THEY'LL LOSE THE CAPACITY TO WAGE WAR.

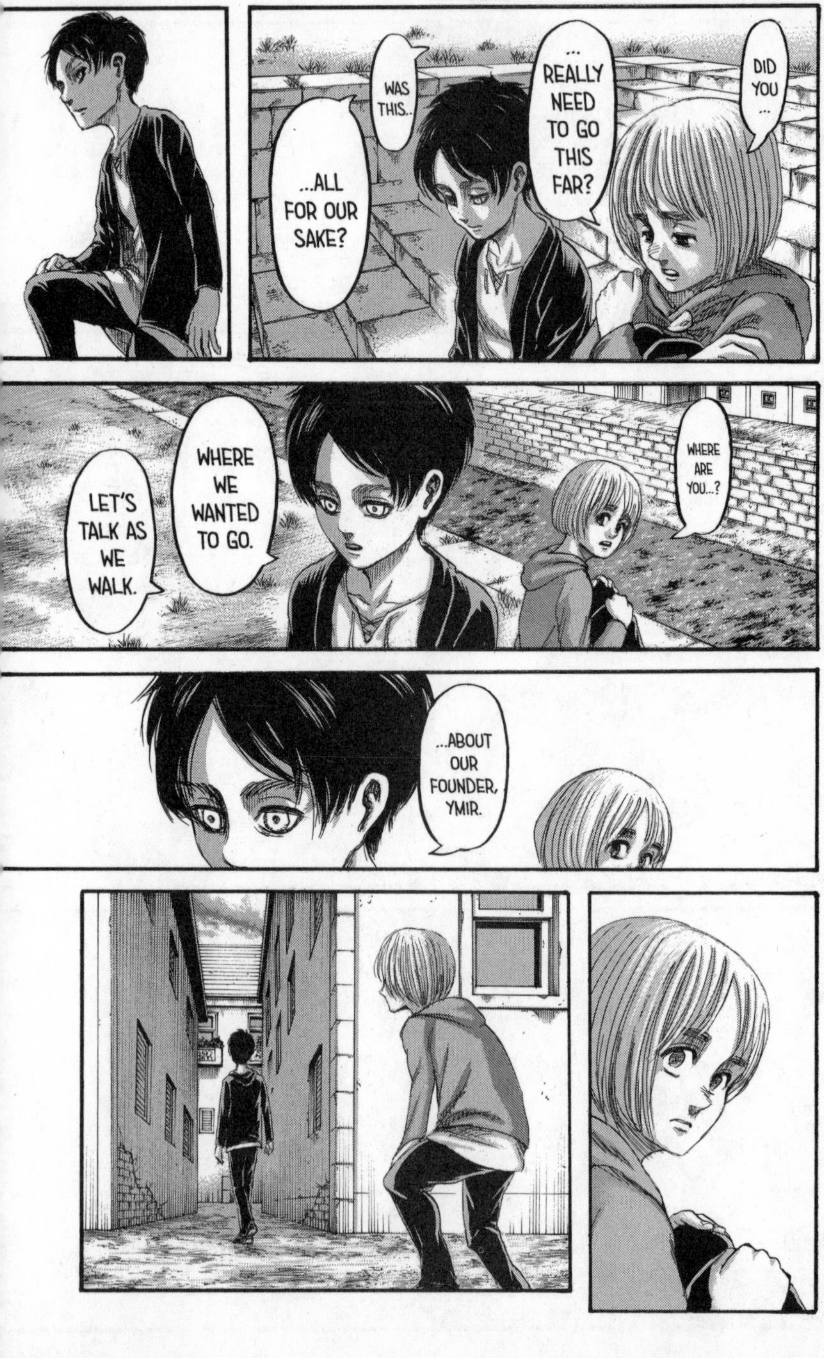
DID YOU ...
... REALLY NEED TO GO THIS FAR?
WAS THIS..
...ALL FOR OUR SAKE?
WHERE ARE YOU...?
WHERE WE WANTED TO GO.
LET'S TALK AS WE WALK.
...ABOUT OUR FOUNDER, YMIR.

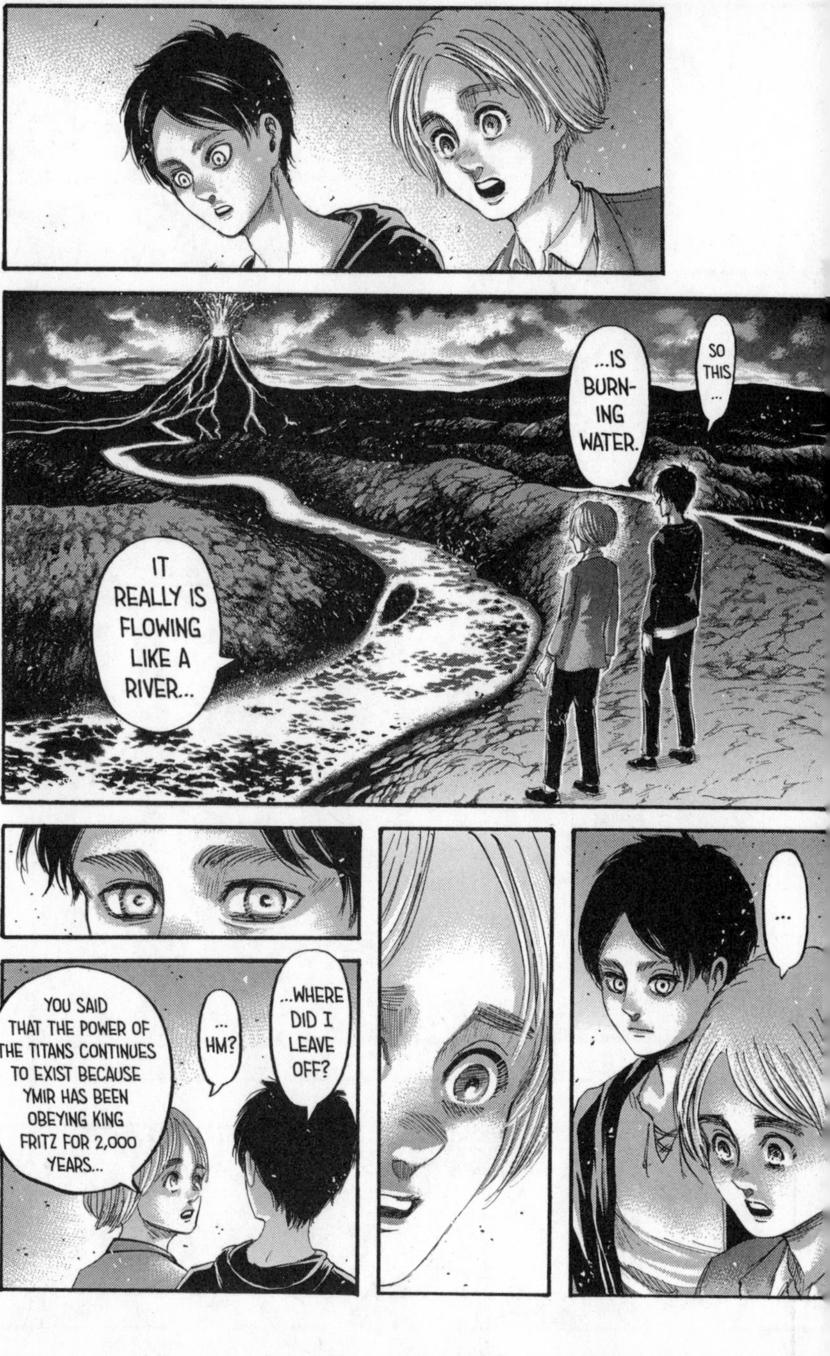
SO THIS...
...IS BURNING WATER.
IT REALLY IS FLOWING LIKE A RIVER...
...
...WHERE DID I LEAVE OFF?
...HM?
YOU SAID THAT THE POWER OF THE TITANS CONTINUES TO EXIST BECAUSE YMIR HAS BEEN OBEYING KING FRITZ FOR 2,000 YEARS...

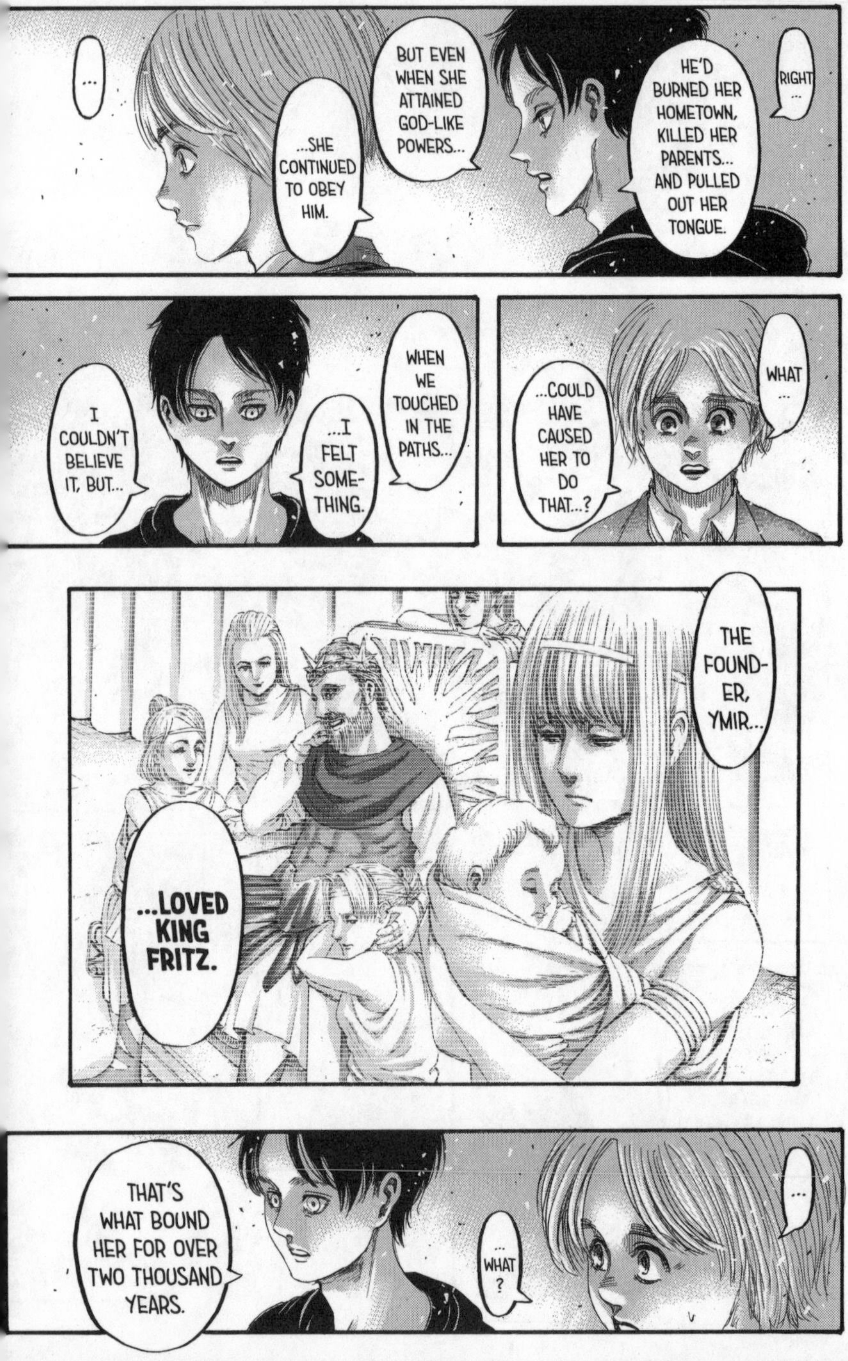
RIGHT...
HE'D BURNED HER HOMETOWN, KILLED HER PARENTS... AND PULLED OUT HER TONGUE.
BUT EVEN WHEN SHE ATTAINED GOD-LIKE POWERS...
...SHE CONTINUED TO OBEY HIM.
...
WHAT...
...COULD HAVE CAUSED HER TO DO THAT...?
WHEN WE TOUCHED IN THE PATHS...
...I FELT SOMETHING.
I COULDN'T BELIEVE IT, BUT...
THE FOUNDER, YMIR...
...LOVED KING FRITZ.
...
...WHAT?
THAT'S WHAT BOUND HER FOR OVER TWO THOUSAND YEARS.

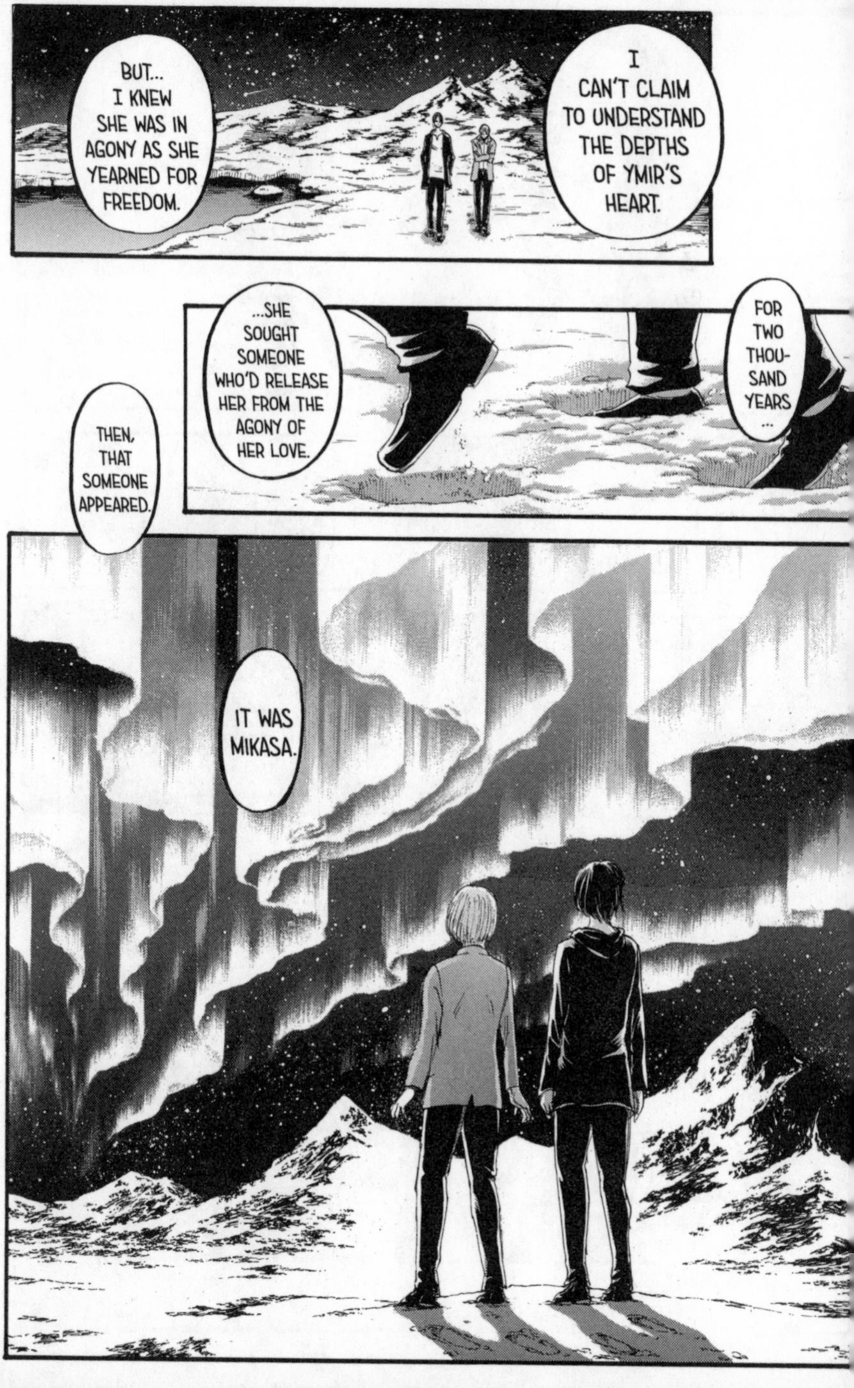
I CAN'T CLAIM TO UNDERSTAND THE DEPTHS OF YMIR'S HEART.
BUT... I KNEW SHE WAS IN AGONY AS SHE YEARNED FOR FREEDOM.
FOR TWO THOU-SAND YEARS...
...SHE SOUGHT SOMEONE WHO'D RELEASE HER FROM THE AGONY OF HER LOVE.
THEN, THAT SOMEONE APPEARED.
IT WAS MIKASA.

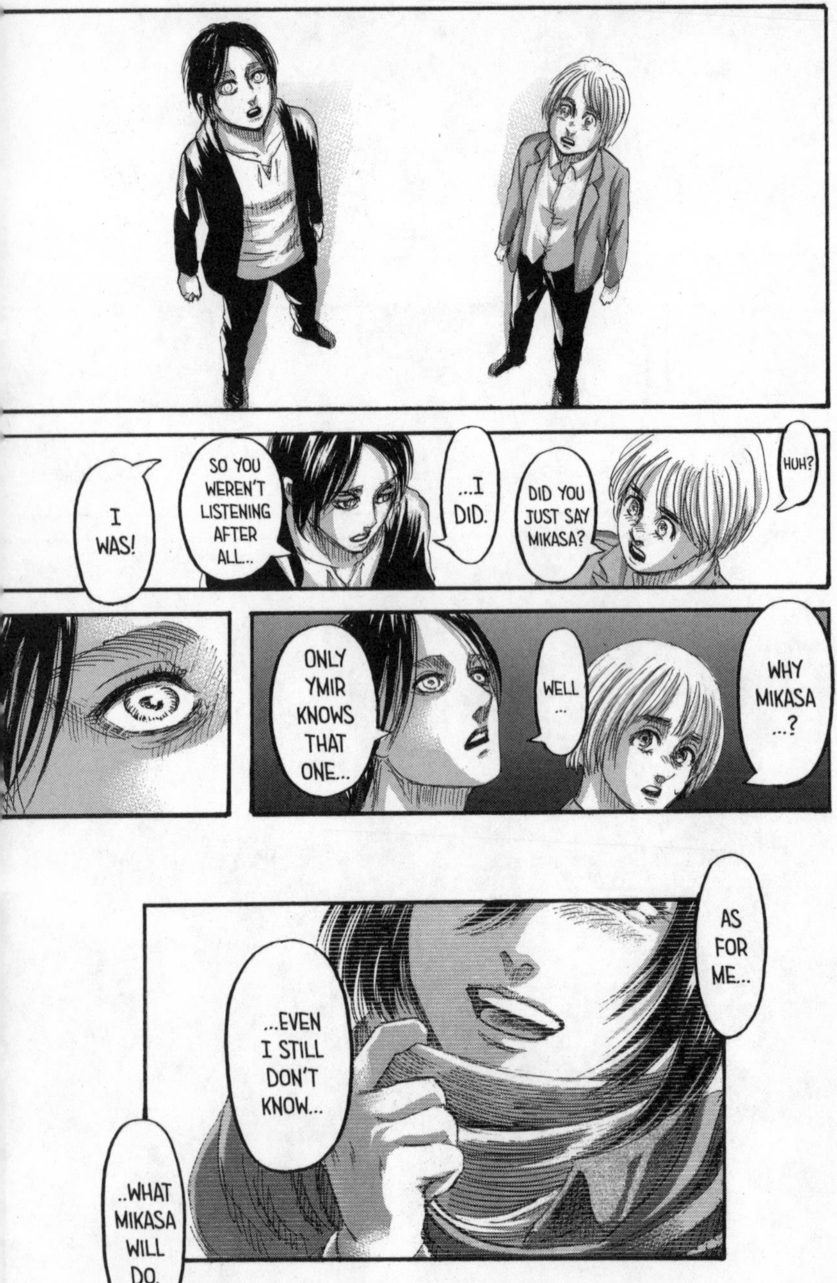
HUH?
DID YOU JUST SAY MIKASA?
...I DID.
SO YOU WEREN'T LISTENING AFTER ALL...
I WAS!
WHY MIKASA ...?
WELL ...
ONLY YMIR KNOWS THAT ONE...
AS FOR ME...
...EVEN I STILL DON'T KNOW...
..WHAT MIKASA WILL DO.

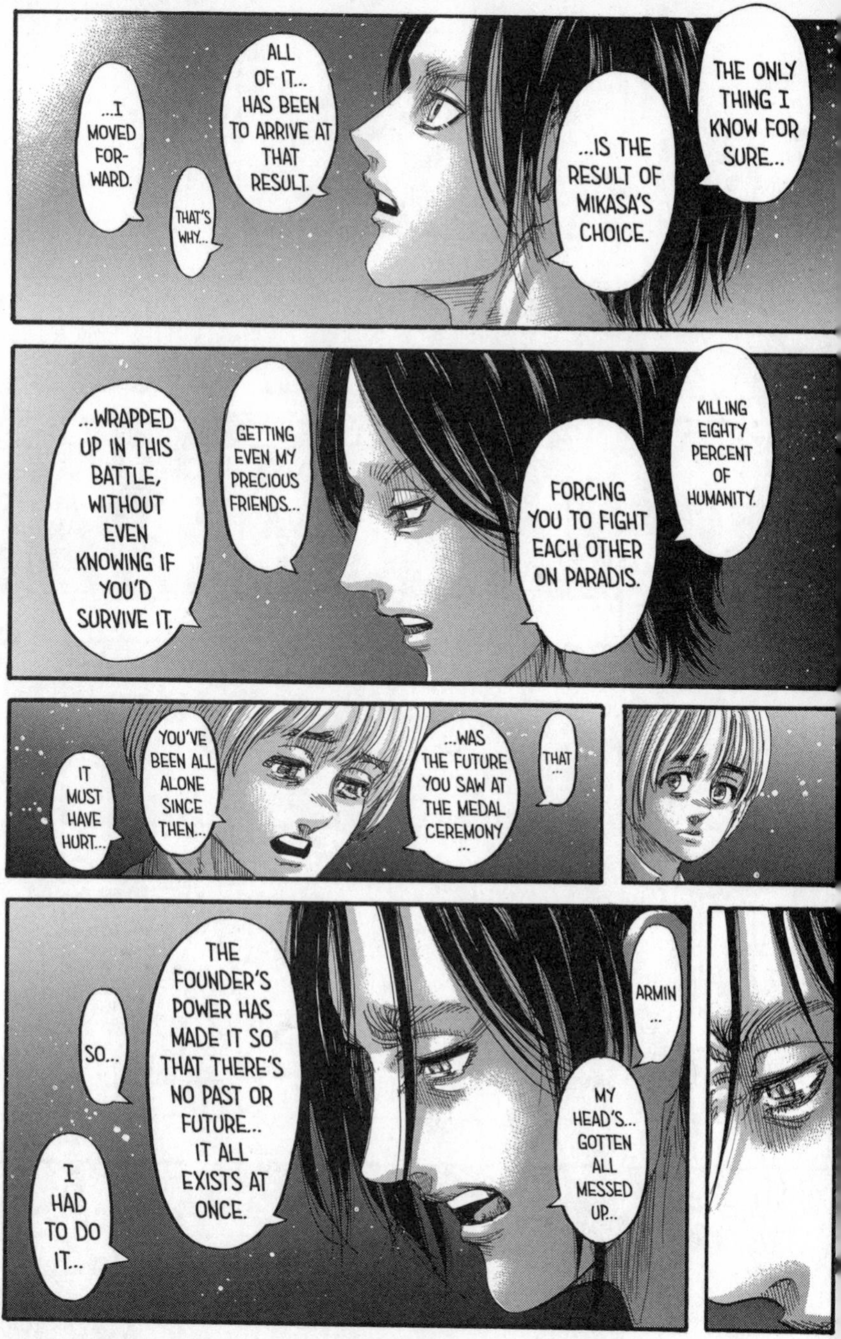
THE ONLY THING I KNOW FOR SURE...
...IS THE RESULT OF MIKASA'S CHOICE.
ALL OF IT... HAS BEEN TO ARRIVE AT THAT RESULT.
THAT'S WHY...
...I MOVED FOR-WARD.
KILLING EIGHTY PERCENT OF HUMANITY.
FORCING YOU TO FIGHT EACH OTHER ON PARADIS.
GETTING EVEN MY PRECIOUS FRIENDS...
...WRAPPED UP IN THIS BATTLE, WITHOUT EVEN KNOWING IF YOU'D SURVIVE IT.
THAT...
...WAS THE FUTURE YOU SAW AT THE MEDAL CEREMONY...
YOU'VE BEEN ALL ALONE SINCE THEN...
IT MUST HAVE HURT...
ARMIN...
MY HEAD'S... GOTTEN ALL MESSED UP...
THE FOUNDER'S POWER HAS MADE IT SO THAT THERE'S NO PAST OR FUTURE... IT ALL EXISTS AT ONCE.
SO...
I HAD TO DO IT...

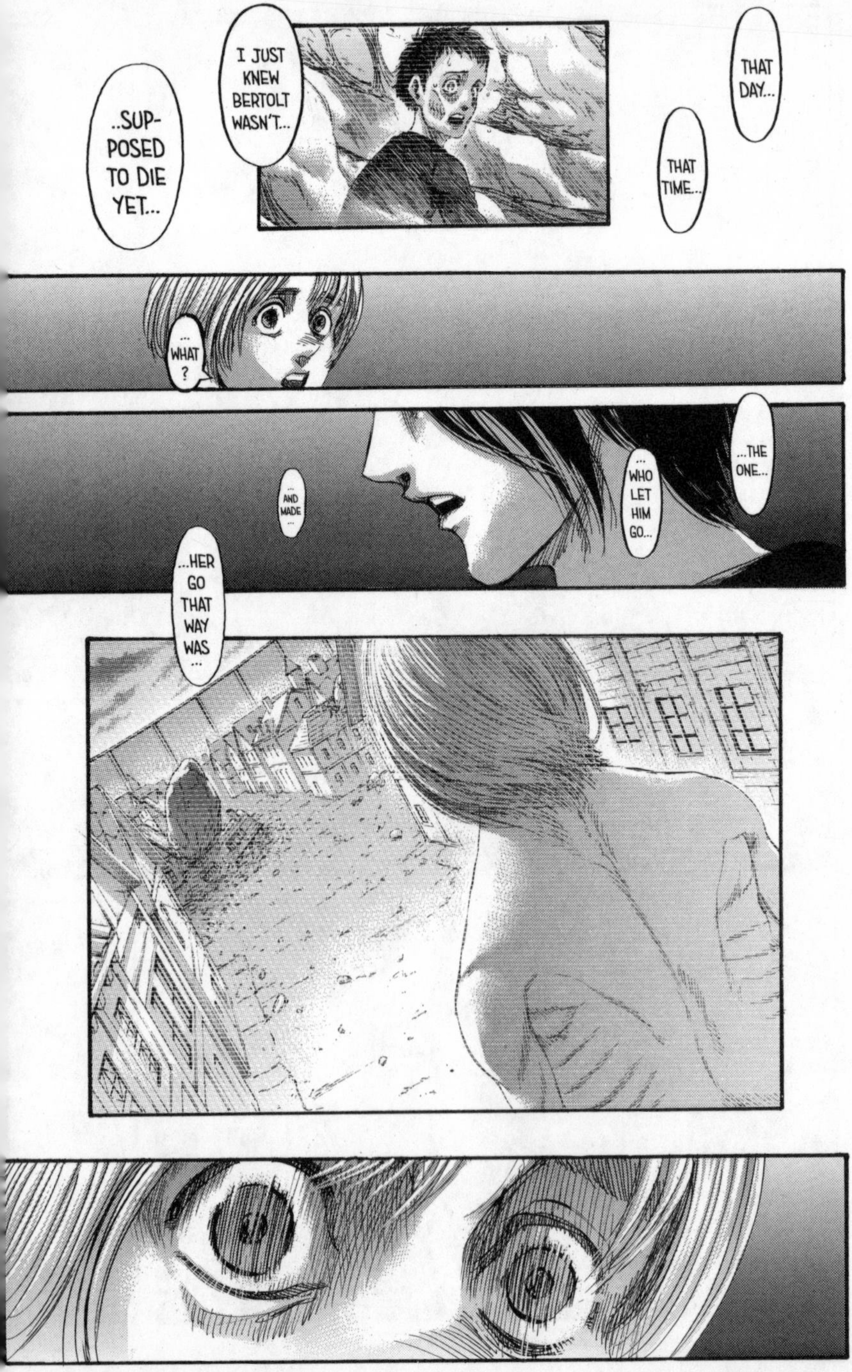
THAT DAY...
THAT TIME...
I JUST KNEW BERTOLT WASN'T...
..SUP-POSED TO DIE YET...
...WHAT?
...THE ONE...
...WHO LET HIM GO...
...AND MADE...
...HER GO THAT WAY WAS...

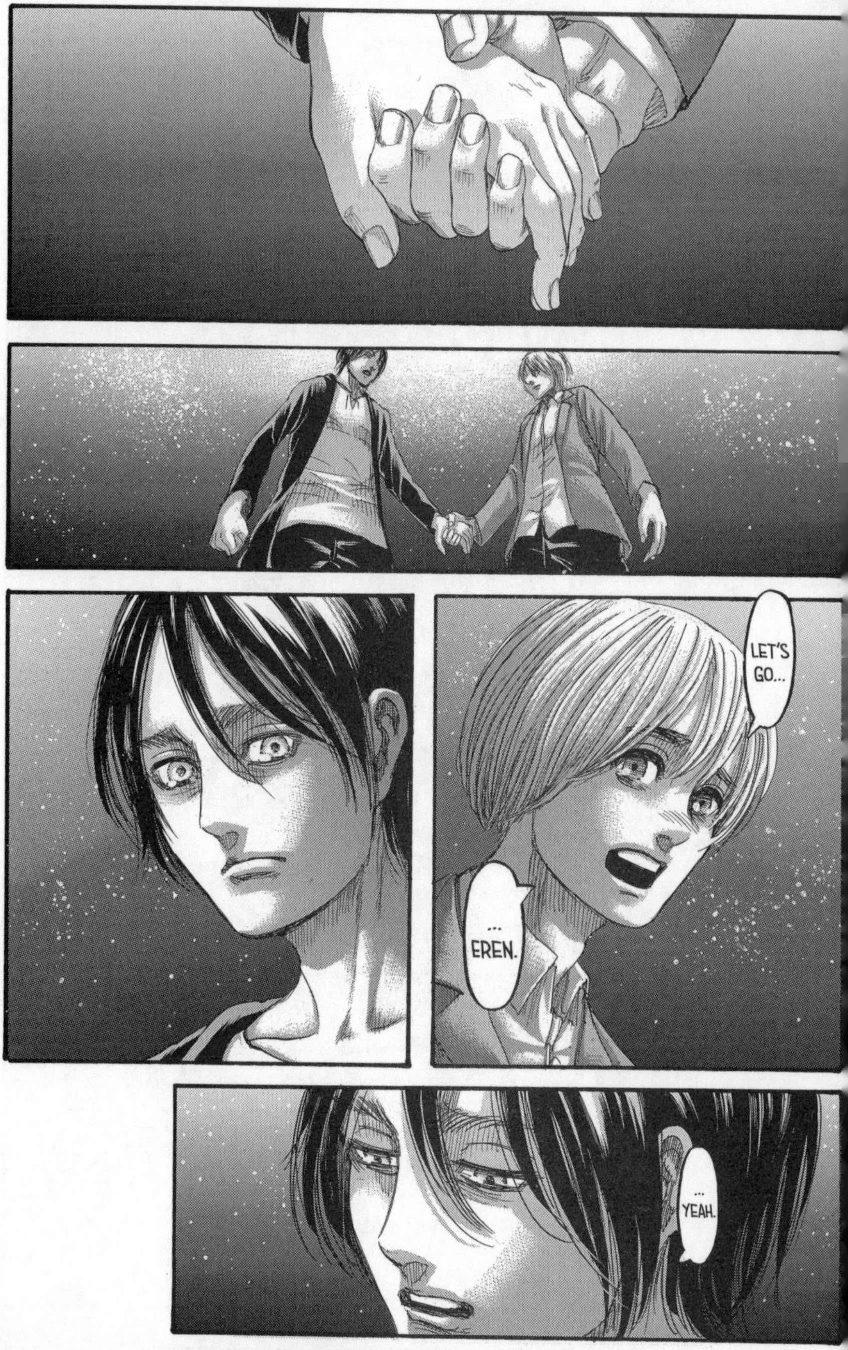
LET'S GO...
... EREN.
... YEAH.

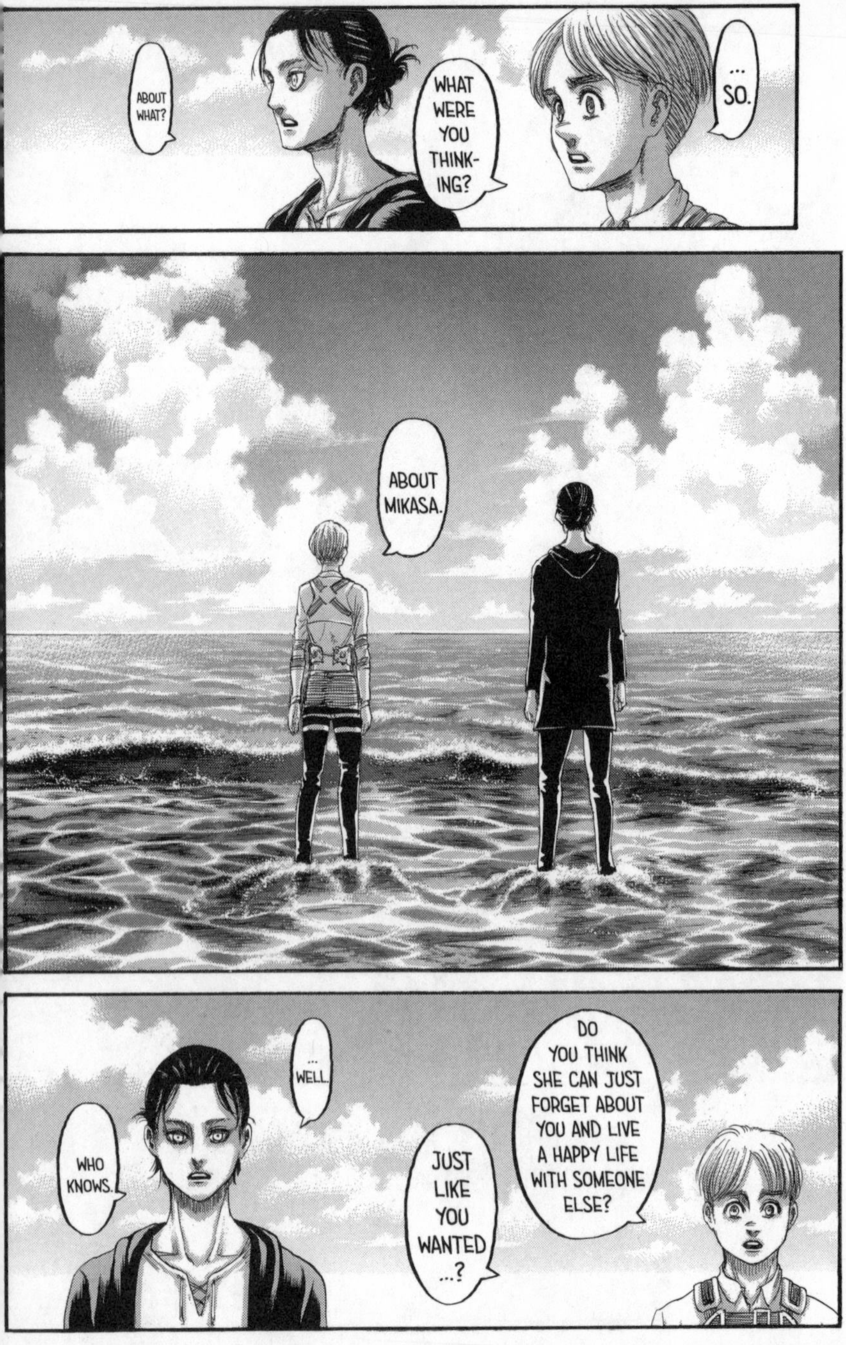
... SO.
WHAT WERE YOU THINKING?
ABOUT WHAT?
ABOUT MIKASA.
DO YOU THINK SHE CAN JUST FORGET ABOUT YOU AND LIVE A HAPPY LIFE WITH SOMEONE ELSE?
JUST LIKE YOU WANTED ...?
... WELL.
WHO KNOWS.

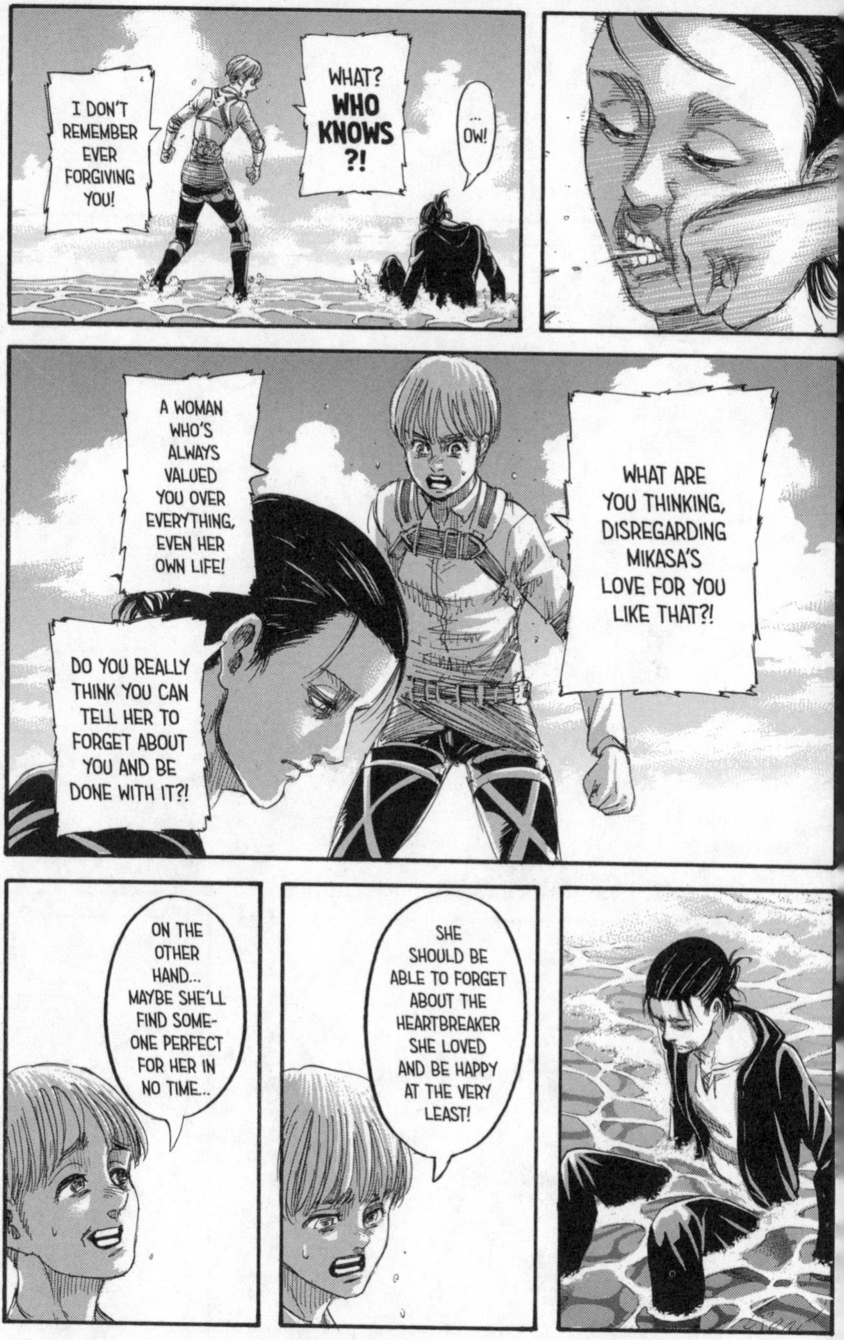

... OW!
WHAT? WHO KNOWS ?!
I DON'T REMEMBER EVER FORGIVING YOU!
WHAT ARE YOU THINKING, DISREGARDING MIKASA'S LOVE FOR YOU LIKE THAT?!
A WOMAN WHO'S ALWAYS VALUED YOU OVER EVERYTHING, EVEN HER OWN LIFE!
DO YOU REALLY THINK YOU CAN TELL HER TO FORGET ABOUT YOU AND BE DONE WITH IT?!
SHE SHOULD BE ABLE TO FORGET ABOUT THE HEARTBREAKER SHE LOVED AND BE HAPPY AT THE VERY LEAST!
ON THE OTHER HAND... MAYBE SHE'LL FIND SOME-ONE PERFECT FOR HER IN NO TIME...

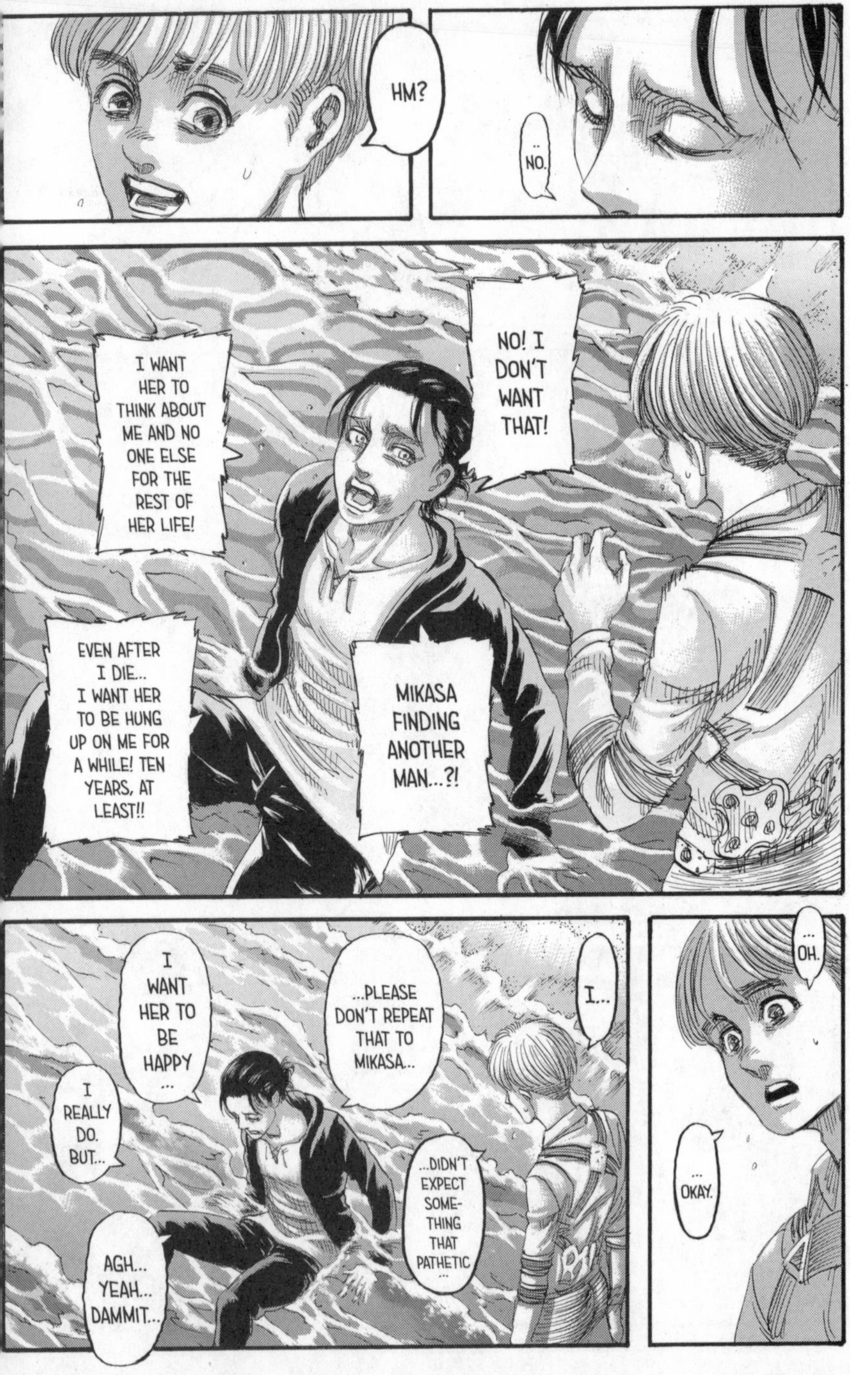
...NO.
HM?
NO! I DON'T WANT THAT!
I WANT HER TO THINK ABOUT ME AND NO ONE ELSE FOR THE REST OF HER LIFE!
MIKASA FINDING ANOTHER MAN...?!
EVEN AFTER I DIE... I WANT HER TO BE HUNG UP ON ME FOR A WHILE! TEN YEARS, AT LEAST!!
...OH.
...OKAY.
I...
...PLEASE DON'T REPEAT THAT TO MIKASA...
I WANT HER TO BE HAPPY...
I REALLY DO. BUT...
...DIDN'T EXPECT SOMETHING THAT PATHETIC...
AGH... YEAH... DAMMIT...

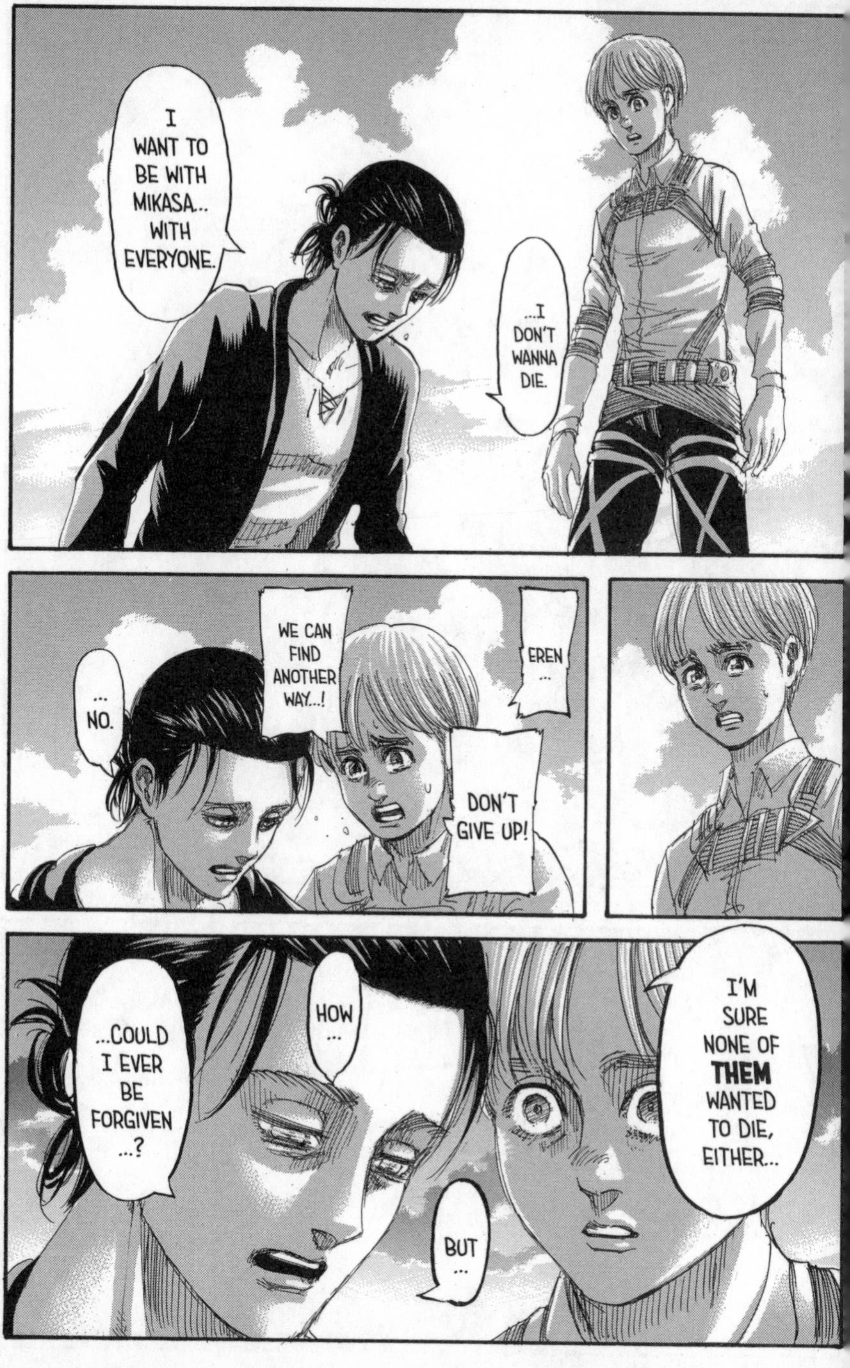
...I DON'T WANNA DIE.
I WANT TO BE WITH MIKASA... WITH EVERYONE.
EREN...
WE CAN FIND ANOTHER WAY...!
DON'T GIVE UP!
... NO.
I'M SURE NONE OF **THEM** WANTED TO DIE, EITHER...
BUT...
HOW...
...COULD I EVER BE FORGIVEN...?

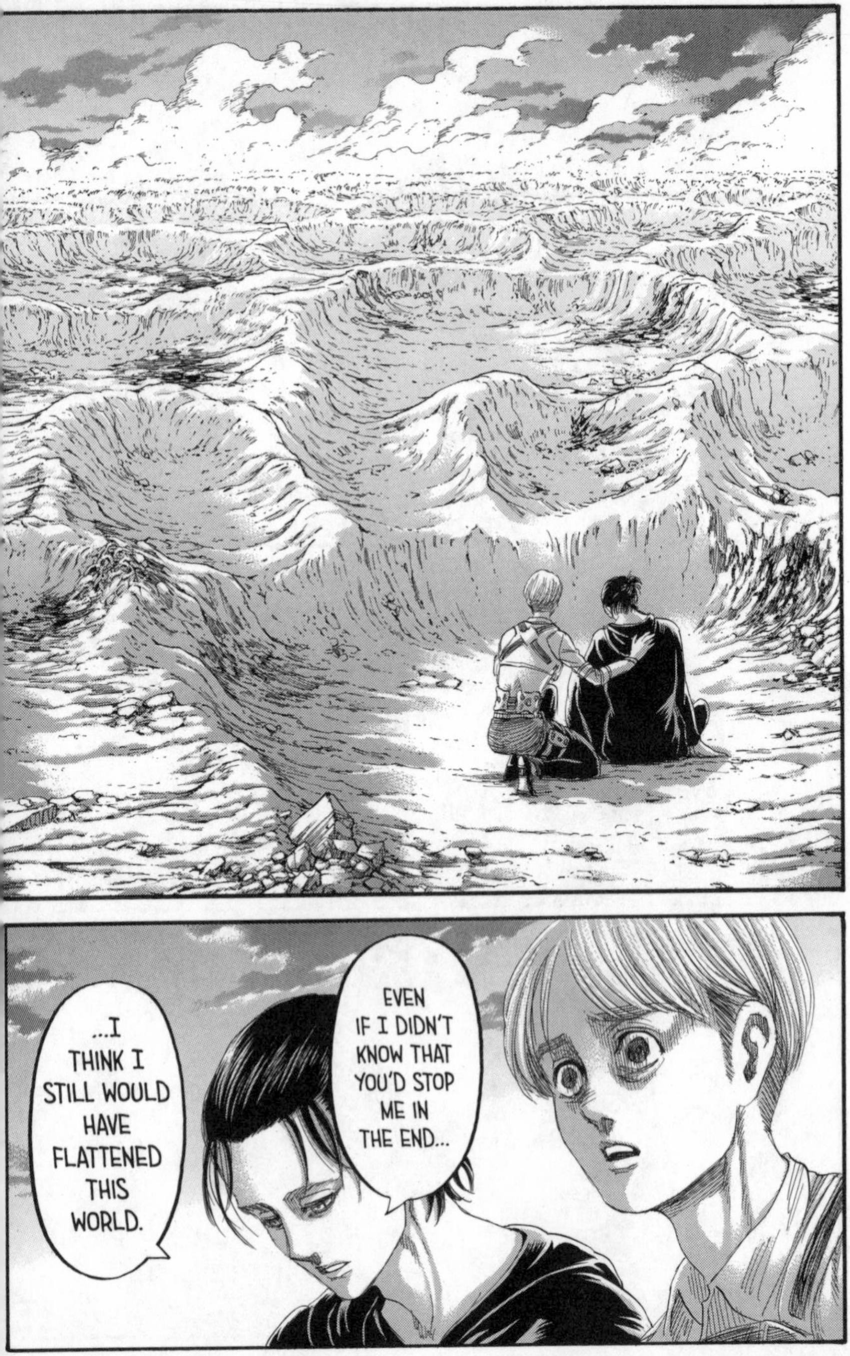
EVEN IF I DIDN'T KNOW THAT YOU'D STOP ME IN THE END...
...I THINK I STILL WOULD HAVE FLATTENED THIS WORLD.

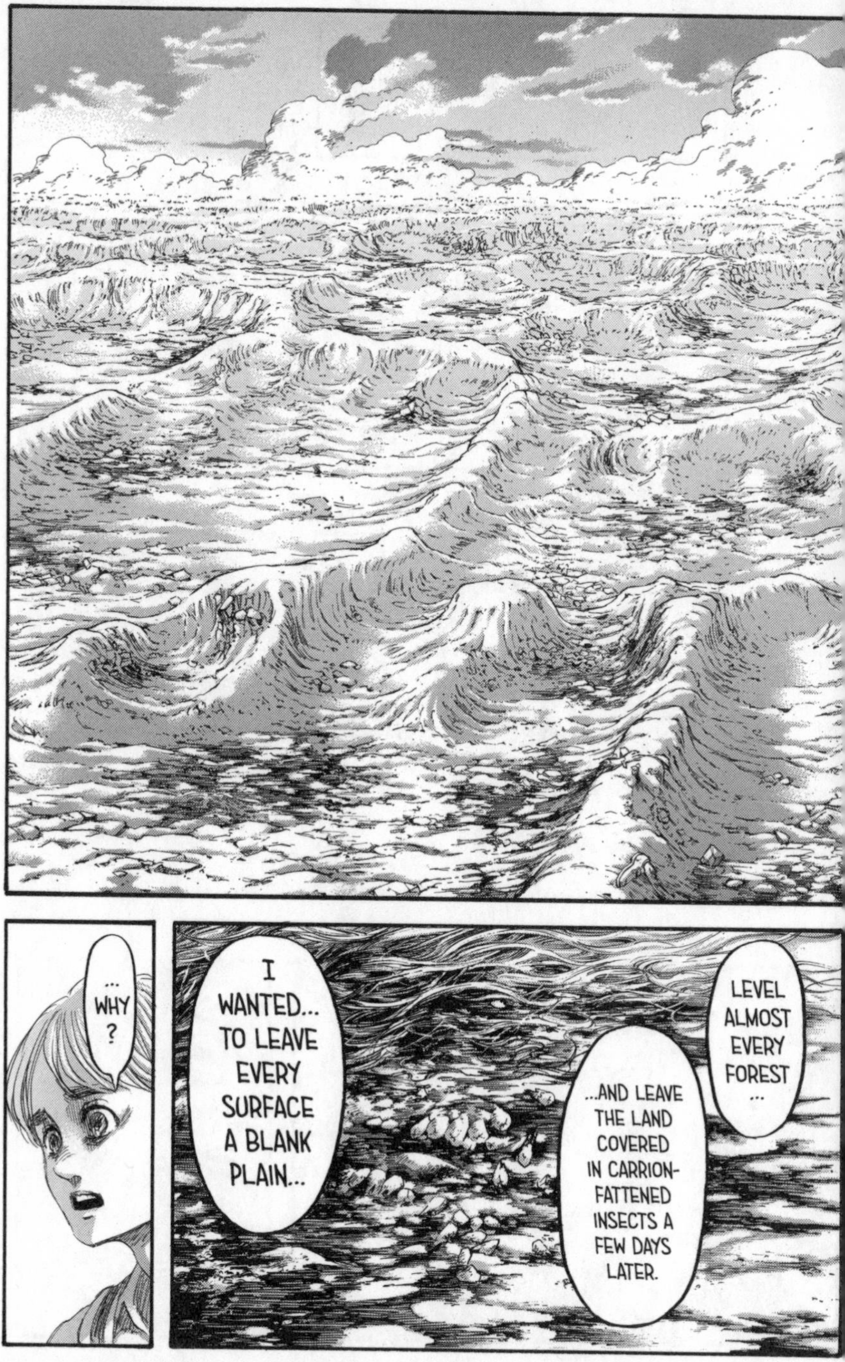
LEVEL ALMOST EVERY FOREST...
...AND LEAVE THE LAND COVERED IN CARRION-FATTENED INSECTS A FEW DAYS LATER.
I WANTED... TO LEAVE EVERY SURFACE A BLANK PLAIN...
... WHY?

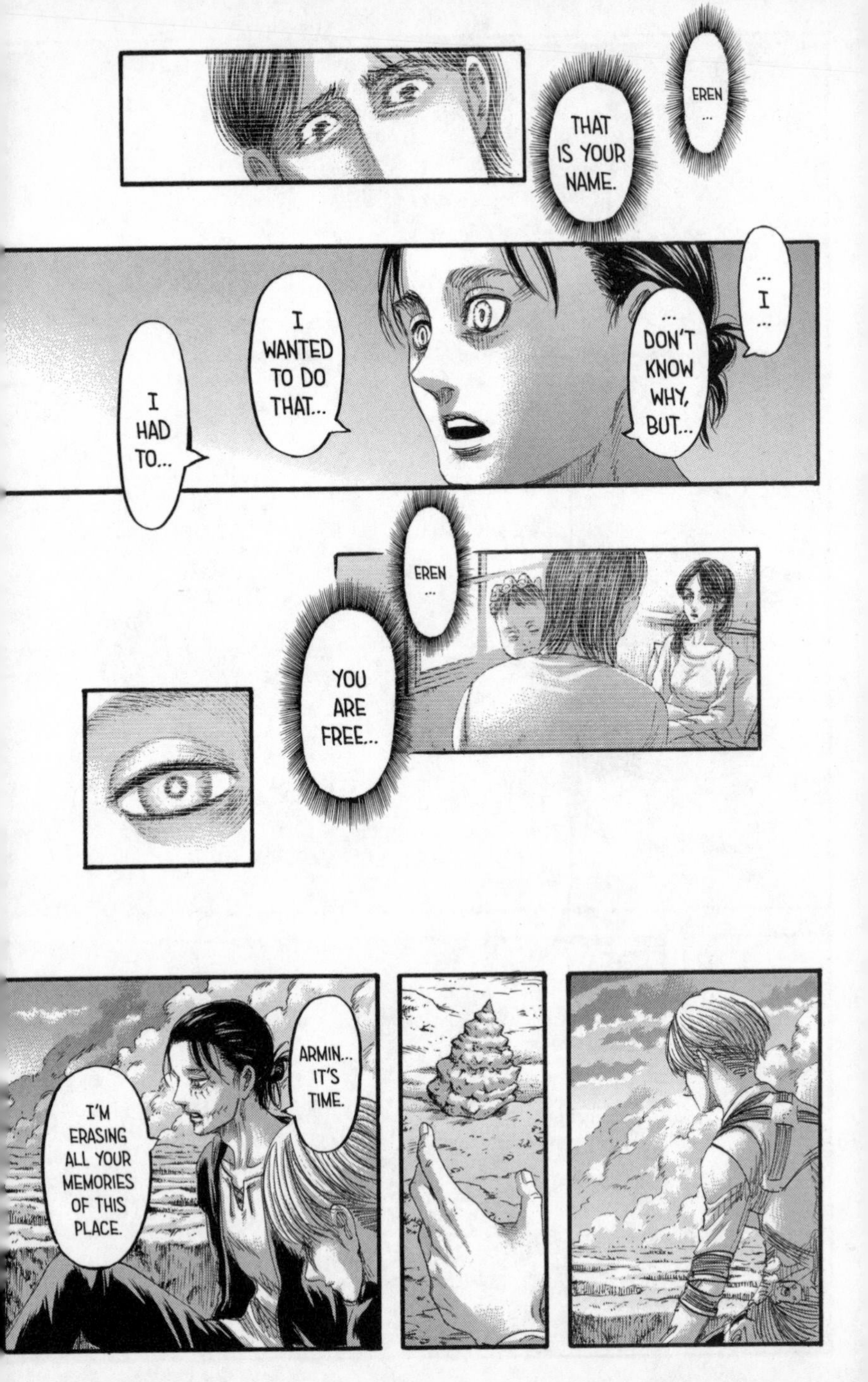
EREN ...
THAT IS YOUR NAME.
... I ...
... DON'T KNOW WHY, BUT...
I WANTED TO DO THAT...
I HAD TO...
EREN ...
YOU ARE FREE...
ARMIN... IT'S TIME.
I'M ERASING ALL YOUR MEMORIES OF THIS PLACE.

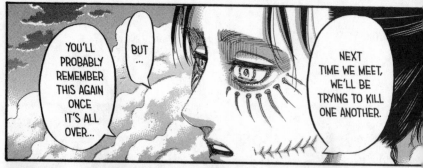

NEXT TIME WE MEET, WE'LL BE TRYING TO KILL ONE ANOTHER.
BUT ...
YOU'LL PROBABLY REMEMBER THIS AGAIN ONCE IT'S ALL OVER...
... EREN.
THANK YOU.
YOU BE-CAME...
...A MASS MURDERER FOR OUR SAKE...
I SWEAR I WON'T LET THIS TERRIBLE MISTAKE YOU'RE MAKING BE IN VAIN.

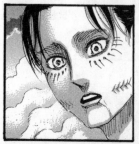

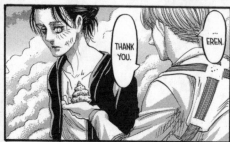

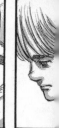

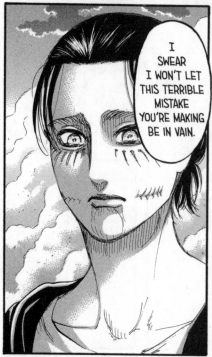

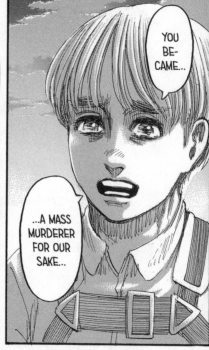

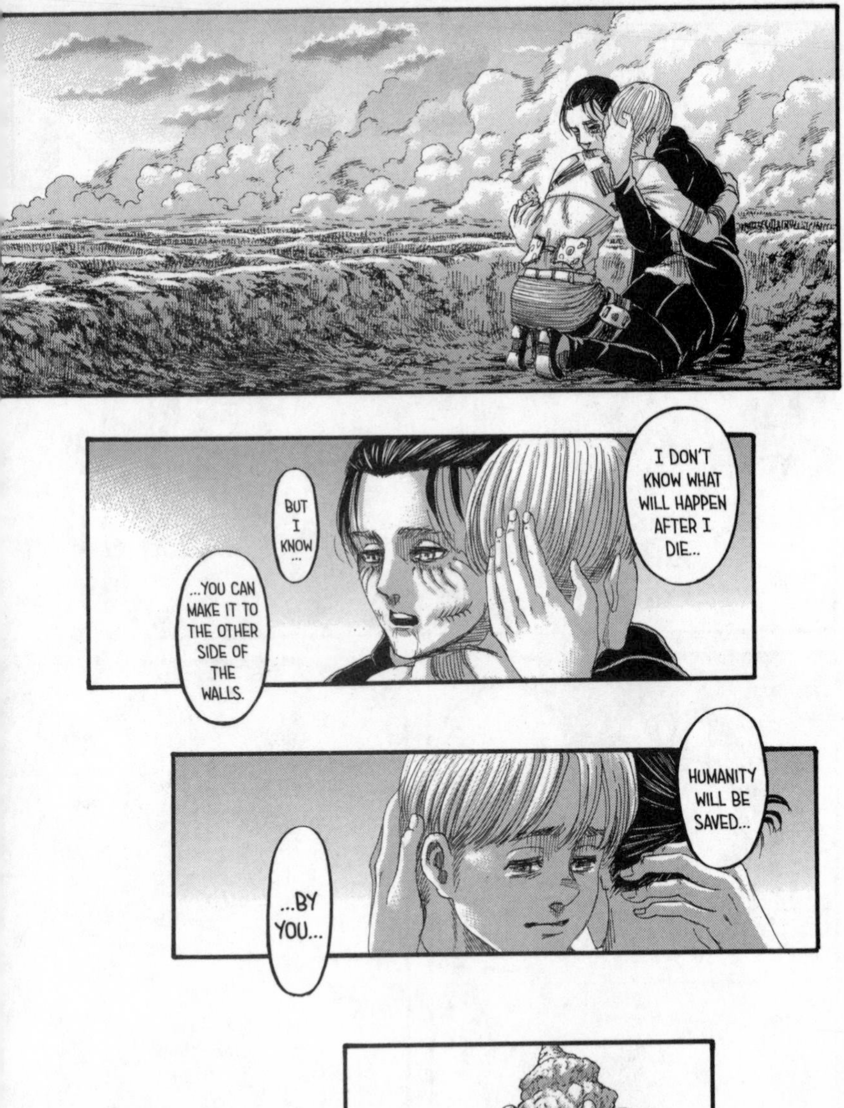
I DON'T KNOW WHAT WILL HAPPEN AFTER I DIE...
BUT I KNOW...
...YOU CAN MAKE IT TO THE OTHER SIDE OF THE WALLS.
HUMANITY WILL BE SAVED...
...BY YOU...
... ARMIN.

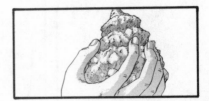

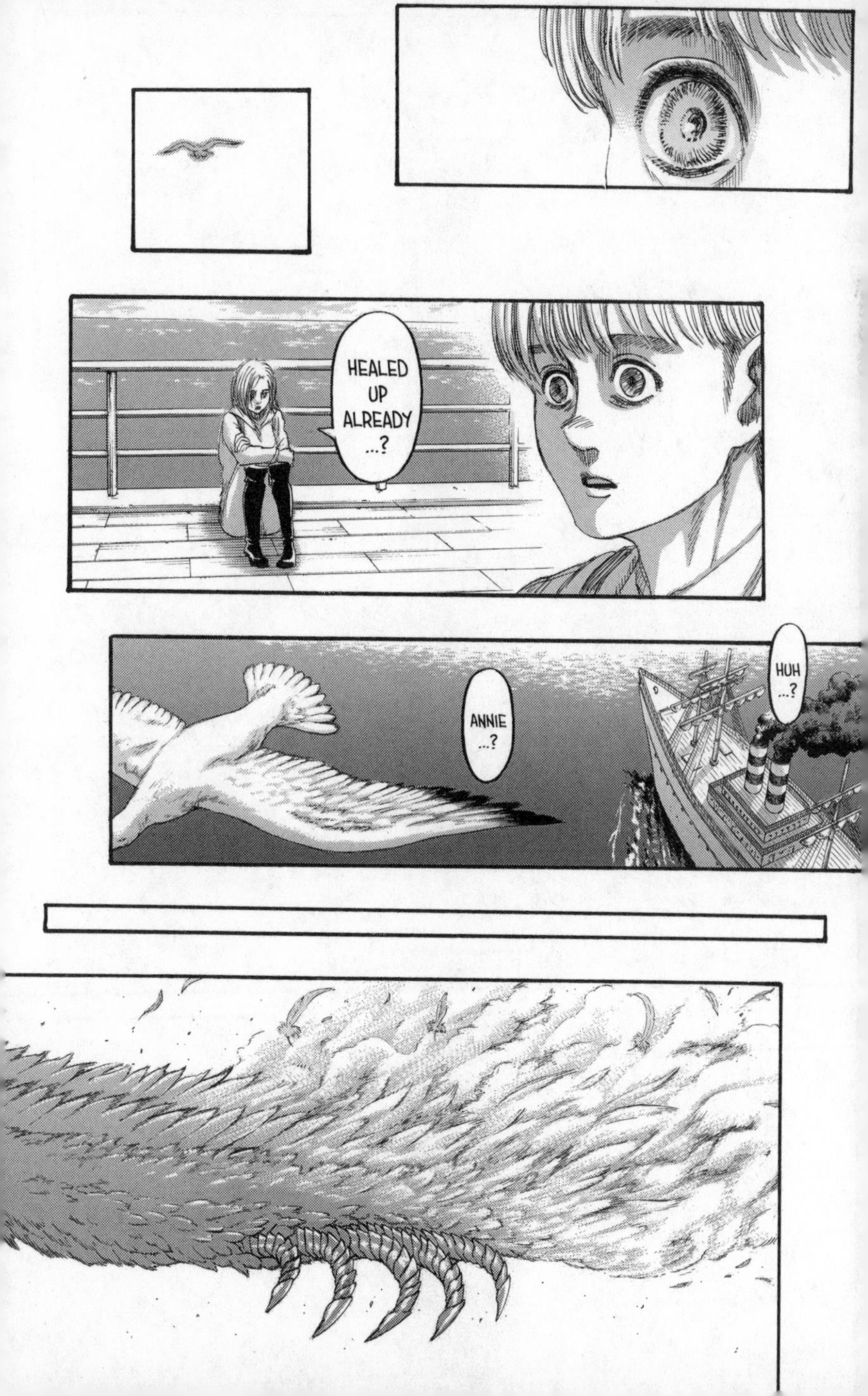
HEALED UP ALREADY ...?
HUH ...?
ANNIE ...?

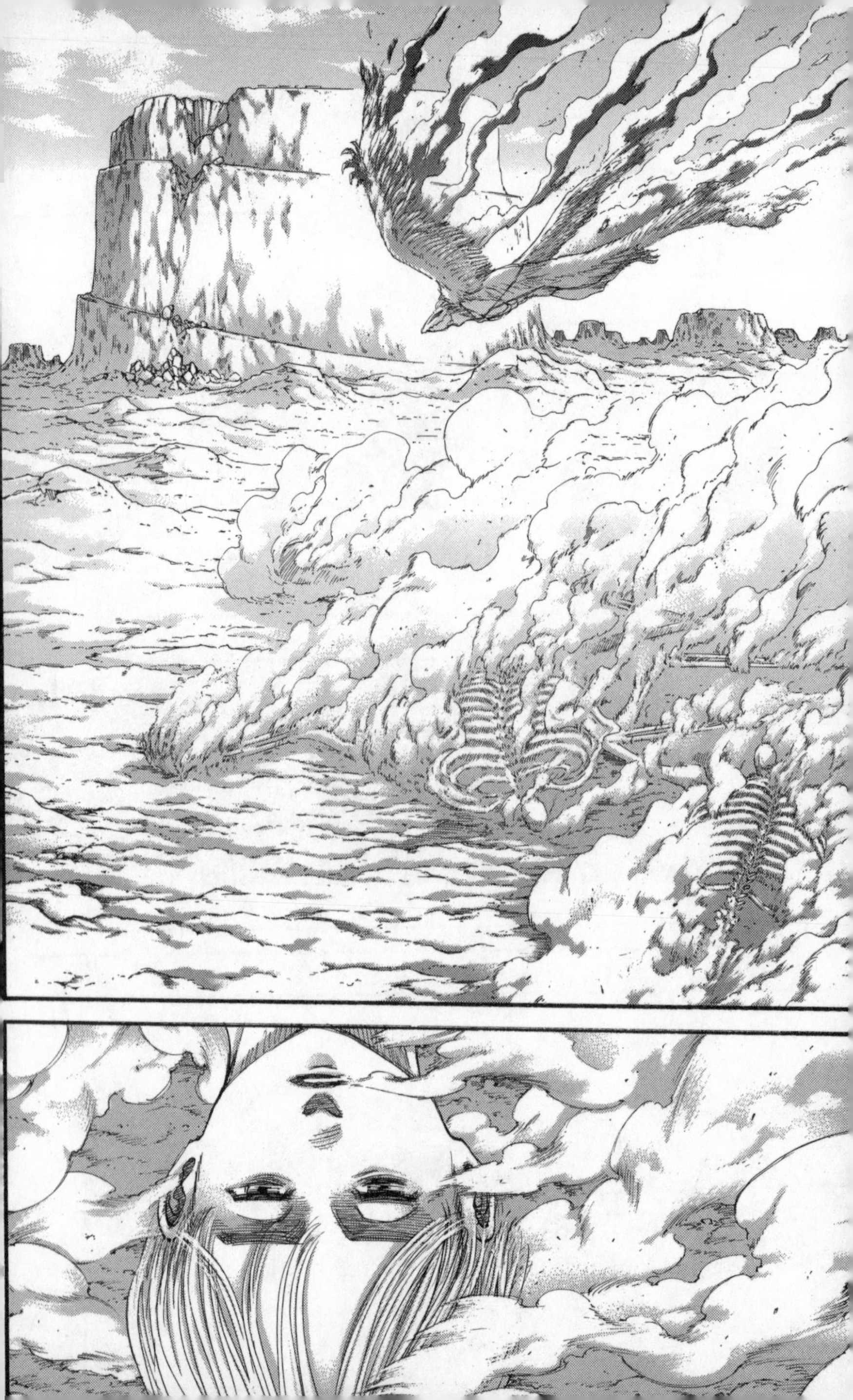

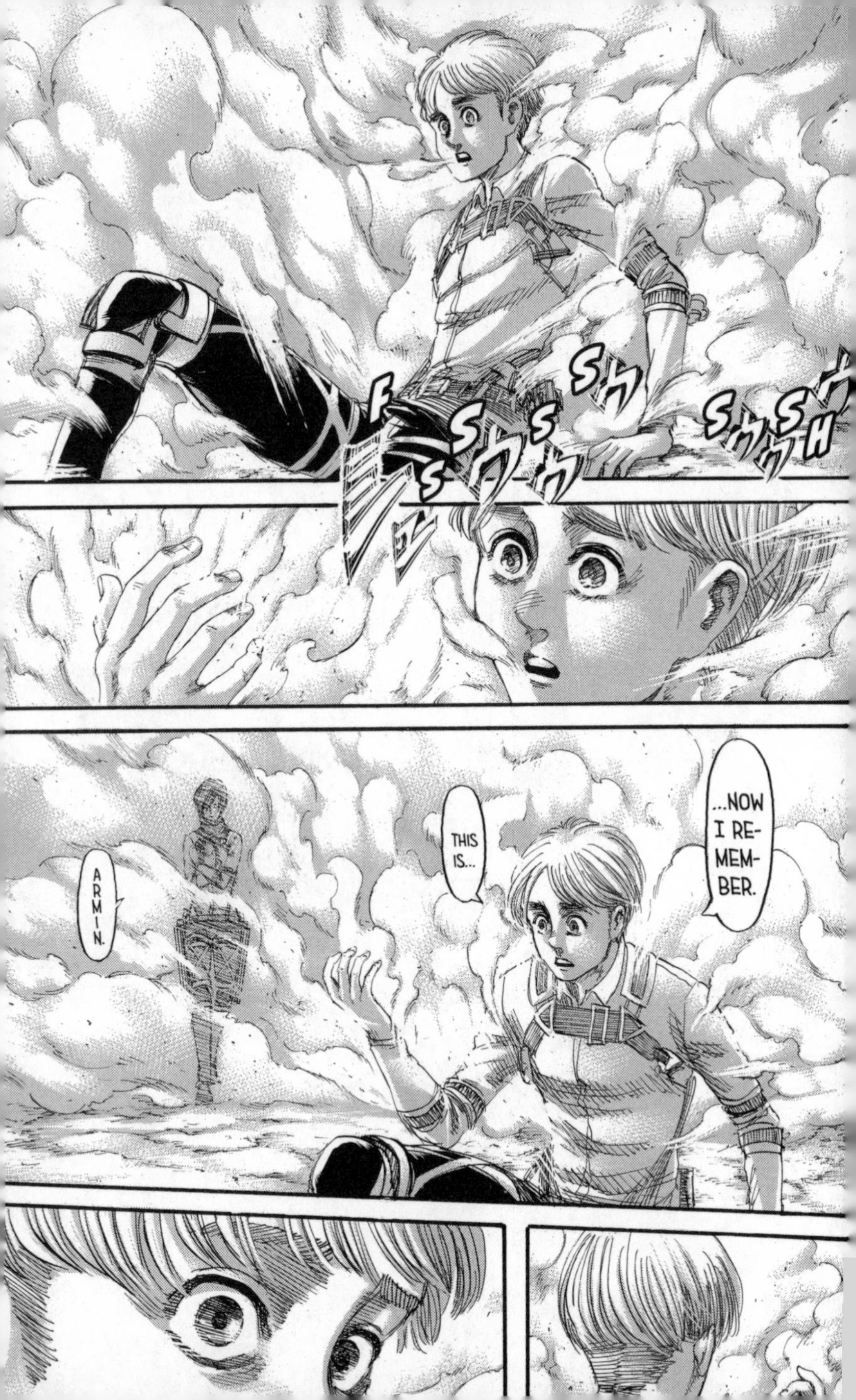
FSSSSH
SSSH
...NOW I RE-MEM-BER.
THIS IS...
ARMIN.

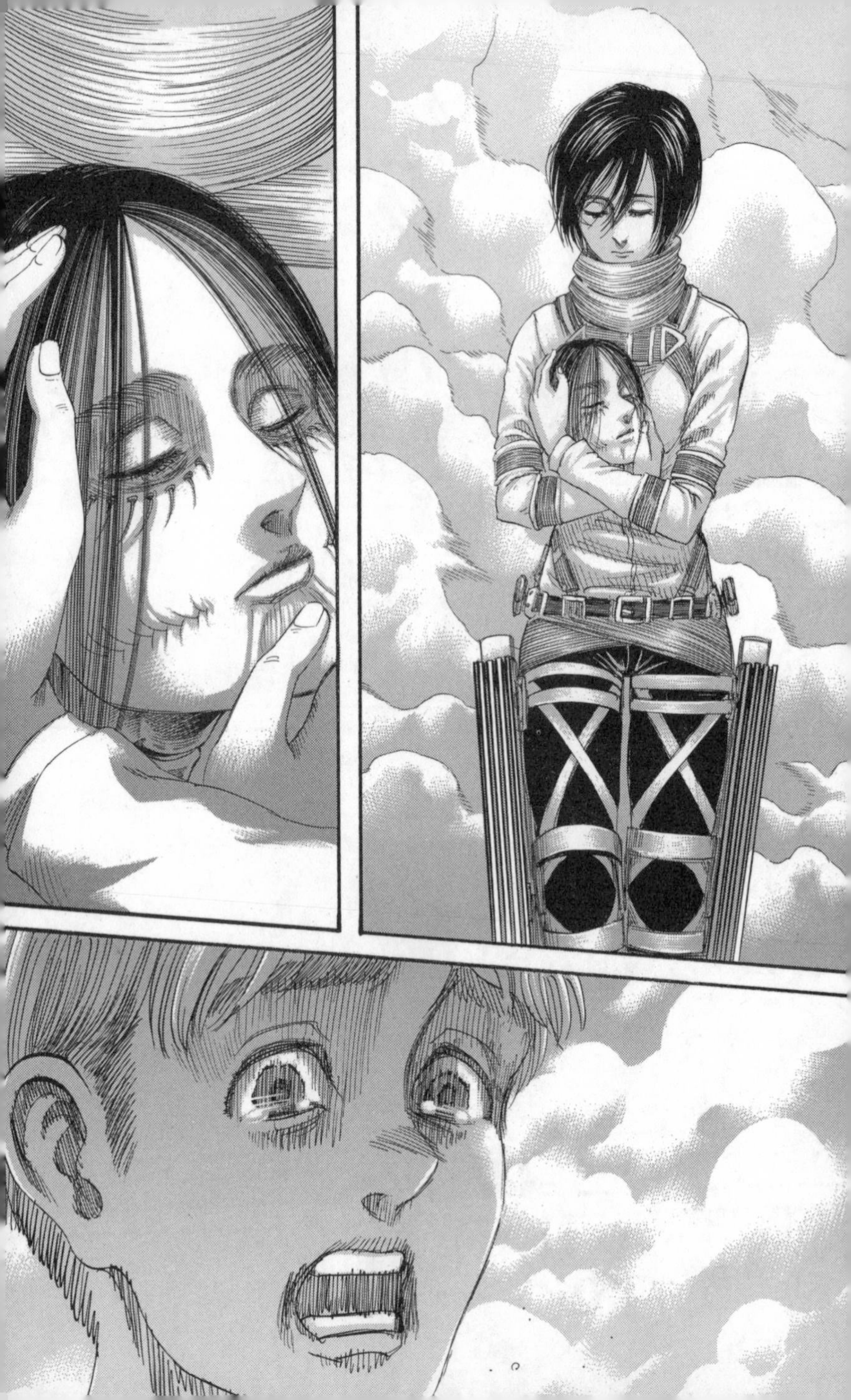

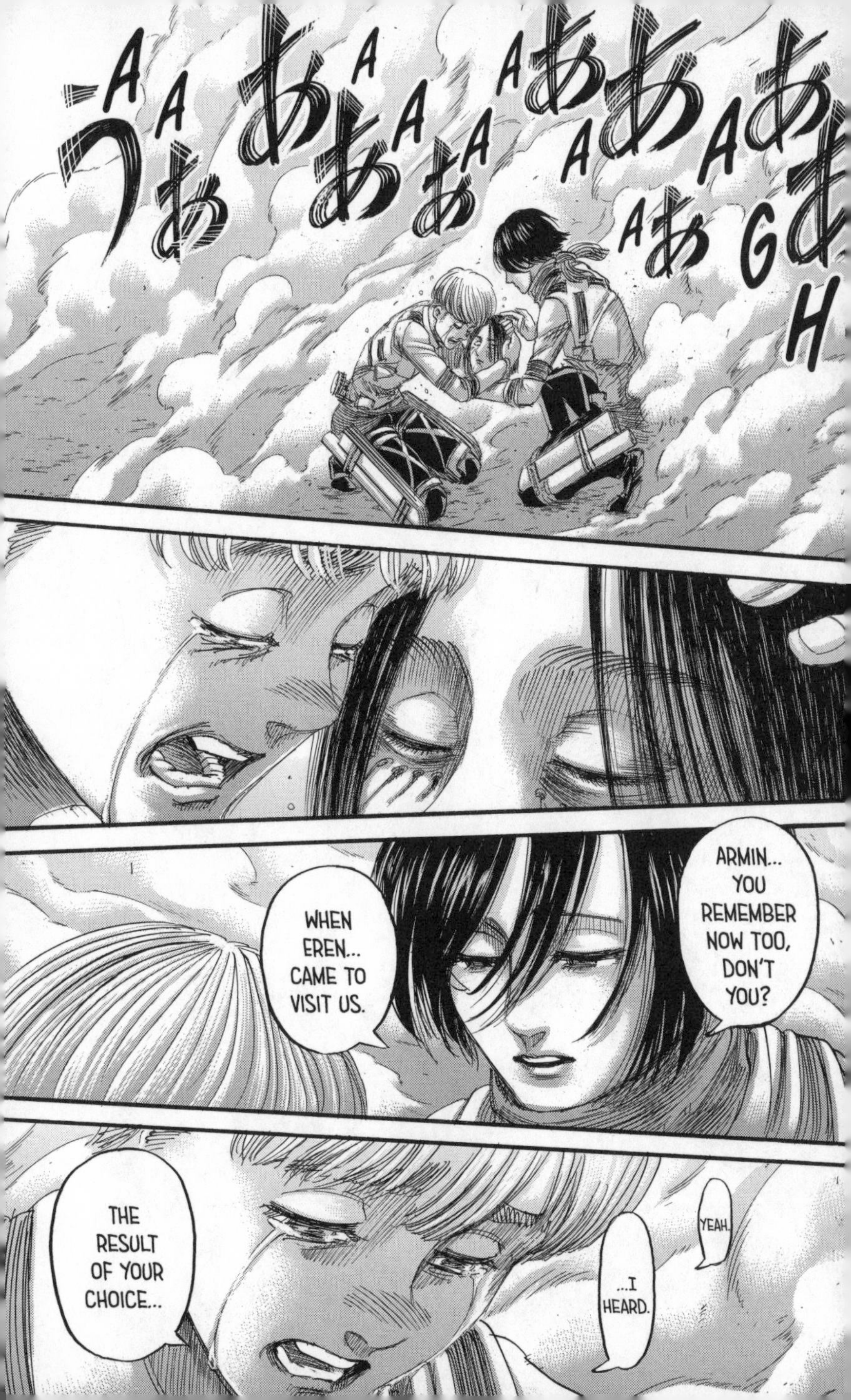
うあああああああああ
AAAAAAAAAAGH
ARMIN... YOU REMEMBER NOW TOO, DON'T YOU?
WHEN EREN... CAME TO VISIT US.
YEAH.
...I HEARD.
THE RESULT OF YOUR CHOICE...

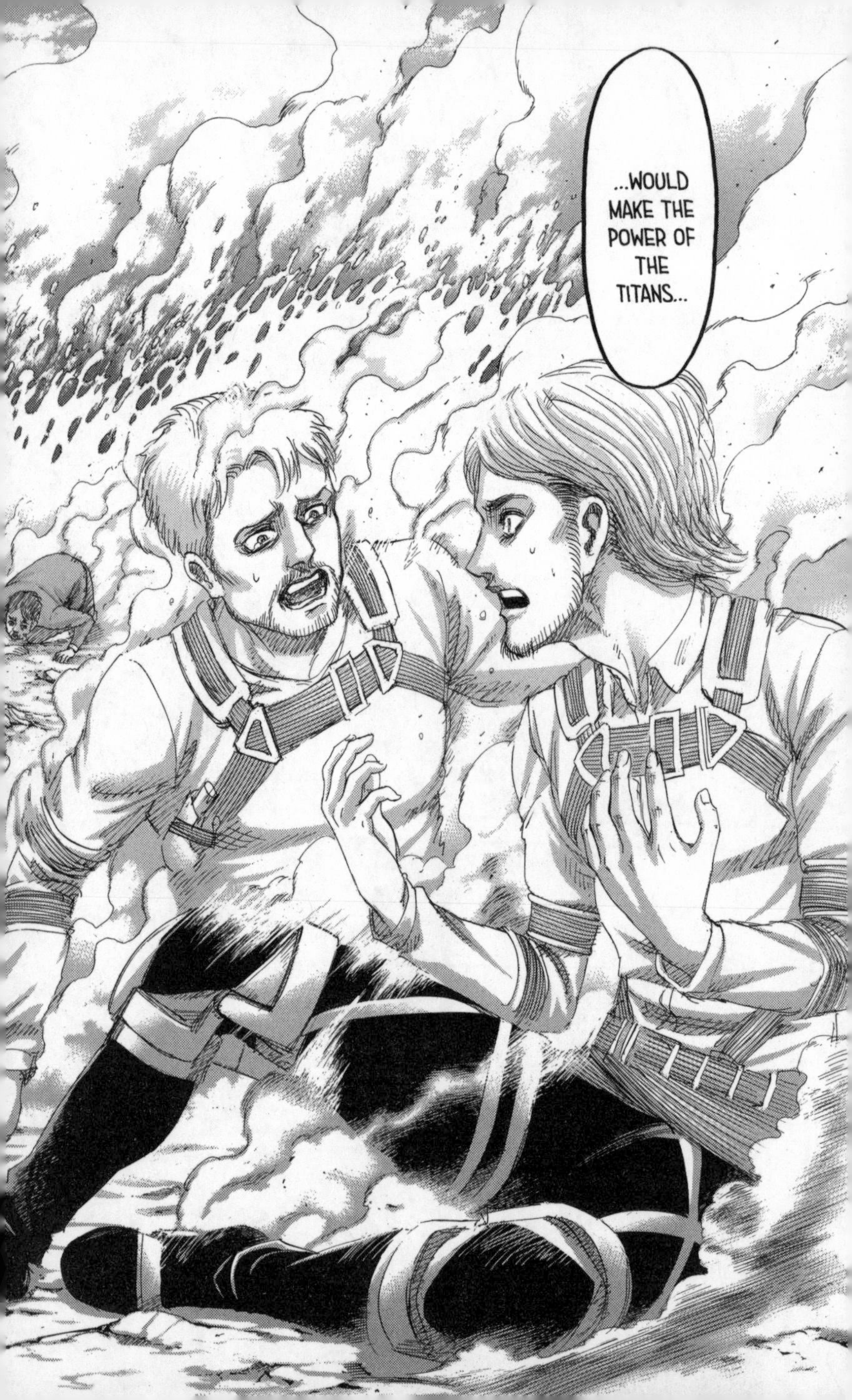
...WOULD MAKE THE POWER OF THE TITANS...

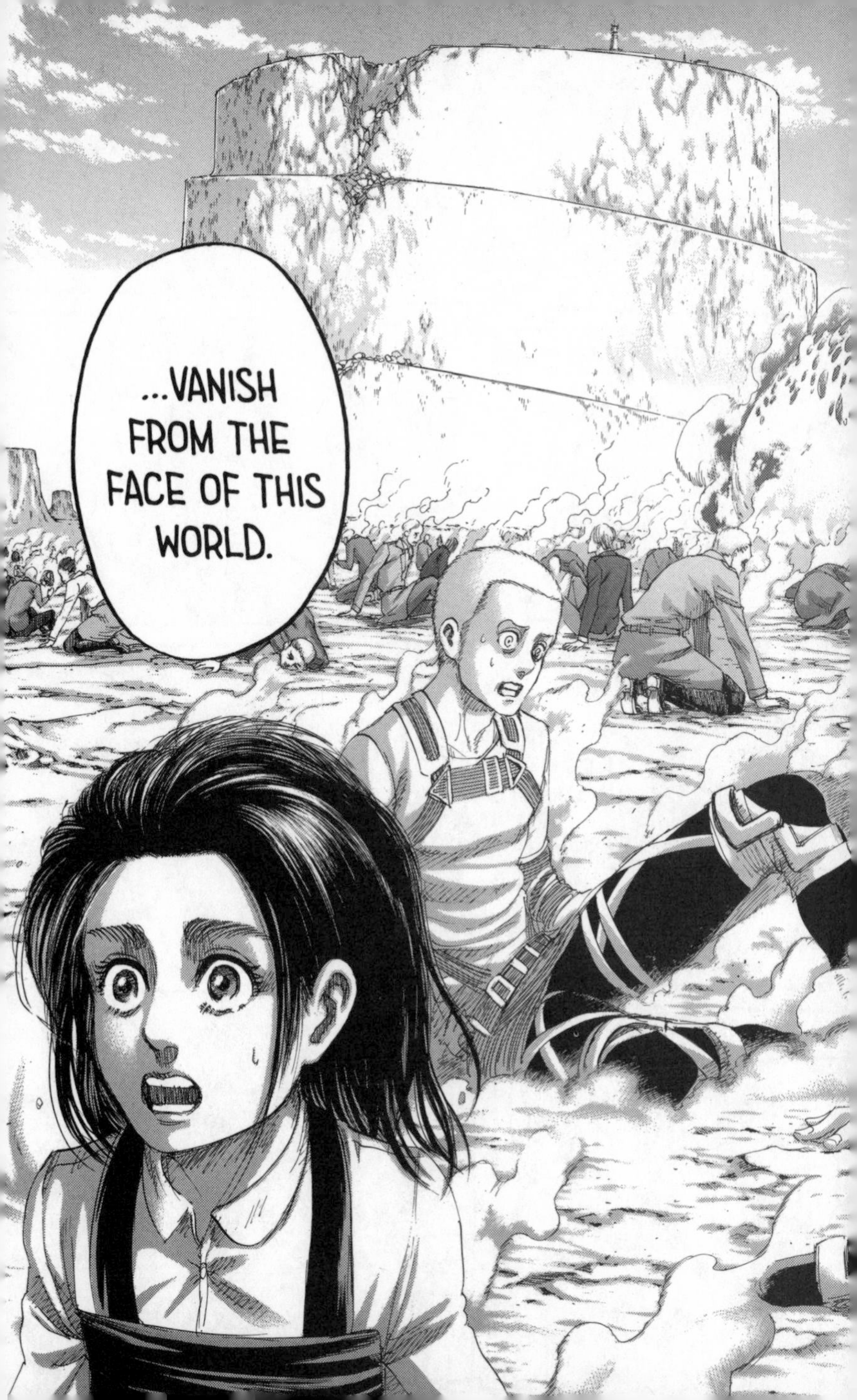
...VANISH FROM THE FACE OF THIS WORLD.

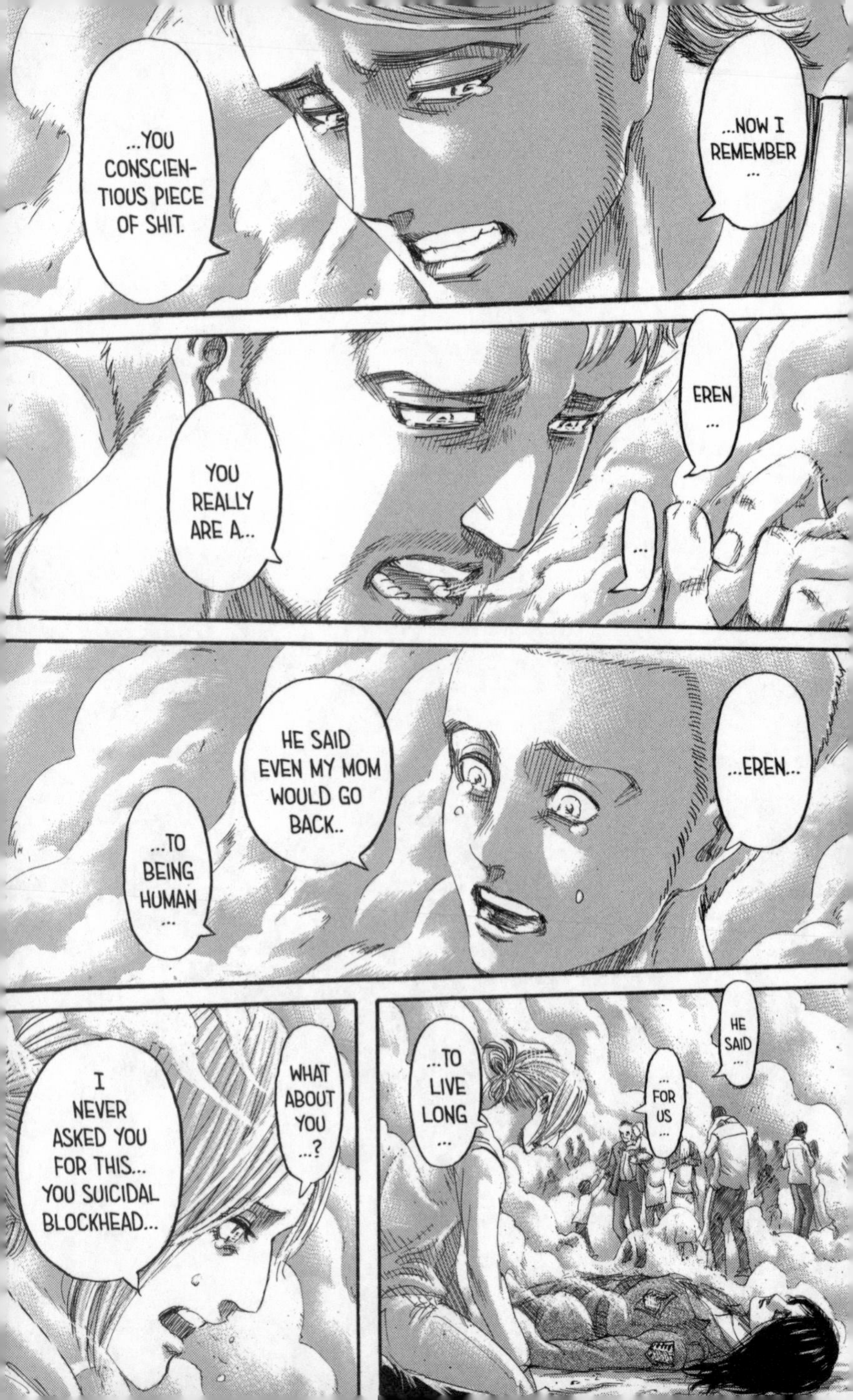
...NOW I REMEMBER ...
...YOU CONSCIEN-TIOUS PIECE OF SHIT.
EREN ...
...
YOU REALLY ARE A...
...EREN...
HE SAID EVEN MY MOM WOULD GO BACK..
...TO BEING HUMAN ...
HE SAID ...
... FOR US ...
...TO LIVE LONG ...
WHAT ABOUT YOU ...?
I NEVER ASKED YOU FOR THIS... YOU SUICIDAL BLOCKHEAD...

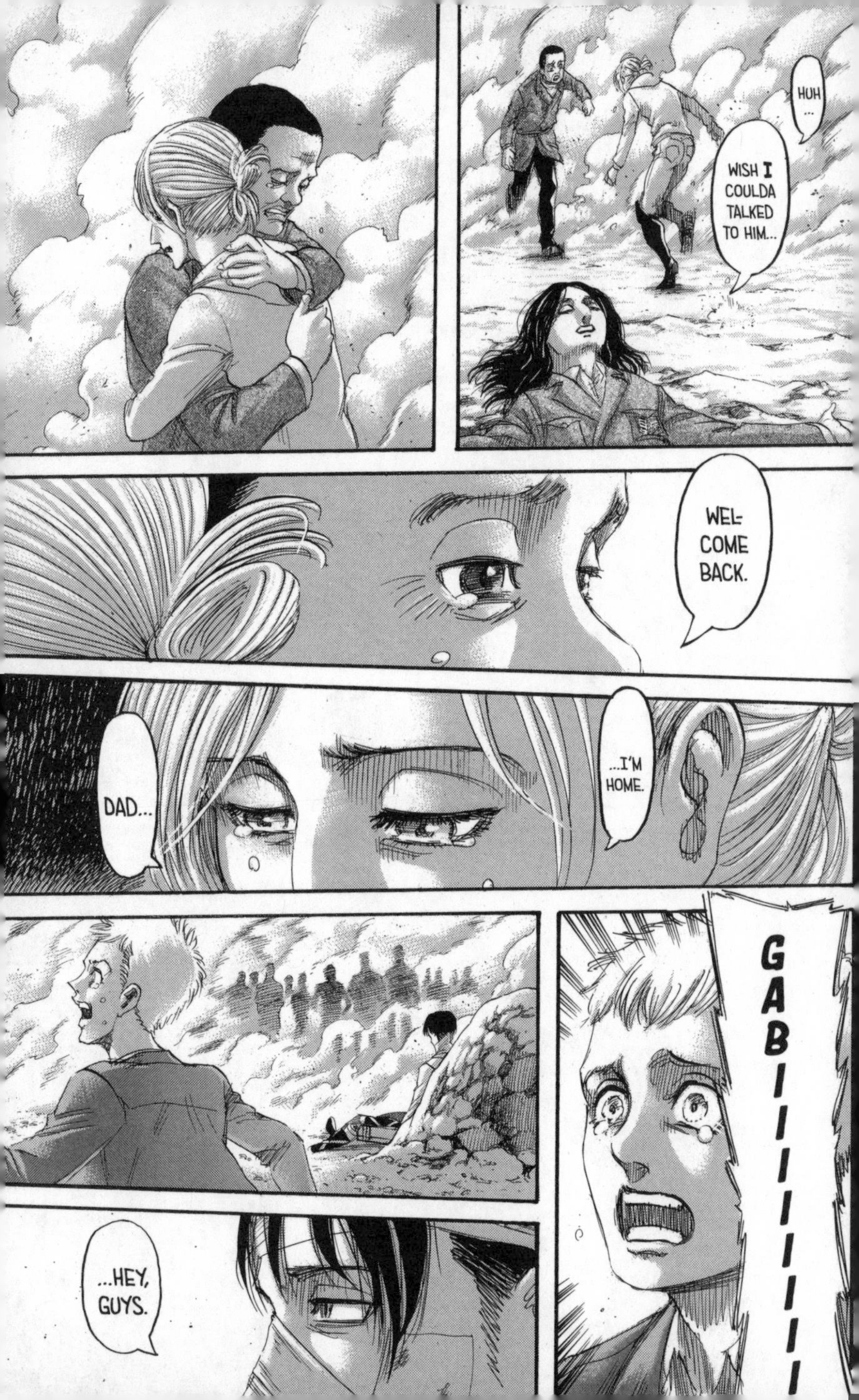
HUH...
WISH I COULDA TALKED TO HIM...
WEL-COME BACK.
...I'M HOME.
DAD...
GABIIIIIIIIIIII
...HEY, GUYS.

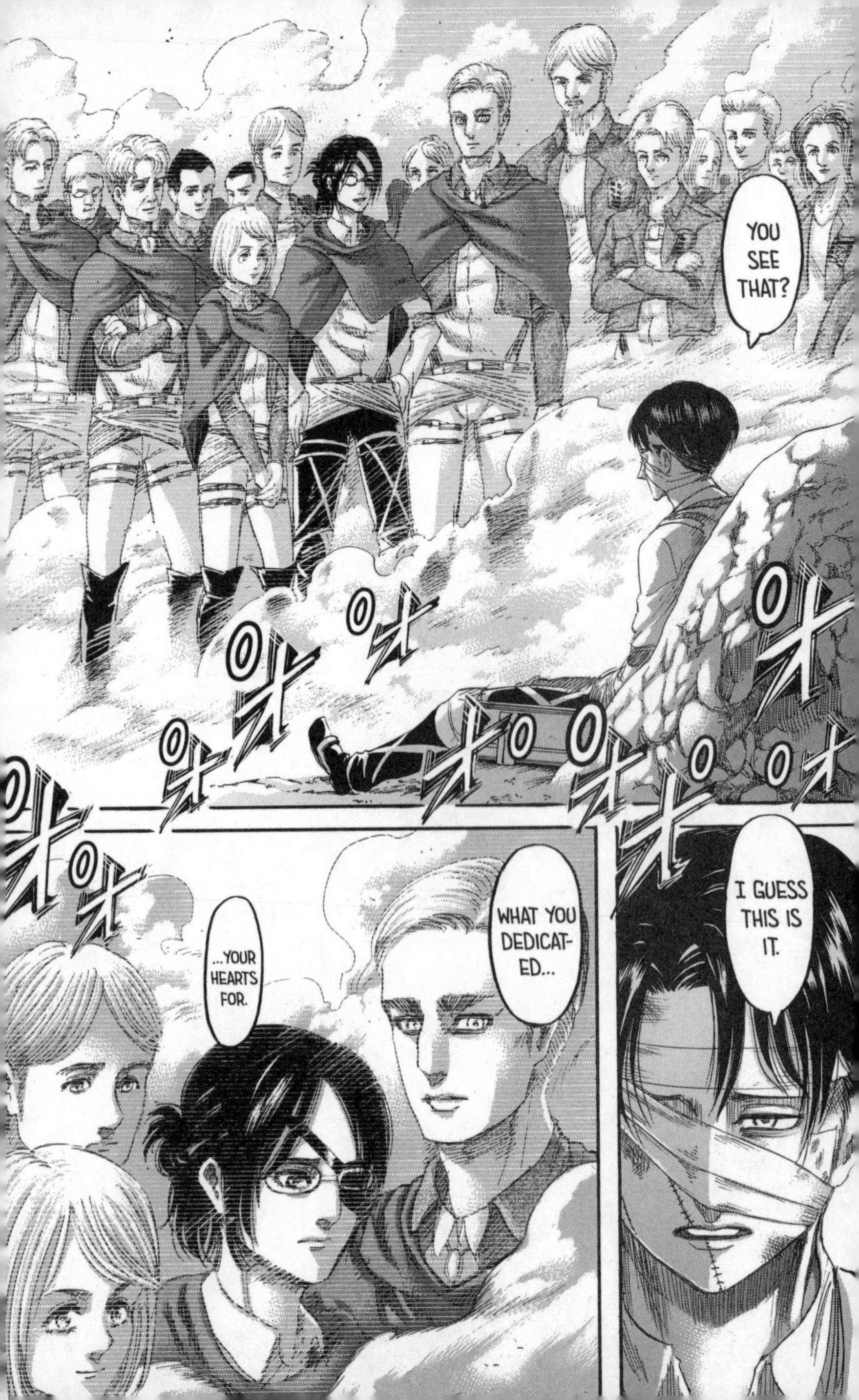
YOU SEE THAT?
Oオ Oオ Oオ Oオ Oオ Oオ Oオ Oオ Oオ Oオ
I GUESS THIS IS IT.
WHAT YOU DEDICAT-ED...
...YOUR HEARTS FOR.

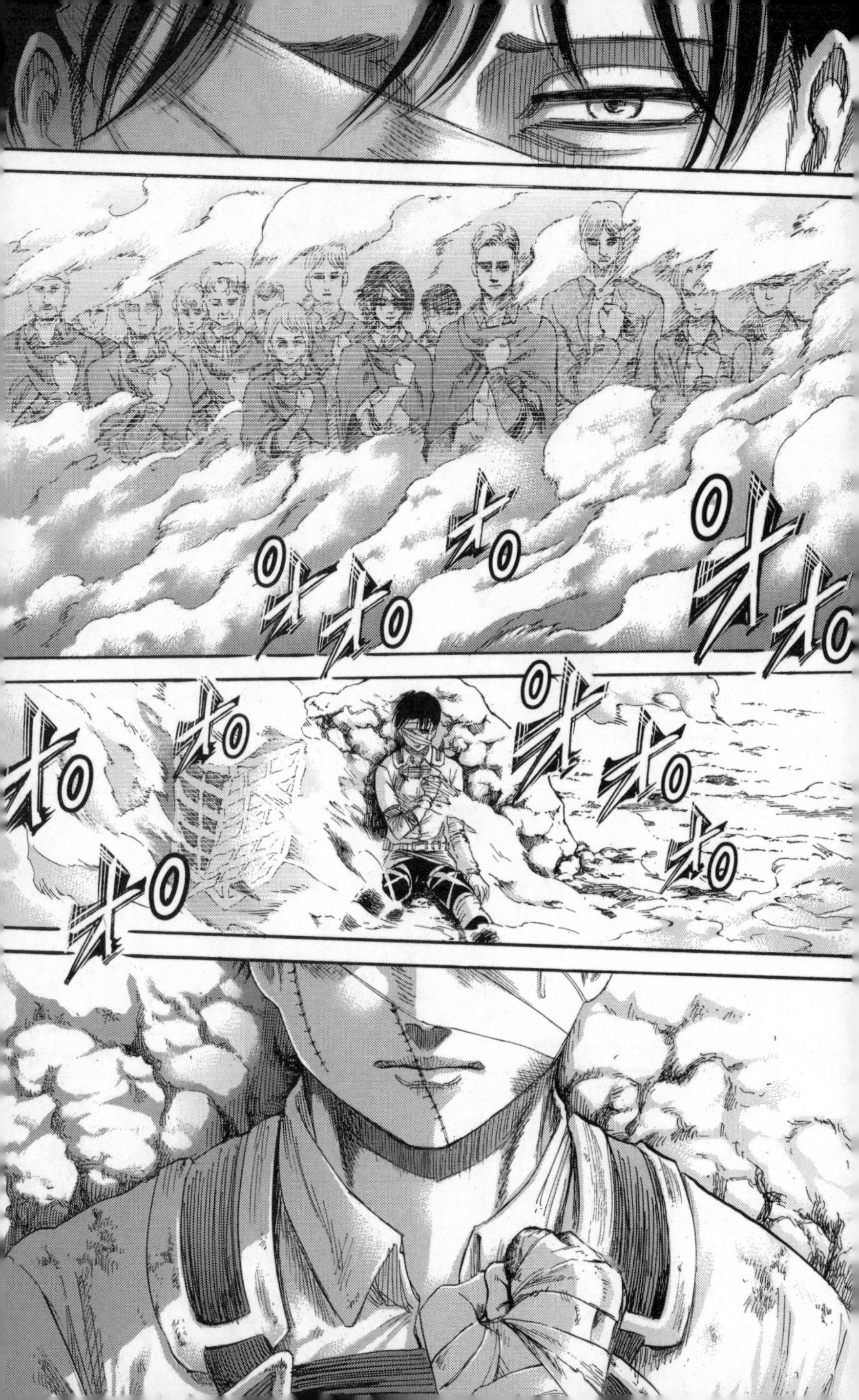

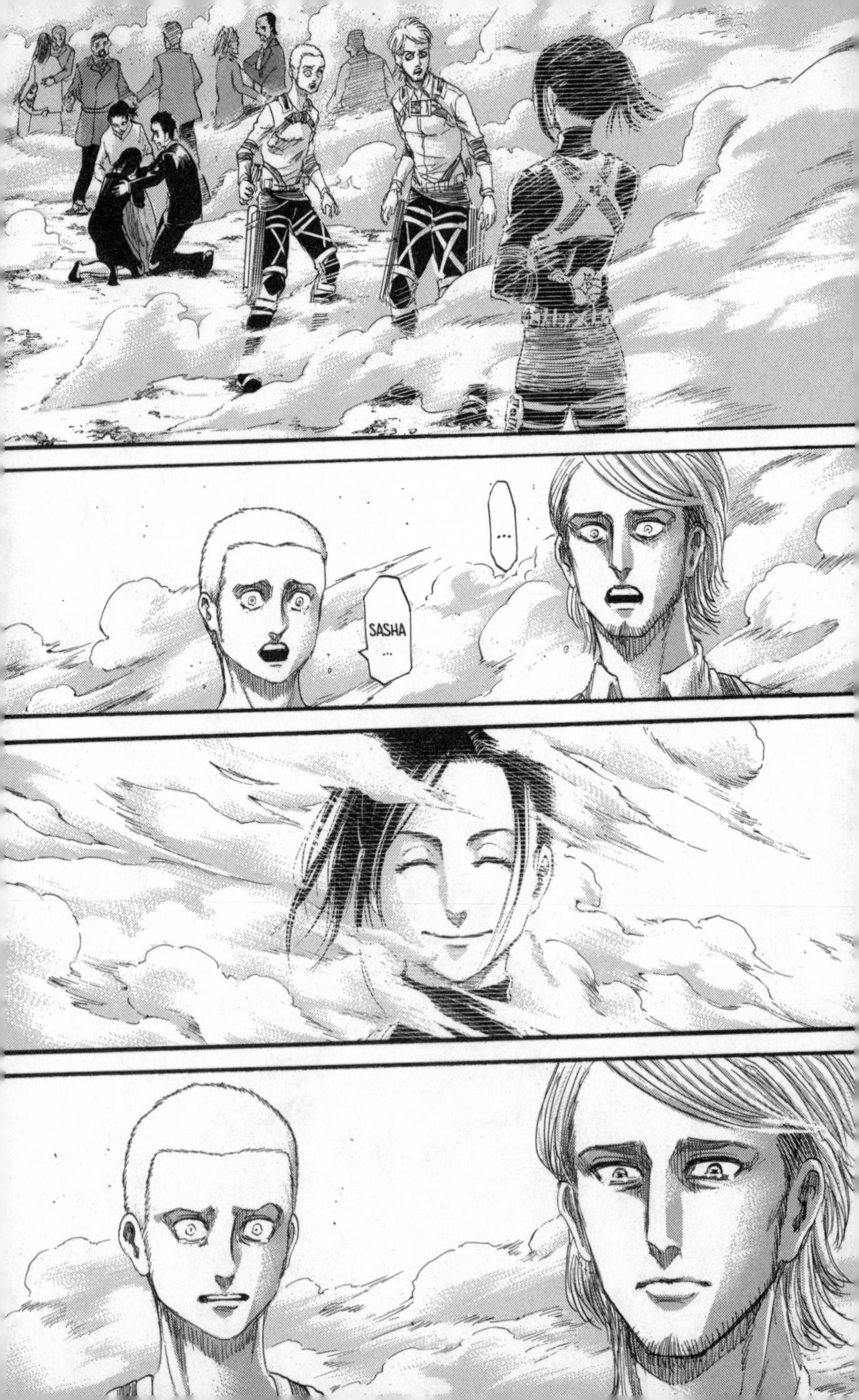
...
SASHA
...

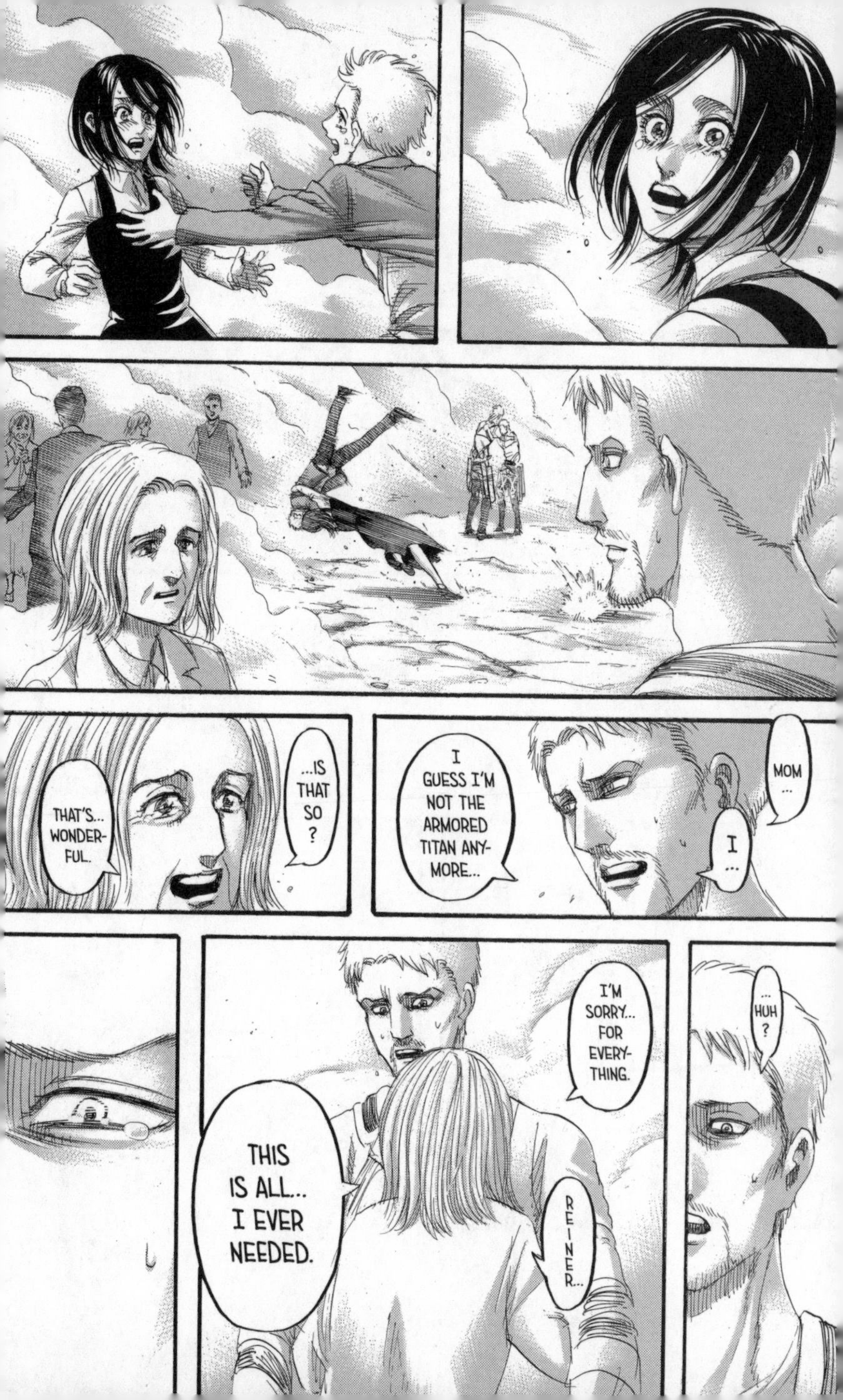
MOM ...
I ...
I GUESS I'M NOT THE ARMORED TITAN ANY-MORE...
...IS THAT SO?
THAT'S... WONDER-FUL.
...HUH?
I'M SORRY... FOR EVERY-THING.
REINER...
THIS IS ALL... I EVER NEEDED.

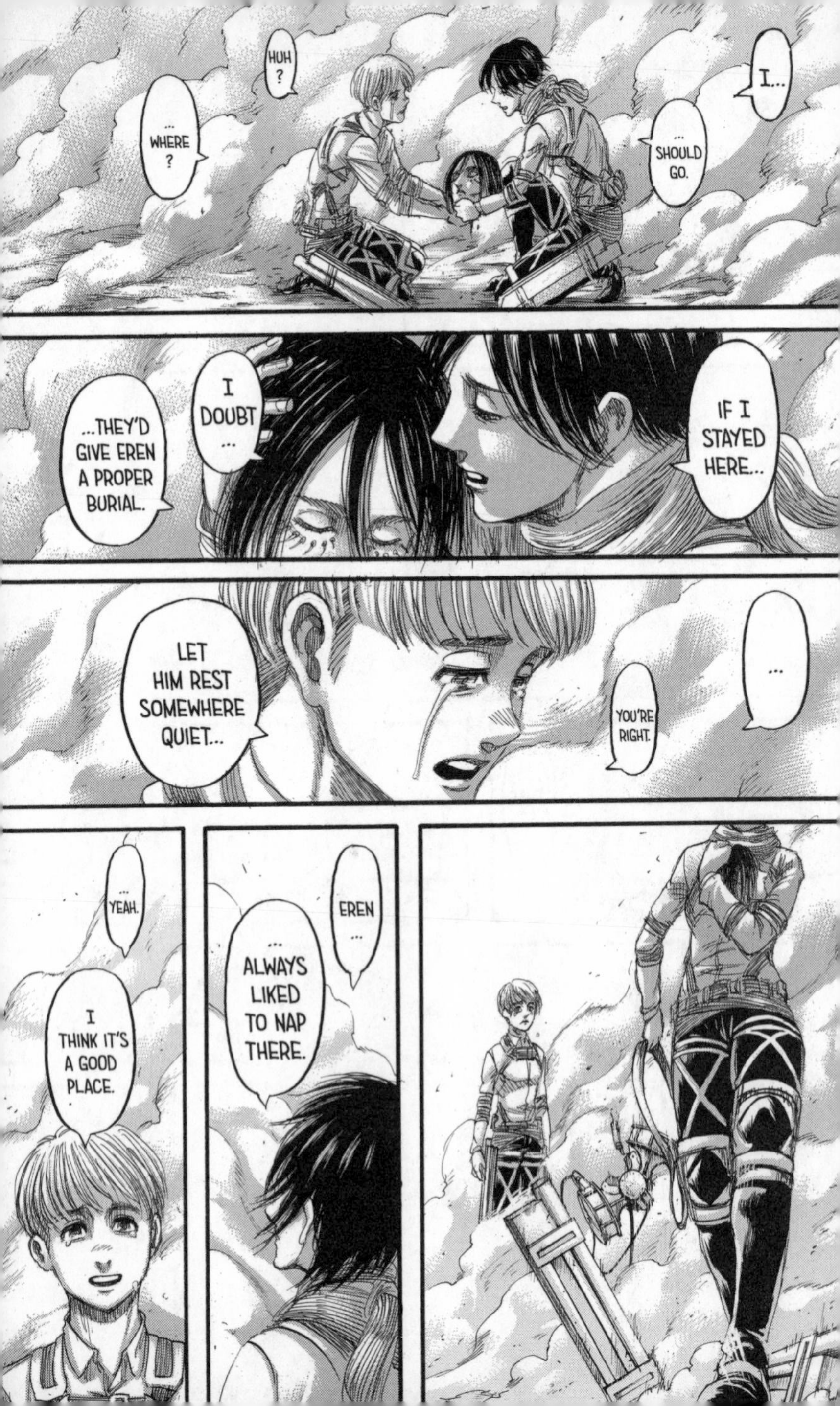
I...
...SHOULD GO.
HUH?
...WHERE?
IF I STAYED HERE...
I DOUBT...
...THEY'D GIVE EREN A PROPER BURIAL.
...
YOU'RE RIGHT.
LET HIM REST SOMEWHERE QUIET...
EREN...
...ALWAYS LIKED TO NAP THERE.
...YEAH.
I THINK IT'S A GOOD PLACE.

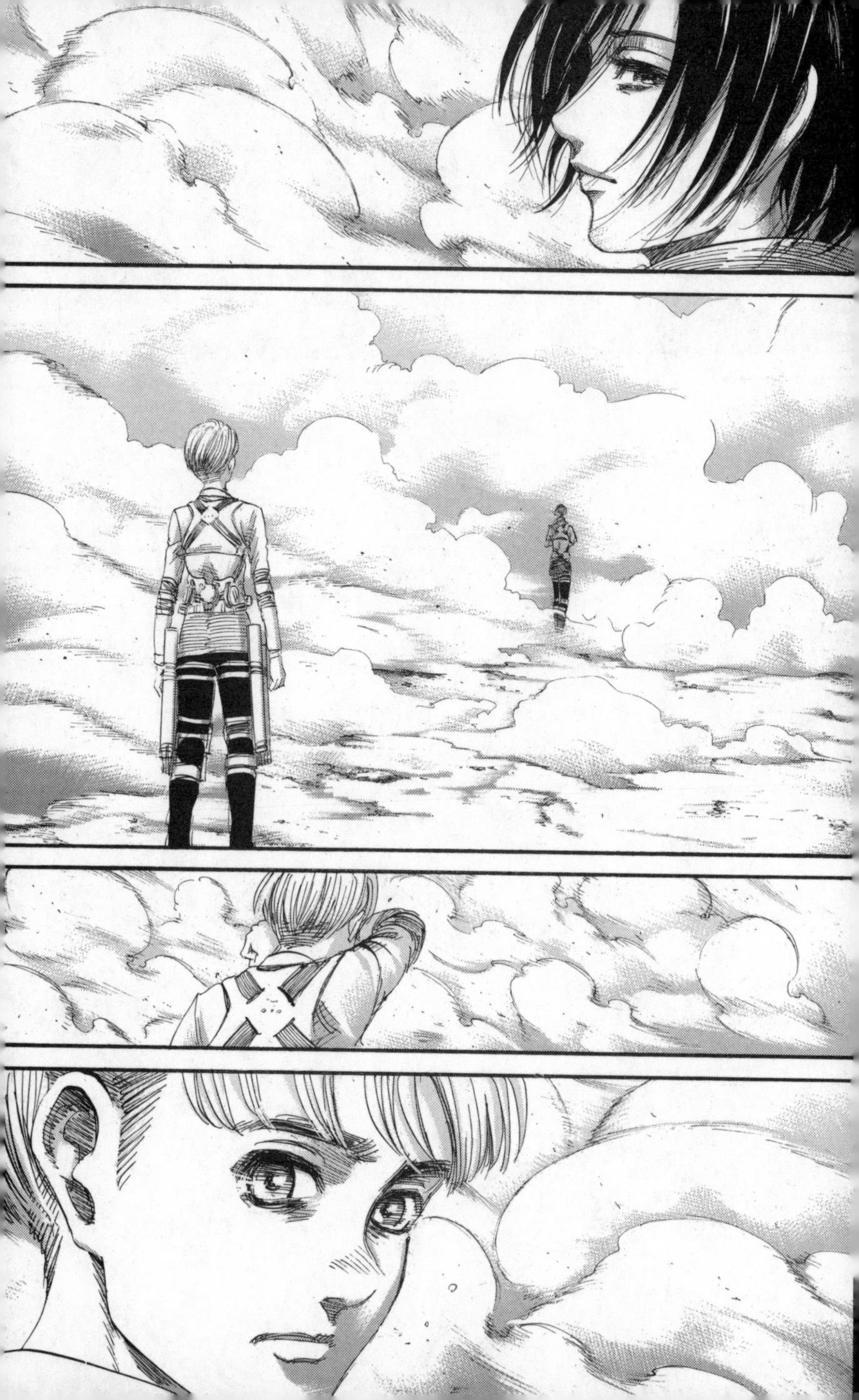

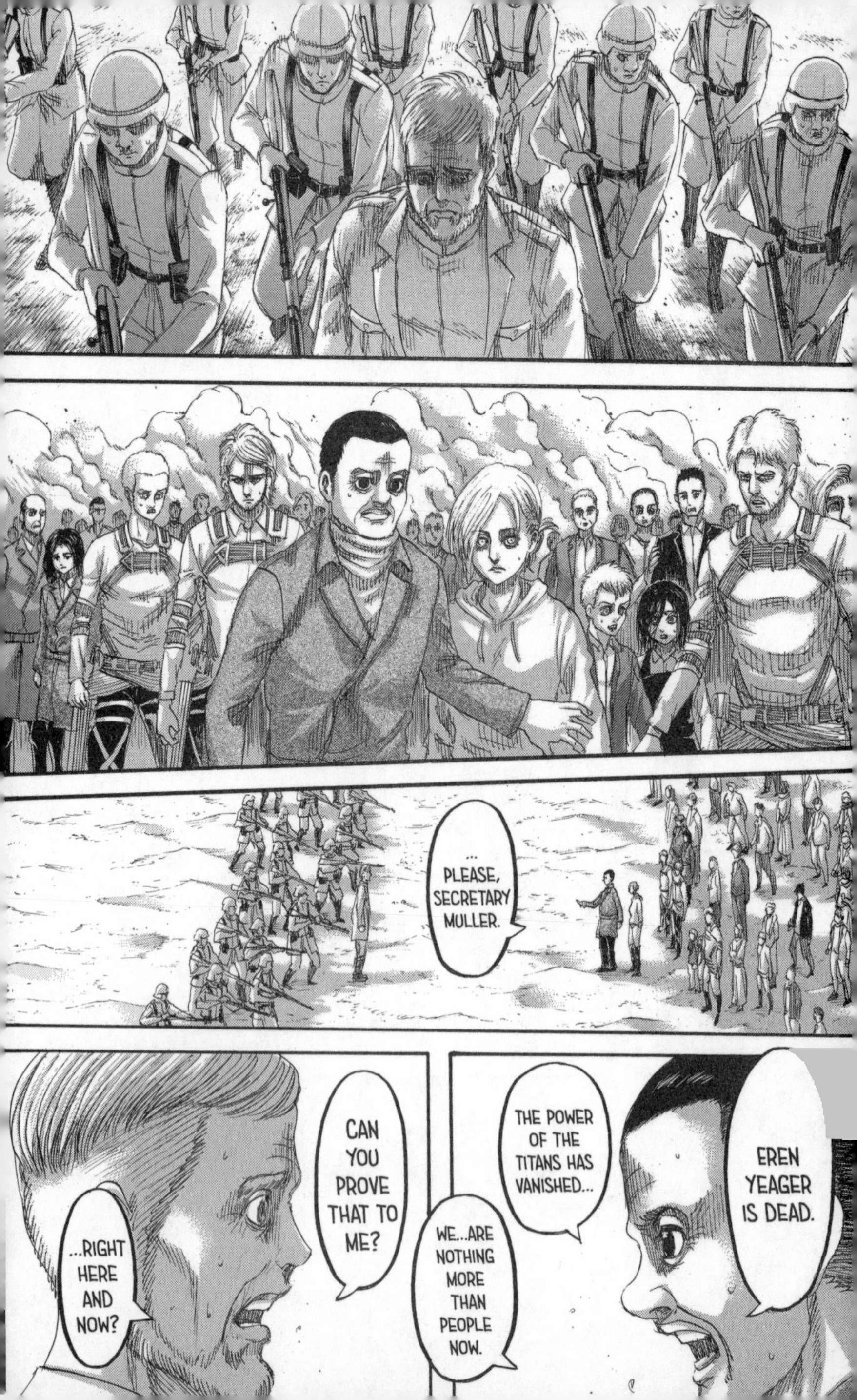
...PLEASE, SECRETARY MULLER.
EREN YEAGER IS DEAD.
THE POWER OF THE TITANS HAS VANISHED...
WE...ARE NOTHING MORE THAN PEOPLE NOW.
CAN YOU PROVE THAT TO ME?
...RIGHT HERE AND NOW?

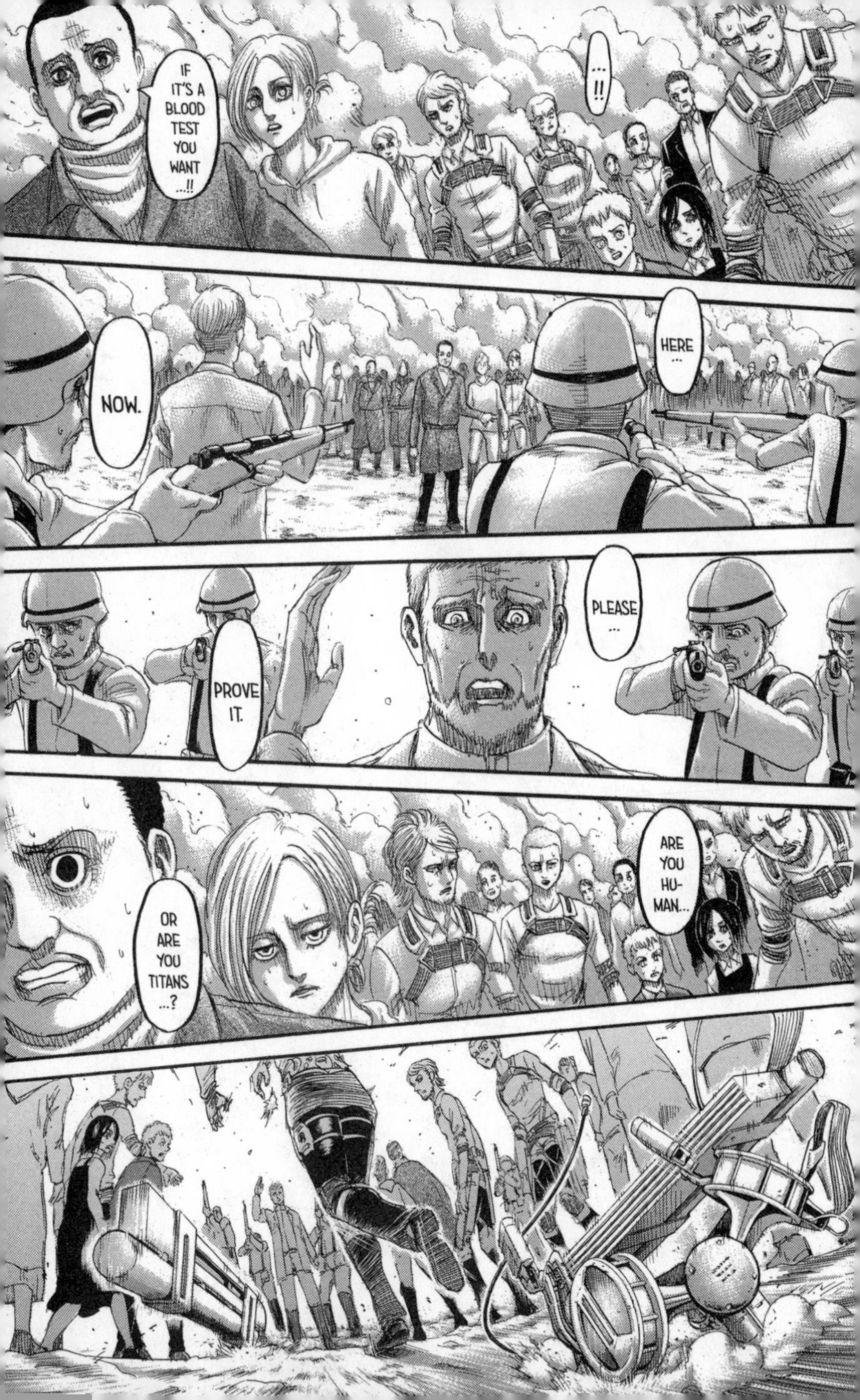
...!!
IF IT'S A BLOOD TEST YOU WANT ...!!
HERE ...
NOW.
PLEASE ...
PROVE IT.
ARE YOU HU-MAN...
OR ARE YOU TITANS ...?

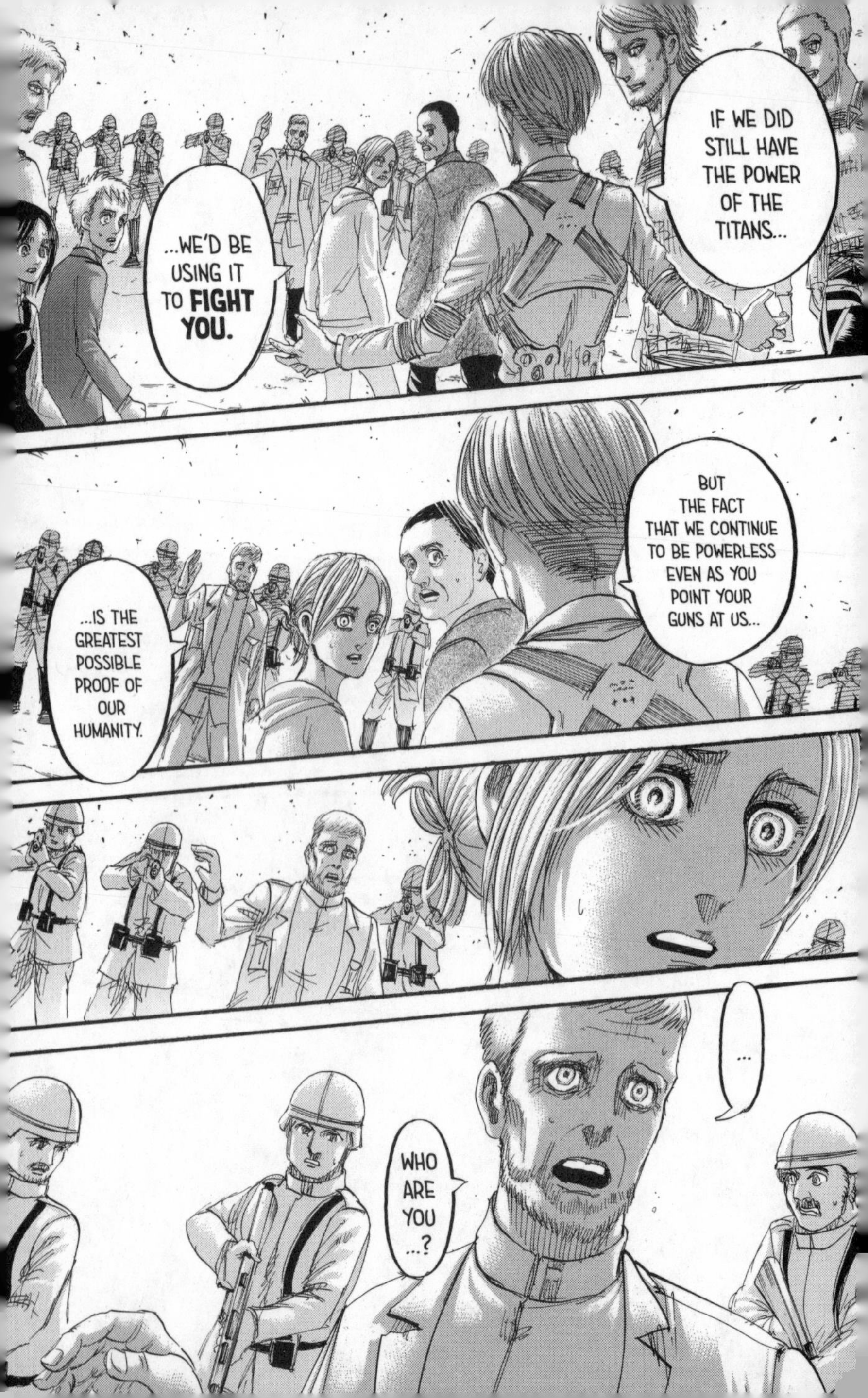
IF WE DID STILL HAVE THE POWER OF THE TITANS...
...WE'D BE USING IT TO **FIGHT YOU.**
BUT THE FACT THAT WE CONTINUE TO BE POWERLESS EVEN AS YOU POINT YOUR GUNS AT US...
...IS THE GREATEST POSSIBLE PROOF OF OUR HUMANITY.
...
WHO ARE YOU ...?

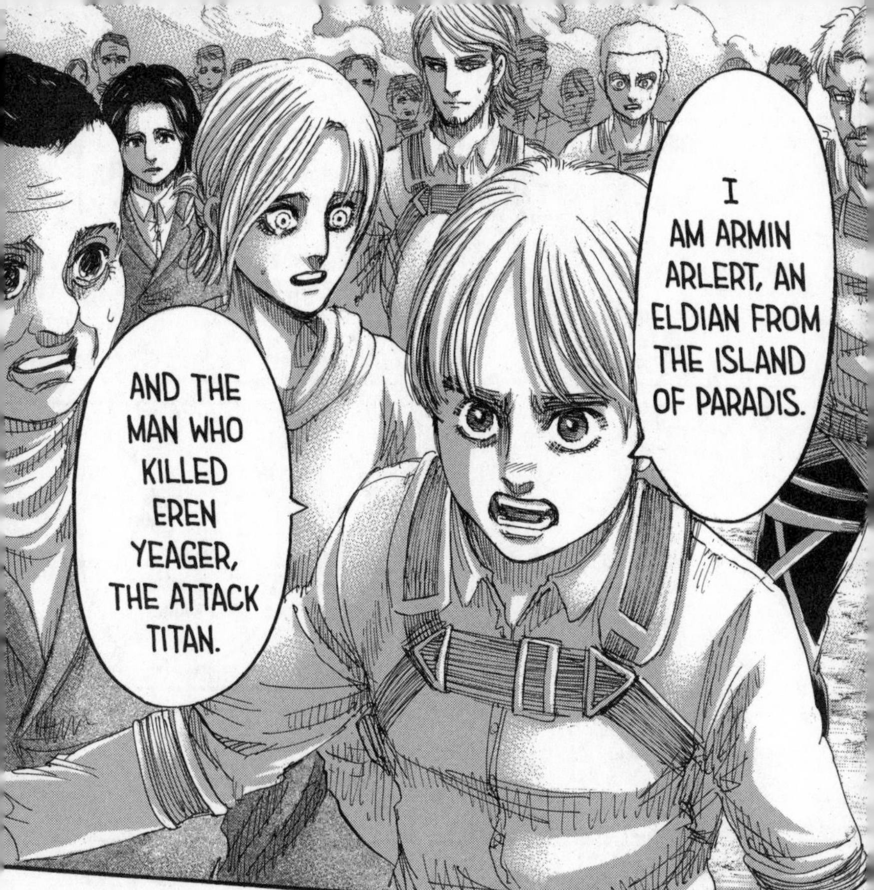
I AM ARMIN ARLERT, AN ELDIAN FROM THE ISLAND OF PARADIS.
AND THE MAN WHO KILLED EREN YEAGER, THE ATTACK TITAN.
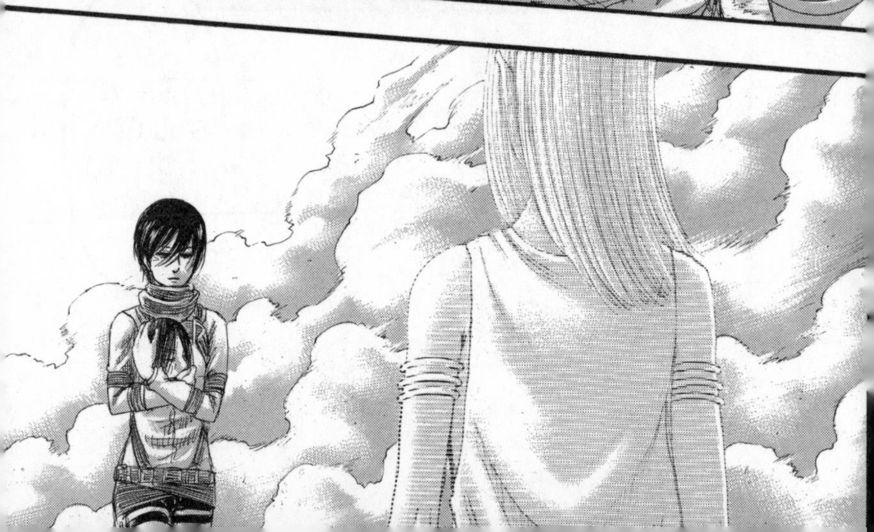

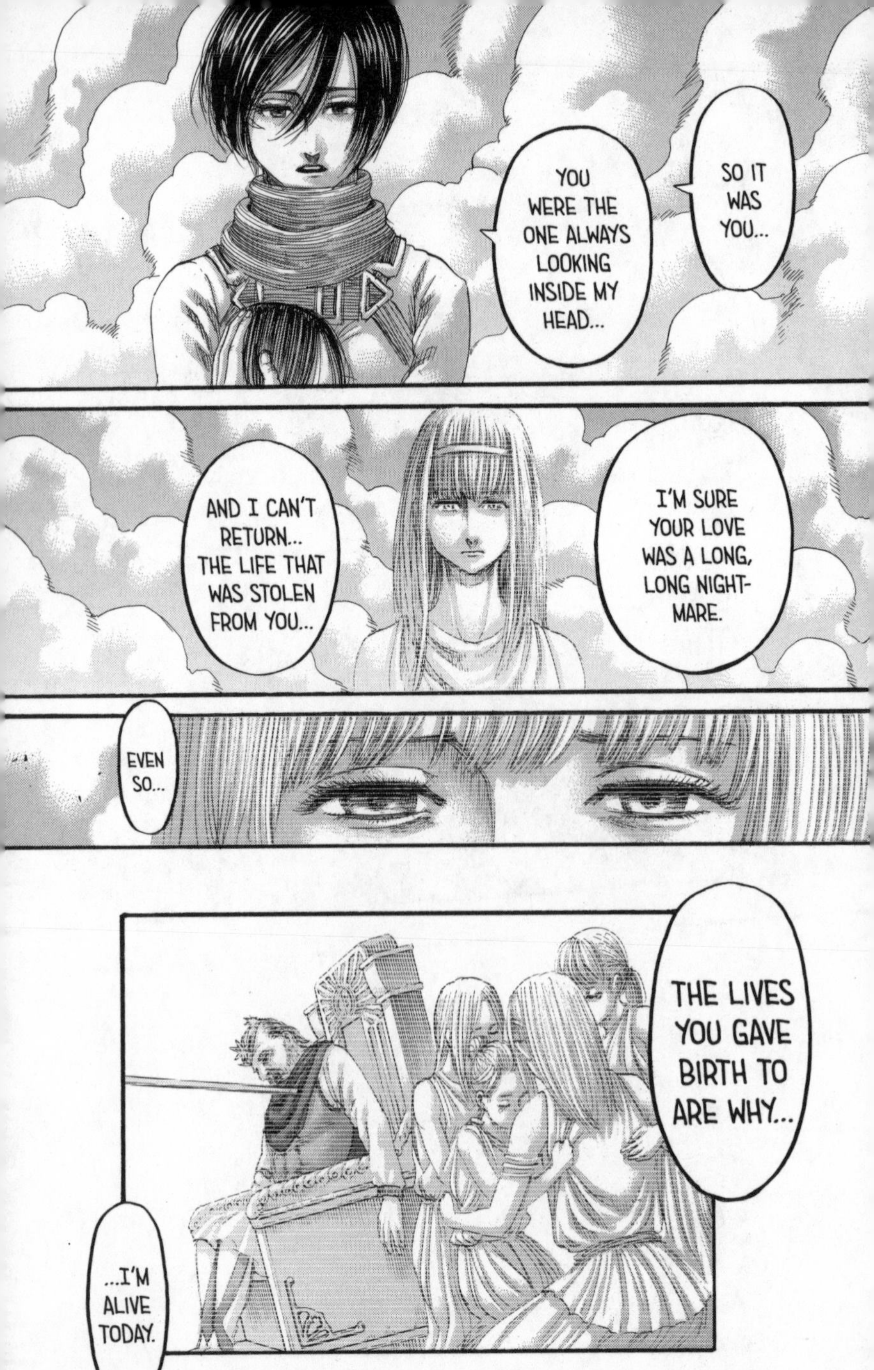
SO IT WAS YOU...
YOU WERE THE ONE ALWAYS LOOKING INSIDE MY HEAD...
I'M SURE YOUR LOVE WAS A LONG, LONG NIGHT-MARE.
AND I CAN'T RETURN... THE LIFE THAT WAS STOLEN FROM YOU...
EVEN SO...
THE LIVES YOU GAVE BIRTH TO ARE WHY...
...I'M ALIVE TODAY.

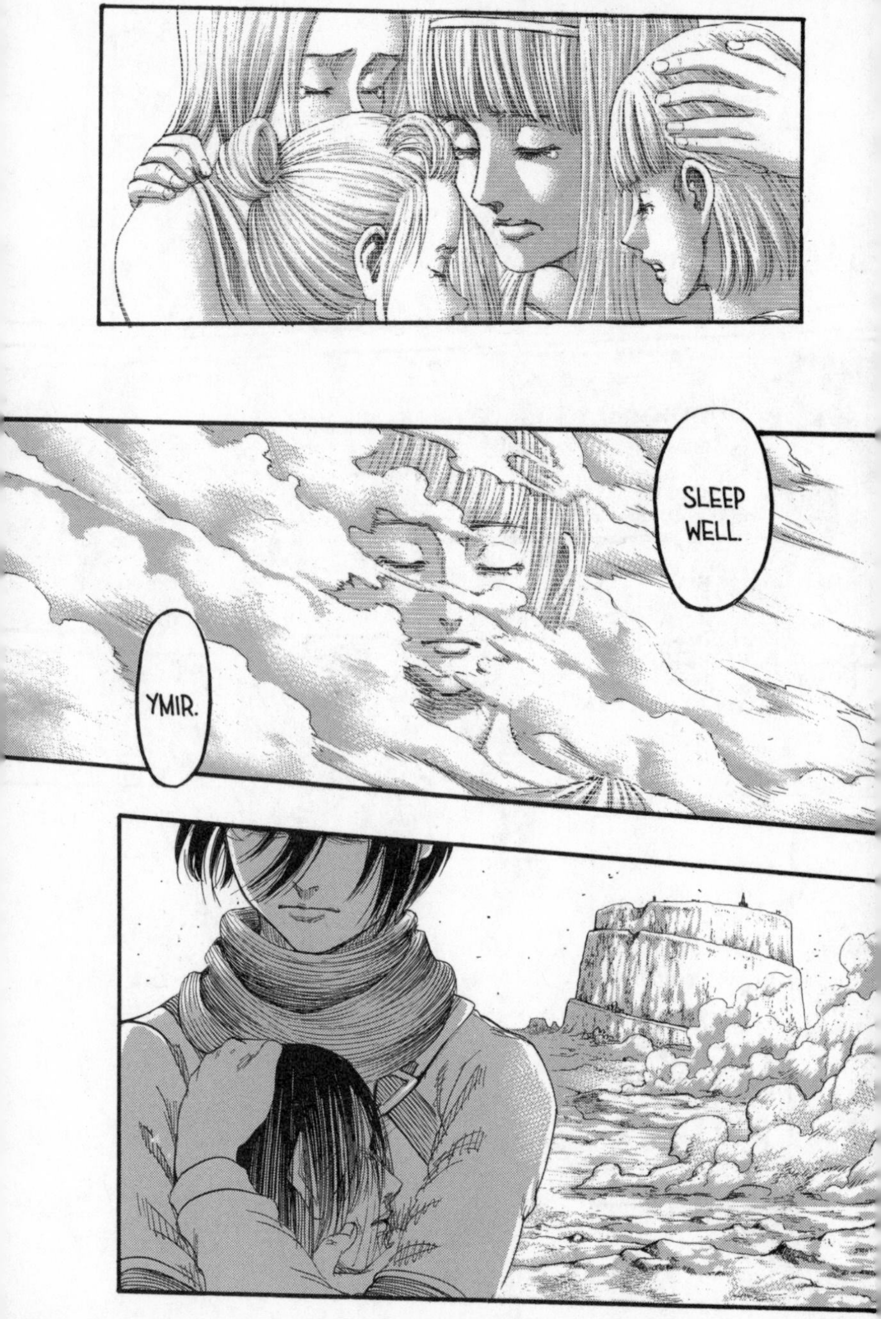
SLEEP WELL.
YMIR.

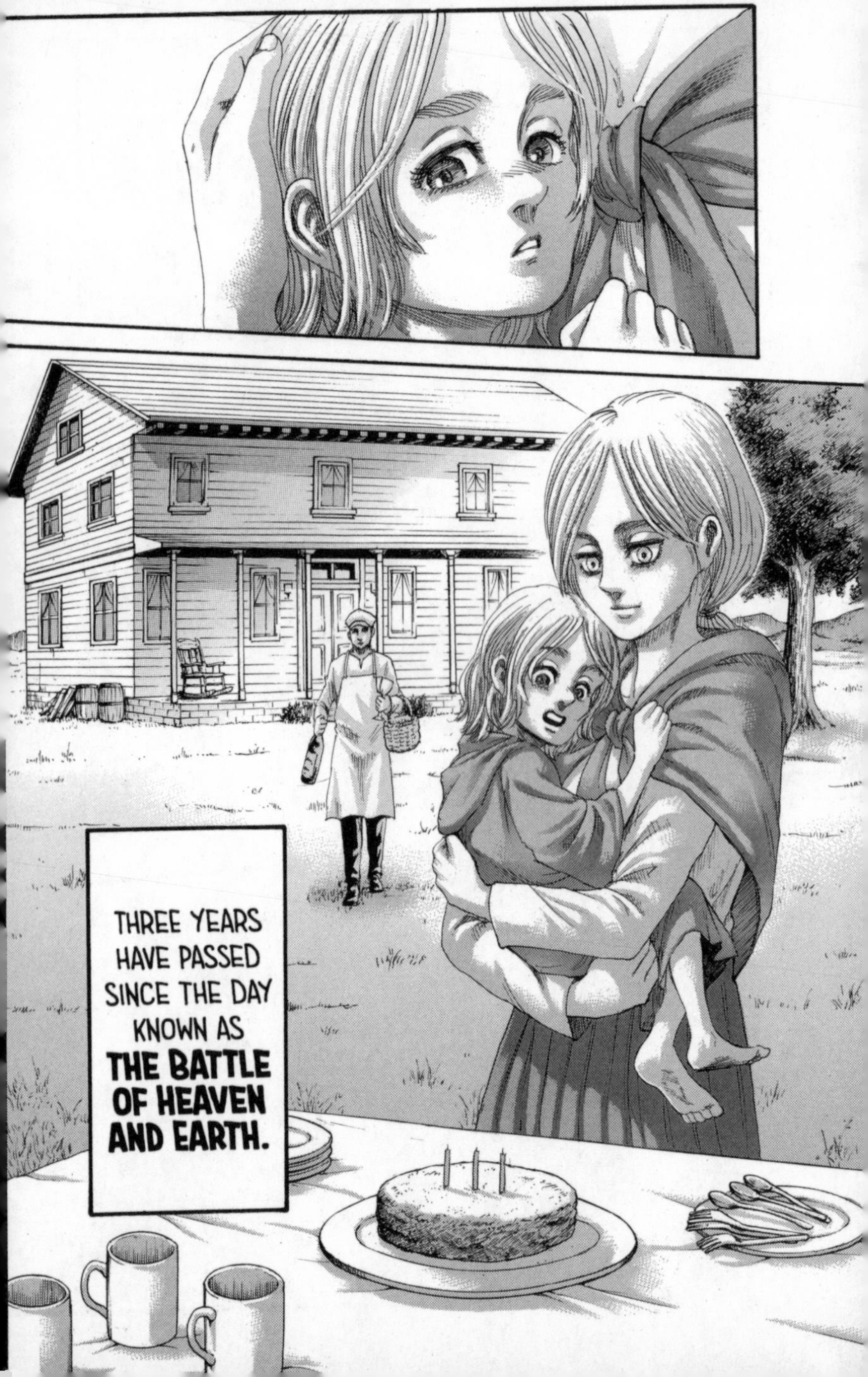
THREE YEARS HAVE PASSED SINCE THE DAY KNOWN AS **THE BATTLE OF HEAVEN AND EARTH.**

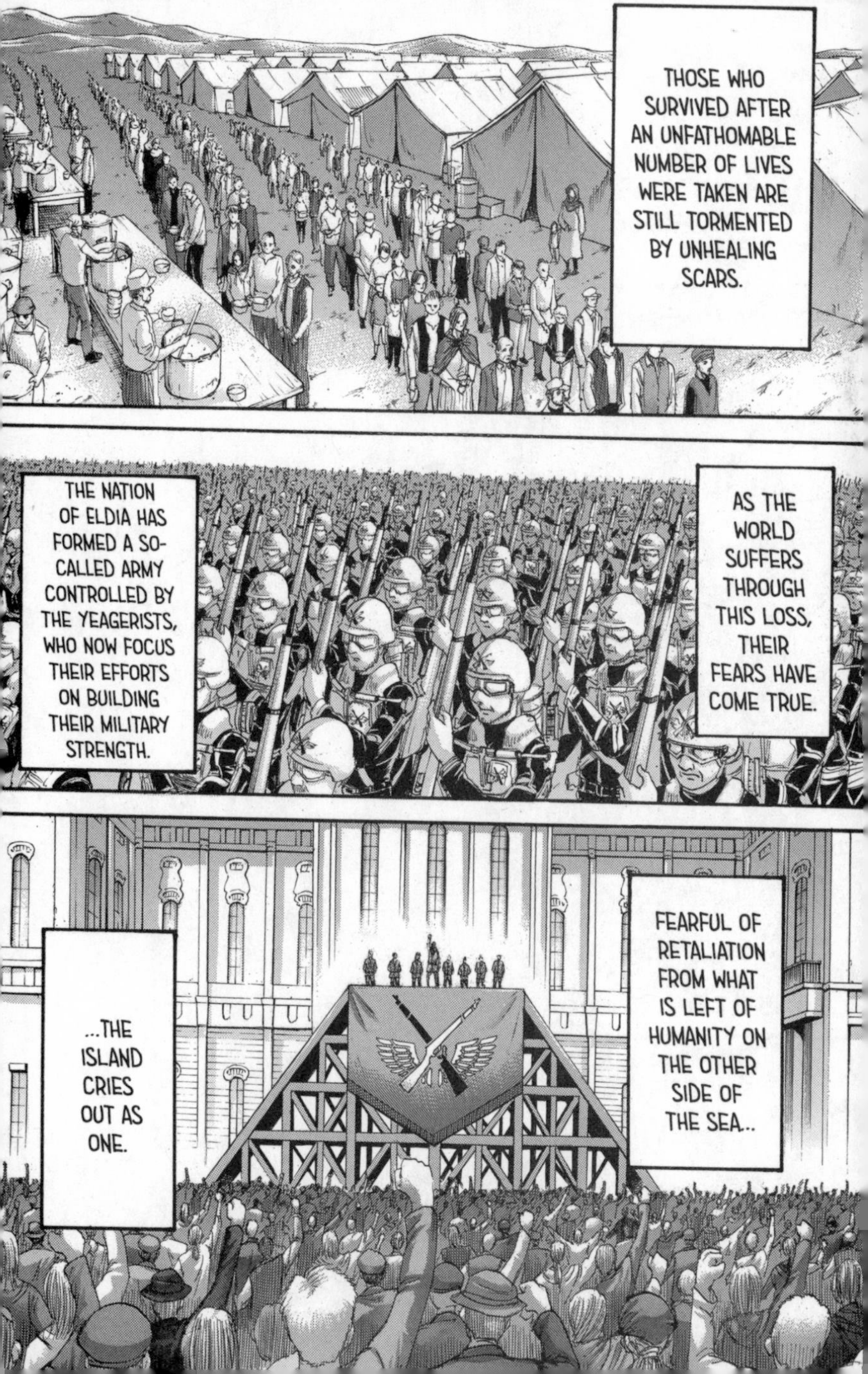
THOSE WHO SURVIVED AFTER AN UNFATHOMABLE NUMBER OF LIVES WERE TAKEN ARE STILL TORMENTED BY UNHEALING SCARS.
AS THE WORLD SUFFERS THROUGH THIS LOSS, THEIR FEARS HAVE COME TRUE.
THE NATION OF ELDIA HAS FORMED A SO-CALLED ARMY CONTROLLED BY THE YEAGERISTS, WHO NOW FOCUS THEIR EFFORTS ON BUILDING THEIR MILITARY STRENGTH.
FEARFUL OF RETALIATION FROM WHAT IS LEFT OF HUMANITY ON THE OTHER SIDE OF THE SEA...
...THE ISLAND CRIES OUT AS ONE.

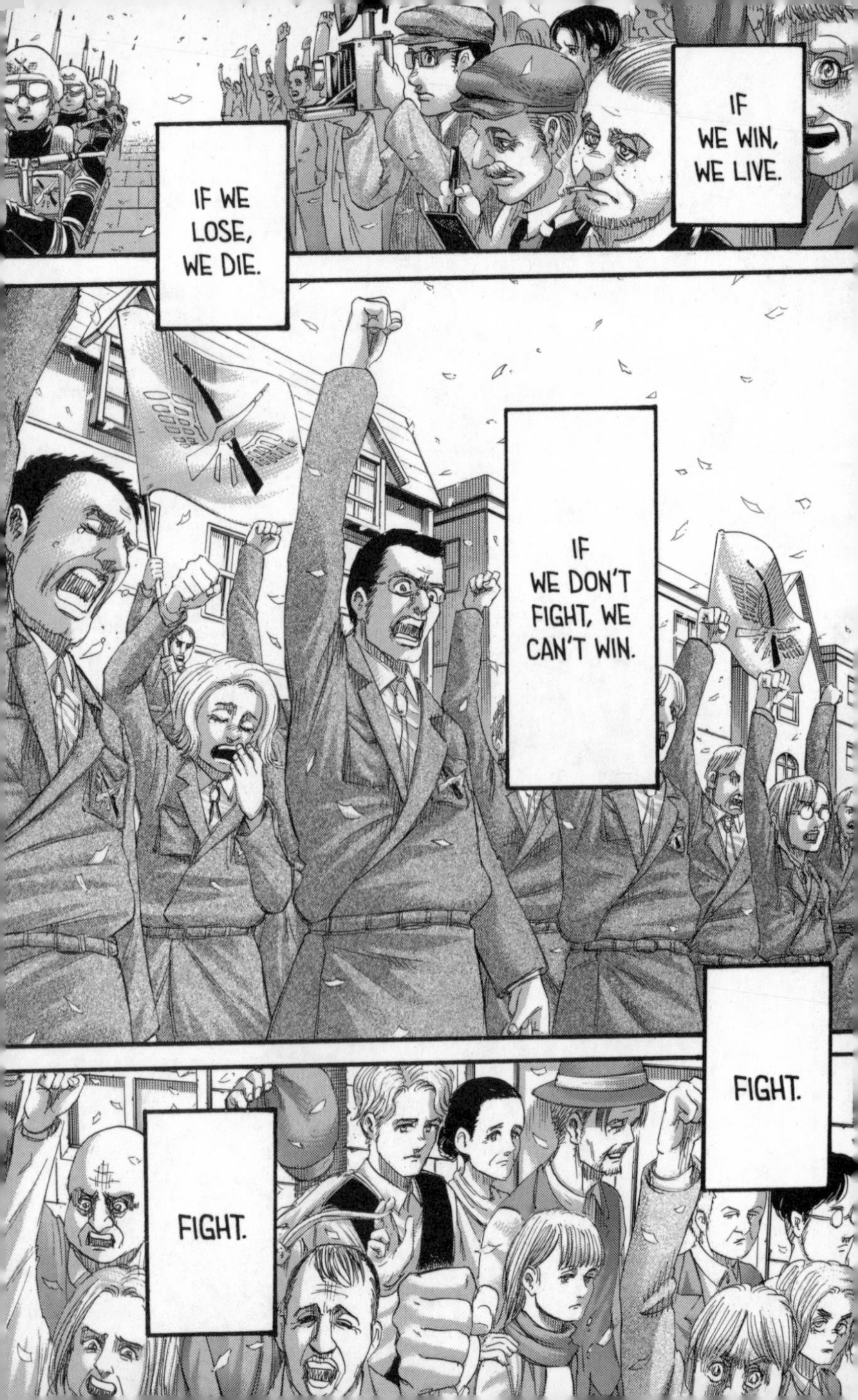
IF WE WIN, WE LIVE.
IF WE LOSE, WE DIE.
IF WE DON'T FIGHT, WE CAN'T WIN.
FIGHT.
FIGHT.

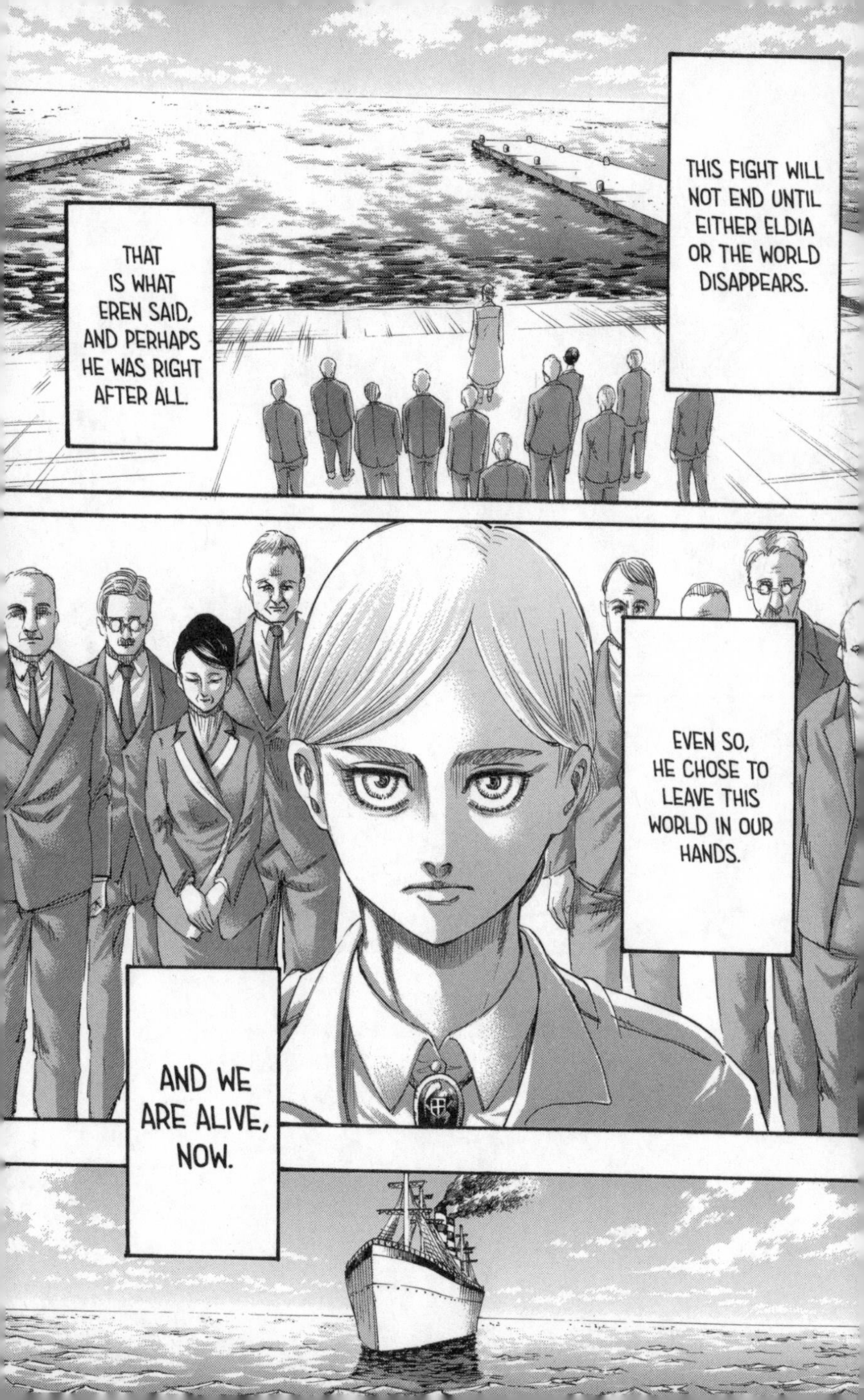
THIS FIGHT WILL NOT END UNTIL EITHER ELDIA OR THE WORLD DISAPPEARS.
THAT IS WHAT EREN SAID, AND PERHAPS HE WAS RIGHT AFTER ALL.
EVEN SO, HE CHOSE TO LEAVE THIS WORLD IN OUR HANDS.
AND WE ARE ALIVE, NOW.

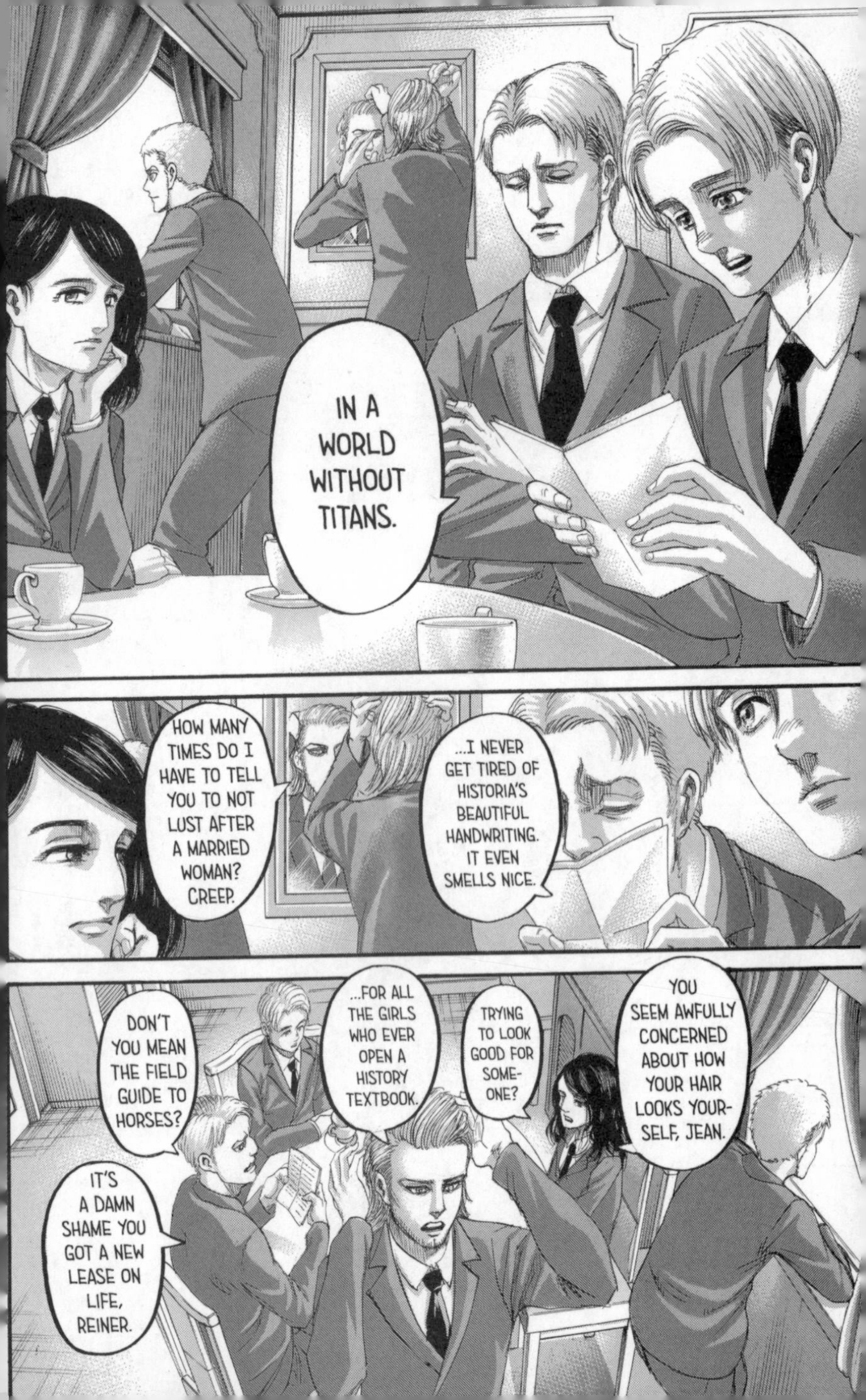
IN A WORLD WITHOUT TITANS.
...I NEVER GET TIRED OF HISTORIA'S BEAUTIFUL HANDWRITING. IT EVEN SMELLS NICE.
HOW MANY TIMES DO I HAVE TO TELL YOU TO NOT LUST AFTER A MARRIED WOMAN? CREEP.
YOU SEEM AWFULLY CONCERNED ABOUT HOW YOUR HAIR LOOKS YOURSELF, JEAN.
TRYING TO LOOK GOOD FOR SOMEONE?
...FOR ALL THE GIRLS WHO EVER OPEN A HISTORY TEXTBOOK.
DON'T YOU MEAN THE FIELD GUIDE TO HORSES?
IT'S A DAMN SHAME YOU GOT A NEW LEASE ON LIFE, REINER.

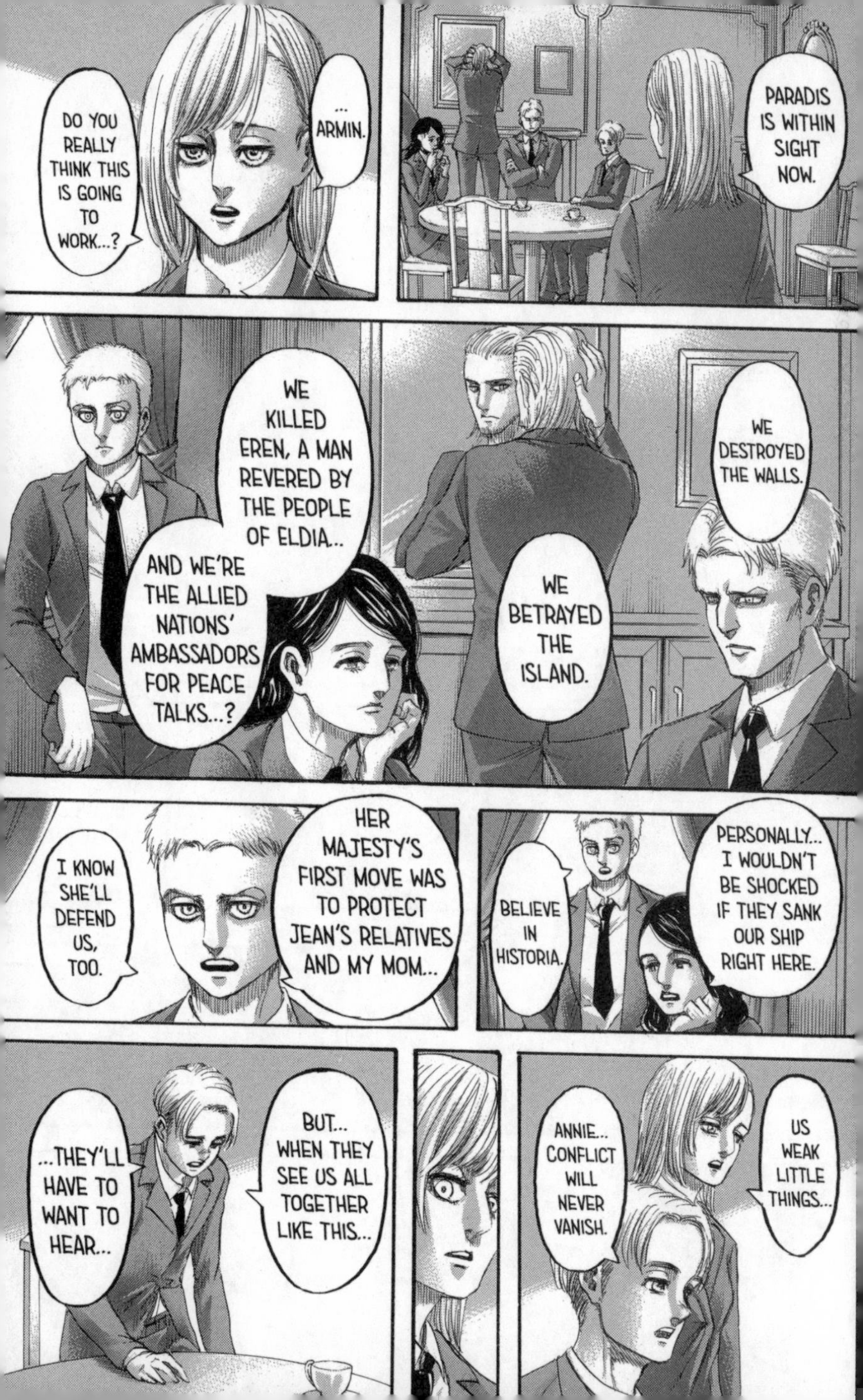
PARADIS IS WITHIN SIGHT NOW.
... ARMIN.
DO YOU REALLY THINK THIS IS GOING TO WORK...?
WE DESTROYED THE WALLS.
WE BETRAYED THE ISLAND.
WE KILLED EREN, A MAN REVERED BY THE PEOPLE OF ELDIA...
AND WE'RE THE ALLIED NATIONS' AMBASSADORS FOR PEACE TALKS...?
PERSONALLY... I WOULDN'T BE SHOCKED IF THEY SANK OUR SHIP RIGHT HERE.
BELIEVE IN HISTORIA.
HER MAJESTY'S FIRST MOVE WAS TO PROTECT JEAN'S RELATIVES AND MY MOM...
I KNOW SHE'LL DEFEND US, TOO.
US WEAK LITTLE THINGS...
ANNIE... CONFLICT WILL NEVER VANISH.
BUT... WHEN THEY SEE US ALL TOGETHER LIKE THIS...
...THEY'LL HAVE TO WANT TO HEAR...

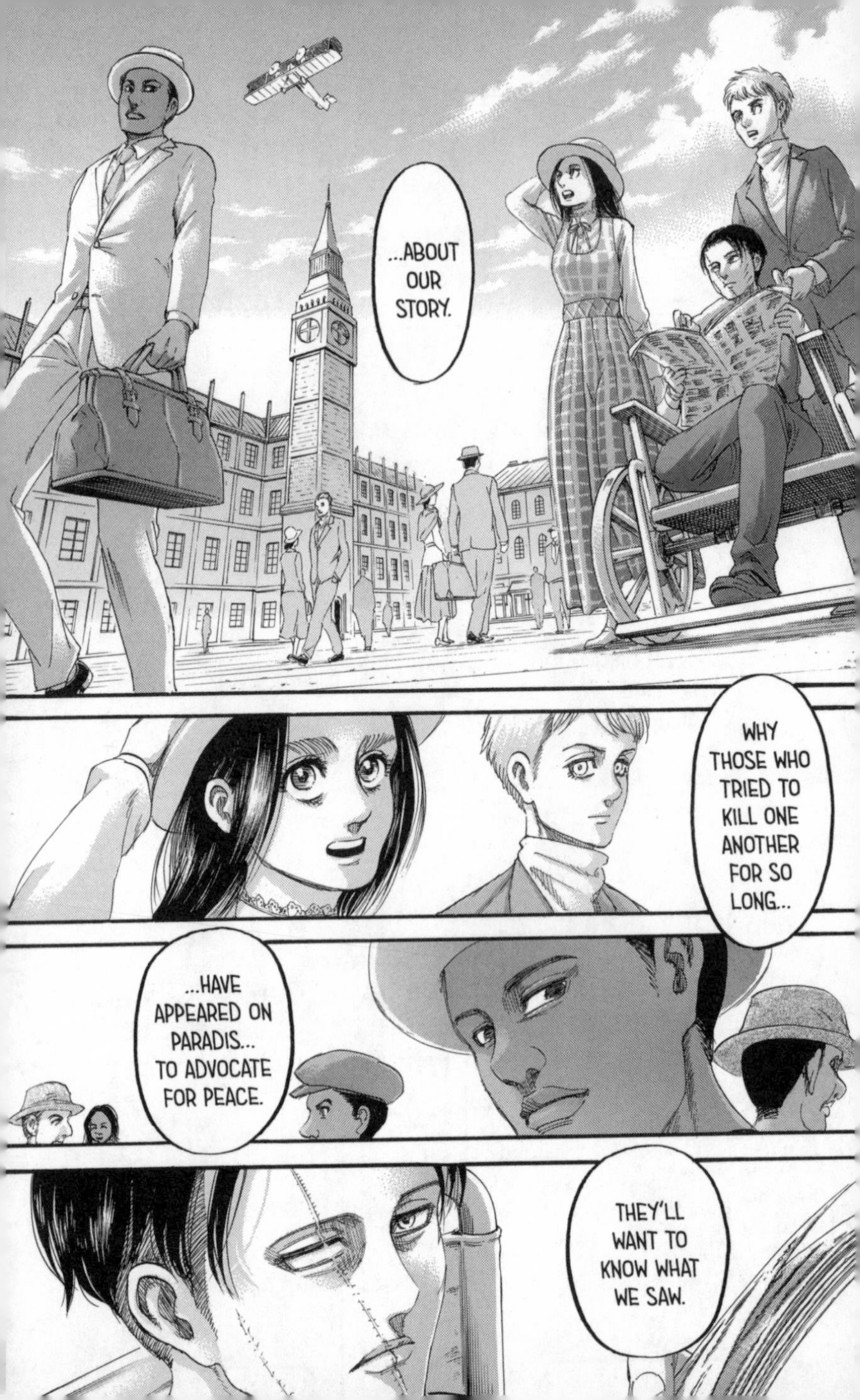
...ABOUT OUR STORY.
WHY THOSE WHO TRIED TO KILL ONE ANOTHER FOR SO LONG...
...HAVE APPEARED ON PARADIS... TO ADVOCATE FOR PEACE.
THEY'LL WANT TO KNOW WHAT WE SAW.

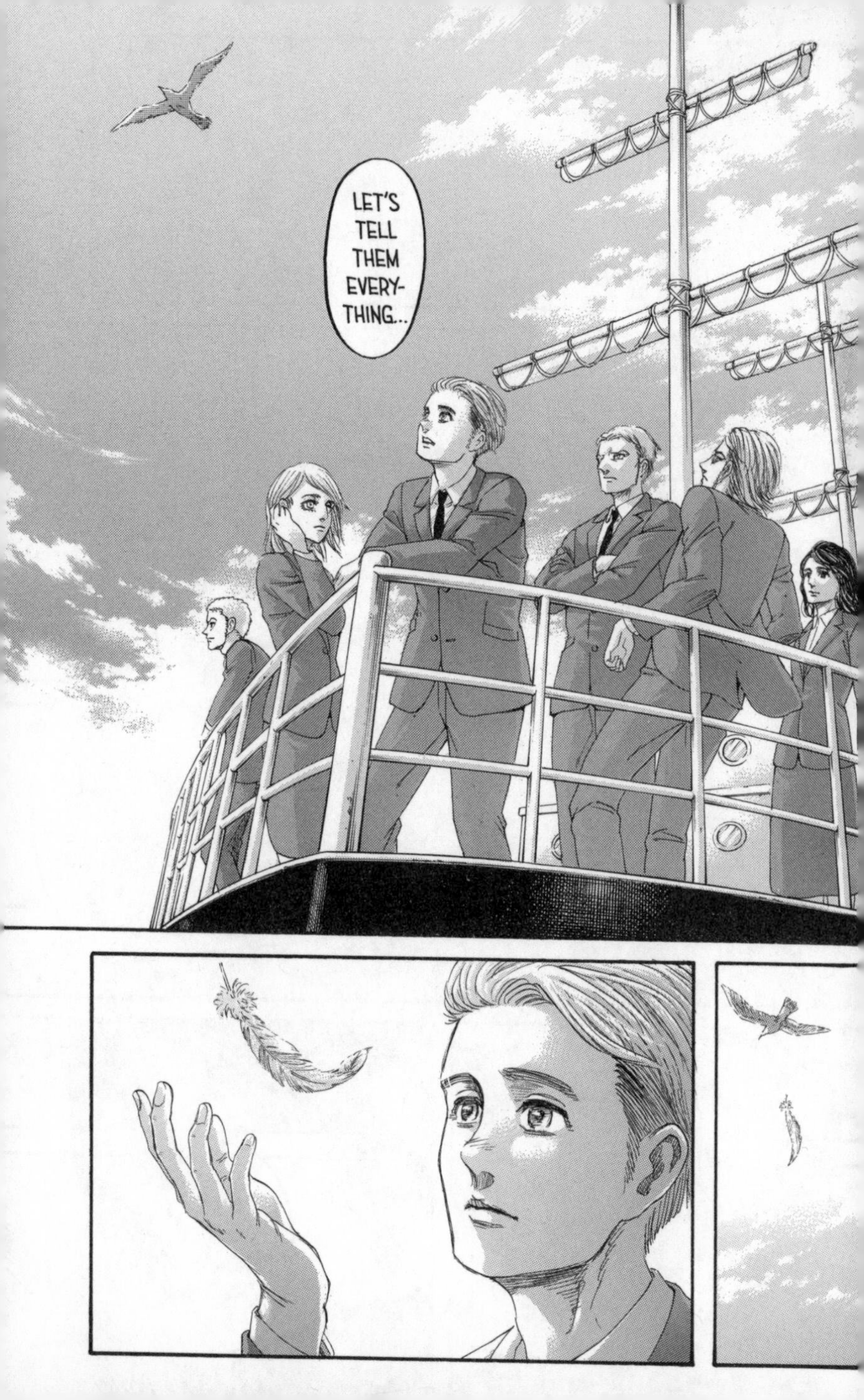
LET'S TELL THEM EVERY-THING...

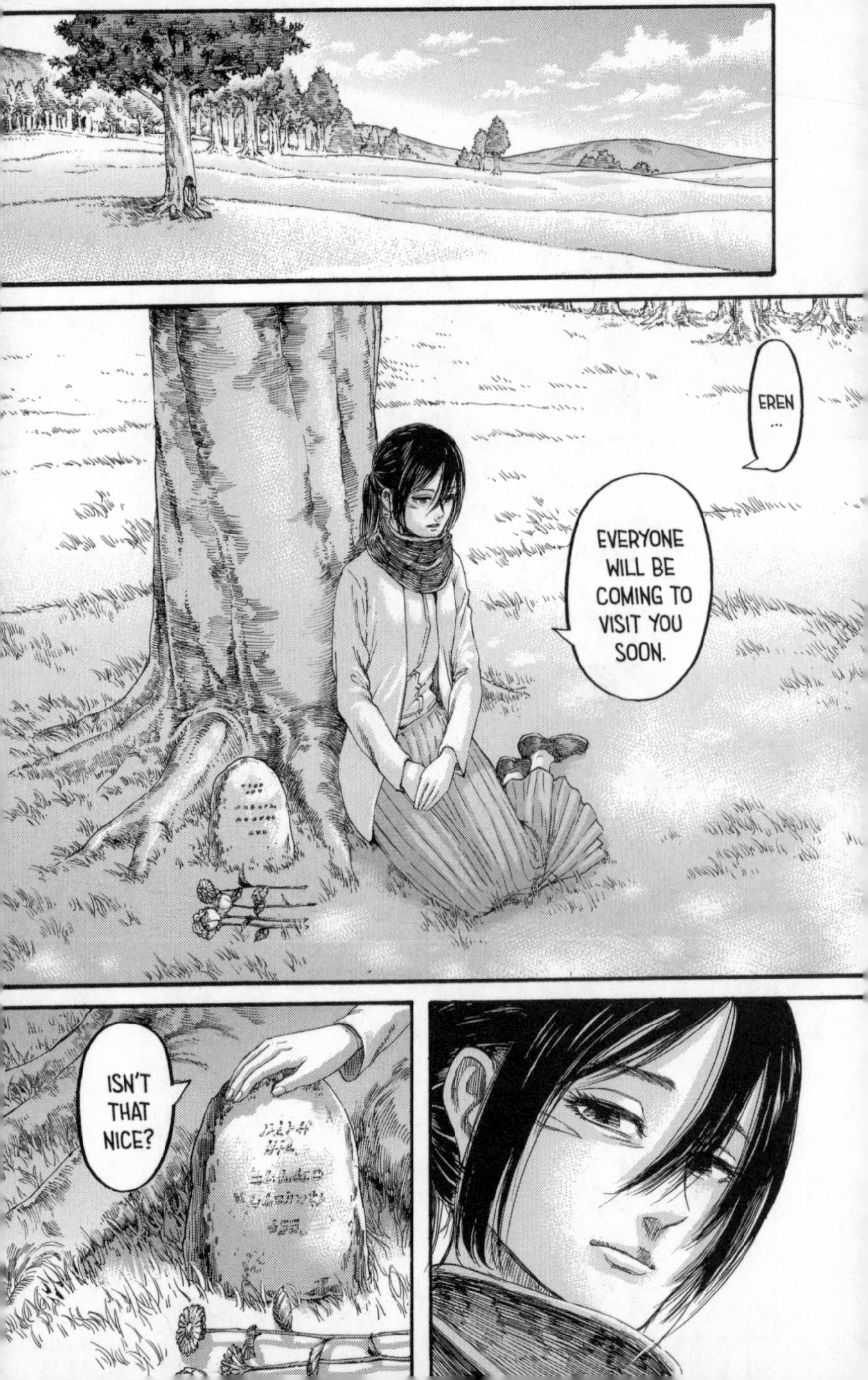
EREN ...
EVERYONE WILL BE COMING TO VISIT YOU SOON.
ISN'T THAT NICE?

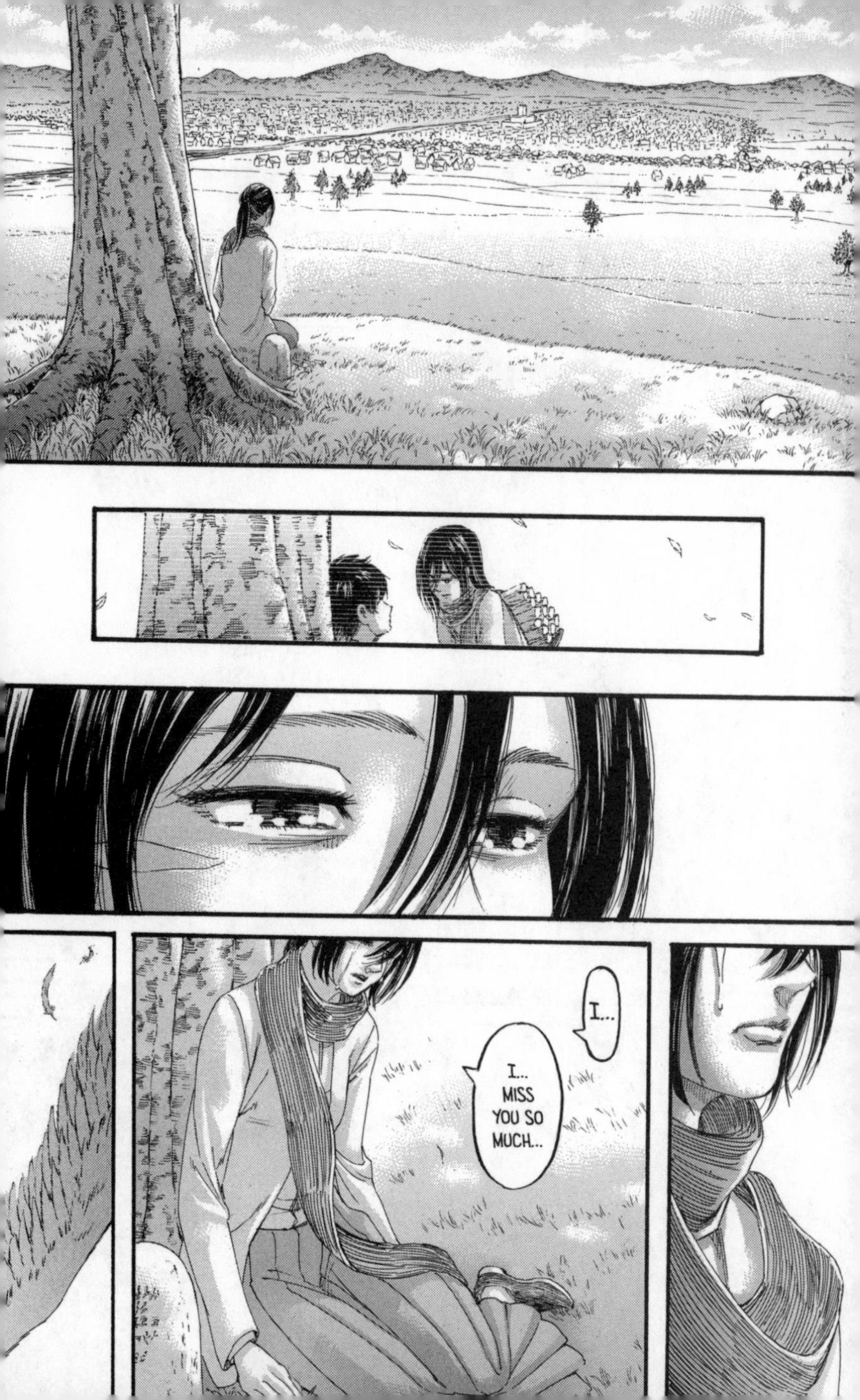
I...
I... MISS YOU SO MUCH...

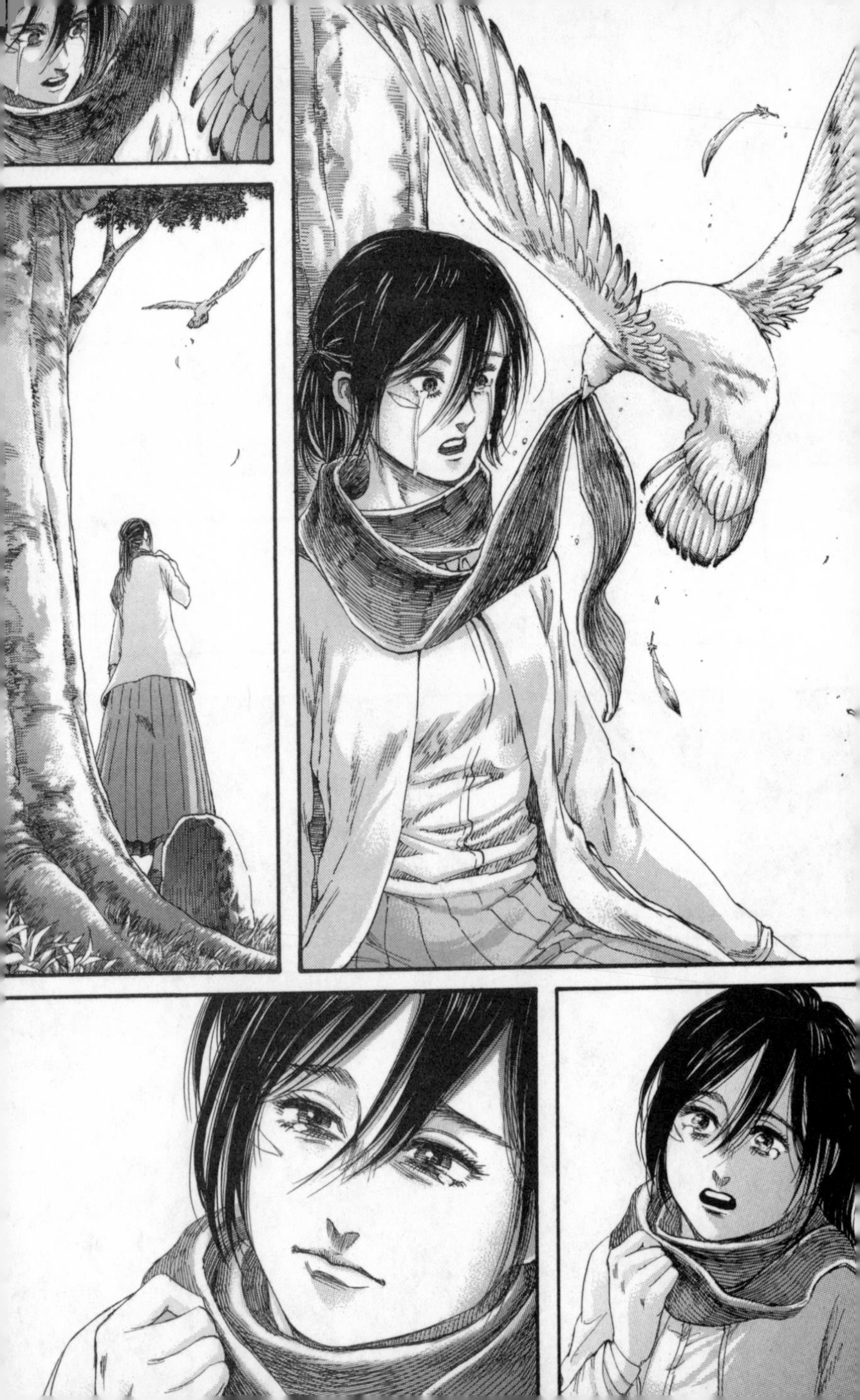

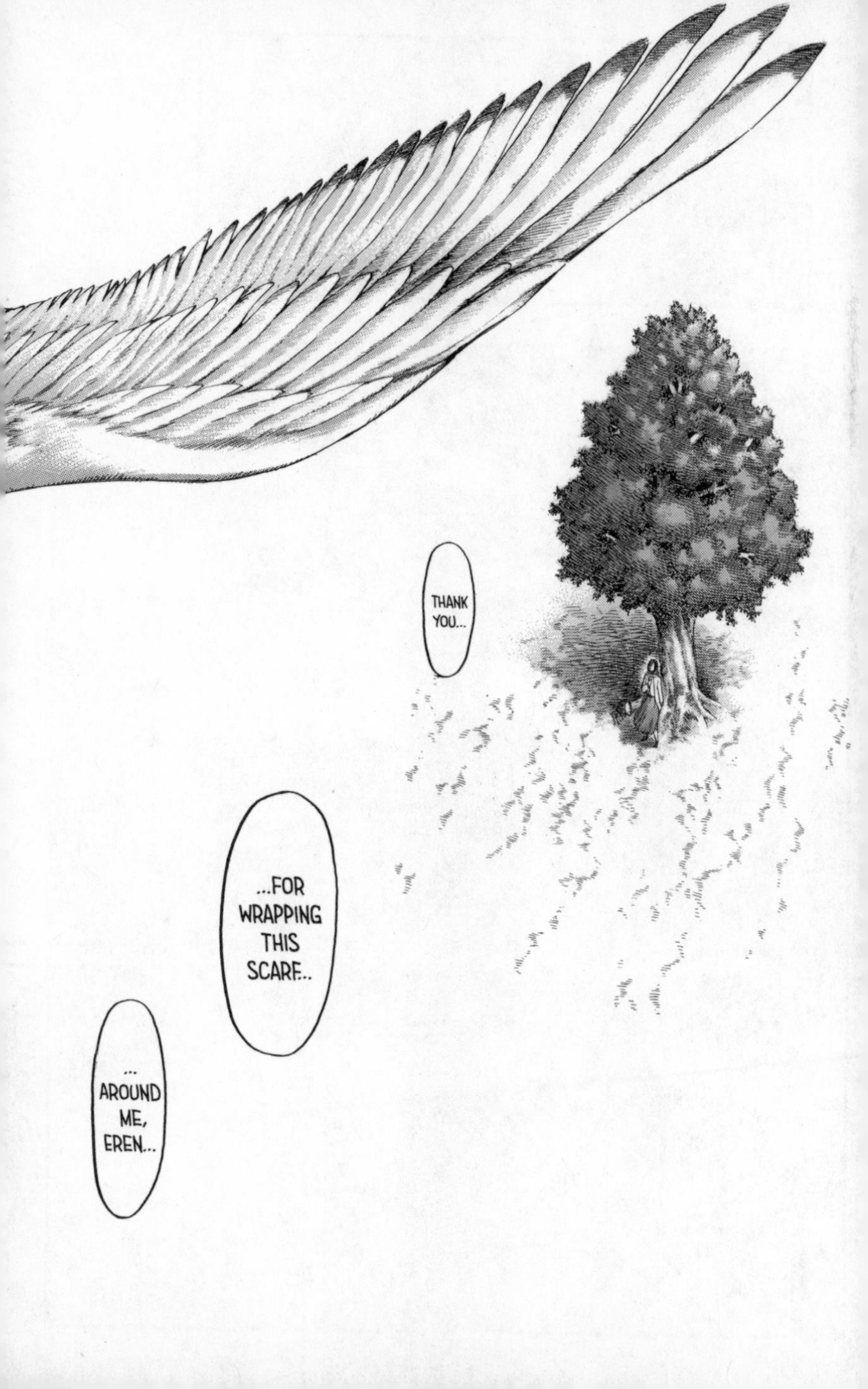
THANK YOU...
...FOR WRAPPING THIS SCARF...
... AROUND ME, EREN...

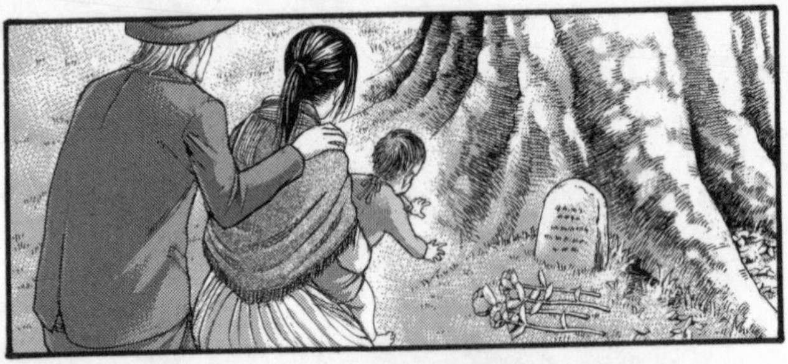
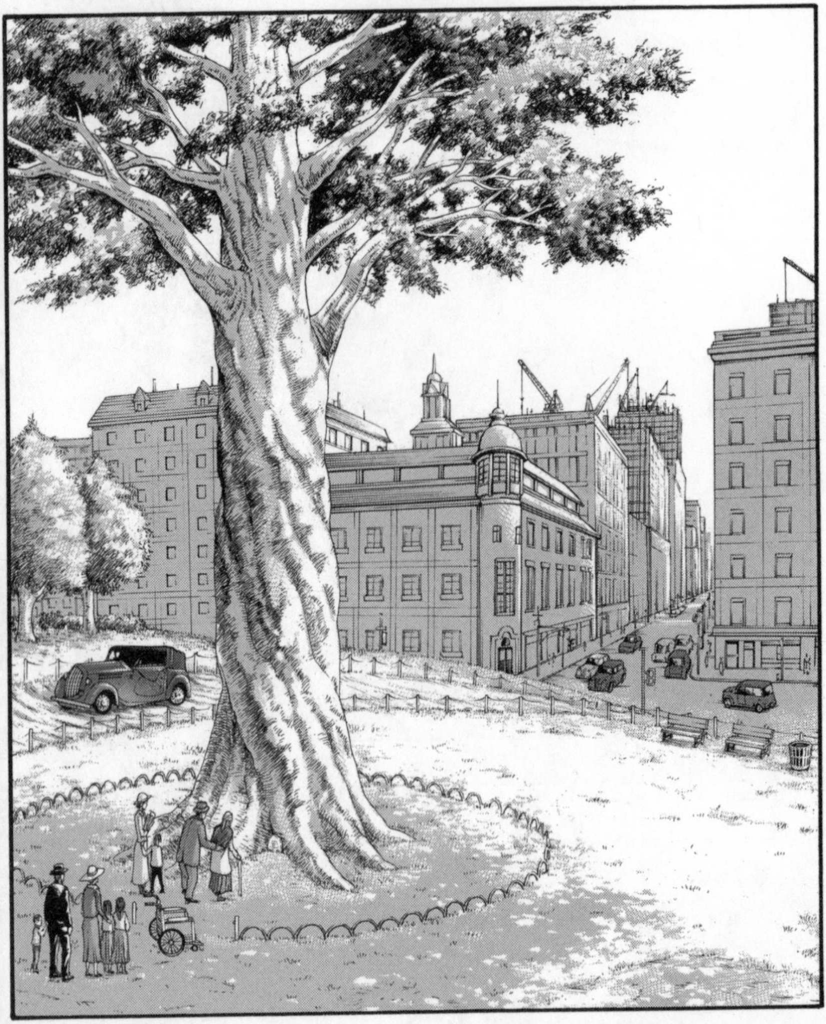

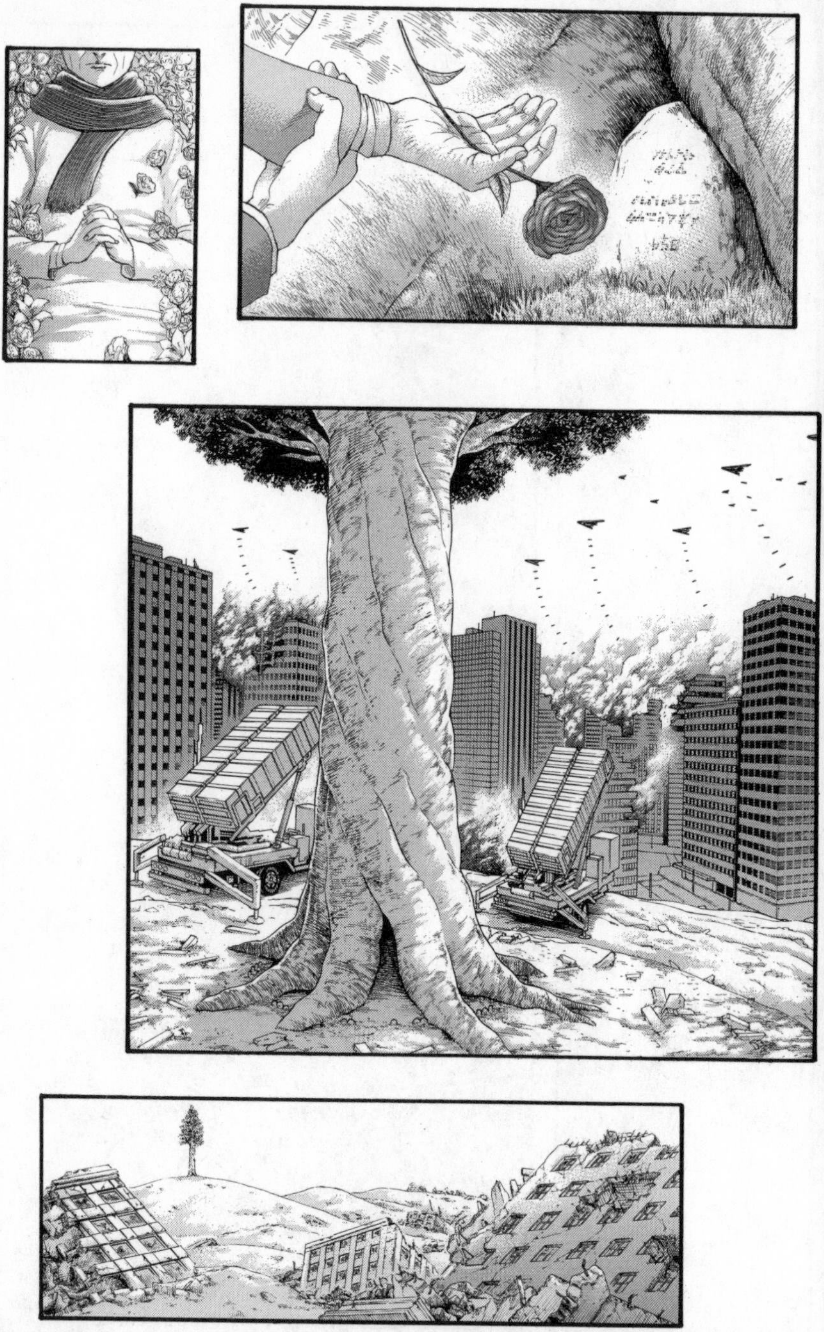

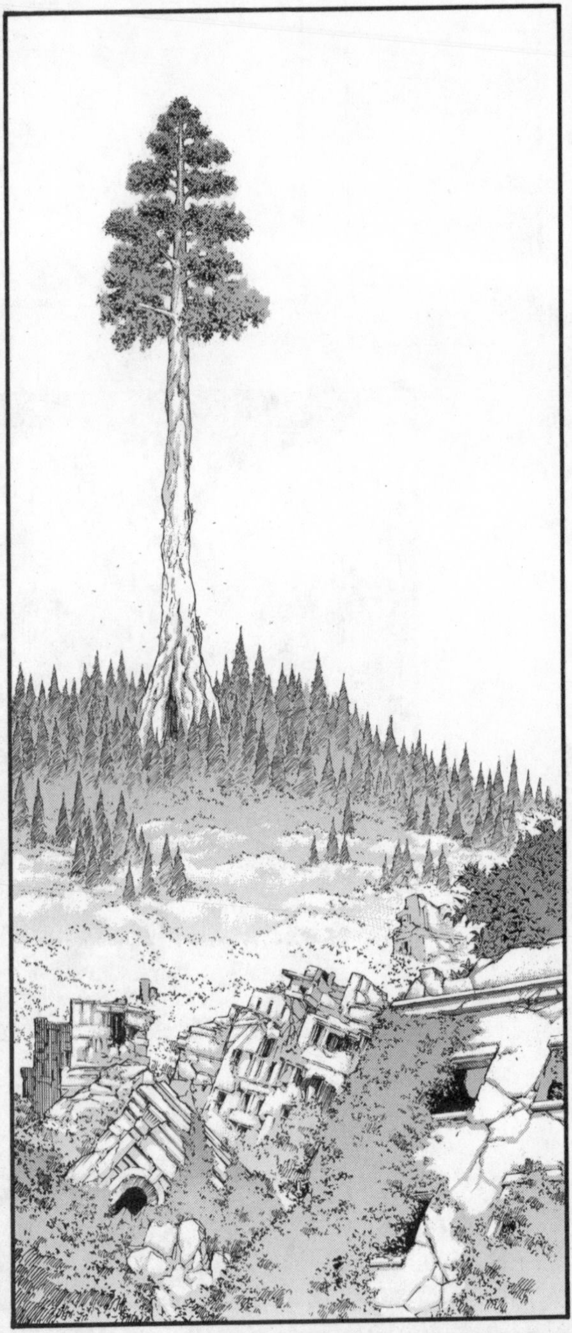

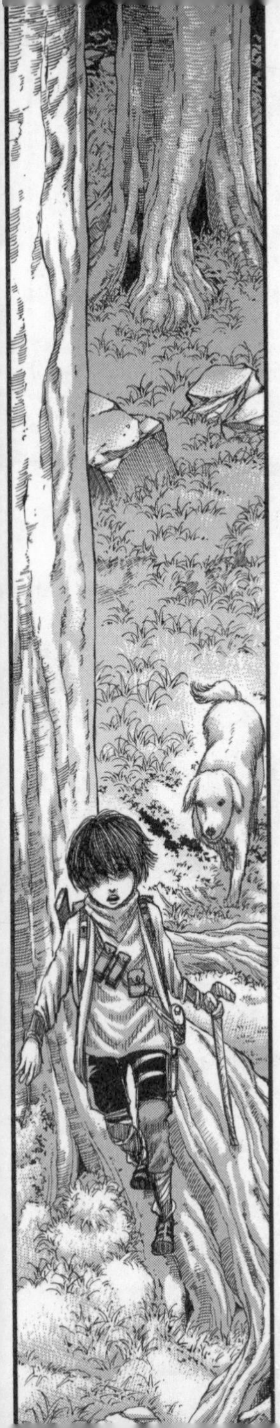

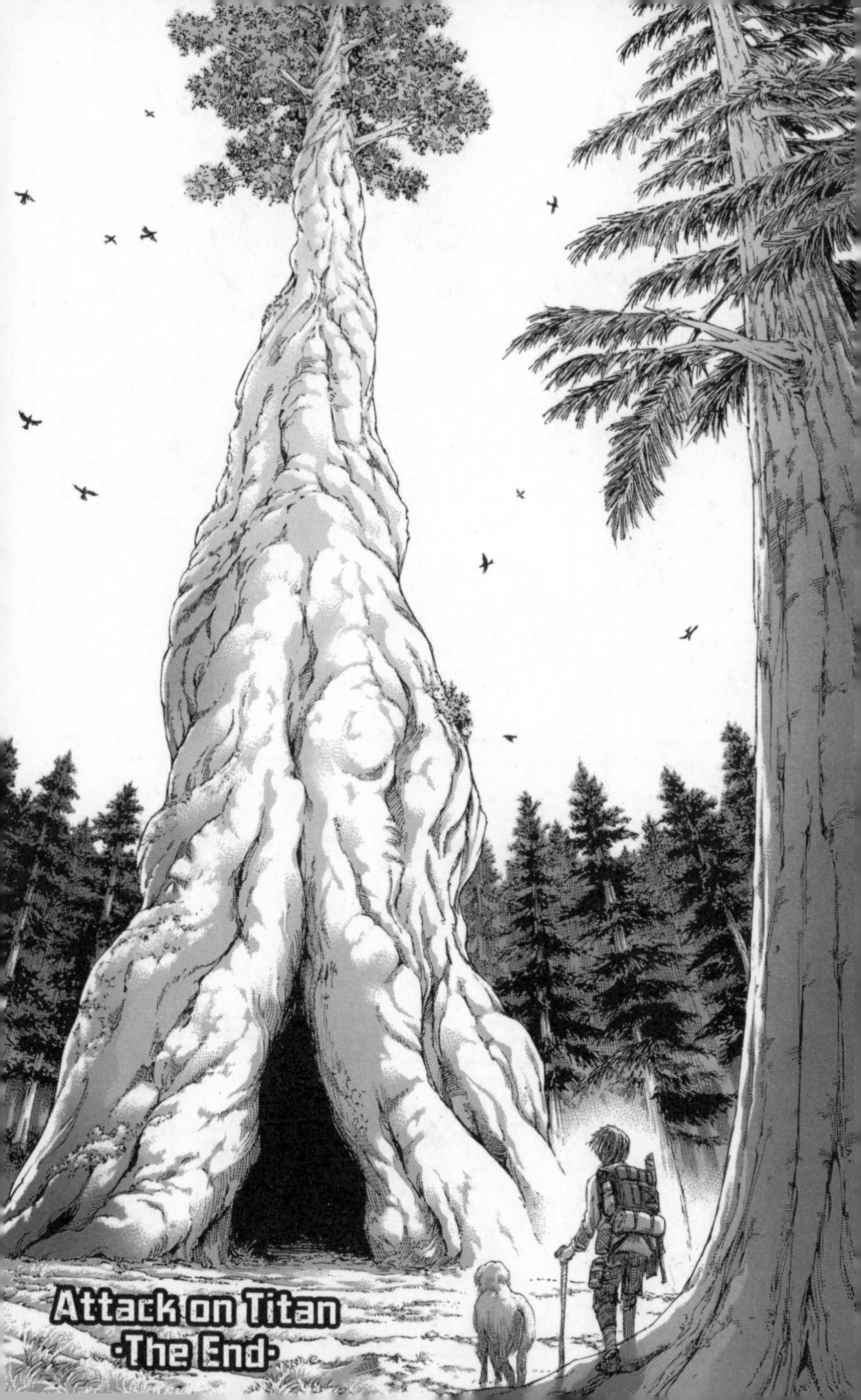
Attack on Titan
-The End-

THE END CREDITS!

ATTACK ON SCHOOL CASTES

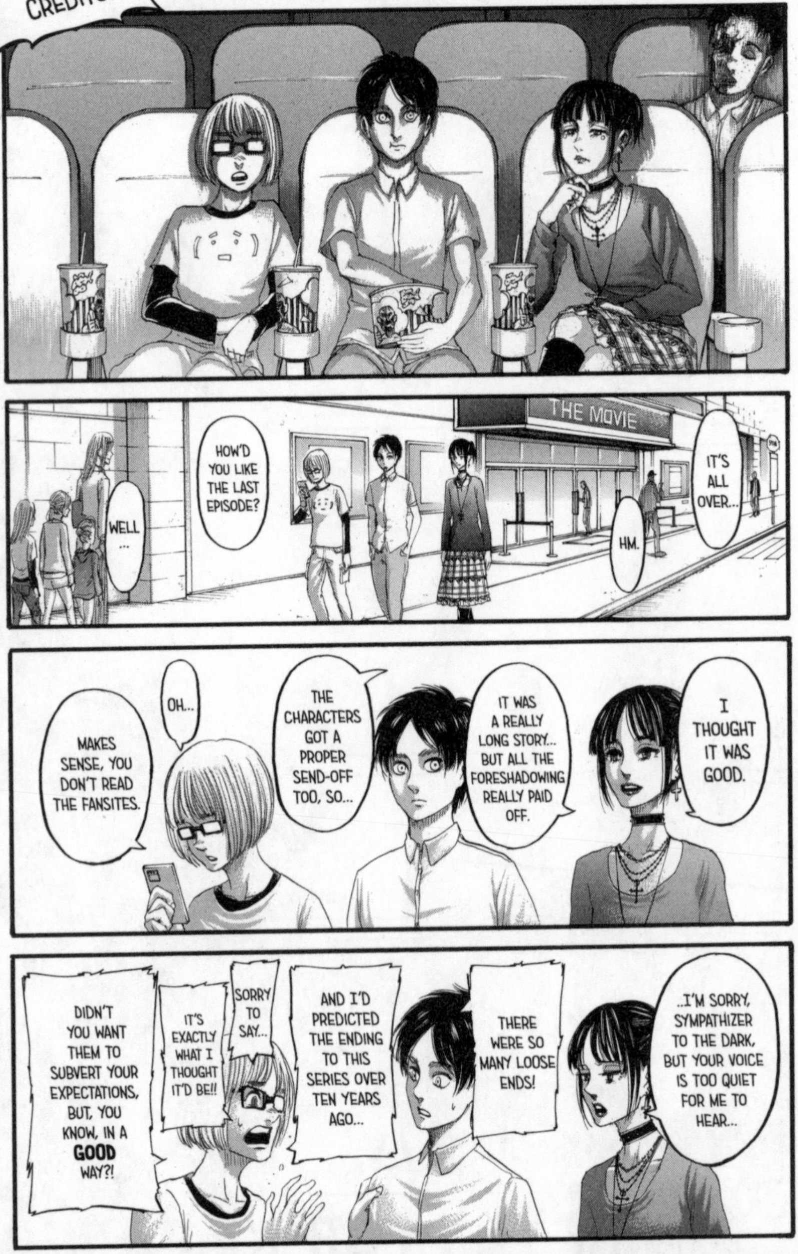
THE MOVIE
IT'S ALL OVER...
HM.
HOW'D YOU LIKE THE LAST EPISODE?
WELL ...
I THOUGHT IT WAS GOOD.
IT WAS A REALLY LONG STORY... BUT ALL THE FORESHADOWING REALLY PAID OFF.
THE CHARACTERS GOT A PROPER SEND-OFF TOO, SO...
OH...
MAKES SENSE, YOU DON'T READ THE FANSITES.
..I'M SORRY, SYMPATHIZER TO THE DARK, BUT YOUR VOICE IS TOO QUIET FOR ME TO HEAR...
THERE WERE SO MANY LOOSE ENDS!
AND I'D PREDICTED THE ENDING TO THIS SERIES OVER TEN YEARS AGO...
SORRY TO SAY...
IT'S EXACTLY WHAT I THOUGHT IT'D BE!!
DIDN'T YOU WANT THEM TO SUBVERT YOUR EXPECTATIONS, BUT, YOU KNOW, IN A **GOOD** WAY?!

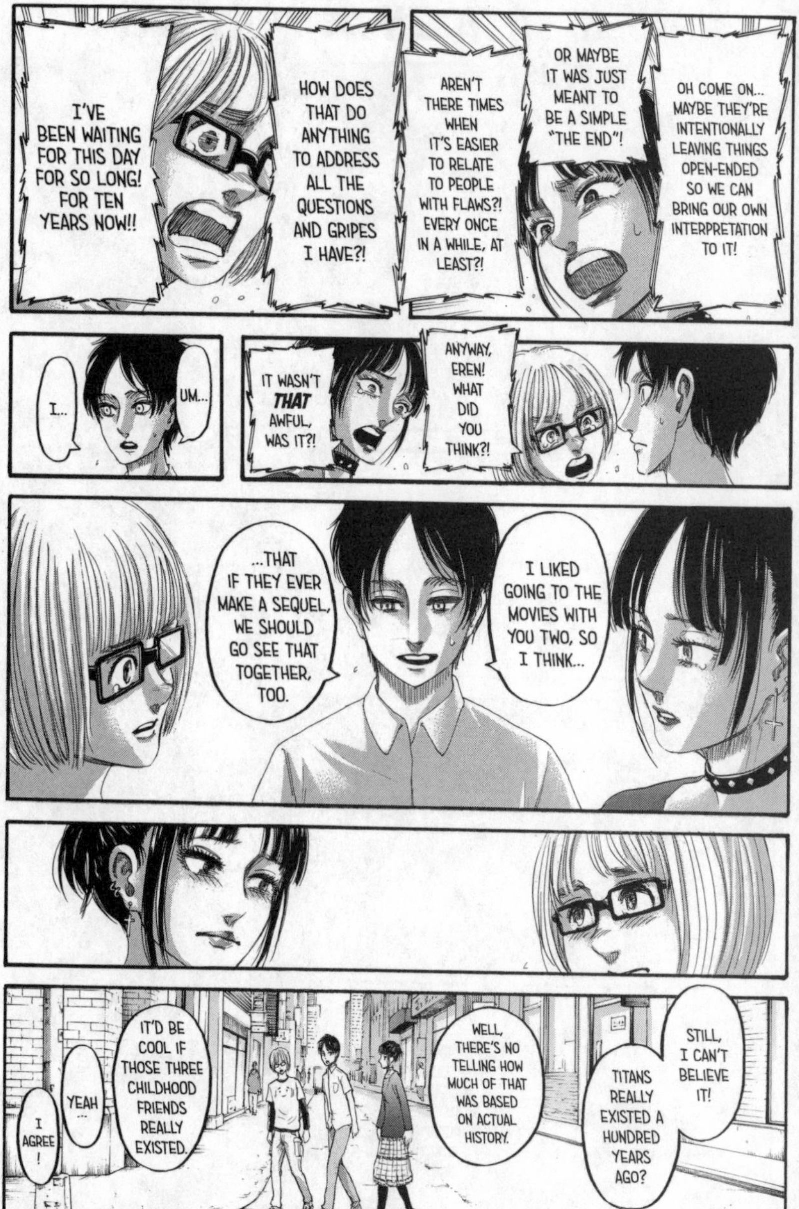
OH COME ON... MAYBE THEY'RE INTENTIONALLY LEAVING THINGS OPEN-ENDED SO WE CAN BRING OUR OWN INTERPRETATION TO IT!
OR MAYBE IT WAS JUST MEANT TO BE A SIMPLE "THE END"!
AREN'T THERE TIMES WHEN IT'S EASIER TO RELATE TO PEOPLE WITH FLAWS?! EVERY ONCE IN A WHILE, AT LEAST?!
HOW DOES THAT DO ANYTHING TO ADDRESS ALL THE QUESTIONS AND GRIPES I HAVE?!
I'VE BEEN WAITING FOR THIS DAY FOR SO LONG! FOR TEN YEARS NOW!!
ANYWAY, EREN! WHAT DID YOU THINK?!
IT WASN'T ***THAT*** AWFUL, WAS IT?!
UM...
I...
I LIKED GOING TO THE MOVIES WITH YOU TWO, SO I THINK...
...THAT IF THEY EVER MAKE A SEQUEL, WE SHOULD GO SEE THAT TOGETHER, TOO.
STILL, I CAN'T BELIEVE IT!
TITANS REALLY EXISTED A HUNDRED YEARS AGO?
WELL, THERE'S NO TELLING HOW MUCH OF THAT WAS BASED ON ACTUAL HISTORY.
IT'D BE COOL IF THOSE THREE CHILDHOOD FRIENDS REALLY EXISTED.
YEAH...
I AGREE!

THANK YOU FOR READING!

ATTACK on TITAN

A SMART, NEW ROMANTIC COMEDY FOR FANS OF *SHORTCAKE CAKE* AND *TERRACE HOUSE!*

LIVING ROOM

MATSUNAGA-SAN

Keiko Iwashita

A romance manga starring high school girl Meeko, who learns to live on her own in a boarding house whose living room is home to the odd (but handsome) Matsunaga-san. She begins to adjust to her new life away from her parents, but Meeko soon learns that no matter how far away from home she is, she's still a young girl at heart — especially when she finds herself falling for Matsunaga-san.

Knight of the ICE

Yayoi Ogawa

Knight of the Ice ©Yayoi Oga...

SKATING THRILLS AND ICY CHILLS WITH THIS NEW TINGLY ROMANCE SERIES!

A rom-com on ice, perfect for fans of *Princess Jellyfish* and *Wotakoi*. Kokoro is the talk of the figure-skating world, winning trophies and hearts. But little do they know... he's actually a huge nerd! From the beloved creator of *You're My Pet* (*Tramps Like Us*).

Chitose is a serious young woman, working for the health magazine *SASSO*. Or at least, she would be, if she wasn't constantly getting distracted by her childhood friend, international figure skating star Kokoro Kijinami! In the public eye and on the ice, Kokoro is a gallant, flawless knight, but behind his glittery costumes and breathtaking spins lies a secret: He's actually a hopelessly romantic otaku, who can only land his quad jumps when Chitose is on hand to recite a spell from his favorite magical girl anime!

KC KODANSHA COMICS

PERFECT WORLD

Rie Aruga

A TOUCHING NEW SERIES ABOUT LOVE AND COPING WITH DISABILITY

An office party reunites Tsugumi with her high school crush Itsuki. He's realized his dream of becoming an architect, but along the way, he experienced a spinal injury that put him in a wheelchair. Now Tsugumi's rekindled feelings will butt up against prejudices she never considered — and Itsuki will have to decide if he's ready to let someone into his heart...

"Depicts with great delicacy and courage the difficulties some with disabilities experience getting involved in romantic relationships... Rie Aruga refuses to romanticize, pushing her heroine to face the reality of disability. She invites her readers to the same tasks of empathy, knowledge and recognition."
—Slate.fr

"An important entry [in manga romance]... The emotional core of both plot and characters indicates thoughtfulness... [Aruga's] research is readily apparent in the text and artwork, making this feel like a real story."
—Anime News Network

KC KODANSHA COMICS

THE SWEET SCENT OF LOVE IS IN THE AIR! FOR FANS OF OFFBEAT ROMANCES LIKE *WOTAKOI*

Sweat and Soap © Kintetsu Yamada / Kodansha Ltd.

In an office romance, there's a fine line between sexy and awkward... and that line is where Asako — a woman who sweats copiously — meets Koutarou — a perfume developer who can't get enough of Asako's, er, scent. Don't miss a romcom manga like no other!

Young characters and steampunk setting, like *Howl's Moving Castle* and *Battle Angel Alita*

A boy with a talent for machines and a mysterious girl whose wings he's fixed will take you beyond the clouds! In the tradition of the high-flying, resonant adventure stories of Studio Ghibli comes a gorgeous tale about the longing of young hearts for adventure and friendship!

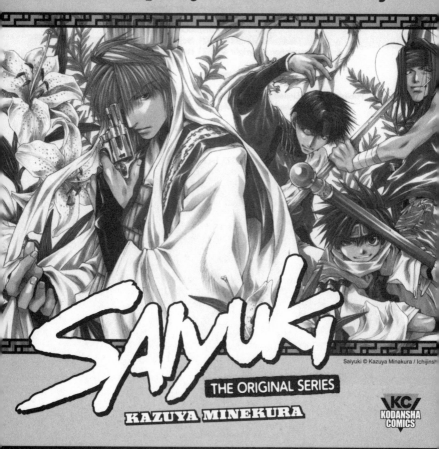

A Kodansha Comics Tra~~nslation~~
Attack on Titan 34 copyright © ~~2021 Hajime~~ Isayama
~~English translation copyright © 2022 Hajime~~ Isayama

~~, an imprint of~~
~~York.~~

~~ed through~~

~~publish~~ed ~~in 2021 by~~ Kodansha Ltd., Tokyo
as *Shingeki no kyojin*, volume 34.

Standard Edition
ISBN 978-1-64651-236-2

Barnes & Noble Edition
ISBN 978-1-64651-459-5

BAM Edition
ISBN 978-1-64651-460-1

Kinokuniya Edition
ISBN 978-1-64651-461-8

Original cover design by Takashi Shimoyama/Manami Fukunaga (Red Rooster)

Printed in the United States of America.

www.kodansha.us

9 8 7 6 5 4 3 2
Translation: Ko Ransom
Lettering: Dezi Sienty
Editing: Tiff Joshua TJ Ferentini, Ben Applegate
Kodansha Comics edition cover design by Phil Balsman

Publisher: Kiichiro Sugawara

Director of publishing services: Ben Applegate
Associate director of operations: Stephen Pakula
Publishing services managing editors: Alanna Ruse, Madison Salters
Production managers: Emi Lotto, Angela Zurlo